MINORITY ECONOMIC, POLITICAL AND SOCIAL DEVELOPMENT

Jesse E. Gloster

University Press
of America™

Library of Congress Catalog Card Number: 78-62738

To Norma, Carol, Janice,

Regina, and Millie

Preface

This book is a continuation and enlargement of _Economics of Minority Groups_, which was first published in 1973, with a second edition in 1976. Suggestions from readers and students resulted in additional chapters on ethnics, politics, higher education and the cultural milieu of this country. Trying to accommodate these requests of readers and students, this volume more than doubles the size of _Economics of Minority Groups_.

Emphasis on the ethnic spectrum in the economy of this country is still gaining momentum. Egalitarianism, that is equal opportunity, is held valid in our system of political economy and the free market.

The famous case, Brown vs School Board, handed down by the unanimous decision of the U. S. Supreme Court in 1954, leads off the book in Chapter One. The part blacks played in the communication industry is presented in the final chapter. Between these two chapters, the plight of the American Indian and Spanish speaking Americans, as well as that of the elderly is described. The seeming trauma of a large segment of blacks is covered on pensions, employment, unemployment, business, housing and land ownership along with parallel discussions of Spanish speaking Americans.

Politics among ethnics and women has taken on a new dimension. Increasingly we see them running for office on

the local, state, and national level. Three chapters are
devoted to this phenomenon.

Crime in the cities is covered in Chapters XVIII and
XIX. Racism, which envelops this country like a fog, shows
itself in the disproportionate number of blacks incarcerated
in jails in this country as compared with the number of
whites. If an ethnic is poor, black or a Chicano and is
confronted by the law he is more apt to come out on the short
end than a white Anglo-Saxon Protestant. Texas is a prime
example of this disproportion.

The part played by blacks in professional sports is
covered in horse racing, baseball, football, basketball,
tennis and golf. The last three chapters cover the minorities in colleges and higher education, the military and the
communication industry.

Acknowledgments are in order for the many individuals
who have assisted me and given me constructive criticism,
during the production of this book. Among them have been my
colleagues at Texas Southern University. A few of them are
Dr. John Biggers, head of the Art Department, Dean Walter
McCoy of the School of Public Affairs, Mr. Charles Johnson,
instructor of black economic development at the University
of Houston, Mr. Joe Mack, Associate Professor of Art, at
Prairie View University, my brothers and sisters, wife and
daughters.

Mrs. Leonia Dorsey, retired teacher of Houston Independent School District read the entire manuscript and made

valuable suggestions. Mr. Walter B. Quetsch, Executive
Director of the National Advisory Council on Economic
Opportunity read the chapter on the War on Poverty. Miss
Judy Bryant typed the first draft and Mrs. Virgil Mae Kenney,
Assistant Professor of Education at Texas Southern University,
also made valuable suggestions and typed the final draft.

Houston, Texas

January 24, 1978

TABLE OF CONTENTS

LIST OF TABLES

LIST OF TABLES (continued)

Table   Page

LIST OF TABLES (continued)

CHAPTER I

The Decision That Shook The World

Time, in its inexorable quest for space and distance, appears, never to look back. But man, who is possessed and processed by time, must always look back to see where he has come from, and to plan on where he is going. It is in the context of time and space that one of the greatest decisions of this country, which affects all of us, was handed down by the Supreme Court of the United States in May, 1954. This case was "Brown vs. Board of Education of Topeka."

Topeka, the capital and the third largest city in Kansas was the place situated on the Kansas River, seventy miles west of Kansas City. Topeka is a middle-sized somnambulant city of about 130,000 people. Since about 1940, the city has doubled in population. It is known for its flour milling and meat packing. Prior to World War II, it was also known as a railroad center, having been served by four railroad systems.

It was ironic that Brown vs. School Board of Topeka, ever came to Topeka. Topeka had come into being in 1854 as a "free state" town. In 1856, about the same time that the Republican Party was formed by free blacks and whites in Racine, Wisconsin, an antislavery convention was held in the town, and the Topeka constitution was adopted. This constitution would have set up Topeka as a state, but it was aborted by Federal troops.

Not only was a suit filed for desegregation in Topeka, but also in other areas of the country, namely, Virginia, South Carolina and Delaware. Law suits were in process in four separate and distinct sections of this country. Black citizens were challenging the old hoary decision of Plessy vs. Ferguson. This decision of 1896, had become a blight on this democracy. It was somewhat similar to the infamous Dred Scott decision of 1856. These decisions were a setback to our great democracy. Here, the plaintiffs were testing the purity of a democracy and the democracy was found lacking in its application to all citizens.

Why was Topeka cast into the spotlight when three other areas had similar cases pending? Topeka got there first. For years, the lawyers who had specialized in Constitutional Law had urged the NAACP to come in well prepared for its assault on Plessy vs. Ferguson. The U. S. Supreme Court had remanded case after case back to appellant courts because of poor preparation. The separate but equal doctrine was a myth. Lawyers and educators knew this. But ideas that have vectored in on vested interests have a way of dying hard. The NAACP also knew that the timing had to be just right in order to get a decision that could hardly be gainsaid. The Gaines Case in St. Louis had set a precedent of a black trying to obtain an equal education in law. The St. Louis decision only resulted in a separate law school being set up at the black Lincoln University in Jefferson City, Missouri. A Chinese student had brought suit, but again the case was remanded to appellant courts.

World War II had come and gone, but again we had seen an evil genius such as Hitler try to decimate a race of people. Now the attitude of the nation was changing because of the service of blacks and millions of other minorities in World War II. It was also apparent that Generals George C. Marshall and Eisenhower and President Truman had integrated the troops without causing any kind of "blood running in the streets." This "blood running in the streets" was an argument advanced by the southern press without any kind of foundation. It was a sort of scare, or sensational tactic so often used by the opposition to delay, retard or obfuscate issues. The Korean War had ended in 1952, and now the forces of law challenging the separate but equal doctrine were about to be joined.

The local quarterback for the legal team was Attorney Charles S. Scott. Scott came from a legal family. His father was an attorney as well as his brother. This family had previously handled earlier, little known civil right cases in the Topeka area.

Although Kansas was classed as a "liberal" state, it had never been as "liberal" as people thought it was. It had been the itinerant home of John Brown and the Pottawattamie massacre. Jim Crowism was practiced all over town as late as 1951. When NAACP officials such as the late Walter White and Roy Wilkins came to town they stayed at "friends" homes because the local hotel practiced Jim Crow.

Scott prefaced his case on the evils of segregation in and of itself as a forced policy, bulwarked by law. The issue here was not one of voluntary segregation, but of a community of interest. It is only when a thing is forced, when the law enhances and implements it, that it brings in its train abuse, corruption and evils that do irreparable harm to oppressed individuals. Scott and his staff held that the white and black schools in Topeka were in fact equal; teachers, book equipment and classrooms. But they also held that although physical equality existed, the separation of races during the educational process was inherently unequal. Although this was a null hypothesis it was far reaching. It was not a new assumption. Educators and psychologists had long held to such a belief and the junior high schools and high schools in Topeka were integrated a long time before Brown vs. Board of Education. Only the elementary schools were confined to all-white or all-black children.

Not a whimper was raised against segregation at this time. Topeka had only four grade schools of all black students and eighteen white schools with a total enrollment of 6,019 students. The four black grade schools had only 658 pupils and twenty-seven teachers. This was a student teacher ratio of twenty-four pupils to each teacher. From an educational viewpoint, it was an ideal teaching situation as well as an ideal learning situation. The white schools were overcrowed and had untold problems of increasing size.

However, a strange thing happened that led to forebodings of things to come. The Topeka school system hired a new superintendent for the black schools. First he took the musical instruments away from the students in the elementary schools. Here we see a fool at work. Not only is music a part of the soul of most human beings, but it is especially strong in black people. Music is one of the main contributions of blacks to this western culture. Now, the superintendent took the instruments away. This raised the wrath of the parents against the school system. Then, the school superintendent of the black schools compounded his case by going to a Rotary Club meeting and stating that black children were not ready to go to white schools. The superintendent was going backwards racially and educationally. This was in 1948. First the NAACP got rid of the superintendent and suggested to the Topeka School System that the elementary schools should be integrated.

Scott and his staff now made their move. The case was first argued before a three-judge federal court in Topeka. The case was decided in favor of the Board of Education. This defeat did not daunt Scott. Immediately he began working on his appeal to the U. S. Supreme Court. Scott made the first trip to Washington at his own expense. This was in 1952. By the time the train got to St. Louis, it was learned that the case was postponed. When the case came up again before the U. S. Supreme Court, Scott and the local NAACP president, Burnett, drove to Washington.

Appearing before the Supreme Court and representing the national office of the NAACP was the celebrated lawyer, Thurgood Marshall. Marshall, in his trips throughout the South on civil rights cases had created a kind of legend. He had won so many cases that the white citizens' councils and the KKK feared him more than they did the president of the United States. When Marshall came to a small southern town, the word spread rapidly, and often,he had to high-tail it out of town carrying his civil rights in his brief case lest the KKK or the white citizens council got hold of him. On the U. S. Supreme Court sat Chief Justice Earl Warren, former Governor of California; Hugo Black, a former KKK member from Alabama, but who had gone through a transformation process; William Douglas, Felix Frankfurter, Potter Stewart, John Harlan, William Brennan, Tom Clark and Sherman Minton.

Facing Marshall was the renowned constitutional lawyer, John W. Davis. Davis had run for the presidency in 1924, on the Democratic ticket, and had lost to Calvin Coolidge. Since all of these cases were of similar import and were lumped together, Davis was representing South Carolina also, as a personal favor to the Governor of South Carolina. This was the chivalry and the quixotic mien of the south. The decision of the Court was unanimous. Not even a dissent was prepared. Chief Justice Warren, who wrote the opinion, held that in the field of public education the doctrine of "separate but equal" has no place and separate education facilities are inherently unequal.

The decision came as a shocker to the nation. The South was stunned. The NAACP was overjoyed. It was thought by the NAACP that school systems would comply throughout the country where enforced segregation had previously existed. But such was not the case. The Court had suggested implementation with all "deliberate speed." This was a loophole for the south and they proceeded to delay implementation. The basic error made by the U. S. Supreme Court was the failure to state a time of implementation. The late Supreme Court Justice Hugo Black admitted this omission. The great question remains: what has this decision meant to blacks, other minorities and to the country as a whole?

First we must deal with the blacks, because it is to them we give credit for bringing up this question for solution. At the present time it is not clear whether this decision has improved black education or education in the elementary and high schools in this country. The findings have not revealed the improvement the psychologists had expected. There are problems much deeper than integration which lie imbedded in the framework of the milieu of this country. For example, the intransigeance of the whites has certainly been a deterrent. Roy Wilkins, former NAACP Chief, thought that the north would accept the decision of the Court.[1] But probably nowhere has desegregation been fought so hard as it had been in the north. The State of Michigan is a prime example. The City of Boston, Massachusetts is another. Blacks in the north had blinders on their eyes when the decision was handed down. They only looked at the south. But the south was the thorny ground over which integration has walked these past twenty-four years. The benefits in education which were supposed to be derived from the Brown case will, for a long time, be from indirection rather than from direct planning for a solution.

Black social scientists in the late forties and early fifties predicted accurately that the direct benefits from the Brown case would be the final sundering of segregation in this country with the emphasis on merit and achievement. And who stood ready to move into the vacuum created by the Brown decision? The black middle class was ready. As we tick off the momentous decisions in civil rights that flowed from the Brown decision all of them brought benefits to the black middle class first. The latent skills acquired by the black middle class in teaching, home ownership, the professions and the technical crafts could now be employed. The poor black and poor minorities who lacked training were left on the "siding" and their situation is getting worse rather than better. After Brown, came the 1957 Civil Rights Act which was shepherded through Congress by the wily Lyndon B. Johnson in the Senate and Sam Rayburn in the House. From the 1957 Civil Rights Act came the 1964 and 1965 Civil Rights Acts on Voting and Equal Employment Opportunity. Since 1965, we have had the Affirmative Action clause as well as open housing legislation. The black middle class was the cutting edge in this gut struggle. But the real benefactors were the children of the black middle class born during and after

World War II. These children, born in the late forties and early
fifties, are now moving into much better jobs than were available
to their fathers and mothers. Those who were competent and who
had the minimum of a bachelor's degree were launched into careers
with incomes in five figures. At times with the wife also working,
these young families had earnings as high as $25,000 annually. Below
is a table showing how blacks have moved up the ladder in clerical,
managerial and professional jobs. There have been large declines
in occupational opportunities for blacks in the areas of household
workers, farmers and farm workers.

Table I

Percent of Change in Black Employment
and Various Occupations 1960-1970

Occupation	1960	1970	% Change
Professional/technical	331,000	766,000	+131
Manager official/proprietor	178,000	331,000	+67
Clerical	503,000	1,113,000	+121
Sales	101,000	179,000	+77
Craftsman/foreman	415,000	691,000	+67
Operative	1,414,000	2,004,000	+42
Service workers, except Private household	1,214,000	1,547,000	+27
Private household workers	982,000	653,000	-34
Nonfarm workers	951,000	866,000	-9
Farmers and farm workers	841,000	328,000	-61
Total	6,927,000	8,445,000	+22

Source: U. S. Dept. of Labor, Bureau of Labor Statistics, 1974

The above table shows that the black middle class has moved
into the areas of management and professional work.

In the executive suites of this country, however, blacks
must still make their mark. Nowhere do we find blacks being
trained to run General Motors or A. T. & T. or General Foods.
The young blacks that are working on their MBA's are usually
hired as junior managers in marketing, accounting, finance, personnel and administration. What is needed after the academics
are completed, is on-the-job training for blacks in the real
executive suites. If the executive suites continue to remain
closed to blacks, then blacks must once again resort to use of
power where it is felt the most: consumer power. Black consumers
with a $60 billion market, consume a far greater proportion of the
following categories: liquor, soft drinks, clothing, housing,
entertainment, autos, gasoline, air-travel, cosmetics, radio-TV,
stereo, movies, tobacco, appliances, and household wares than their
percentage of the population in this country.

Whereas the black middle class has improved considerably
economically and politically in the past twenty-five years, what
has been the impact of the Brown decision and other subsequent
civil rights measures upon whites? The basic impact has been shown
by the changes in the behavior of whites. Where it was formerly
legal to segregate, now it is not. Segregation and discrimination
are no longer the way of life which was in the past extolled by
whites and apologized for by some blacks. This does not mean to
say that racism is ended in this country. Far from it. Institutionalized racism is difficult to overcome, but measures are being

taken to change the institution of racism. Such institutional
racism is so subtle that even whites at times are unaware that
they are racists. Kenneth Clark, a psychologist, and past president of the American Psychological Association, holds that:

> Unlike Southern white supremacists, who make no
> bones about their feelings, the strongest supporters of
> institutional racism have an exactly contrary personal
> image. These proponents of invidious racism--as I call
> it--think they're free of it, or if they acknowledge it
> at all, they claim the distinctions they make are empiri-
> cally based. They really think they're not like other
> whites.

> Therefore, given that self-image--a powerful defense
> mechanism--any attempt of discussing the subject evokes
> an emotional polemic, and probably an attack on the
> questioner for being a racist himself. That, cf course,
> postpones coming to grips with reality or with facing the
> real issue, for you first have to deal with the question
> of who is a racist. Such people will then trot out their
> credentials. Basically, this is all diversionary, and by
> the time you've dealt with the diversion, you're emotionally
> exhausted before you get at the real issue.

> The intensity of the delusion you're dealing with is
> really a deep unwillingness to change. The psychological
> devices that are used merely indicate the depth of the
> racism. For these people have invested so much of them-
> selves in the emotional part of all this, that any signifi-
> cant change would make them admit much more than they can
> possibly admit about themselves. [2]

Middle class blacks who have become mobile and have benefited
from the Brown decision, as well as subsequent legislation, still
are confronted with obstacles erected by whites. It is apparent
now that blacks and other ethnic groups of middle income stature
are moving into the mainstream, whites still want to call the shots
and determine policy affecting these blacks. Racism comes to the
fore when it is observed how whites talk about blacks and how they

treat blacks. Even when there are black management personnel in a company or union, there is usually white person who will invariably checkmate the black on issues involving equal employment opportunity, promotions and assumption of posts on boards of directors. Deeply imbedded in the black middle class are dire thoughts that whites think they should rule because they are white, not because they are competent. These attitudes on the part of whites will delay the development of a society based on meritocracy. Racism will wither away as ethnics in this society gain higher self-esteem, greater education, business expertise, professional competence and voting skills. The consequences of Brown vs. School Board are still unfolding. Results from this great decision will be beneficial to blacks and whites, contingent upon the follow-through of the Civil Rights Act of 1964, Affirmative Action and other subsequent legislation that bears on these basic issues.

From Brown vs. School Board, which brought minorities back into the mainstream of this society, we must now review poverty, one of the dragons that plague the minorities.

REFERENCES

1. New York Times, Magazine, May 12, 1974, pp. 43 - 60.
2. Ibid.

CHAPTER II

The War on Poverty

President Johnson signed the Economic Opportunity Act on
August 20, 1964. It was a declared policy of this country to
eliminate the irony of poverty in an affluent society. It is
quite obvious that the swelling rhetoric on poverty was not joined
by implementation. The country did not try hard enough to conquer
poverty. One of the basic flaws in setting up the war on poverty
was that it came under the aegis of the Executive Branch of the
Government. It was never given an independent cabinet status. This
was the way it was meant, even from the beginning. Quite early the
program came under severe criticism from the conservaties in the
Democratic and Republican parties. Local politicians, also, began
sending out their hatchet men to cut up and carve the OEO out of
existence. The conservative Democrat and Republican always thought
such expenditure of funds was a waste. Poverty would be with us
always, so why do anything about an underclass, one that would
not help itself? The local politician in this country thought
Community Action Agencies were a threat to him at city hall. The
local politician in this country thinks in terms of precincts and
head hunting. His weakness has been in numbers and not in quality.
The local politician had thought the CAA's would alienate the poor
from city hall which had always taken care of the poor in its own
way--permitting the numbers games and other forms of gambling,

getting individuals on relief, getting a chosen few out of jail, fixing traffic tickets and finding jobs for the party faithful.

In getting off on the wrong path, the war on poverty, unlike so many other government sponsored programs alienated other ethnic groups in the population. At first glance, the war on poverty was looked upon as a solution to the black man's problems in economics. Immediately this turned off the vast number of ethnic groups such as the "hard hats" as well as the whites who thought that blacks were going to get something they would not get. It was never propagandized in this country that most of the poverty people were white, not black. But the press and government edicts always stressed that blacks would be beneficiaries from the war on poverty.

Location of the Poor

Where were the poor located? The data below show the country divided into four sections: Northeast, North Central, South and West. The West has the least poverty, about sixteen percent of all the poor in the nation and eleven percent of the population in this region. The Northeast, which includes New England and the Middle Atlantic states of New York, Pennsylvania and New Jersey, has 4,200,000 people with about seventeen percent of the poor in the nation and with ten percent of its population in this category. In the South is found the heaviest incidence of poverty. It has more than 12,000,000 on the poverty level. Houston, the largest city in the region has one out of five on the poverty level, a percentage of twenty percent. The South including Texas has about half of the poverty recipients and the North Central has seventeen percent.

As late as November, 1975, a report from Shreveport, Louisiana, revealed that the Caddo Parish Police Jury, in an application for federal funds, stated that one-third of its residents lived on incomes below the federal poverty level. The population of Caddo Parish is 232,699. Of this number 79,510 or about thirty-four percent were living below the poverty level. At this time the poverty level for a family of four was $4360.[1]

The Other War

A second subtle cause of the drop in interest in the war on poverty was the Vietnam War. After President Johnson was elected in 1964, he stepped up the war in Vietnam. It was bandied about in Washington by Robert McNamara, the Defense Chief, and the Pentagon, that within two years the little brown people in southeast Asia, fighting tenaciously on rice and dried fish, and proving a match for the United Nations Forces, would be subdued. So, a massive build-up went on, with more troops and war goods being sent to South Vietnam. After about two years of intensive fighting, President Johnson became so exasperated with the war effort that he called in John J. McCloy, the CIA Chief. He asked McCloy why it was that his CIA, who know everything, was so derelict in not knowing the potential of these "ragged-ass brown people" in Vietnam. McCloy could not answer Johnson. Later he resigned from the CIA. As the war deepened and demonstrations began to focus on Johnson and the administration, he decided not to run for the office of the Presidency in 1968.

Poverty Guidelines

Poverty guidelines were issued by OEO at the beginning of
the program. Sources of these guidelines were derived from the
Department of Agriculture, based on the minimum subsistence needs
of family size running from one person to seven. Non-farm families'
guidelines were higher than farm families because the farm family
could augment its income by raising some of its food. The non-farm
family is severely limited as to the amount of its own food it can
grow. Alaska and Hawaii have higher allotments for both categories
of non-farm and farm families. Cost of living is higher in these
states.Family size runs from one to seven persons. A family can be
one person if that person is maintaining a household.

Table II

OEO Poverty Guidelines for all States
Except Alaska and Hawaii for 1971

Family Size	Non-farm Family	Farm Family
1	$2,000	$1,700
2	2,600	2,100
3	3,300	2,800
4	4,000	3,400
5	4,700	4,000
6	5,300	4,500
7	5,900	5,000

For families with more than 7 members, add $600 for each
additional member in a non-farm family and $500 for each
member in a farm family.

Table III

OEO Poverty Guidelines for Alaska

Family Size	Non-farm Family	Farm Family
1	$2,500	$2,125
2	3,000	2,550
3	3,650	3,100
4	4,400	3,750
5	5,200	4,425
6	5,850	4,975
7	6,500	5,525

For families with more than 7 members, add $750 for each
additional member in a non-farm family and $650 for each
additional member in a farm family.

Table IV

OEO Poverty Guidelines for Hawaii

Family Size	Non-farm Family	Farm Family
1	$2,300	$1,975
2	3,000	2,550
3	3,650	3,100
4	4,400	3,750
5	5,200	4,425

Table IV (continued)

Family Size	Non-farm Family	Farm Family
6	$5,850	$4,975
7	6,500	5,525

For families with more than 7 members, add $650 for each additional member in a non-farm family and $550 for each additional in a farm family.

Source: OEO November 19, 1971

Other Events

Since Lyndon B. Johnson said he would not run, Robert Kennedy, who had taken soundings on the office of the president, and in the meantime,became the U. S. Senator from New York, made a stronger bid. Robert Kennedy was assassinated in Los Angeles, California, in May, 1968. Hubert Humphrey, who was Vice President, stepped into the breach and made the race. However, in April, 1968, Martin Luther King was assassinated in Memphis, Tennessee. The malaise of this country had begun with the assassination of John F. Kennedy in Dallas, Texas, November 22, 1963. It was now deepening and spreading. Under the impact of these bizarre, tragic events, the War on Poverty was placed on the sidelines by government and the people. It no longer had a clear direction of where it was going. R. Sargent Shriver, Jr. was the director, and any number of political appointees knew less than he. This statement is not to demean the true, faithful workers in the war on poverty who knew what it took to overcome poverty. Many of these people had been poverty-stricken themselves, and they were able to discuss poverty and the social and economic issues involved. The political hacks from city hall and the state capitals of the nation, however, did not serve the poor but served themselves. The "short rope trick" was being played on the poor.

The Other War, Again

The presidential election of 1968, was a close one. Hubert Humphrey, the politician of joy, was defeated by less than 200,000 votes by Richard Nixon, the dour, convoluted politician who had a long history of a poor press, and a form of paranoia that was unusual in a United States president. Again, the new president became absorbed in Vietnam. Although he had campaigned like Johnson to end the war in Vietnam, he actually stepped up the war with increased bombing, and dropping of napalm, a jelly-like substance that burned intensively. People upon whom it was dropped, actually were incinerated. Although we had enough on our hands in Vietnam, President Nixon, without consulting Congress, ordered the bombing of Cambodia in 1970. Exhibiting the paradoxical nature of his administration, Nixon was also trying to end the war in Vietnam. Henry Kissinger, his able National Security Chief and minister without portfolio, made many trips to South Vietnam to seek to negotiate a peace. After many, many, many demonstrations against

the war and its legacy of immorality, military intervention, and
desertion by the young men of this country, a compromise-negotiated
settlement was reached. Troops began to be withdrawn from South
Vietnam in stages. While this was taking place, more and more of
the American people became disenchanted with the War on Poverty.
Running on a platform of peace with honor in Vietnam, and a lack-
luster campaign by George McGovern, Nixon won the presidency again
in 1972 by a majority vote of sixty-four percent, one of the largest
pluralities since Franklin Roosevelt defeated Alf Landon in 1936.
The victory by Nixon was not a victory won by Nixon. It was a
Pyrrhic victory. A victory of the hard hats, blue collar, conservative forces who wanted to put the black man and woman in their
place. George McGovern had used so many long hairs, nondescript
people, in his race that his campaign rhetoric even turned off
liberals and blacks.

Dismantling OEO

After Nixon's victory in 1972, the man had hardly been
inaugurated before he began to scuttle the Office of Economic
Opportunity. Although some of the criticism was valid, such
as drug addicts using OEO funds for rehabilitation and the use
of funds to undermine political candidates, yet one does not
usually throw the baby out with the bath water.

After a succession of five OEO directors in twenty-four
months: Donald Rumsfeld, Frank Carluci, Philip Sanchez, Howard
Phillips and Alvin Arnet, the poverty program began a holding

action. When Nixon, in 1972-73 sent to Congress bills designed to
dismantle the agency, the local politician, the social worker and
the community action activist resisted these changes, with the
result that Congress began to look a little harder at what had
been accomplished by the OEO. In its short, hectic, ten-year
history the Office of Economic Opportunity had produced a new perspective toward overcoming poverty.

The most successful innovation was Head Start. This program of basic education for the ghetto child has done more to
enlighten the child and to make him aware of his responsibilities
to himself and his fellow man, than any similar program. The
teachers in Head Start exerted consummate skills to reach this
child. A counterpart to this program was Upward Bound. This
program concerned itself with the ghetto teenager, and was involved
in early skills, recreation during summer on the baseball field,
swimming pool and basketball court. Other innovations were the
Job Corps, community action agencies, the concentrated employment
program, concern for migratory labor, health care, economic development, operation mainstream , training paraprofessionals, providing
legal services, an awareness of self-help in the ghetto, tutorial
educational   programs and a plethora of other services that
were basic to needy Americans. The unseen factor that has been
overlooked is that the poverty program was the springboard for
thousands of Americans into other careers such as politics for
Ronald Dellums of California, Parren Mitchell of Maryland, Coleman

Young of Detroit and Theodore Berry of Cincinnati. In the areas of education, business and job careers, OEO was the launch pad for many individuals.

Seeking to restructure society in its own image was one of the flaws of OEO. The radical left, who got control of some of the programs, meant to turn things around. They failed because people could not be restructured in the way they wanted, and also because of the costs of the Vietnam war. Donald Rumsfeld, the first director appointed by Nixon, tried to restructure OEO by omitting the words poverty and the poor. He called poverty people low income. Rumsfeld, as a Congressman was from Chicago's north sector. He had voted against OEO in 1964. Concurrent with Rumsfeld's appointment was an underlying suspicion of the staff people on OEO that Rumsfeld was appointed as the undertaker of the agency. Under such a cloud of apprehension, the agency, during the Nixon regime, never could become an effective representative of the poor. Rumsfeld made a large number of political appointees, among them were YAFER's, or Young Americans for Freedom. This junior college segment of the Nixon campaign of 1968, really surfaced after Nixon was heavily reelected in 1972. Sensing that he could take McGovern, Nixon went all out, not only with the YAFER's, but waded into Watergate which was ultimately his Waterloo. Rumsfeld was followed in quick succession by Frank Carluci and Philip Sanchez. All three of these OEO Directors later served as ambassadors: Rumsfeld to NATO, Carluci to Portugal and Sanchez to Colombia. Howard Phillips

was appointed director in January, 1973. Phillips' avowed purpose
was to destroy OEO. In his appearance before the National Advisory
Council on Economic Opportunity, in January, 1973, Phillips let
it be known that OEO was to be split up among a half dozen government agencies, and only a skeleton force was to remain under White
House jurisdiction. Since the die had been cast now, forces began
to rise to oppose Phillips and the administration. OEO employees
went to court to block Phillips' action because he was serving
illegally. His name had never been submitted to the Senate for
confirmation and thus could only legally serve thirty days. He
probably would have been rejected by the Senate. Phillips lost
this battle before he had served six months. A year later, Phillips was seeking to arouse Republican conservatives against Nixon
because of the refunding of the legal services for the poor.

After the demise of Phillips, Nixon appointed Alvin Arnett,
a man who had greater empathy for OEO. Arnett wanted to preserve
OEO and actually lobbied for its continuance. However, he was
fired by Nixon while the president was in the throes of Watergate,
just before his resignation in August, 1974.

Speaking at the "New Day with Community Action Programs"
Conference at Chatham Center in Pittsburgh on Friday, April 25,
1975, Alvin Arnett blamed the federal government for undercutting
the fight on poverty. There was no real commitment on the part
of the federal government, the former OEO head lamented. The
poverty war was a "skirmish."

From 1964 to 1975, poverty was reduced from 36 million to 23 million. In 1964, there were 180 million United States citizens on the poverty level. The poverty class comprised twenty percent or one out of every five United States citizens. In 1975, poverty was reduced to eleven percent or about one out of every ten people in the United States. In 1964, the poverty income level for a family of four was $3,000. By 1975, the poverty income level was $4,000. Credit for reducing the poverty class should be given to the community action programs according to Arnett. "We don't know what worked, but all we know is that it did work. There's no way to accurately document it," he declared.[2]

Reorganization of Poverty Act

After Gerald R. Ford assumed the presidency in August, 1974, and Nixon returned to San Clemente, Bert Gallegos, a Denver lawyer, was appointed director of OEO. Gallegos had formerly been OEO's general counsel. In previous meetings he had been optimistic that OEO would continue intact. However, President Ford and Congress planned to complete the transference of certain programs under OEO to other government agencies. Some agencies had been previously transferred by amendments to the original act in 1969 and 1971. The new Community Services Act of 1974 (Public Law 93-644) completed the transformation of OEO. The title of the new law was Head Start, Economic Opportunity and Community Partnership Act of 1974; the short title: Community Service Act of 1974.

The National Advisory Council on Economic Opportunity

The advisory arm of the Office of Economic Opportunity has been the National Advisory Council on Economic Opportunity (NACEO). The NACEO was created by Congress in 1966 under Section 605 of the Act. Its twenty-one members, including the Chairman, were appointed by the President. The first Council was appointed in March, 1967, by the late President Lyndon B. Johnson. The main function of the Council is to report to Congress through the President each year what the Council thinks collectively is necessary to ameliorate poverty and eventually to eradicate poverty.

The so-called War on Poverty was started in 1964. But it was not a war, it was a skirmish. The Council did not get going until three or four years later, because it did not get going until March 31, 1968. One aspect of the Council's work is to focus its attention each year on a segment of the poverty problem. The Council appoints various subcommittees to zero in on the problem and come up with recommendations to Congress. A note must be made here of the members of the Council. Judges, executives, labor leaders, professors, lawyers, housewives, Indians, blacks, Chicanos, entertainers and whites have been members of the Council at one time or another since 1967. Some of the outstanding people who have served on the Council have been the late Whitney Young, Jr., when he was Executive Director of the Urban League and Sammy Davis, Jr.

The first Council had twenty-one members:

1.	Morris I. Leibman, Chairman	Attorney	Chicago, Ill.
2.	Morris Abram	Attorney	New York, N. Y.
3.	Horace Busby	Consultant	Sandy Springs, Md.
4.	John Patrick Cardinal Cody	Archbishop	Chicago, Ill.
5.	George R. Davis	Minister	Washington, D. C.
6.	Otto Eckstein	Economist	Cambridge, Mass.
7.	Buford Ellington	Governor	Tennessee
8.	Hector P. Garcia	Medical Doctor	Corpus Christi, Tx.
9.	Walter Lane	Medical Doctor	Temple Terrace, Fla.
10.	Sidney Marland, Jr.	Supt. of Schools	Pittsburgh, Pa.
11.	Donald H. McGannon	Pres. and Chairman, Westinghouse Broadcasting Corp.	New York, N. Y.
12.	Theodore McKeldin	Attorney	Baltimore, Md.
13.	Mrs. Robert McNamara	Housewife	Washington, D. C.
14.	Albert Rains	Attorney	Gadsden, Ala.
15.	Carl Sanders	Attorney	Atlanta, Ga.
16.	James A. Suffridge	Pres., Retail Clerks, AFL-CIO	Washington, D. C.
17.	David Sullivan	Pres., Building Services Employees International Union AFL-CIO	Washington, D. C.
18.	Cato W. Valandra	President, Rosebud Sioux Tribe	Rosebud, S. Dak.
19.	Louie Welch	Mayor, City of Houston	Houston, Tx.
20.	Whitney M. Young, Jr.	Executive Director Urban League	New York, N. Y.
21.	Jesse Kellam	(Resigned from the Council before years end)	

Lawyers outnumbered any other occupation on the first Council. This is not because they are seeking employment, but because of their presence. But the cross section of the Council and the geographic distribution show a wide dispersion. However, the region that has the greatest incidence of poverty, the South, had about seven on the Council or one-third of the total membership.

The first Council, in their report in 1968, reviewed the massive amount of literature on poverty. Assisted in their review of the literature by a professional and research staff and through their own observations, the Council affirmed among other things that:

1. The Office of Economic Opportunity is an essential tool in the national effort to eradicate poverty.

2. The Office of Economic Opportunity represents a unique governmental approach towards solving a major social problem. Its programs have been experimental and innovative and they must remain so.

3. The Community Action Programs of the Office of Economic Opportunity are the most promising development of the war on poverty because they have:
   **proved the need for total community involvement, including government, the poor, the private business sector, and the traditional social agencies in multiple approaches to solving local problems;
   **provided a forum and a vehicle for representatives of the poor to be involved in local decisions affecting their lives;
   **emphasized local initiative and maximum feasible participation of the poor in planning and executing the programs designed to help them break out of poverty;
   **developed and tested new techniques for combating poverty including neighborhood centers, neighborhood corporations, resident nonprofessional workers,and "outreach" as a new mode of communications to the poor;
   **encouraged flexibility, innovation, and creativity in approach, method, organization, and operations.

The recommendations of the Council were that:

1. The antipoverty programs, especially community action, remain flexible, multifaceted, and experimental in nature, whether executed by existing or new organizations. No single-strategy approach will work.

2. The basic idea of community action--community involvement and maximum feasible participation by all elements of the local community--be preserved and strengthened.

3. At least 50 percent of funds appropriated for the community action programs be made available for funding locally initiated projects, in order to strengthen the principles of local initiative and maximum feasible participation.

Focus of the first Council was on Community Action and the "issues surrounding the goals and purposes of the Office of Economic Opportunity."[3]

The Second Report of the Council was virtually a follow-up to the First Report. Although members of the Council are appointed to three-year staggered terms, virtually the same Council that initiated the first report also wrote the second report. Even before the election of Richard Nixon in 1968, the Office of Economic Opportunity began to undergo changes. Contrary to the Council's recommendation, Upward Bound and the Foster Grandparents program under legislative mandate were transferred to the Department of Health, Education and Welfare.

By the time the Third Annual Report was published in 1970, terms of fourteen members of the Council had expired. Also, it must be remembered that the Economic Opportunity Act of 1964, as amended, had expired June 30, 1969. Congress did not extend the Act which included the operation of the Council until late December, 1969. No formal meetings of the Council had been held since March, 1969, because there were not enough members to constitute a quorum. Once the legal mandate had been given for continuation of the Council after December, 1969, the Council in its recommendations to Congress continued to stress the need of continuing the community action program. It emphasized that local initiative in planning and operation was necessary for fulfillment of the objectives of the program.

The Fourth Annual Report of the Council was more of a holding action than one of pointing out solutions to the poverty problem. The new chairman of the Council was John E. Rosson, senior partner of Liebman, Williams, Bennett, Baird, and Minow, a law firm with offices in Chicago and Washington, D. C. Other members of the Council are listed below.

1.	Harold H. Anderson	Retired Publisher	Chicago, Ill.
2.	Ruth N. Atkins	Community Development Specialist	New York, N. Y.
3.	Robert A. Arkison	Executive Vice Pres. Coenen and Co., Inc.	New York, N. Y.
4.	Edward C. Banfield	Professor-Harvard University	Cambridge, Mass.
5.	William W. Bradley	Professional Basketball player New York Knickerbockers	New York, N. Y.
6.	Damasio C. Cano	Relocation Officer Mercedes Urban Renewal	Mercedes, Tx.
7.	Sammy Davis, Jr.	Professional Entertainer	Los Angeles, Calif.
8.	Warren H. Day	Day and Brown Insurance	Long Beach, Calif.
9.	Patricia H. Dunbar	Executive Committee Admin. Board Society of Memorial Sloan-Ketterng Cancer Center	New York, N. Y.
10.	Owen B. Echo-Hawk	Consulting Geophyicist	Tulsa, Okla.
11.	Gustave C. Gilg	General Manager Trans Parts and Motor Parts	San Juan, P. R.
12.	William Gorham	President The Urban Institute	Washington, D. C.
13.	Donald R. Hayes, M. D.	Retired General Surgeon	Longmeadow, Mass.

14.	Richard G. Lugar	Mayor	Indianapolis, Ind.
15.	Woodrow W. Mathna	Mayor	Lorain, Ohio
16.	Ruth G. Melton	President and Treasurer-Southside Day Care Action Group	High Point, N. C.

One of the significant changes on the Council was the death of Whitney M. Young, Jr., Executive Director of the Urban League. Coming from the Atlanta School of Social Work, where he had served as Dean, Young did a remarkable job in bringing the League into a position where he had the ear of the executive suite in the corporate structure of this country. He was working for more jobs in industry for blacks and minorities in this country. While on a trip to Africa along with a group of professionals including Ramsey Clark, Young died while swimming off the coast of Ghana. President Nixon ordered an Air Force jet to Africa to fly Whitney's body back home. Lieutenant General Daniel "Chappie" James, the highest ranking black, in the military piloted the jet. President Nixon delivered the eulogy at Young's funeral in Kentucky. Replacing Young on the Council was the celebrated entertainer, Sammy Davis, Jr.

Along with changes in the Council were changes in the professional staff that began service in 1970-71.

PROFESSIONAL STAFF

Bradley H. Patterson, Jr., Executive Director (on leave)
Walter B. Quetsch, Deputy Director
Kenneth L. Adelman, Research Specialist
Jack Nelson, Research Specialist
Margery Sorock, Research Specialist
Victoria B. Oliver, Administrative Officer

CONSULTANTS

Harold Segal   Jeanne Viner

SECRETARIAL AND CLERICAL

Maxine M. Snyder   Marie Ann Rausa
Mathhew Phillips, Jr.   Shiela Diane Peterson
Diane Graham

GOVERNMENT REORGANIZATION

Because of the proposals on executive reorganization, the
NACOEO was cast into temporary limbo. Reaching back into history
it was found that almost every new administration weighs in with
innovations on government restructuring. It is almost like
moving pieces around on a chessboard. In 1937, the Brownlow
Commission suggested a Conservation Commission. Gifford Pinchot,
governor of Pennsylvania, and Teddy Roosevelt were two of our
earliest conservationists and environmentalists.

For example, after World War II, the Hoover Commission made
recommendations when Harry Truman was President. These recommendations were carried over into implementation during Dwight D.
Eisenhower's tenure in office, along with suggestions from the
Rockefeller Commission. A new Department of Health, Education
and Welfare was created. Mrs. Oveta Culp Hobby, a former Colonel
in the Women's Army Corps in World War II, and owner of the
Houston Post, was appointed the first Secretary over this new
government department.

During the Kennedy administration, a task force on government reorganization recommended new departments of Transportation

and Housing and Urban Development. Before these could be implemented, Kennedy was assassinated in Dallas, Texas, and it was
left to Lyndon B. Johnson to implement these new departments in
his administration.

Among the recommendations of the Ashe Council, which was
appointed by President Nixon, was a phase-out of the Office of
Economic Opportunity. The Ashe Council recommended that the
on-going programs of OEO be turned over to new departments and
evaluation be conducted by the Domestic Council and the Office of
Management and Budget. President Nixon changed his mind in 1973
because the agency resisted this proposed role and decided to
abolish it. One of the Ashe Council's recommendation was
accepted. This was the creation of the Environment Protection
Agency.

Proposed Four New Departments

On March 21, 1971, President Nixon,in the most sweeping
proposal for government reorganization since the Hoover Commission,
suggested or recommended four new departments to Congress.

The President's Proposals

An understanding of how the executive reorganization
would affect the Office of Economic Opportunity requires
some understanding of the reorganization in its entirety.
The proposed purposes of the four new departments as
described by the President in his March 25, 1971, message
to Congress were:

1. The Department of Natural Resources to
***bring together the many natural resource responsi-
bilities now scattered through out the federal
government. This Department would work to conserve,

manage and utilize our resources in a way that would
protect the quality of the environment and achieve
a true harmony between man and nature.

2. The Department of Community Development to
***help build a wholesome and safe community environ-
ment for every American. This process would require
a comprehensive series of programs which are equal
to the demands of growing population and which provide for balanced growth in urban and rural areas.

3. The Department of Human Resources to
***unify major federal efforts to assist the development
of individual potential and family well-being. This
Department would be subdivided, in turn, into
three major administrations: Health, Human Development, and Income Security.

4. The Department of Economic Affairs to
***promote economic growth, to foster economic justice,
and to encourage more efficient and more productive
relationship among the various elements of our
economy and those of other nations. As this single
new department joined the Teasury Department, the
Council of Economic Advisers and the new Federal
Reserve Board in shaping economic policy, it would
speak with a stronger voice and would offer a more
effective, more highly integrated viewpoint than
four different departments can do at present.

The President recommended these four new departments
in order to reduce the present "fragmentation of Federal
responsibility." The existing structure often precluded
a coordinated attack on complex problems because no one
agency has the overall responsibility, authority and
organization for coping with a particular problem and for
implementing solutions and longrange policies. As a
result, there was often duplication of effort in some areas,
neglect of pressing issues in others, as well as over-
centralization of decision-making. This was accomplished
at great inconvenience, expense and diminished effectiveness
of state and local public officials who have to deal with
multiple Federal agencies. Such diffusion of authority
and responsibility makes it difficult and sometimes impossible to insure that the intentions of the Congress and
the President are executed.
The proposed reorganization was aimed at structuring
the executive branch around delineated functional areas

designed to eliminate or reduce the duplication and deficiencies of the present organization.

The Effects on NACEO and the Fourth Report

Once it was known that OEO would be dismantled, a further

holding action set in with the NACEO. Just as subsequent reports

wanted OEO to continue in its original role, so the issue was

advanced in the Fourth Report. Included in the report was the

part OEO could play as an advocate for the poor. However, the

report was redundant in that OEO would be involved in the presi-

dential plans for reorganization and revenue sharing. How OEO

would survive was not answered. Regional meetings and committee

assignments and studies on executive reorganization and special

revenue sharing ended the Fourth Annual Report.

The Fifth, Sixth and Seventh Annual Reports of NACEO were

transitory. Whereas the members of the Council in November, 1972,

had a full complement of members, by the time of the Seventh

Report, the Council had dwindled down to nine active members and

in September, 1974, this number had been cut to seven.

The Fifth Annual Report of NACEO

The Fifth Annual Report was devoted almost in its entirety

to the involvement of the poor in the broadcast media. In his

letter of transmittal to President Nixon, John E. Robson, Chairman,

stated that:

> In your inaugural address you stressed the importance
> of learning from one another by speaking so that our words
> as well as our voices can be heard. This report examines

communications among and about the poor, antipoverty programs and the people who administer these programs. Particular attention is paid to the words that are heard
and the way they are interpreted by the listeners. [4]

Realizing the need of communication with the poor, the

Fifth Annual Report reflected the impact of TV and Cable TV in

particular. "Black Perspective" carried an article on "What

Cable TV can mean to the Black Community." [5]

Blacks and the Media

As a sort of confirmation of Black Perspective and inves-

tigations of TV in the Fifth Annual Report, 1972, it was found, in

a special survey by the A. C. Nielson Co., that the percentage of

time TV was viewed by blacks was much higher than that of the

general population. Surveys were conducted in Chicago, Washing-

ton, Detroit, Philadelphia and Cleveland. These cities have high

black population densities.

Taking one city from the survey, it was found in Chicago

that black families watch TV on an average of almost fifty-two

hours a week. The general population, according to Nielson,

watches TV forty-three hours per week. At the time of the survey

the top ten shows that blacks preferred were: Sanford and Son, All

in the Family, Good Times, Streets of San Francisco, Maude, Flip

Wilson (cancelled), Kojak, Soul Train, M*A*S*H and Barnaby Jones. [6]

Also, during 1974, the National Black Network, this country's

only black controlled radio network, formed the National Black

Network Wire Service. The service started in the spring of 1975 with New York as the location for headquarters. Bureaus were planned for Chicago, Washington, D. C., Los Angeles and Atlanta.

Because of a lack of communication among the poor and a need for establishing better communications, NACEO, in its Fifth Annual Report, found that, after virtually tons of material such as brochures and flyers were distributed together with the use of Outreach Workers, information still did not reach the poor. These results mean that either the poor don't read, cannot understand what is read or they do not have confidence in the Outreach Worker. It has been found,however,that it is possible for the Outreach Worker to become a potent force in Community Action Agencies.

Underscoring Community Action Agencies was the second major recommendation of the Fifth Annual Report. By recommending emphasis on this part of OEO overall program, the NACEO upstaged the demand for continuation of the CAA's when the OEO came under severe stress in 1973-74.

The Sixth Annual Report

As the Fifth Annual Report was completed in the spring of 1972, almost a whole new National Advisory Council on Economic Opportunity was convened in November, 1972. Norman A. Hodges, a personable black man with a graying Afro, was named chairman. Hodges was president of the California Green Power Foundation, and the first black chairman of the council. Later he ran for Congress in the 31st Congressional District on the Republican ticket in California in November, 1974,and was beaten by a democrat.

The Council which was convened in November, 1972, was highly representative of the ethnic groups in this country. The Council had thirteen whites, four blacks, three Mexican-Americans, and one Indian. Within these twenty-one individuals there were fifteen men and six women. On the Council were lawyers, judges, economists, investment specialist, bankers, labor union representatives, community development specialists and housewives. A list of Council members is below.

1.	Norman A. Hodges, Chairman	President, California Green Power Foundation	Los Angeles, Calif.
2.	Robert A. Arkison	Lehman Brothers Investment Bankers	New York, N. Y.
3.	Ruth N. Atkins	Community Development Specialist	New York, N. Y.
4.	Rita Crocker Clements	Civic Leader	Dallas, Tx.
5.	Damasio C. Cano	Relocation Officer-Mercedes Urban Renewal	Mercedes, Tx.
6.	Americo V. Cortese	Attorney-at-Law Fell, Spaulding, Goff & Rubin	Philadelphia, Pa.
7.	Msgr. Joseph A. Dooling	Archidocesan	Newark, N. J.
8.	Patricia H. Dunbar	Board of Directors and Vice President, Tellco Information Services, Inc.	New York, N. Y.
9.	Owen B. Echo-Hawk	President	Tulsa, Okla.
10.	Thomas E. Geraghty	Professor University of Tennessee	Signal Mountain, Tenn.
11.	Jesse E. Gloster	Professor Texas Southern University	Houston, Tx.
12.	Willis D. Gradison, Jr.	Partner W. D. Gradison and Company	Cincinnati, Ohio
13.	Morris Herring	Board of Directors Banco de las Americas	Tucson, Ariz.

14.	Dorothy E. Kyle	Civic Leader	Waterloo, Ia.
15.	Richard G. Lugar	Mayor	Indianapolis, Ind.
16.	Frank C. Padzieski	President Dearborn Underwriters, Inc.	Dearborn, Mich.
17.	Stella C. Sandoval	Commissioner Fair Employment Practices Commission	Anaheim, Calif.
18.	Paul A. Tranchitella	Judge Court of Common Pleas	Philadelphia, Pa.
19.	Joseph Trerotola	President Joint Council #16 International Brotherhood of Teamsters	New York, N. Y.
20.	Sherman Unger	Attorney-at-Law	Cincinnati, Ohio
21.	Ruth V. Washington	Commissioner New York State Workmen's Compensation Board	New York, N. Y.

The staff which served the Council and completed the Sixth Annual Report are listed below.

Walter B. Quetsch, Deputy Director
Fritz Baskett, Special Assistant to the Chairman
Matthew Phillips, Jr., Administrative Officer
Margery Sorock, Research Specialist
Dolores A. Washington, Executive Secretary
Jeanne Viner, Editor and Special Consultant
James M. Crothers, Consultant
Eunice Meredith, Consultant

After the appointment of committees which focused on households headed by women, children of the poor, American Indians and the unemployed in the Southwest, reports were written and submitted for Council review. Below are the conclusions of the Council in its Sixth Annual Report. Conclusions:

It is the general conclusion of the Advisory Council that the economic development aspects of the Economic Opportunity Act have had only a marginal impact on improving the long-term well-being of the poor.

The Council found that it was attempting to compare a variety
of economic development programs that were short-term,
under-funded, poorly managed and functioning in poor
market areas with programs outside of the poverty sector
that have demonstrably provided economic development.

Further, the constraints on the programs the Council was
examining have resulted in built-in mechanisms for failure
that must be eliminated before any substantial economic
progress can be made.

The Council has concluded that the most crucial element
to the longrange success of economic-development programs
is an immediate and intense effort to educate the disadvantaged to understand and use the economic opportunities that exist in the free enterprise system.

In addition, a change of attitude is needed on the part
of the federal government and those implementing economic
and business development programs for the poor. In order
to achieve any meaningful business or economic development in this country, the private sector must participate.
This participation can be enlisted only when those promoting government-sponsored economic development projects
convey the idea that their efforts are in concert with
successful private enterprise approaches.

Further, economic development programs should be designed
to establish profitable enterprise; federal agencies
administering economic development programs should not
impose social goals on business development programs.
The Council is convinced that social goals will be
achieved and the quality of life will be improved as
valid economic opportunities raise the income level of
the poor.

Aside from the findings and recommendations on economic
development and the specific groups set forth in this
report, the Council directs attention to the need for an
on-going national concern about the plights of all the
poor. Poverty in the midst of plenty still abounds in
this country. Although many of the programs examined
had minimal impact and some of the successful models
are to be continued, the demise of the Office of Economic
Opportunity leaves the poor without an identifiable
advocate at the federal level. The Council feels that
another structure must be formed to continue the attack
on poverty.

All of the time that Hodges was seeking to organize the
Council during his tenure, the OEO was undergoing changes. After
the Nixon landslide in 1972. the Office of Economic Opportunity
came under extreme criticism. The downplay of OEO was now in
effect. All during 1973 and through 1974, the Council having
its funds provided through Congress and dispensed by the General
Accounting Office, operated on almost a month to month basis.
Although such spasmodic funding placed constraints on the work
of the Council, the advocates of the poor continued to meet and
carry out their assignments.

The Seventh Report

The Seventh Annual Report under the chairmanship of Norman
Hodges had as its theme the delivery of services to the poor. It
must be remembered that during the construction of the Seventh
Annual Report, this country underwent, for the first time in its
history, the resignation of a president of this country and the
government turned very slowly, if at all. Over the whole Federal
Government in Washington, there was an air of uncertainty. The
televised Watergate hearings of 1973 led up to the publication
of the presidential transcripts. The chain of events accelerated
until a sustained clamor from the public, Congress and leaders
from his own party, called for Nixon's resignation. It was under
these conditions that the Seventh Annual Report was completed.

In his letter of transmittal to Congress, President Gerald R. Ford noted that "many of the observations and conclusions of this report are at variance with policies of this Administration."[7]

Because of the very nature of the political process and the nuances of human behavior, there are bound to be differences. President Ford was no exception. Variances would have to be resolved, if poverty was to be conquered in this society.

Since the Sixth Annual Report revealed glaring deficiencies in the program of economic development which was designed to overcome poverty as well as constraints that produced failure, the Seventh Annual Report showed how ineffective were the delivery systems that were organized to alleviate poverty. While the Seventh Annual Report was being written, inflation as well as recession hit the country simultaneously. In the winter of 1974-75, high unemployment hit the auto industry. In Detroit, 190,000 auto workers were laid off. The timber industry in the northwest also suffered high unemployment. The textile industry in the southeast and its manufacturing outlets in New York City were hard hit. The construction industry in New Jersey and the northeast reached an unemployment rate of fifteen percent. It was under these conditions that a reduced staff of seven people met in November, 1974, to plan research for 1975. The need of solving the problem of poverty was now uppermost. How it would be done could come under the advice of the Council to OEO, the Administration and the Congress.

The New Economic Opportunity Act of 1975

The new Economic Opportunity Act of 1975, came out of the Congress hopper and was approved on January 4, 1975. The new act in its preamble says:

> To provide for the extension of Headstart, community action, community economic development, and other programs under the Economic Opportunity Act of 1964, to provide for increased involvement of State and local governments in anti-poverty efforts, and for other purposes.

> Be it enacted by the Senate and House of Representatives of the United States of America in Congress Assembled, That this Act may be cited as the "Headstart, Economic Opportunity and Community Partnership Act of 1974."

> STATEMENT OF PURPOSE

> Sec. 2. It is the purpose of this Act to extend programs under the Economic Opportunity Act of 1964, including Headstart, community action, and community economic development programs; and to provide for increased involvement of State and local governments in anti-poverty efforts by authorizing a community partnership program.

From the preamble and the statement of purpose, the new Act has changed the title of the old Economic Opportunity Act of 1964, but has brought into sharper focus the involvement of local government in the solving of the poverty problem in this country.

Title II of the Act covers research and demonstrations. It is the purpose of Title II to definitely focus attention on State and local as well as on the Federal Government with regard to the responsibility to help low income families and low income individuals to get out of poverty through self help by attaining skills, knowledge and motivation necessary to enable them to become productive citizens.

Under the demonstration community partnership agreements which involve the matching of local and state funds, $50,000,000 was authorized to be appropriated for the fiscal year 1975, and such sums as might be necessary during each of the two succeeding fiscal years. However, no funds have been appropriated for these programs todate. Not more than twelve and one-half percent of such amounts could be used in any one State.

Recognizing that good health and adequate medical care are necessary to success in overcoming poverty, the Act established within the Department of Health, Education and Welfare a Comprehensive Health Services program. This program was designed to coordinate all government agencies involved in preventive medical and diagnostic treatment, rehabilitation, family planning, narcotic addiction and alcoholism prevention and rehabilitation, mental health, dental care and follow-up services. The health program was to be implemented in urban and rural areas with a high density of poverty population and highly visible inadequate health services for the poor. Counseling services for alcoholism and drug rehabilitation were provided for in Section 402 of the Act.

Head Start

This highly successful program, which aided pre-school poverty children, was developed in the early stages of the old Economic Opportunity Act, was later transferred to HEW, and now

became a major part of the new act. Title V is labeled Head-
start and Follow Through. Its avowed purpose is to focus primarily on children of low income families with health, nutritional,
educational and social problems that will require aid so that
these children may develop their full potential.

The act provides that any local public or private non-
profit agency can be designated as a Head Start Agency. The
thoroughness of this act covers allotment of funds (Sec. 513)
designation of head start agencies (Sec. 514) powers and functions of head start agencies (Sec. 515), submission of plans to
governors (Sec. 516), administrative requirements and standards
(Sec. 517), and participation in head start programs (Sec. 518).
The Act further provides for tight controls in audits, records,
technical assistance and in training, research, demonstration
and pilot projects, evaluations and follow through. To carry
out this portion of the act $60,000,000 was appropriated for
1975.

Community Services Administration

The Community Services Administration is the successor
agency of the Office of Economic Opportunity. The Director of
this agency is appointed by the President with the advice and
consent of the Senate. In this office there is one Deputy
Director and Assistant Directors. They are all appointed by
the President. The Director of the Community Services Administration

is the umbrella agency over Titles II, III, VI, VII and IX of this act. These would include previous titles dealing with research and demonstration, Comprehensive Health Services, and Head Start. For carrying out Title VII of this act $39,000,000 is appropriated. Title VII is classed as Community Economic Development. Section 701 of the CED specifically involves the community in helping to solve its economic problems through social participation in the community life. A community development corporation is defined as a nonprofit organization that is responsible to the residents of the area and of which fifty percent is owned by these residents. Financial assistance is to be provided in grants to both nonprofit and profit community development corporations. Programs for such CED's can include business development programs, providing equity capital to start, expand or locate businesses in or near the area served so as to provide employment and ownership opportunities for residents of such areas. All of these programs are designed to eventually eliminate poverty and to establish permanent economic and social benefits in such areas.

Rural Programs

It is the intent of this act to aid rural poverty areas through self help and economic cooperation. Such aid can be done through financing cooperatives, improving the operation of family farms, and financing non-agricultural enterprises which will enable a family to derive income from activities other than farming.

A major feature of the CED is the development loan concept. In recent years there have been suggestions for a development bank, but the development loan and revolving fund will suffice. Loans can be made either direct or through banks. Loans made by the Director will bear interest at a rate determined by the Secretary of the Treasury. The Secretary will determine such a rate based on the market yield of treasury obligations. In other words, if the treasury bills are selling at .055, or five and one-half percent, then direct loans can be made at this rate. All such loans will be repayable in a period of not more than thirty years. For the purpose of carrying out portions of this act pertaining to the Community Development Loan Fund, $60,000,000 will be made available from appropriations.

All of the programs coming under Community Economic Development carry provisions for technical assistance in management, entrepreneurial development, legal services, and capital outlays. Limitations on assistance for financial services are conditioned on feasibility studies, fulfilling a need for services which are being met.

Provisions for Indians on Federal and State Reservations

Title VIII makes provisions for financial aid to native Americans such as Indians, Hawaiian natives and Alaskan natives. Financial assistance under this title is made available to a nonprofit or profit agency up to eighty percent of cost. The

Secretary has the option of providing more than eighty percent
if he deems it necessary to carry out the project. Non-Federal
contributions shall be in cash or in kind. All projects under
this act which are approved for implementation will be in addition
to the project and not in substitution thereof. As in other
titles which have been mentioned, similar constraints are placed
on these funds to native Americans. Plans must be submitted to
state and local officials for approval. These would include
research, demonstration and pilot projects. Scrupulous care must
be given to records and audits.

Summary

The Community Services Act of 1974 is an all-embracing law
designed   to be used to overcome poverty and to improve near
poverty in the United States. With its large number of amendments,
the new act is likely to be better than its predecessor. The
reason for this is that, throughout the act, it is spelled out
that poverty must be ameliorated or overcome. The ways and means
of doing this are also spelled out. The great hope of the act
is the Head Start program where the children of the poor are given
a chance to receive a hot meal at breakfast at the day care center
where they can also obtain adequate medical care and good recreation.

Another development in this act is the commitment of
various government departments and agencies to bring to bear

their immense knowledge and expertise to help solve the problems
of poverty. With such a coordinated effort and a given time
span, it is possible that poverty can be reduced to a level as
low as five percent of the population within five years. A
third strong point in the act is economic development. The
establishment of a separate director for economic development
places the responsibility for achievement directly upon those
individuals who are the administrators of the program. The
direct loan feature is a definite plus with the interest rate
to be set by the Secretary of the Treasury based on the Federal
funds rate. The administration of the revolving fund by the
Director is another plus for the act.

Perhaps the major innovation of the act is Title IX,
Evaluation. Without appraisal of the effectiveness of an act,
some of the major contributions provided for have been eliminated.
Now this does not have to be done. Advisory Councils have long
advocated an evaluation procedure. We have now developed a
PERT analysis--program evaluation review technique. Such
evaluation can pin responsibility and can stop a program before
it gets botched.

The welfare syndrome in this country came with the Great
Crash in 1929, and has accelerated since. Not only in numbers,
that is, but also in the controversy on who should be on welfare
and who should be off welfare. The great question surrounding
welfare is does the system feed upon itself? There is evidence
that it does.

Pernicious myths about welfare only make the problem more difficult to handle. Some of these myths are: welfare recipients are lazy and shiftless, those on welfare are cheats, the poor will remain poor and people in rural areas will leave for the urban areas where they will get more welfare money than if they stayed home. On a true and false examination all of these answers would be no. However, they persist in the milieu of this country.

About 11,000,000 people are now on welfare, with a cost to the government of more than $10 billion dollars. The great majority are women and children, numbering about 9,500,000. Only about 150,000 are males and these males are handicapped either physically or educationwise. Research has shown that many able-bodied people would like to get off welfare, but if the man lacks skills as well as education he is trapped. The children on welfare are usually pre-schoolers. Their mothers would like to work, if their children could be cared for while they are working.

Census data show that as of 1970, the southern states are gaining in population faster than the northeast. This means that poor rural blacks are not leaving the south for New York or the east, but staying home where a more pleasant wholesome life can be lived than in the urban areas.

On any bureaucratic state program there are bound to be abuses. Some cheats on welfare are those who receive two checks for the same month through computer error, and who do not return the extra check. Also, other cheats on welfare have usually been working middle income individuals who were formerly on welfare, but got a job, and continue to receive the welfare check. Better quality control would eliminate a great majority of the cheating.

The Puritan Ethic states that the poor will be with us always. This is a true statement, but the poor are a fluid population. Research has already shown earlier in this chapter that the poor are not constant. Aberrations in the economy help to produce welfare as well as poverty. Poverty and welfare are in direct proportion to the gross national product, national income and implementation of the bureaucracy in laws applicable to welfare.

A fifth persistent myth is that most people on welfare are black. This is a vicious allegation. In April, 1977, the Department of Health, Education and Welfare reported Aid to Families with Dependent Children was received by 50.2 percent whites, an increase from 46.9 percent in 1973. Blacks decreased from 45.8 percent to 44.3 percent. American Indians received 1.1 percent and other minorities such as Mexican-Americans and Asians went down from 6.2 percent to 4.3 percent.

Other statistical data released by HEW show that there is an increase from 24 months to 31 months average months on the welfare rolls. The number of welfare families headed by women has increased from 75.8 percent to 81 percent.

The wide variations in income received by the welfare recipient in different regions is a further flaw in reconciling the welfare problem. Comparisons between Texas and New York as well as cities such as Houston, Chicago, Philadelphia and Detroit magnify these differences.

In Texas, only about 18 percent of the Lone Star State's 500,000 poor will be eligible for aid in 1977. In contrast, New York has about the same number of poor as Texas, but will help 80 percent of that number or four times as many as Texas. The complete irony of this contrast between New York and Texas is that the Welfare Department in Texas spends far less than is allocated. For fiscal 1977, it will show a surplus of $40,000,000 in its food stamp and aid to dependent children programs.[8]

This amount of $40,000,000 is just half of what the State Constitution allows for welfare. The Welfare Department in Texas shows that recipients of both food stamps and welfare fall in the bracket of $3,300 per year. This is forty percent below the poverty level of $5,500 per year for a non-farm family of four. As a further comparison of the paucity of the average welfare payment in the Lone Star State, here are some cities in other parts of the country:

City	Annual Amount Dispensed on Welfare Resident
Houston	$ 15.93
New York	159.00
Chicago	170.00
Philadelphia	170.00
Detroit	222.00

Welfare payments to families in Texas average about
$140.00 per month. These are families with two children and
who have no other income. Only three states are lower than
Texas. They are Alabama, South Carolina and Mississippi. These
four states have the largest numbers of blacks, and Texas has
the largest number of Mexican-Americans with the possible
exception of California.

A recent study by a University of Michigan economics
staff found that there is not a persistent traumatic
poverty in this country, but instead there is a pernicious poverty
which is pervading and extensive. This research in depth by the
Michigan economists sought to destroy the myth that people in
poverty are usually lazy and did not want to work. The Puritan
ethic which has been extant in this country for decades held to
this myth.

James N. Morgan, the leader of the research team,surveyed
5,000 United States families. The studies ranged over ten years,
dating back to 1967. Team members followed up the respondents
in this country and in foreign countries. From the respondents,
it was also found that families move in and out of poverty. The
interviewers found that only one in five people who came under
the definition of poverty in 1975, were classed as poor in all
of the nine years covered by the study. Another derivative from
the study showed that almost one-third of the individuals in the
study were below the poverty line at least once during the nine
years.

From the study it was also gleaned that poverty is harder on women, children and the disabled than on other components in the population. Divorced women who had not remarried almost invariably fell below the poverty line. White women were more vulnerable to this change in family dysfunction than black women. One implication from this shows that black women as a group show a higher propensity for employment than white women; another implication is that black men earn less than white men. Research has shown that the black family income is about sixty percent of the white family income.

A further penetrating analysis of the study shows that the present welfare program which amounts to $30 billion anually is ineffective in getting people out of poverty. There is a need for a broad-based workfare program and a recognition of the diverse needs of the people in poverty.

Poverty rose in this country by ten percent from 1974 to 1975. This increase was a reflection of the high unemployment rate of 8 - 9 percent during this period. The actual number increased by 2,507,000 from 1974 to 25,877,000 in 1975. The number on poverty in 1974 was 23,370,000.

An analysis of the census report shows that 12 percent of all U. S. citizens were below the poverty level of $5,500 in 1975. The cutoff for an urban family of four on the poverty level in 1974 was $5,038. This increase of 11 percent reflects the twin scourge of high inflation and unemployment during this period.

REFERENCES

1. Houston Post, Friday, November 28, 1975, pg. 13A

2. Pittsburgh Courier, Vol. 67, No. 17, Pittsburgh, Pa., April 25, 1975

3. Third Annual Report, National Advisory Council on Economic Opportunity, March, 1970, p. 7

4. Fifth Annual Report, The National Advisory Council on Economic Opportunity, 1016 16th St., N. W., Washington, D. C. 20036, p. iii, May 31, 1972

5. Black Perspective, Spring, 1972, Vol. 1, No. 1

6. From an article by Irv Kupcinet, Chicago Sun-Times, as reported in the Atlantic Constitution on October 26, 1964

7. Letter of Transmittal To The Congress of the United States, October 9, 1974, Seventh Annual Report, October 9, 1974

CHAPTER III

Economics of the Aged

At the turn of the century there were only about three million United States citizens over 65. Today there are about 22
million. In this category of the elderly over 65, women outnumber
men by 143 to 100. Women usually outlive men by about seven years.
Since women usually marry men who are older than they are, this
age differential accounts for the much higher proportion of widows.
Of this 22 million, thirty-eight percent suffer from some kind of
chronic ailment with about five percent confined to the home.

About 7,000,000 of the aged live in poverty. Notwithstanding the fact that Social Security will disburse about $72 billion
to about 34 million individuals this year, about 4,750,000 of the
aged live on less than $2,000 a year. This amount is well below
the poverty line. Of this 4,750,000 aged who are getting along on
less than $2,000, more than half are blacks, and they are living in
the southeastern part of the country.

The brightest spot in the lives of the aged is that about
seventy percent of these individuals own their homes. The national
average on homeownership in the nation is sixty percent among the
white population and forty percent among the black population.

Benefits for a sixty-five year old couple entering the Social
Security program for the first time in 1975, and satisfying all
requirements for full benefits would amount to $474 per month. This

amount places the couple above the poverty level. The average couple aged 65 receives $310 per month. This amount is well below the poverty level.

If all of us live long enough we will become old, aged, a part of the vast legion which society has cast aside without realizing that there is a chasm of difference in being old, or aged,and persons are placed in a separate category. Assigning individuals to a niche distinct from the general population is an econo-social-genic state of mind. In short we will call this an esg situation.

The people of this country, because of its long history of growth, its millions of immigrants, and its population explosion after World War II, has become youth oriented. This extreme development reached its highest point after World War II. The sixties were the high water mark. With the birth rate receding, and bench marks pointing to a modest growth economy, the nation may be over the hump on its youth culture.

The first of the three basic age groups in this country is the period from birth to pre-college. The number of siblings and those in the period of puberty is declining. The second age group, and it is the largest, is from age eighteen to fifty-five. The third group is composed of those over 55. The age of fifty-five is being used because increasingly this age is becoming the target for early retirement. The United Auto Workers have adopted this termination point in their contract negotiations with the auto companies in collective bargaining.

Not only has there been a mythos about the limitation of
achievement beyond sixty-five, but it has been reinforced by
modern psychology--that the learning process appears to decline
after age sixty-five. The data of these testers may be valid,
but their interpretation is in error. There is a vast difference
between a person sixty-five, an old person and an aging person. A
person can be sixty-five, but he is not old nor is he aging. Pre-
liminary research shows that males would like to continue to work
beyond age sixty-five if they are professional men--engineers,
dentists, physicians, college professors, salesmen to name a few
of these professions. Women with some exceptions want to retire
at age sixty-five or prior to sixty-five. Men who want to retire
prior to sixty-five are usually bored with their jobs. The boring
nature of auto production may explain why members of the United
Auto Workers want the age fifty-five clause in their contracts.
They want out. If they can get at least one-half of their monthly
take home pay in social security and private pension funds they are
satisfied. This does not mean they will remain satisfied. Subsequently in this chapter we will discuss pensions in great detail.

The science of gerontology--the study of aging--is still in
its infancy as is also the study of geriatrics, the science of
diseases of the aged. By an infant state it is meant that there
are still open questions about the findings from these studies.

In the Center Magazine, a publication of the Center for the
Study of Democratic Institutions, for March/April 1, 1975,[1] a

section was devoted to "Aging in the American Society." Four
articles were written on this problem by Carl Eisdorfer, Alex Com-
ford, Harry S. Ashmore and an interview with Maggie Kuhn. Some of
the basic problems of the aged were amplified in these articles as
well as new light thrown on ways of solving these problems. These
problems were:

1. Insufficient money. This is the most frequent complaint
of the aged. However, it is possible for a person's income to
increase with retirement. For example, a teacher who has teacher
retirement and social security coverage may at retirement, receive
an income greater than the take home pay when she was working. It
is possible that retirees need much more money when retired than
working, because they spend more with less retirement than when in
pre-retirement they spent less with greater earnings. Organizations
such as the National Council on Senior Citizens, the American
Association of Retired Persons, the National Retired Teachers
Association are urging Congress to look at Social Security and the
Supplementary Security Income program.

2. Health. The aged are constantly suffering from some
chronic health problems. But the term chronic, as used by the
health professions, can mean any ailment. Thus that does not tell
us very much. More specifically are the aged disabled? About half
of those over 65 are. This disability impairs their getting around,
driving and doing for themselves.

3. Most older people fear long, chronic illness. It is not death that the older fear as much as they fear dependency and inability to do for themselves. The finger points at the nursing homes that give poor care, while exacting money from the aged in social security pensions as well as private pensions for their inadequate care. In mid-1975, there were about 1,000,000, or five percent of the elderly, living in nursing homes. Jack Anderson, that acerbic columnist who rawhides the Washington scene, in one of his columns in August, 1975, states that one Chicago nursing home administrator boasted that he fed his senior citizens on fifty-four cents a day per person. Even the Chicago jails spent sixty-four cents a day per inmate. Senator Frank Church's Aging Committee has found that the elderly are dying from lack of proper health and medical care.

4. A third problem is violence. In the central cities, this is a major problem for the elderly as the young toughs living in the inner cities prey upon them. In certain cities and apartment complexes, the youthful gangs exact a high tribute from the elderly who cannot protect themselves, and who cannot obtain adequate police protection.

Crime hovers over the elderly in the ghetto areas.[2] Shills and flim-flam artists prey upon the elderly when pension checks are received. Hugger-muggers await the elderly women and steal their purses, or way-lay them in elevators and dark halls in the high rises. The high rise apartment houses constructed in the 70's may be a delight to the architects and designers, but a snare and a

trap for the elderly. It has been found by researchers such as
Newman and Cappon that when the elderly are in the minority in
the high-rise apartment projects, they are victimized by burglaries,
muggings and felonies at a greater rate than the non-elderly. Another
hardship on the elderly are the frequent elevator breakdowns. Some
of these breakdowns are caused by teenage vandalism.[3]

It is highly probable that the least unhappy people among
the aged poor are those individuals who have a hobby or an avoca-
tion. It is highly possible that very few of the urban aged poor
have developed such hobbies as caring for their flowers, or garden-
ing or looking after animals. People who have been brought up in
the country are likely to have these hobbies, whereas the aged in
the city have not.

As previously stated, the first basic problem of the aged
is having sufficient money. This is a constant problem of all
minorities, but it becomes extremely serious the older one becomes.
To obtain an adequate income, and how it will be used will be taken
up in the next chapter. Pensions, Social Security, institutional
and private, will be our next area of investigation.

In 1974, the cost of living for retired couples was generally
higher in the Northeastern United States than in other parts of the
nation. A retired couple has been defined as a husband 65 years of
age or over and his wife, who had been self-supporting and were in
general good health. Data furnished by the Department of Labor's
Bureau of Labor Statistics, show a lower and higher budget for the

the retired couples. The lower level budget of $4,756 was $528, or twelve percent, above the national average retirement income. This lower level budget for the Northeastern areas was exceeded by Anchorage, $5,872; Hartford, $4,811; and Honolulu, $4,801.

The upper or higher level budget was $10,665, which was $1,696, or nineteen percent, above the national average. These living costs were higher in all areas except Anchorage, Alaska, which was $11,000; and Boston $10,972. Personal income taxes were not included in the totals because of differences in the various states. Life insurance premiums were included in the higher budgets.[4]

Political Power and the Elderly

As older people grow in numbers and begin to realize the power of technique of organization, they are increasingly bringing pressure to bear on Congress and state legislatures to ameliorate the problems of the elderly. These basic economic problems extend beyond the so-called retirement years. Extending the privilege of working beyond age 65, the mandatory retirement age in industry and government, is one of their prime objectives. Changing the Social Security laws, whereby people over age 65 can work without sacrificing any cut-off in Social Security benefits, is another objective, as well as permitting a woman to marry after her husband predeceases her without losing the social security benefits from first husband. They also wish to obtain a national health care bill in lieu of Medicare and Medicaid.

Three main elderly groups are pursuing these gains. They
are the American Association of Retired Persons, the National
Council of Senior Citizens and the Gray Panthers. These three
organizations alone have members totalling more than 10,000,000.
Their lobbyist are located in Washington, D. C. and they are urging
their representatives to do something about the above problems.
Aware that there are 22,000,000 people in this country that are
65 or over, these organizations are commanding more attention
from legislators on the need of giving more consideration to the
problems of the aged.

It is revealing that today one-fourth of the population in
this country are over 65. It is also revealing that poverty claims
one out of four of the elderly. It is an ironic fact of life that
the twenty-five percent of the elderly who are in poverty reach
this condition at 65. This indicates that our Social Security
system as well as government and private industry pensions are
below the poverty scale in this country. It is also a great
reflection on our government as well as the ethos of this system
that would permit the elderly who have previously lived above the
poverty level to move into a much lower economic status when they
reach the retirement age. As has been mentioned previously, ennui
has characterized the thinking of the conventional wisdom in this
nation about the elderly. A further revealing factor contributing
to poverty among the elderly is the fact that they lose a certain
portion of their Social Security income if they work beyond age 65

and up to age 72. That amount is $2,400. However, a pensioner who wants to work beyond age 72 will not lose any of his social security benefits. The source of about half of their income is from pensions and the great majority of that comes from social security. The average monthly payment is about $314 for a couple. A single person's average is about $184 per month.

Besides income, another problem of the elderly is inadequate housing. One of the basic reasons for nursing homes is not that the children or relatives do not want to look after the elderly, but it is because of inadequate housing. It is estimated that we will need 120 thousand new low income housing units for the elderly over the next twenty years. A deterrent to good housing for the elderly is the Department of Housing and Urban Development which is trying to change the terms under which financing is arranged for housing for the elderly. At the present time the money is used by non-profit agencies that sponsor housing for the elderly with long term loans with low interest. HUD would like to see the money used for construction only.

The high cost of Medicare which now reaches $750 per year takes a large bite out of the income of the elderly. The elderly would like to see a National Health Program instead of the Medicare program.[5]

The elderly are increasingly mounting a sustained political thrust on Congress and the administration for improving their economic status. In the spring of 1975, elderly men and women visited their Representatives in Congress to make clear to their

Congressmen that the elderly are not seeking a hand-out but an

opportunity to become first-class citizens. This was the opinion

of Bernard E. Nash, Executive Director of the American Association

of Retired Persons and National Retired Teachers Association.

The philosophy of Mr. Nash is in direct conflict with that

of Hobart Jackson, former Chairman of the National Caucus on the

Black Aged. Mr. Jackson feels that older people must receive the

benefits that will come from the political process. Mr. Jackson

further emphasizes that programs for the elderly are not welfare.

He is adamant in maintaining that these economic programs for the

elderly are due the elderly for their past contribution to society.

When the Pension Reform Act was enacted by Congress in 1974,

this was the first piece of major legislation directed twoard those

individuals in our society who can make provisions for their old

age without being penalized for doing so. This new law will per-

mit a pensioner to establish his own retirement plan.

---

1. The Center Magazine, Vol. VIII, Number 3, March/April, 1975, pp. 11 - 25.

2. A Plague Upon the Penthouse, Roger Rapport, Oui Magazine, Vol. 3, No. 8, August, 1974, pp. 92.

3. The New York Times, Vol. CXXV # 43,177, April 11, 1976, pp. 1 - 42.

4. U. S. Bureau of Labor Statistics, Regional Office, 1515 Broadway, Room 3400, New York, N. Y. 10036.

5. The New York Times, Vol. CXXIV, June 22, 1975, pg. 37.

CHAPTER IV

Pensions

At what age should a person start planning for retirement? Age thirty-five is a good guess. Realizing that more and
more early retirement is taking place and that corporations should
give personnel time to plan for retirement. At thirty-five a
working person would have twenty years in which to start seriously
thinking of job jumping and experimentation.

The word pension is taken from the Old French. The word
pension means a gratuity, a sum to tide one over. Pensions go
way, way back into the dawn of man and the written word. Making
a gratuity to a person was for faithful service, to tide a person
over until death came knocking at the door. The pension is the
oldest fringe benefit. American Express started giving pensions
as early as 1875. The usual standard pension paid is forty-five
percent of the best years income of the pensioner while working
who retires at age 65. Some companies pay up to sixty-five percent
for thirty years service. The longer the service, the larger the
pension. In an agricultural economy a man's pension was his children who would take care of their parents. Such is not the case
in a highly industrial-money economy.

A comparison of the pension as a percentage of the best
five years average income of the United States and some foreign
countries shows Sweden leading the list with 131.6 percent,

followed by Switzerland, 95.6; Finland, 95.5; Austria, 90.5; West
Germany, 84.3; Great Britain, 81.6; Netherlands, 80.4; United
States, 71.4; Canada, 62.1 and Belgium 60.6.[1]

In Chapter Four we have seen that this is a youth oriented
economy. It is changing, but not fast enough. Since this is so
at the present time, then the youth are concerned with taking care
of themselves. Their parents must shift for themselves. In an
agricultural economy there was little need for insurance. In an
industrial-money economy, insurance is a necessity. Thus we see
that insurance companies, which provide pensions or annuities
are the great financial giants in this country. Prudential,
Metropolitan Life, New York Life, Equitable Life are some of the
giants in the world of pension management. Among minorities there
are the giant North Carolina Mutual, Golden State Mutual, Atlanta
Life and Universal Life. In an industrial-money economy people
are interdependent, hence the need for pensions, a form of
insurance--private as well as social.

Pensioners on fixed incomes are highly vulnerable to inflation. During the period 1973-75, when inflation in the United
States was running at an annual rate of twelve percent, pensioners
were hard put to make ends meet on an income of $500-$600 per
month. Once a style of living has set in, it is very difficult to
reduce one's living standards. But reduce the pensioner must,
unless he takes another job to supplement his pension. Those
retirees between 65 and 72 can only earn $2,520 above their Social

Security pension without having their pension reduced. An individual who retires on Social Security receives about $300 maximum monthly benefits. If his wife has worked she receives about half of that. However, those retirees who are over 72 on Social Security can earn as much as they are capable of without losing any Social Security benefits.

During 1973-75, another severe economic situation affecting pensioners was the falling stock market. On some very blue chip stocks, price-earning ratios fell as low as four. All during 1974, there was a constant erosion in stock values. Watching values melt away, although dividends remained good, was traumatic for pensioners who had previously invested in the stock market as their nest egg.

The remainder of this chapter will include discussion of Social Security pensions, other government pension systems such as Civil Service, pensions for Congressmen-Women and Senators, State retirement systems, teacher retirement systems, private industry retirement systems and pensions for baseball players and sports figures.

Social Security Pensions

The Social Security pension fund was established in 1935. It is the largest pension entity in this country. The following shows the monthly retirement benefit schedule of June,1974.

Social Security System Retirement Benefits

June 1974

Average Yearly Earnings	For Workers Retirement				Dependents				Family Benefits
	at 65	at 64	at 63	at 62	Wife at 65 or Child	Wife at 64	Wife at 63	Wife at 62	
$923 or less	93.80	87.60	81.30	75.10	46.90	43.00	39.10	35.20	140.80
1150	114.40	106.80	99.20	91.60	57.20	52.50	47.70	42.90	171.60
1500	138.70	129.70	120.40	111.20	69.50	63.80	58.00	52.20	208.40
2000	157.20	146.80	136.30	125.80	78.60	72.10	65.50	59.00	235.80
2500	175.70	164.00	152.30	140.60	87.90	80.60	73.30	66.00	263.60
3000	194.10	181.20	168.30	155.30	97.10	89.10	81.00	72.90	296.80
3500	220.40	196.40	182.40	168.40	105.20	96.50	87.70	78.90	341.30
3750	220.50	205.80	191.10	176.40	110.30	101.20	92.00	82.80	368.20
4000	228.50	213.30	198.10	182.30	114.30	104.80	95.30	85.80	390.50
4250	238.70	222.80	206.90	191.00	119.40	109.50	99.50	89.60	417.40
4500	246.90	230.50	214.00	197.60	123.50	113.30	103.00	92.70	439.60
4750	257.10	240.00	222.90	205.70	128.60	117.90	107.20	96.50	466.70
5000	264.90	247.30	229.60	212.00	132.50	121.50	110.50	99.40	488.90
5250	274.70	256.40	238.10	219.80	137.40	126.00	114.50	103.10	513.50
5500	282.10	263.30	244.50	225.70	141.10	129.40	117.60	105.90	524.60
5750	291.50	272.10	252.70	233.20	145.80	133.70	121.50	109.40	538.20
6000	299.40	279.50	258.50	239.60	149.70	137.30	124.80	112.30	549.30
6250	306.90	286.50	266.00	245.60	153.50	140.80	128.00	115.20	560.50
6500	316.30	295.30	274.20	253.10	158.20	145.10	131.90	118.70	573.90
6750	325.40	303.80	282.10	260.40	162.70	149.20	135.60	122.10	585.70
7000	335.50	313.20	290.80	268.40	167.80	153.90	139.90	125.90	597.90
7250	345.60	322.60	299.60	276.50	172.80	158.40	144.00	129.60	610.30
7500	355.70	332.00	308.30	284.60	177.90	163.10	148.30	133.50	623.20

Source: Social Security Administration. 1974

From the table you can see that retirement benefits are greater at age sixty-five than at any other age. Thus it is advantageous for a person to wait longer for his/her retirement benefits under covered employment. A second feature of the Social Security retirement fund is that benefits are slanted towards the lower earnings than the higher earnings. That is, the lower the average yearly earnings, the greater the retirement benefits. This is why the word <u>social</u> is inserted. The intent of the act was to benefit the lower income earner in relationship to his contributions on an increasingly higher scale than that of the higher income earner in relationship to his contributions. The lowest amount a person can receive at age sixty-five is $75.10. The highest for family benefits is $623.20.

In periods of recession, the Social Security pension fund wades out into deep water. It was the first time in ten years that outgo exceeded income. In 1975, the deficit was expected to hit $2,500,000,000. In 1976, the deficit is expected to hit $6,100,000,000 and in 1977, the deficit is expected to rise to $8,300,000,000. When these expected deficits were announced by the fund managers, actuaries and economists, it came as a shock to Congress. It is possible for the pension or trust fund for the present 30,000,000 recipients to become exhausted, but this probability is remote as long as the number of workers outnumber the number of beneficiaries.

At present the number in the work force is 87,000,000. About 8,000,000 are unemployed. It is unlikely that any of these 8,000,000 are receiving benefits from the fund. Taxes are paid into the fund by those who work and those employers who are covered by the Social Security act. This covers nearly all employers in this country who employ at least one person under covered employment earning at least $50.00 per quarter. Payroll taxes paid into the fund by employer and employee are 11.70 percent. Half is paid by the employer on his wages and half is by the employee under covered employment. Taxes are levied on maximum earnings of $15,300 per year. All earnings above this amount are exempt from Social Security taxes. Hence, the point is made here that Social Security taxes are oppressive on all those employees earning $15,300 or less.

Of the 30,000,000 individuals who benefit from the fund, the major concern is for the 26,500,000 aged widows, widowers of decreased persons, as well as the dependent children. These aged individuals over sixty-five and dependent children comprise twelve percent of the population. They are paid a maximum benefit of $316.30 and a minimum of $93.80 per month. If we average these two, the benefit comes to about $200.10 per month for each of the recipients. This would amount at about (30,000,000 x $200.10) = $6,003,000,000 for 1975 alone. Payments to Medicare patients would raise this by another $2,500,000,000 hence, the expected deficit in 1975.

It is logical to assume that so long as the basic assumptions in the program are relevant to the real life situation, then the system is not in jeopardy. But if the **assumptions** prove incorrect then the Social Security system is in deep trouble. Now, how has this happened? First, as long as more people are working than those receiving benefits from the fund, there is no problem. Second, those that are working are contributing to the fund as well as the employers, so that taxes received are greater than the proceeds paid to the beneficiaries, good. Third, if the wages paid by American industry increase relevant to prices this is excellent because, barring any legislative fiats, the fund will not become exhausted.

The third assumption made by the managers has reversed itself. Since the end of the Vietnam War, prices have increased at a rapid rate, leaving the level of wages far behind. This is a situation that no crystal ball gazer can project. Most of the economic models abstract out of their equations such natural phenomena as droughts, foreign relations, wars, discoveries, inventions, weather cycles and innovations.

There is nothing inherently flawed in the financing of the Social Security system so long as wages increase at a greater rate than prices. But there is no guarantee that these conditions will go on forever. To control such a program for Social Security would mean total control of the economy. The American people are apparently not yet ready for such controls. One solution to the problem would be to raise taxes or the wage scale so there is enough money in the fund to pav those beneficiaries without a deficit each year. A second solution would be to put Medicare or early retirees on the general revenue budget.

Federal Civil Service Pension Plans

Federal Civil Service Pension Plans are similar to those in private industry. After thirty years of service or at aae sixtv-five, a person can retire. Benefits are based on the best five years. The pension is figured like this: Say the best five years average is $10,000. Two percent of this amount is $200. With thirty years service, this would amount to thirty times $200 which would equal $6,000 per year. Of course, persons with terms of service beyond thirty years would obtain a higher pension. Civil Service not only covers all the GS classifications, but service in the post office. Incomes of government workers in the higher classes would also mean higher pensions. Those earning as much as $20,000 a year for the best years' average would receive as much as $12,000 per year. In these two examples the recipients are receiving about sixty percent of their gross pay.

Congressional Pensions

Members of Conqress with as little as five years service can retire on pensions that are at least twelve and one-half percent of their annual salary and up to eighty percent of their annual salary, depending on length of service. The Federal government matches the members of Congress's eight percent of his annual salary.

Since salaries of members of Congress were raised eight years ago from $35,000 to $57,000, there has been a greater urge to retire. Retirement pay is now based on the best three years average salary of a member of Congress, The computation goes like this. If Congressman/woman has been earning $42,000 on average over the past three years, then .025 multiplied by amount would be ($42,000 x .025) = $1,050. If the member of Congress has been serving for twenty years, then (20 x $1,050) = $21,000. Maximum retirement would be $34,000. Now if comparisons are made with standard government Civil Service retirement as well as private industry, the the members of Congress have good retirement plans going for them. In private industry, teacher retirement systems and civil service systems, it is the best five years' average salary. But, as Congress makes our federal laws, it may not be asking too much for them to reserve the right to determine their own pension plans and salary levels. However, it is always good politics to consider the voters and the source of Congress's income which comes from the taxpayers.

State and Teacher Retirement Systems

We shall use Texas as our model for a state-teacher retirement system. This state does not pay the highest state pension nor the lowest. In Texas if a teacher works for twenty-thirty-forty years, the pension is figured thusly:

Best five years' earnings average: $13,000

Thirty years service x 1.75 = 52.50

$13,000 x 52.50 = $6,825 annual pension.

In Texas the typical pension is about fifty-two percent of the
best five years with thirty years' service. Of course with more
years of service, the higher percentage-wise, is the pension. In
all pension systems, the longer the work period the higher the
pension becomes. State employees follow virtually the smae pattern.

Private Industry Retirement Systems

Retirement systems in private industry are constantly pushing early retirement. Companies are suggesting early retirement
to rid themselves of obsolete executives, static employees and non-
productive personnel. The usual early retirement age is 55, or
those with at least twenty-five years of service. Increasingly
the 30 and out retirement system is gaining momentum. Another
reason for early retirement and retirement before 65 is to make
room for younger workers. Such conditions usually obtain during
economic slow-downs. A third reason for early retirement is to
reduce payrolls of the most highly paid personnel and those with
long seniority. In the 1971-72 recession IBM gave two years'
salary to those employees with twenty-five years or more of
service who would retire early. Of the 6,500 individuals eligible,
2,000, or thirty-eight percent, took advantage of the offer. For

the employees who desire early retirement, it offers an opportunity for a new career, or the opportunity to overcome the boredom of the job and to enjoy leisure. My example of early retirement for an executive of a multinational corporation is used. Our company is an acronym: AIRCO, (Amalgamated International Research Corporation). Any resemblance to an on-going American corporation is purely incidental. J. Ellsworth Henderson is applying for early retirement. He is 55 and worked as a vice-president in charge of defense contracts. The employee who retires early will be getting a smaller pension which is reduced actuarially over a greater number of years. Costs to the employer are no greater than the normal pension at 65. Incentives may be given for early retirement. The pension for the early retiree is spread over a longer time with smaller payments. Early retirement has short term benefits and long term hazards. If J. Ellsworth Henderson is unaware of these conditions, he may rue an early retirement. But he has made up his mind, so here goes his computation of benefits. AIRCO figures his pension this way. Take one and two-tenths percent of the first $14,200 (Social Security maximum pay) and one and three-tenths of the remainder of his salary which was $22,500 over the past five years. Hence: 1.2 percent of $14,200 is $170.40. One point three percent of the remainder $8,300 is $107.90. The total here is $107.90 plus $170.40 = $278.30 x 30 = $8,349. Now because he is retiring at 55,

twenty-five percent discount is taken which reduces his pension to
$6,261.25. His $6,261.75 is much lower than his $22,500, while
working for AIRCO. His social security will not start until age
62, or in seven years. At age 62 his pension from AIRCO and
Social Security will be about $10,000 per year. Now, if J. Ells-
worth has his home paid for, his children educated and having
families of their own, all of his wife's mink stoles paid for,
and no large debts, he can look with satisfaction on his retirement years. He can go into a new career such as teaching, consulting, business or parttime employment. If another career is
not taken, then J. Ellsworth Henderson will encounter serious
income deficiencies over the next 20 years. The Bureau of Labor
Statistics says that the cost of living for retirees has gone up
fifty percent since 1967.[2] Within ten years, present retirement
pensions such as Henderson's may not even pay the utility bills.
It is obvious that unless this former executive has some outside
source of income, or other kinds of annuities, he and his wife
will barely be able to make ends meet. The hazard of early retirement is, of course, again inflation. The example given above is
an exceptional one. In 1973, a survey was made for the United
States Senate. It was found that only ten percent of the enrollees
in private pension plans stay long enough with a firm to have
vested pension privileges. Whereas Civil Service pensioners
and state retirement systems guarantee the pensions to the
retirees, no such guarantee is given to a pensioner in a private

plan. Although private pensions plans in this country have about $157 billion in assets and are growing at the rate of about $10 billion a year, there have been many pitfalls in these plans. If a company goes bankrupt, the pension plan can run out of money. Or if a merger takes place, the pension plan can dry up. The new pension legislation passed by Congress is seeking to overcome these deficiencies. Benefits paid to private pensioners average only $1,605 per year. This is a far lower amount than government pensions. However, it must be said that Social Security is added to the private pension plan. But the reason for the low pension is that only one percent of private pensions are supported solely by the workers themselves. In private industry not many pension plans are vested or contributory as they are in government and teacher retirement systems.

Miners' Pensions

Miners' pensions average about $140 per month. In 1970, funeral expenses and widows and survivors' benefits cost the fund $8.7 million. Over the last twenty-five years, the miners' pension fund has paid out $353.8 million. Administrative costs of the fund have averaged about three percent including medical offices in the ten areas that administer the pension.

Baseball Pensions

Of all the heroes in this country, it is probable that our sports heroes, those superstars on the baseball diamond, gridiron,

basketball court, hockey and other sports are the most fortunate
pensioners. But if pensions are a guideline, than the baseball
players are treated among the best. Pensions for baseball players
listed in the following table, show that:

Table VI

Baseball Pensions

Baseball's Pension: What it Pays

All figures in this table are rounded off to the nearest
dollar. The column headings going across represent years of service in the major leagues. The figures in the first column represent the age at which a player elects to start collecting his
pension. For example, a player with eight years service who begins
his pension at age 55 would collect approximately $659 per month.

Years	4	6	8	10	15	20
Age
45	$174	262	350	436	509	582
47	198	296	396	494	577	659
49	224	338	450	562	656	740
50	240	360	480	600	700	800
51	256	384	513	641	748	854
53	291	437	582	728	848	968
55	329	494	659	824	959	1091
57	372	559	745	931	1088	1224
59	421	631	842	1052	1212	1372
60	447	671	895	1119	1286	1452
61	476	715	953	1191	1364	1538
63	541	812	1082	1358	1540	1726
65	618	927	1236	1545	1745	1945

even at age forty-five, if a major leaguer can survive four years,
he can draw a pension of $174 per month. If he waits until he
is sixty-five he can draw $582 per month. But if he can stay in
the majors for twenty years, at age sixty-five he can draw $1,945
per month. So, a journeyman ball player, once he gets in the
majors, hits an average of 240, has a good arm, and is a terror
on defense, can stay with the majors for five or ten years and
retire with a good pension at the age of his choosing once
he reaches forty-five. The exceptional youth of today can play in
sports and come out with a pension that not only is more than private industry offers, but one that revals the government pension.

Pension Fund Managers

Managers of pension funds are judged on their ability to
enhance or appreciate the value of the fund as well as turning a
profit on the fund. Fund managers are lodged in the insurance
companies, banks, investment trusts, mutual funds and brokerage
houses. Large pension funds in the range of $100,000,000 - $700,-
000,000 are managed by teams of investment experts who make it
their responsibility to monitor the economy. The real object of
the team is to beat the averages. This is impossible for all of
them, because the managers themselves help to make the averages.
So, about half of them will manage investment portfolios that will
be above the averages and about half will be below the averages.
This is performance management. Costs of managing a fund run from

0.2 percent to 0.3 percent. For managing a $100,000,000 fund at 0.3 percent would cost $300,000. This amount after deduction for overhead costs by the management company, would be paid to the specific managers of the fund, the team. The salary is around $30,000 per year. It could range up to $50,000 including bonuses and commissions.[3]

The recent new pension law placing direct responsibility on the managers of pension funds as to prudence, care and performance has brought more respect to the pension fund industry. Managers can be sued now for not protecting the fund, or for doing what a prudent man would not do.

Investment of Pension Funds

One of the hazards of pension funds during the 1973-75 recession was the precipitous decline in the stock market. Funds that had heavily invested in the stock market came out with a depreciation in the fund with as much as fifty percent. The whole notion of a pension fund is the ability to pay the pensioner a fixed income when he retires which he will receive until he dies. If the pensioner cannot be paid because of a decline in assets or income of the fund, then the whole pension concept becomes counter productive. Canny pension fund managers have by no means given up on the stock market or bonds. They are not diversifying into real-estate investment trust or REITS. The REITS were seriously damaged in the 1973-75 recession because they loaned money to builders

and contractors in a high priced market. The builders and contractors got caught in the inflationary spiral, and could not
meet their amortized payments. Let it also be said that many
of the REITS borrowed high interest loans from banks and insurance
companies.

The pension fund managers are buying into already built
apartments and shopping centers. These are income producing.
Furthermore the fund managers do not use borrowed money but cash.
Properties that are purchased are sound.

Various businesses that contract with an insurance company
or bank to manage their funds are being introduced to pooling their
funds for diversification. Under the new pension law, fund managers
can be held responsible for not pursuing a prudent investment
policy. Under our present economic system with all of its possibilities and hazards, prudent investment policy means that,within
a closed system, stability can be maintained. Although inflation
and recession are the poles within which values fluctuate, the
shrewd investment manager should be able to keep his equilibrium
within these extremes. Inflation is the bane of fixed income
investments. Recession is the monster which dries up liquidity.
Keeping off the shoals of these perils is the duty of the pension
fund managers. The problem of the fund manager is not to fall
victim to the fallacy of composition.[4]

Pension Reform

Serious thinking on pension reform legislation came in
Congress in 1971, when Senator Javits of New York introduced
in May, 1969 a proposed Pension and Benefit Act.[5]

Severe criticism of the private pension system resulted
in the Employee Retirement Income Security Act of 1974. Already,
practitioners of the art of pension management are dubbing the act
ERISA or "Theresa."[6] This acronym is similar to Fannie Mae of
the Federal National Mortgage Association and Ginnie Mae, Government Mortgage Association.

The years of uncertainty over private pensions has not
necessarily ended. But the new law is seeking to make employee
benefits more certain and hold accountable those individuals
who are responsible for managing these pension funds. The basic
features of the law seek to guarantee to employees who are covered
by pensions basic pension rights to their pensions after they have
worked for a covered employer. Controversy surrounding the law
is the fiduciary relationship pension managers have to pensioners.
Pension managers can be sued in a Federal Court by participants
in pension plans where a manager does not exert responsibility
in the management of the fund. Because of the great measure of
probability in investment management, it is likely that investment
pension managers will stop seeking speculative returns while trying to build a pension fund at a fast clip and in so doing
jeopardize the soundness of the fund. The new law does not force

a company to have a pension fund. It says if it has a pension
plan, it must be well managed to protect the interests of the
participants in the pension. The stringent requirements placed
on the managers are sending shock waves through the cult
of the pension managers. It is not that the large corporations
in this country are not already in compliance with the law, but
when the country is in a period of inflation or a stock market
slump, it means a larger contribution from the companies to the
pension fund. Once a pension has been projected actuarially and
the economy goes into doldrums, current income from the fund may
not be able to match current outgo. When this happens, the difference must be made up by the corporations.

It is assumed that for the first few years under the plan,
fixed income investment will prevail. Equity positions in
pension funds are still about sixty percent.

Management of funds is the crucial aspect of pension plans.
Smaller companies will seek more sophisticated investment advice
from insurance companies, banks and brokerage houses. Overcoming
conflicts of interest will be the manager's most difficult preventive. Defining what a prudent man would do will also tax the
most circumspect individual when he is trying to earn money for
the fund.

---

1. Parade Magazine, June 19, 1977.

2. Money, November, 1974, pg. 50, Vol. 3, No. 11.

3. _Wall Street Journal_, Vol. LV #39, February 26, 1975, pp. 1-23.

4. _Business Week_, Number 2364, January 20, 1975, pg. 64.

5. _Wall Street Journal_, February 12, 1971, pg. 6.

6. _Business Week_, Number 2373, March 24, 1975, pg. 144.

CHAPTER V

Indians-The First Americans

.   How is it that the Indians on the Massachusetts shore who
helped the Pilgrims to survive, should now be regarded in such a
controversial plight? How is it that Squanto, of the Pawtuxet
tribe, who educated this group of settlers from Holland in survival,
and was regarded as a saint, if he should return today would see
his descendants held in such low esteem? Squanto spoke English.
He knew the art of survival. He arranged a peace treaty with
Massosoit, Chief of the Wamponoags, to insure the survival of the
Pilgrims. When the Pilgrims landed at Plymouth Rock in 1620, fall
was setting in. Because Squanto knew how to fish and hunt, he
enabled the first settlers in New England to subsist through the
winter of their first year in the new world. In the spring of
1621, Squanto taught the struggling survivors how to plant corn, and
how to use fish as fertilizer. The Thanksgiving of 1621 was held in
the appreciation of Squanto and blessings from God.

How is it that these things have come to pass in a great
land, a land blessed by God for its natural resources, its beauty,
the majestic folds of its mountains, and the sough of the winds
as they blow over the plains? Before the white man, the brown man
and the black man came to these shores, the Indian alone dwelled
herein, coming thousands of miles across the seas, through Alaska,
Canada, and into the United States and Mexico. Anthropologists

tell us that he came this way. Also, modern researchers say that
the Indian, or his ancestors, migrated from Africa or the Islands
in the Pacific which could have been the sources of Indians in
Central and South America.

But it is in the United States where the Red Man resided,
that our story begins. In the United States, east of the Mississippi there lived the tribes of the lush woodlands. With the
Great Lakes, the Ohio and Mississippi Rivers. as their highways, with
lesser highways such as the Susquehanna, Hudson, Delaware, Mononga-
hela, Allegheny, Tennessee and Wabash Rivers, this area was the
hunting ground of more than sixty tribes. Some of the more famous
tribes were the Iroquois, Cherokees, Creeks, Illinois, Kickapoo,
Seminole, and Miamis. These tribes and their sub-bands hunted in
the virgin forests. They fished the clear streams for trout and
bass. During the day the air was pure. At night the dark velvety
sky was pinpointed by twinkling stars. They staked out their own
territory, and woe befall the enemy who breached the boundary
or broke the treaty.

The lush woodlands were the territory which was breached
by Daniel Boone, as he sought to find out what was beyond the Blue
Ridge mountains. His explorer's passion carried him into Kentucky,
and there he found life so elemental, so simplistic, and the Indian
in his natural state, so that he was charmed for the remainder of
his life. When Boone returned to Reading, Pennsylvania, he told
the settlers that Kentucky was a dark and bloody ground.

In the plains region, stretching from Texas and the western portion of the Gulf of Mexico to the Canadian border, were the hunters. These nomadic tribes were the great horsemen, who hunted buffalo, deer, elk and the other denizens of this vast land. The plains Indians made forays into each other's camps, and provoked intermittent skirmishes because of an aggressive chief or a hot headed brave. The plains hunters had almost their entire existence centered in the buffalo. These great animals that roamed the prairie were the Indians' food supply. Not only did they provide food, clothing, and shelter for the tribes, but these ungainly beasts with a small rump and huge shoulders carved trails for the Indians through the terrain which were later used by the stagecoach and the railroads. Because the hunters of the plains depended on the buffalo, they had become virtually a prisoner of this animal. The Indian followed the animal, the animal did not follow him. Always, the Indian would slaughter only the number of animals necessary for his sustenance. The herd was allowed to reproduce itself. This is why in carrying out the implacable order of the United States Army to subdue the Indians, the food supply of the Indian was the first objective. The buffalo was slaughtered without any consideration for the Indian. The doom of the Indian on the the Great Plains was now sealed.

Also, the region of the Great Plains was the scene of the great Indian wars. Probably the most publized was the defeat of Custer by Chief Crazy Horse and Red Cloud's war against the Army.

In 1865, the United States government decided to construct a road in Montana to the gold fields. The road was through Indian territory where the Sioux hunted buffalo. The road was through the territory of Red Cloud, Chief of the Oglala Teton Sioux. He saw that such a road was a threat to his people's existence. For three years, skirmishes and battles were fought over what later came to be known as the Bozeman Trail. The army lost heavily to the Oglala Teton Sioux. Red Cloud's warriors put such great pressure on the Army that the Bozeman Trail was closed and a treaty was made with the Indians. This was one of a few victories won by the Indians over the Army. Other well known Indian tribes living in this region were the Crows, Blackfeet, Comanches, Utes, Arapahos, Nez Perce and Cheyennes.

In the northwest states of Washington and Oregon lived the salmon fishermen. Some of these tribes were the Klamath, Yakima, Chimakuan, Kusa and Alsea. In the California-Nevada region were the seed gatherers as characterized by the Haskell Indian Junior College. Some of these well known tribes were the Shasta, Moduc, Shosoni, Paiute, Mono and Mohave.

In the diverse state of Alaska were found the Point Barrow Eskimo, Bering Strait Eskimo, the interior woodsmen of Alaska and the salmon fishermen of the peninsula. In the area of Valdez, Alaska were found the Pacific Eskimo.

In the Southwest, the Indian lived a hard and spartan existence. This area is divided into three groups: the desert dwellers, the Pueblo farmers and the Navajo shepherds. Tribes familiar to this region in the Southwest, which covers the three states of west Texas, New Mexico and Arizona, were the fearsome Apache with their bands of Mescaleros, Jicarillos Lipons, Chiricahuas, Hopi, Zuni and the largest tribe of Indians on the North American continent--the Navajos.

Long before Anglos came west, the Navajos had made contact with the Spaniards. Raids were made on Spanish supply trains for horses and cattle. The first treaty negotiations came prior to the War with Mexico. The man responsible for this treaty was Charles Bent of Bent's Fort on the Upper Arkansas, who followed General Stephen Watts Kearny into Santa Fe which later became the state of New Mexico.

Entering Santa Fe without firing a shot, General Kearny had with him two lawyers, Willard P. Hall and A. W. Doniphan. Doniphan, a red head from Missouri, was the more notorious of the two. However, these two men drew up a code of laws for the new territory of New Mexico. The time was 1846, in late August.

On orders of the War Department, Kearny set out with 300 dragoons for California. He left Charles Bent in charge as governor of New Mexico Territory. Doniphan's mission was to proceed south with his assortment of volunteers clearing the territory of the Mexican forces and joining General Wood at Chihuahua. Before his departure, Bent had one request. Reports were coming to him of trouble with the Navajos. Bent induced

Doniphan to make a treaty with the Navajos. Doniphan headed a force to the foothills of the Rockies. He persuaded the Navajos to sign a peace treaty at Val Verde on November 22, 1846. This was the first treaty in the West signed by an Indian tribe with United States forces.

The treaty signed at Val Verde with the Navajos provoked a continuous misunderstanding of the Army with the Navajos for about twenty years. The Army interpreted a treaty signing with one Navajo leader as covering all Navajos. The leader of the band who signed the treaty with Colonel Doniphan was responsible for his own people, not all Navaios. Because of such misunderstanding there were raids, retaliations. skirmishes, more treaties. The Army became so exasperated that Colonel Kit Carson was given the job of rounding up all Navajos and killing them. History records that Carson was a man of his own mind and would not commit a My Lai. He did not kill the Navajos, but escorted them to Canyon de Chelly, where they almost died of starvation. Recognizing the experiment at Fort Sumner had failed, the Navajos were permitted to reestablish themselves on their reservation. Because of stamina and industry the Navajo has survived.

However, the Navajos around Taos, New Mexico, remember Kit Carson as a tramp and killer. In a coalition joined by Chicanos and the Mescaleros, the Taos GI Forum is now seeking to change the name of Kit Carson Memorial State Park. A bill to do this was introduced in the New Mexico legislature in January, 1974, to change the name to Lujan, a Taos Indian who was a Sergeant in World War II.

The GI Forum President, David Fernandez of Taos, hopes that a new perspective can be cast on Kit Carson, the tramp who came from nowhere. Kit Carson is described as such by Dee Brown in Bury My Heart At Wounded Knee, who pictured Carson as an unbridled character who used a scorched earth policy in Navajoland and committed genocide against the Navajo nation.

Committing themselves to eventual self determination, the Navajos organized a General Council in 1921 in order to negotiate oil leases on their land. The present council structure which was adopted in 1938, is composed of seventy-five representatives elected from 100 communities. The presiding officers are a chairman and vice-chairman who are elected at large from the entire reservation.

Probably the wealthiest Indian tribe on the North American continent is the Aqua Calientes of Palm Springs, California. This small tribe of 125 landowners control title to more than 20,000 acres. From the land that they have already sold or leased the tribe has realized $6 million. As a separate entity of its own, the Aqua Calientes receives $25,000 a year from leased properties which include lease income on the Spa Hotel, which is built around the hot springs from which the tribes derives its name.

. The area around Palm Springs, California, has been under development for more than forty years. Since World War II, growth

and development have accelerated. The fortunes of the Agua Calientes are inextricably interwoven with the real estate developments of the area. The remarkable thing about such wealth flowing
into the tribe is that it is tax free. No taxes are paid on tribal
land.

As the Agua Calientes become more involved with the growth
of the Palm Springs area, they are in the process of losing their
identity. Gradually fading are their traditional dances and festi-
vals. Their language and culture are fast eroding in the wake of
population pressures in the area, fast-paced living and hamburgers
and milk shakes. In its vast wealth, the bells are tolling for the
tribe.

In contrast to the Agua Calientes, as one of the smallest
and wealthiest of the Indian tribes, is the largest and least
wealthy--the Navajos.

The Navajo Indian Tribe, is also called, the "Navajo Nation,"
a name suggested by Peter MacDonald, the President of the Navajos.
The name Navajo Nation has instilled pride and self-esteem in the
Navajos.

The Navajos are the largest Indian Tribe in this country--
numbering between 135,000 and 140,000. The second largest is the
Oglala Sioux in South Dakota. The Navajos are related to the
family of Athobascan Indians, who are found in California and
Alaska. Apaches are also related to the Navajos through language,
if not by family. Th early history of the Navajos show that they

arrived at their present reservation about 500 years ago. These
nomadic people spread throughout the Southwest and acquired
horses and sheep and dogs from the Spaniards.

The name Navajo was given to the tribe by the Spaniards
as they made their way through the Southwest looking for the seven
cities of gold. The name stands for raiders. Analyzing the Navajos
and their economic development gives insight into the plight of
the Indian tribes in this country.

Because of this country's new concern for minorities, we
approach briefly the Indians' contributions to this country, their
oppression, and a beginning recovery. When Sir Walter Raleigh came
to this country in 1607 his colony could not have survived without
the help of the Powhatans in Virginia. At the beginning of this chapter it was mentioned Pilgrims landed at Plymouth Rock from Holland.
They could not have survived the first hard winter in the new world
without the help of the Massosoit Indians. The Indians made their
main contributions in agriculture. They raised wild rice, pumpkins,
maple syrup, sugar, squash, turkey, tomatoes, tobacco, pineapples,
sweet potatoes, chili-peppers, cacao, tapioca, avocado, beans, corn,
(maize) gourd, cashew nuts, potatoes, rubber, peanuts and coca.

A much more recent contribution to American culture, the
protection of our environment was derived from the Indians. The
Sierra Club and the Friends of the Earth derived their cause from
the Indians. Indians were our first nature boys. They learned to
live with nature. When the Navajos perform the Yeibichai dance,

they seek to develop sereneness and beauty as they execute the dance. The dance brings together man and nature in harmony. The Navajo religion strives to create beauty and happiness.

Another form of practical Indian art is the tipi. The tipi is a Sioux word which means to dwell in, to be used. The "teepee," which is the way the word is commonly pronounced, now enables the Indian to make peace with his environment. The teepee is in direct relationship to the tribe. Harmony exists in the group. Earth and nature are as one. The cone-shaped feature of the teepee represents the sky; the earth or floor, the mother; the poles, the father that link earth (mother), sky (cover), poles, (man), with the universe or the heavens.

In the world of art, it is found that western art is pragmatic and practical. There is usually a cause and effect relationship. Understanding abstract art comes harder for Western man. For the Indian, abstraction is a part of his life. The American Indian's abstract art is embedded in his culture. Man's relationship in Indian art and painting show no given shape. Such shapes are symbolic and are not usually recognizable. Abstraction gives meaning to universality.

The Navajo blankets symbolize such abstraction. The vast sweep of the southwest with its canyons, arroyos, mountain and mesas is reflected in their blankets. The blanket not only symbolizes nature, but shows the handiwork of the weaver. Weaving is done exclusively by women. This ancient craft was handed down through the Spider Woman.

Because of the abstractions of the Indians and the pragmatic nature of the Western world exemplified by the white man's arrival on these shores looking for gold, it was inevitable that these two cultures would clash with dire results. Thus, the Indian was oppressed and hounded from the land by the Army, restrictive laws and broken treaties. The buffalo, which was his food supply, was slaughtered. The clear cool streams and rivers were dammed and diverted. He was placed on barren land from which it was difficult to get a crop. However, the Indian was able to survive all of these forms of repression. But in surviving, he has had to exist on the most meager subsistence. Such levels of living have produced for the Indian some of the most severe forms of trauma that any ethnic group has had to encounter.

CHAPTER VI

Health And Education Of The Indians

Health Care

In order for a person, or group, to move on the "green light,"
he must first have good health. This, the Indian has not had. The
Senate Permanent Investigation Sub-committee in its research on
Indians, has found that they have the greatest incidence of diseases than any group in this country.[1] They suffer in greater
degrees from dysentery, strep throat, hepatitis and tuberculosis
than other Americans.

The birth rate among Indians is 38.5 live births per thousand. The national average is 17.5. Life expectancy is 64 years
whereas the general population is 70 years. The infant mortality
rate as surveyed by the Albuquerque Area Indian Health Services
is 37.1 per thousand but the rate for the United States population
is 22.4.

A two-year health study for HEW, showed that ten percent of
all Indian children suffer from chronic otitis media, a serious ear
malady that comes from simple ear infections which are not cared
for. On Navajo reservations alone, 24,195 visits to clinics in
1974 came from children suffering from otitis media.

Inadequate medical and health care among Indians is so acute
that on January 30, 1973, six armed Indians, allegedly from the
American Indian Movement, took over the Indian Medical Center in

Gallup, New Mexico, demanding adequate health care. The Indians took over the hospital for seven hours. After stating their demands, the Indians surrendered to law enforcement officers.

One of the most severe reasons for such poor medical care for the Indian population is the vast distances that the Indians must travel to obtain medical care. In the states which the sub-committee visited, Oklahoma, New Mexico, Arizona and Nevada, it was found that, among 260,000 Indians, thirty-three percent of the Indian population, distances of travel to medical facilities was in some cases more than twenty-one miles. In one case, a mother with three children ill of pneumonia and congestive heart failure, had walked fifteen miles to notify Indian police.

Because of the low standards of the Indian Health Service even when the Indians reach their havens, the patients face inferior medical care. Of fifty-one Indian hospitals, only twenty-two have been accredited. Only sixteen of the hospitals meet fire and safety standards on a national basis. The DJ Associates who did the research and study for the Senate Sub-Committee found that thirty-three of the hospitals were in such poor condition that nineteen need to be replaced and fourteen should be refurnished and brought up to date. The cost for such reconstruction would amount to $200 million. It was found that funds for Indian hospital construction had been cut consistently by the HEW and Office of Management and the Budget.

Under the Handicapped Persons Bill of Rights, $1,000,000 in aid has been granted to handicapped Indian children. It is expected that $3,000,000 more will become available after October 1, 1977, when the law will become fully operational.

Alcoholism and Suicide

As a corollary to poor health care, the suicide rate on reservations is one of the highest in the country as are also the rates for homicide and alcoholism. Alcoholism is so acute among Indians that a protest demonstration was held last August, 1974, at Window Rock, Arizona, to close the Navajo Inn, a liquor establishment. The St. Michaels Chapter of the American Indian Movement led the demonstration.

On the Navajo reservation, two new Local Alcohol Rehabilitation Centers opened in September, 1974. One facility opened in Page, Arizona and another in Lupton, Arizona. The centers will provide living facilities for fifteen men and women. The patients will be able to stay at the centers for as long as six weeks.

It was revealed in January, 1975, that Indians in the Canadian northlands were consuming alcohol far in excess of the average consumption in Canada. A bizarre incident revealed that when excessive consumption of alcohol is used by Indians it can destroy the home. Returning to his home, a young Indian boy found his parents drunk. They were jobless. Going into a fit of rage, the boy destroyed the village liquor store in Picture Butte,

Alberta. The incident sent tremors throughout the north country. Across the sweep of this part of Canada, Alcoholics Anonymous chapters are on the increase among the Indian population.[2]

The reservation may be a prime cause of suicide. Dr. Anthony R. Ray, mental health authority of the World Health Organization, holds that personal and environmental factors that are usually connected with suicide are bereavement, social isolation, chronic physical illness, psychotic disturbance, alcoholism and drug addiction.

In order to move on and overcome poverty among the Indians, first a massive health improvement program must be initiated. Along with improvement in health conditions, joining concurrently with health is the need for education. These are the two basic needs in the long-range conquest of poverty. Stress on education from the elementary school through college is now being pushed by the Navajo Nation as well as Apaches. Technical education is being stressed through the Navajo Economic Opportunity Program as well as college education at the Fort Defiance Agency.

Education

The total number of Navajos in college during 1969-70 were 1,100. In this same year 370 were majoring in education.[3]

One of the bright spots in Navajo education is the Navajo Community College located in Tsaile, Arizona. This is the largest college completely controlled and operated by Indians on a reservation in this country. The college is valued at about $15,000,000 located on a 1,200 acre campus. There are 1,365 students of which the great majority are Navajos and the remainder come from twenty other tribes. The college offers courses in the Navajo language, history and culture. Numerous other courses lead to Associate art degrees and Applied Science certificates. Graduates are moving to four year colleges, also.

In the summer of 1974, thirty-five American Indians received A. B. degrees from Arizona State University at Tempe. This was the largest Indian group to graduate at one time from an Arizona University. A special convocation was held on ASU's campus at Grady Gammage Auditorium.[4] Such a large number of graduates could mean a new thrust on the education of Indians in the Southwest. The degree permits the recipients to teach anywhere in Arizona. All of the graduates--a third were over age forty--are expected to teach in school systems on the Fort Apache, Salt River, Gila River, Akchin and Papago Reservations.

The graduates participated in the Career Opportunities Program which was started in 1970 by the United States of Education for a five-year period. These prospective teachers started as paraprofessionals in public affairs, Bureau of Indian Affairs, mission, and Head Start schools on their reservations. They were especially trained to teach special education and elementary education. Since Indian children have been deprived as much or more than all other minorities, the new-found skills of these

graduates will enable them to help the Indian child who has been
handicapped. With the Indian graduate now being used on the
reservations in the S outhwest, stability will come in teacher
turnover. Heretofore, Anglo teachers had a high turnover rate on
the reservation because it was difficult for the Anglo.teacher to
relate to the Indians.

International Business Machines is aiding the Navajos in
their quest for more education in the Athabascan languages. This
multinational corporation has produced a typewriter in the related
Athabascan languages which are spoken and written by the Sarcee
and Chipewyan in the Canadian N orthwest and mid-Alaska, and the
Navajo and Apache in the s outhwestern part of the United States.
A Navajo non-profit organization is introducing the typewriter
to expose the Navajos and Apaches to a deeper appreciation of
their culture. The name of the organization is 'Ak'e'elchiigi',
taken from a Navajo word which means "about writing." Campbell
Pfeiffer, president of the group wants to promote a deeper
appreciation on the Indian langaue.[5]

Navajos as Code Talkers

A white male who knew the Navajo language is credited with
one of the most successful experiments of World War II. The man
was Philip Johnson, an engineer working for the City of Los Angeles.
Johnson grew up on the Navajo Reservation with his missionary
father. Over a period of years, Johnson not only could speak

good English, but also, in his association with the Navajo children and adults, had mastered the Navajo language. Johnson suggested to the Marines that the Navajo language be used in telephone conversations under combat conditions in the Pacific during World War II. The idea was accepted by the Marine brass.

In the spring of 1942, recruiters from the Marine Corps came to Arizona looking for Navajos to implement the project. Two squads of young Navajos were recruited and sent to Boot Camp in San Diego. Their itinerary carried them to Camp Pendleton, then overseas to Marine Combat units in the Pacific. In the great battles the Marines fought on Saipan, Iwo Jima, Tinian, Tarawa, Kwajalein, Eniwetok and Okinawa there were Navajo code talkers. The code was so contrived that even as skilled as the Japanese were in code breaking, they could not break the Navajo code. The Navajos had developed thirty-eight sysmbols and a backup of 411 other terms. At this time the Navajos used an unwritten language, hence a non-speaker of the language could not understand it. However, this was not the first time the military had used Indians as transmitters of information during the war. Choctaws were used in World War I against the Germans. Comanches were with the United States Army in the European theater in World War II. The Choctaws and the Comanches used their mother tongues. The Navajos developed from the base language a special code that was the envy of cryptographers. It could not be deciphered in the time that would be necessary to counter a military thrust. The Navajos worked in two man teams. They pinpointed air strikes and directed artillery

bombardment. Marine commanders praised them highly for their

service in the field. Martin Link, curator of the Navajo Tribal

Museum has found through research that 320 Navajos served in com-

bat in World War II. In his research Mr. Link found that five

Navajos served with the United States Army in North Africa in

World War II.[6]

  In the fall of 1976, the Navajo radio network was estab-

lished. It was opened on December 13, broadcasting to the 150,000

members of the tribe living on the 25,000 square mile reservation

in Utah, New Mexico and Arizona. Broadcasting will be in the

Navajo language as well as local, state and national news. Ray

Gilmore, the tribal council's media director, announced that the

new studio contained $1,500,000 worth of equipment donated by the

Columbia Broadcasting System.

  One of the flaws that has been exposed by the Senate sub-

committee on Indian education is that the reservation school must

teach the Indian, who is looked upon as a "foreigner," the values

of the Anglo-Saxon culture. The Navajo Teacher Education Develop-

ment project at the University of New Mexico is attempting to

overcome that stigma with a project to place more Navajo teachers

in reservation schools.

  On the Navajo reservation covering the three states of New

Mexico, Utah and Arizona, there are 3,000 teachers, but only 180

Navajos, or six percent. The primary goal of NTED is to place

200 additional teachers in reservation schools immediately and 1,000 over the next five years.[7] In the states of Arizona and New Mexico, where twenty percent of the Indian population live, the educational achievement of Indian children is two to three years below the general population. The dropout rate is excessive.

On the San Carlos Reservation of the Apaches, there was only one Apache teacher in the elementary school during the summer of 1973.[8] At the San Carlos school, Indian students complained that teachers were prejudiced against them. The students had a difficult period trying to adjust to a non-Indian culture.

Continuing upgrading of Indian education was reported by Morris Thompson, Commissioner of Indian Affairs in August, 1974. A $1 million contract was awarded to Indian tribal groups in the Great Lakes area. The contracts were awarded through the BIA's Minneapolis office. The Minnesota Chippewa Resource Development Corporation received the largest grant of $863,668. Six Chippewa Indian Reservations will benefit from this grant. They are Bois Forte, Fond du Lac, Grant Portage, Leech Lake, Mille Lacs and White Earth.

Table VII shows funds expended under the Johnson-O'Malley Act for fiscal year, 1970.

The Act of 1934, under which these grants were made, provides that where substantial Indian enrollments in public education exist, supplemental programs are to be used to assist standard education programs. In past years, the use of such funds would

Table VII

State	Total Amounts (Johnson-O'Malley Contracts	Number of Students
Alaska	$ 2,594,000	2,851
Arizona	3,668,843	14,322
California	25,300	-----
Colorado	182,427	733
Florida	28,000	216
Idaho	395,000	1,496
Iowa	113,000	152
Kansas	48,000	134
Minnesota	796,500	2,680
Mississippi	5,250	19
Montana	577,987	4,287
Nebraska	282,000	741
Nevada	141,500	1,593
New Mexico	2,197,487	12,620
North Dakota	441,200	1,630
Oklahoma	1,015,000	16,081
South Dakota	1,197,000	4,058
Utah	11,223	16
Washington	560,000	4,823
Wisconsin	326,500	1,269
Wyoming	70,000	217
Peripheral Dormitories	1,716,069	2,134
Totals	$16,392,286	72,081

Source: Bureau of Indian Affairs

have been determined by the BIA, State Department of Education and the school districts. Now that self-determination is a part of overcoming poverty, the Indian tribal groups determine for themselves where the needs exist.

Self-determination is picking up momentum in education. In the Navajo community of Ramah, New Mexico, the weavers and sheep

herders are educating their children in their own culture. The
people manage and control their own high school. The board is all
Navajo. The teaching staff is over one-half Navajo. This innovation taking place at Ramah is being hailed by Indian leaders, and
at the same time is being watched closely by the BIA. On the
reservation and off, Indians scoff at the BIA Indian boarding
school system. Of the 250,000 Indian school children, about one-
third attend these BIA schools. They were originally established
to assimilate the Indian in western culture. But they have failed.
The concept was to take the Indian children from their parents and
train them (work in a menial capacity) in the white man's ways.[9]
This was similar to taking black students in the south a generation
ago and training them in home economics. Home economics in those
days conditioned the black girl to work in some white woman's kitchen.
The boys were trained in manual arts, not the liberal arts, or the
art of doing his own thinking.

1. Wall Street Journal, Vol. LV #54, March 19, 1975, pg. 1.

2. The New York Times, Vol. CXXIV, # 42,729, January 19, 1975,
    pg. 14.

3. Letter from A. Z. Brown, Teacher, Shanto, Arizona 86049,
    January, 1975.

4. The Navajo Times, Vol. 16, #31, Window Rock, Arizona,
    August 15, 1974.

5. The New York Times, Vol. CXXLV, # 42,729, January 19,
    1975, pg. 20.

6. Wall Street Journal, December 31, 1974, pg. 2.

7. The Navajo Times, Vol. 16, No. 31, August 15, 1974, p. B-14.

8. "Deprivation, Poverty, A Way of Life for Reservation Indians," article by Joel Nilsson for the Associated Press, published in the Pittsburgh Post Gazette's Daily Magazine, August 9, 1973

9. The New York Times, July 15, 1973, pg. E-7. From an article by Richard Margolis, who have made contributions in education and Indian achievements.

CHAPTER VII

Indian Economic Development

Economic development, in a concurrent manner, will help
solve the excruciating Indian problems of health and education.
In a very broad context, economic development implies improving
the quality of living. The stress on economic development also
does not mean that getting more money or goods or enjoying more
creature comforts will simultaneously solve the problems of
suicide, dope addiction, homicide, alcoholism or wife beating.
They would not.

What would be solved would be a reduction in the high rate
of unemployment on the reservations, through the process of creating more jobs through on-the-job training, attracting industry to
the reservations, obtaining water rights,[1] improving farming methods
that will yield larger crops, improving grazing methods, introducing direct sales of Indian jewelry, art, clothing, mining materials,
developing timber resources, and improving the tourist industry.
Economic development can further be extended to the reduction or
complete eradication of exploitation of Indian by whites who
trade and conduct businesses on the reservation.

Through economic development the Indian on the reservations
can accelerate his self-determination and gradually phase out the
Bureau of Indian Affairs more efficiently than through any other
vehicle. Economic development is extensive, and striving for its

implementation means the greater development of the Indian and the denouement of another government bureaucracy.

Census data for 1970 show that there are 827,000 Indians in the 50 states. The five states below have 50,000 or more Indians.

Table VIII

States With 50,000 Or More Indian Population - 1970

State	Indian	Population Total	Percent Indian
Oklahoma	97,731	2,559,253	3.8
Arizona	95,812	1,772,483	5.4
California	91,018	19,953,134	0.5
New Mexico	72,788	1,016,000	7.2
Alaska	51,528	302,173	17.0
Total	408,877	25,603,042	1.6

1. The Navajo Indian Project opened in Farmington New Mexico in April, 1976. The project is designed to convert 110,630 acres of over grazed land into an irrigated system of farmland.

Population Increase

Over a ten-year period, 1960-1970, Indian population increased from 523,591 to 792,730, an increase of 269,139, or fifty-one percent. The percent of increase in the Indian population was double the increase in the national population. Half of the Indian population reside in urban areas and on 115 reservations. Thirty-five percent or 292,301 live in thirteen other states with populations of 10,000 Indians or more. Eighty-five percent of our total Indian population live in only eighteen states.

Table IX

Thirteen States With 10,000 Or More Indian Population

State	Indian Population
North Carolina	43,437
Washington	33,386
South Dakota	32,365
New York	28,330
Montana	27,130
Minnesota	23,128
Wisconsin	18,924
Texas	18,132
Michigan	16,854
North Dakota	14,369
Oregon	13,510
Illinois	11,413
Utah	11,273
	292,301

It is estimated that seventy-five percent of the Indian population reside on reservations. The other twenty-five percent have migrated into the urban areas of this country. With 620,250 living on reservations, it is there that the need for economic development exists. On the reservations, the Indian or the tribal council holds land in trust for him. There is a semblance of control. So, land ownership is the first priority for economic development.

Landownership in New York

One of the latest incidents in land ownership is claimed by Indians in New York State. In early November, 1974, a group of Mohawk Indians created the State of Ganienkeh, a name derived from the Mohawk language meaning "Land of the Flint." The area claimed a 612-acre camp site in Herkimer County in Upper New York state north of Utica. The Mohawk Indians set up the site as the headquarters of the Six Nation Iroquois Confederacy, dating back to the period in United States history prior to the Revolutionary War. This six nation confederacy was composed of tribes of Mohawks, Oneidas, Onondagas, Cayugas, Senecas and Tuscaroras.

Since occupying the land, New Yorkers have been denied access to the area as a recreation spot. The Mohawk Indians claim this land on the basis of the treaty of 1798 which they claim is invalid because it was signed by Joseph Brandt who was a traitor to the Indians. Kakwirakeron, a spokesman for the Indians, claims that all land in Upper New York State was originally the Indian hunting grounds. At present there are about 150 permanent Indian residents in Eagle Bay located in the western Adirondacks.

Seeking to resolve the conflict, the Indians are calling on President Carter, citing a 1794 treaty between the United States and the Six Nation Confederacy. The controversy can only be cleared by the President of the United States. The New York Police would like to evict the "trespassers" but because of the

fallout from Attica, the police are maintaining their composure.
It is also quite obvious that the New York State authorities do
not want another Wounded Knee.[1,2]

The Indians in Maine are claiming that the State of Maine
and a number of cities have false titles to land that really
belong to the reservation Indians. It is estimated that two-
thirds of the State of Maine is claimed by Indians as being their
land and which was taken from them. These claims have tied Maine
up in far-flung litigation. Sales of property in portions of the
state have just about stopped. Trying to get title to a piece
of land is tenuous. Lawyers are not guaranteeing title to property that is under jeopardy.

Indian land claims in Maine and Massachusetts are causing
other Indians to seek to join the Passamaquoddy and Penobscot
tribes in northern Maine and the Wampanoags in Massachusetts.
The Wampanoags are located in the area of Mashpee and Martha's
Vineyard. These tribes are charging that their land was taken
without Congressional approval under the Indian Non-intercourse
Act of 1790. Since the filing of these suits, the BIA in Washington, D. C. has been deluged by inquiries from other Indians on how
they could get on the tribes' rolls. Because of these land
claims, the tribes in Maine and Massachusetts speculate that
Indians who previously passed as whites are now claiming that they
are Indians again.[3]

Choctaw Land in Mississippi

Under a complicated ruling by the United States Government, it was found that the State of Mississippi could not collect state sales taxes from the Choctaws because they were not a tribe. Judge James P. Coleman, who handed down the ruling on a brief filed in May, 1972, held that the United States Government did not have jurisdiction over the Choctaws. As early as 1831, under the treaty of Dancing Rabbit Creek, Choctaws as a tribe ceased to exist in the State of Mississippi. Choctaw land which amounted to more than ten million acres was ceded to the State. In payment for the land, each Choctaw head of a family who chose to remain in the state, was given 640 acres of land. They could also apply for United States citizenship. The tribe itself as an entity migrated to Indian Territory in Oklahoma.

This is another form of termination policy similar to the Klamath Indians in Oregon. In December, 1974, the Federal Government paid the Klamath Indians of Oregon $45,000,000 for 135,000 acres of Klamath land. About a generation ago, the tribe accepted the termination route. In 1961, the Federal Government paid some Indians as much as $43,000. Four years later it had been frittered away. The attorney for the Indians stated that when the Indians were paid off, the government put them off the former reservation. Such action destroyed the tribe. There was no longer any identity.

Indians Love for Land in Illinois

Chief Black Hawk, the Sac Indian chief, believed that land could not be sold. When the settlers in Illinois continued to violate treaties by buying land from individual Indian groups, this provoked Chief Black Hawk to challenge the settlers. In fact, Abe Lincoln was drawn in 1831-32 into the Black Hawk Indian War in Illinois because of the differences between Governor Reynolds and Chief Black Hawk

Indians Land Claims in Alaska

Under the terms of the Alaska Native Claims Settlement Act of 1971, the Indians in Alaska, Eskimos and Aleuts, were compensated for their ancestral claims by a package arrangement of $1 billion in cash and 40 million acres of land.[4] This settlement went to 60,000 Indians and Eskimos. This was the equivalent of $15,000 in cash and 666 acres of land per individual.[5]

Oil companies interested in Alaska helped the Indians get the bill through Congress. Land-claims questions were holding up drilling permits for the trans-Alaska pipeland. Twelve regional corporations were established. Under the terms of the agreement, these corporations were authorized to lease some of the native-owned land for commercial ventures.

Questions of land ownership can be settled if the Indians remain on the reservation and seek to develop the reservation. Those Indians who decide to leave the reservation and merge into the general population do so with all the concomitant hazards of urban living as well as its advantages.

Also, because of the reservation policy, the Indian is somewhat isolated from the general population. Unlike the blacks who developed and parleyed civil rights into human rights and in the process involved labor and other minorities in their struggle, the Indians, until recently have not used this approach. The American Indian Movement is an outgrowth of the black civil rights struggle in the fifties and sixties.

Since the reservation is our starting point, it is found that the greatest problem on the reservation is unemployment. Joel Nilson, a reporter for the Arizona Daily Star, lived on the San Carlos Indian Reservation in Arizona for four weeks. He found unemployment approaching twenty-five to forty percent. Of the homes on the reservation, 923 out of 1,122 were unfit to live in, and 2,000 of the San Carlos Indians were receiving some welfare.[6]

Again and again the government (BIA) has tried to get the Indians to leave the reservation. The BIA in their research have found that eighty percent of the Indians who receive on-the-job training and move off the reservation and seek to merge into the American milieu, eventually return to the reservation.

One Indian who left the San Carlos reservation and went into the city to live was asked why he returned. He stated that he had not seen the sun set in three months. So, it is the great panorama of the prairie, the majestic buttes, the high mesas, the

cool, clear streams and the flowing rivers that attract the Indian.
Nature is so deeply embedded in his soul that it cannot be detached.
But the population of the Indian is increasing. Indian family
size is larger than the national average. Provisions must be made
for living.

In order to reduce unemployment on the reservation where it
reaches forty percent, the Navajos are adopting a policy of bringing industry to the reservation. One of the examples of this is
the contract with Exxon Corporation. Out in Shiprock, New Mexico,
Exxon, U. S. A. will begin prospecting for uranium on the Navajo
reservation. Exxon has negotiated a unique contract with the
Navajos which permits the Indian to participate in a joint venture
in lieu of taking royalty payments. The Navajos will receive $6
million for Exxon's right to develop the deposits.

Because of the energy shortage, American energy companies
are reaching out for sources other than oil. Eleven companies
have bid for the right to prospect for uranium on Navajo land.
The tribe, admits Art Arviso, executive assistant to the tribal
chairman, wanted the best company to develop the deposits. Exxon
fitted the bill and was chosen. Under the terms of the agreement
the Navajos can elect to own forty-nine percent of any Uranium
mined by investing forty-nine percent of the capital. Exxon pays
all exploration costs. Robert Schryver, director of the tribe's
Office of Minerals Development, figures that the tribe got a good
deal. He figures a potential profit of $33.5 million on a $17.2

million investment. It is estimated that 20 million pounds of
U_3O_s, or yellowcake, will be recovered. On a purely royalty
basis the yellowcake recovered would have yielded only $14 mil-
lion.[7]

In August, 1976, hearings began on the proposed Navajo-
Exxon Uranium Development which was proposed as early as January
24, 1974. Approval must be given by the Bureau of Indian Affairs
before exploration can begin. The agreement approved by the
Tribal Council gave the Tribe two options. The Royalty option
would yield the Tribe $8,250,000 a year for not less than ten
years. Under the partnership option, the Navajos' share could
approach $22,000,000 annually, based on estimates by BIA officials.
If the Secretary of Interior approves the Exxon environmental
statement, the Tribe would benefit by a $6,000,000 bonus payment.

The Gallup, New Mexico Independent reports that geologists
estimate that there may be as much as 100 million pounds of
uranium in the area. The price of uranium today would bring the
Navajos $200 million in royalties to the Tribe.[8]

Coal Gasification on the Navajo Reservation

Energy sources? This is the problem of great magnitude
that this country is now facing which will continue into the
future. Where will new energy sources come from? How will they
be developed? One is coal gasification. Processes have been
developed through the Lurgi method. This process was used by

the Germans in the 30's, when they had plenty of coal, but little
natural gas. Natural gas is now in short supply, so the most
plentiful source open for development is coal. Geologists have
estimated that more than 3 billion tons of coal are underground
in the United States. It is waiting to be tapped. On the Navajo
Reservation straddling New Mexico, Arizona and Utah in the four
corners area, about one billion tons of coal lie near the surface
of the ground. The coal can be easily strip mined.

Four companies are involved in creating this synthetic
fuel. They are El Paso Natural Gas Company, Western Gasification
Company (WESCO), Pacific Lighting Corporation, Transwestern Pipe-
line Company. Because of the shortage of natural gas and the need
of synthetic gas, the companies who are seeking to develop this
fuel source expect to run head-on into the environmentalists. The
project on the Navajo Reservation will be a testing ground for the
clashing of these two forces. The stakes in this contest are far
reaching. The Navajos need more industry on the reservation. Once
these plants are established, more than 2,000 people will be
employed,probably as soon as 1978. Support services such as retail
service centers, schools, churches, light manufacturing and ware-
housing will produce another 6,000 jobs. More than 15,000 residents
will live in the area. The Navajo coal gasification companies.
involved envision a new town to accommodate   the workers and
their families.

Challenging the industrialization of the area are the environmentalists, including the Navajos. The voluminous black smoke spewing from plants already generate power in the Four Corners turns environmentalists off. It is suspected that the four company consortium will demonstrate the same disregard for the environment that has been shown in the Four Corners. What are the alternatives? Basically the power is needed for Southern California. That is where the population is. It is needed where the population is. Without a supply of synthetic gas or natural gas, Southern California, with its 12,000,000 people, cannot long live on the standard on which it has been living for more than a generation. El Paso Natural Gas is investing heavily in a plant to produce gas from strip-mined coal in New Mexico. The State of California does not produce any natural gas. Nor does it have any large deposits of coal. It does have oil, but these supplies are already being pumped from the Pacific Ocean.

The second alternative is to maintain the status quo. But already the Tribal Council has overridden some forty or more dissidents. The industrialization of the area will place severe strains on the Navajo culture. The choice is to remain nomadic and in poverty, or to become industrial and improve one's living standards. The Navajos will get first chance at the $30 million annual payroll of the proposed plants. The Tribal Council will make money from the leases and the plants. Taxes that will go to the state of New Mexico will amount to about $7 million a year.

Environmentalists are also concerned with water rights. It
is estimated that the proposed six plants will have available
water from the San Juan River. However, it is possible that the
new population centers will consume the remainder which will not
leave a sufficient amount for irrigation. The companies have
allayed these fears saying that the water needs are exaggerated.
They are pushing ahead. It is felt that the needs of the environmentalists can be solved much more quickly than the continued
dire poverty can be overcome for the Navajos or the needs of
Southern California can be met.

In 1950, oil was discovered on the Navajo Reservation.
Over the 25,000 square miles of New Mexico, Arizona and Utah which
the Navajos control, companies have been drilling for oil. Since
1950, $235 million in oil royalties, bonuses and rents have been
paid to the Navajo Tribe by American oil companies. Thinking in
terms of the total Tribe, the Navajos pooled their resources and
invested the money in building a motel, discount stores, electronics
assembly plant, shoe factory and an utility company. Through the
results of such investing, the Navajo income has tripled. Infant
mortality has dropped fifty percent. The school drop-out rate
has been reduced from sixty to twenty-five percent. For those
Navajos who want to further their education, a $10 million
scholarship fund has been created for any Navajo students who
qualify to attend the college of their choice.

Table X lists the major areas of employment in various industries on the reservation. Public services show the highest number of Navajos employed. These services include food handling, hospitals, BIA operations and tribal functions including education. The next largest industry is construction. Here the employment of non-Navajos is four times the Navajo employment. The individuals employed in this capacity are mostly Anglos. The need for more skilled craftsmen among Navajos reveals itself in the low percentage engaged in the construction industry. In manufacturing and processing the Navajo employment almost matches the non-Navajo. The differences in commercial trades and services are small. More on-the-job training will overcome these differences. The number of Navajos engaged in agriculture and forestry almost matches the number of non-Navajos and shows the highest rate of employment, next to transportation, communication and utilities. Tourism shows a high rate of employment of Navajos but the lowest absolute number employed in any of the categories listed. In subsequent analysis, it will be seen that tourism is one area which can be increased on the reservation. Mining offers the next to the lowest percent of employment. Mining includes metals and coal. Expansion of these industries is now in progress.

The total employment of Navajos is 14,280 out of a total of 29,140. Navajo employment rate in seventy-one percent of the total. However, the unemployment rate as of August, 1974, on the reservation,was as high as fifty percent.

Table X

On-Reservation Full Time Employment By Industry

	Total	Navajo	Navajo Employment Rate
Mining	794	518	65.2
Agricultre and Forestry	890	840	94.3
Tourism	240	217	90.4
Manufacturing and Processing	1,383	1,281	92.6
Commercial Trades and Services	1,156	892	77.1
Transportation, Communication, and Utilities	348	333	95.6
Construction	2,716	741	27.3
Public Services	12,613	9,458	74.9
Total	20,140	14,280	70.9

Sources: Office of Navajo Labor Relations--Equal Employment
          Opportunity Reports, 1974
          Office of Program Development--Inventory of Commercial
          Areas and Employment, 1974

Attracting industry to the reservation should not be a

difficult task, especially where there is a definite need for

development of a natural resource.   The Exxon case is a good

example.   Other examples are oil in Oklahoma, timber in the

State of Washington, coal in the Four Corners, textiles and

tourism.   Rservation Indians are not subject to taxes.   Tax

subsidies could be given to industry for locating plants on

the reservation.   Payment of wages would be paid above the

minimum level and also above the welfare level.   So long as

the industry or business did not immeasurably alter the

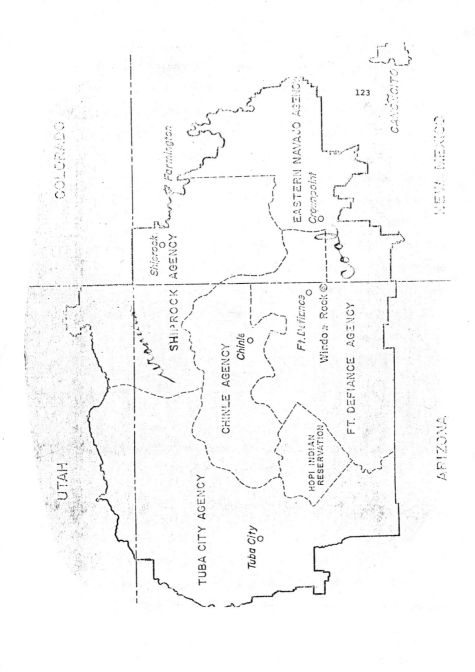

environment, it should be welcome. The goal for employment on the reservation should be a stated reduction in the unemployment rate on the reservation. In some cases, where businesses have located on the reservation, results were disastrous because the project was not researched thoroughly enough, and there was a lack of advanced planning on the part of the company and the Indian leaders.

On the San Carlos reservation a fifty-acre industrial park, completed in 1971, never became viable. One of the lessors backed out before the project was finished, and another one could never get financing. Robert Taylor, one of the BIA's program officers, said that the park was in the wrong location. It was not close to the metropolitan areas of Phoenix or Tucson, nor were there any rail facilities available. A lumber company employs thirty-five Apaches. Salaries range from $2 to $3.50 per hour. Outside of the BIA and the Tribal Work Experience Program, the biggest amount of income is earned from tending government and tribal buildings, grazing and marketing cattle. Cattle sales in 1972 produced $2.5 million. Since the cattle business is the biggest income earner on the San Carlos reservation, it appears that this enterprise should be expanded to its fullest. One of the flaws in such expansion is the leasing of 232,000 acres to private ranches and associations. Land is leased for three percent of gross sales and charges of $4 per head. With a present world demand for beef, it would be possible for the San Carlos Apaches to realize a trebling of income from cattle raising if they could control the production .

Water Rights

Along with agricultural development is the control of water rights, depending on which point of origin of the contiguous water rights of Navajos on the San Juan River. It flows for about 150 miles through the Navajo Reservation in New Mexico and Arizona. The Colorado, in southeastern Utah, also flows, for about 125 miles bordering the Navajo Reservation in Arizona and Utah.

Recognizing that water is the elixir of life. Peter MacDonald, Chairman of the Navajo Tribal Council, has had the Tribe appropriate $665,000 from its funds for a comprehensive water resources study on the reservation. There is a dire lack of water on the Navajo Reservation. In these arid lands, water is "liquid gold." For too long water has flowed past the Navajos into the homes and businesses of people living in Phoenix and Los Angeles. Now, the Navajos want self-determination over these water resources. For a long time, the Navajos have known that the Federal Government has not protected their water rights.[9] In the entire west, water is at a premium. Poplation and the pressure of new towns in the west have placed extra burdens on water resources.

With control over their water resources, the Navajos can then determine their economic development. Industry looks for

water. It is one of the six great energy sources: coal, water,
oil, sunlight, wind, thermal.

Mineral Resources

Since the increase in oil prices by the countries in the
Organization of Oil Producing Countries (OPEC), there has been an
acceleration in the search for power sources. On the Navajos'
land there are adequate mineral resources which need to be
developed. Uranium production is already underway. Other
mineral resources are copper, silver, oil, gas and coal. The
controversy surrounding coal deposits in the Four Corners needs
to be clarified. It has already been discovered that low sulphur coal is found in great quantities in the west. One of
these beds of low sulphur coal is found in eastern Montana.
Peabody Coal Company signed a lease with the Northern Cheyenne
Tribal Council for a $16,000 lease to mine 500 million tons of
Cheyenne coal. The complex would include four coal gasification plants. The total operation would amount to $700 million.
But before the announcement could be made by Peabody, the
Cheyenne Tribal Council instructed the Bureau of Indian Affairs
to break off negotiations. What motivated the Cheyennes to
break off the leases was an offer made by Pittsburgh's Consoli-
dation Coal Company. Consol wanted to negotiate lease at $35
per acre. The BIA, acting for the Tribal Council had negotiated permits or leases on about half the reservation over the
past eight years. These leases were for $1 an acre and royalty

payments of seventeen and one-half cents a ton. Consol had
offered twenty-five cents a ton.

Other American energy companies have entered into
leases with the Cheyennes, American Metals, Climax, and Chevron
Oil. These two companies hold permits on 250,000 acres of the
Northern Cheyenne Reservation. For these initial permits and
leases the tribe has already received $2.5 million.

Logging and Forest Products

Not only can Indians cut and log their own timber, but
can be employed by lumber companies contiguous to the reservation. At the Alabama-Coushatta Reservation in Livingston,
Texas, the members of the tribe work in the East Texas lumber
industry around Diboll and in the Piney woods with Temple Industries. They also engage in lumbering on their own reservation.
The Navajos have developed forest products through lumbering
and processing lumber into millwork. Products produced by their
plant at Navajo, New Mexico, are door frames, casements, bases
and other wood products for the home building industry.

Oregon is the home of the Klamath, Modoc and Snake Indians.
The reservations of these tribes abound in timber land. The
relationship these tribes had with the Federal Government was
terminated in 1961. There were 2,133 members in these tribes
at the time of termination. The tribes owned 862,662 acres of
tribal land and 104,322 acres of alloted land. This forested
land was appraised at $90,791,123. The share to each member of
the tribes was $43,500.

In New Mexico, the Jicarillo Apaches in the northwestern part of the state and the Mescalero Apaches in Ruidoso Downs, and the White Mountain Apaches of Arizona, maintain a thriving lumber industry.

During the fiscal year 1976, 952 million board feet of timber was produced on Indian lands. In 1968, tribal lands had cut only 150 million board feet, but the yield from the sale of timber amounted to $21.1 million. Timber used by the Indians as a fuel source for themselves amounted to $311,000. The BIA reports that the total gross value from agricultural production as of 1967 was $186 million. This income includes crop production, cattle and sheep and the use of fish and hunting.[10]

Tourism

The development of tourism on Indian reservations as a source of income is now being increased. The Alabama-Coushatta Indian Reservation at Livingston, Texas, in early 1973, received a federal grant of $2,123,000. This grant came from the Economic Development Administration to be used for utility improvements on the reservation and for water, sewage, paved roads, gas stations and for crafts. This reservation was created by Sam Houston, as early as 1835. The tribe occupies about 1,000 acres in this East Texas region. It is heavily endowed with timber resources and has a fast developing tourist industry. Nine years ago the tribe started appealing to the tourists traveling up down Highway 59 which runs from Texarkana to the Mexican border.

During this time, tourists have increased from 25,000 annually 200,000 in 1973. Income from tourism has risen from $20,000 in 1965 to $200,000 in 1973. By using federal and state grants and loans from the Small Business Administration, the Alabama-Coushatta Indians have been able to expand their tourist facilities to include restaurants, retail stores and craft shops. The payroll on the reservation amounted to $287,000 in 1972. From an average family income of $1,000 in 1965, the average in 1972 was $4,000. It is estimated that the tourist business will grow to $1.5 million by 1978.

Additional income, from the sale of oil leases by the Alabama-Coushatta Indians to Atlantic Richfield, will produce $27.61 per acre on 4,200 acres in the Big Thicket area. Proceeds from leases will enable the tribe to match available state and federal funds for the building of gymnasium, community meeting facilities and a recreation hall.

For tourists, the great attraction which the Navajos have is scenery. Monument Valley and Canyon de Chelly are two of the most awe-inspiring attractions on the Navajo Reservation. Clement-Smith, in his research on tourism for the Navajos, has described how the Navajos could profit from running buses into the reservation and profiting from these two main attractions. Another main attraction could be a development centered around the great conflicts between the Navajos and the army General Carleton, and the scout Kit Carson. History can be retold to show how Kit Carson,

in carrying out Carleton's order, introduced a scorched earth
policy against the Navajos. Diaramas could be painted showing
the long campaign of attrition and the eventual submission of
the Navajos to the army. Sketches could be made of the trip
to Bosque Redondo and the Canyon de Chelly. A panoramic descrip-
tion could be made of the great Navajo leader Manuelito and his
classic resolution to resist going to the scarred, barren Bosque
Redondo. Then the hated Carleton was relieved and with the
coming of General Sherman, the order was given for the Navajos
to return to their homeland in Northern New Mexico. In these
great trials of endurance against a persistent foe, the Navajo
story could be viewed with awe. These are the things the
tourists crave--stark tragedy, pathos, survival of the spirit.

In far West Texas, in the area around El Paso, live the
Ysleta Indians. Just a few years ago, this tribe was so desti-
tute that there was fear that it would die out, but today, the
tribe is thriving. To keep the memories of the past from fading,
in 1975 the tribe dedicated a tourism and cultural center. The
purpose of the center is to portray traditional arts, crafts
and native skills. The intent is to make provisions for a major
tourism center which will serve as a ceremonial and governing
enclave. Antigua Community Building, which was built between
1692 and 1744, is an outstanding example of a museum which shows
the background and deep culture of the Pueblos dating back
before Columbus.

Economic Exploitation

A throwback to the old, outmoded, company stores, which were in vogue in isolated mining and steel towns up to World War II, has now come to the Indian reservations. A withering thick report, issued by the Federal Trade Commission, presented evidence that white operating trading posts are gouging the Indians who trade with them. On the 15,000,000 acres in the latter part of 1972, it was found that the Navajos were victims of excessive pricing, usurious interest rates and confiscation of government welfare and unemployment checks. Because the Indians are geographically isolated, these stores are the only source for purchasing staples. The post operators use "credit saturation." This means that the operators find out the value of the welfare check or unemployment check, then issue credit up to the amount of the check. When the check arrives, the operator pockets it, then the cycle of debt or indenture begins again. This feature is quite familiar to the foreign born and the blacks who lived in company (captive) towns mining coal and making steel a generation ago.

Many of the trading posts also act as postoffices. The store operator opens the mail in clear violation of federal law. He knows the amount on the check. The Indian signs the check face down, sometimes not knowing the face amount.

As a follow-up to the 1972 investigation by the FTC another one was made in 1974. The same practices were still being used against the Indians. Nineteen trading posts were found to be the worst of the lot. Although the posts are in violation of truth-in-lending legislation, it is doubtful that the Navajo Nation can even prosecute the traders.

Because of a conflict in law, the white traders cannot be prosecuted by the Navajos. The white traders are not Navajos but citizens of the United States government. Of course, the Federal Government could prosecute the traders for violating federal laws, but who will testify against the traders? Certainly not the Indians who in some cases may not be able to understand legal conditions and may not be able to speak English or they may fear that they will not be able to purchase staples at the store, or if the store is closed, a longer distance must be made to buy goods and services. It is not uncommon for a Navajo to travel 35 miles to purchase a loaf of bread.

This economic trap can be broken. The Navajos are fast developing their own stores on the reservation in cooperatives. Reservation status should not limit bargaining power. Also, the Bureau of Indian Affairs, which has jurisdiction over the reservation, can do a much better policing job.

Conclusion

Economic and industrial development on Indian Reservations was begun as early as 1950 by the BIA. Cooperation was initiated with Tribal Councils and states. In 1950 on the Navajo Reservation a pact was entered into with the Hopi for $1 million. This money was for industrial development, but now that the Hopis and the Navajos are having differences over the use of land this development is at a standstill.

However, recognizing that there must be a money source, the Indians organized the first bank controlled by Indians in Washington in 1973. The name of the bank was the American Indian National Bank. Barney Old Coyote, a Crow Indian and an economics professor at Montana State University was elected president. Charles W. Swallow, an Oglala Sioux was elected senior vice-president. W. W. Keller, Chief of the Cherokee Nation of Oklahoma, became chairman of the board.

The recognition that capital is the first need for economic development has started the Indians on the way toward solving their economic problems. Other minorities in the United States are also doing this now; Blacks, Mexican-Americans, and Orientals.

Aiding the Navajos in their economic development is the National Science Foundation. A grant of $40,000 was made to the Navajo Nation in August, 1974, for investigation and the possible development of geothermal power resources on the reservation. The project would also include a study of no-resistance under-ground power lines. An all Navajo panel of six will be heading the project. The project will be coordinated by Fred Young, a physicist with Los Alamos Scientific Laboratory. He was the first Navajo to receive a doctorate in science. Other members

of the panel are Thomas Atcitty of Tsaile, Arizona; Dr. Gahe
Billy; Dr. Taylor-MacKenzie, Priscilla Mowrer, and Jimmy
Shorty.   The members of the panel represent a cross section
of health, agriculture, academia and law.[11]

1. The New York Times, Vol. CXXIV # 42 m 659, November
   10, 1976, pg. 68.

2. The Kootenai Tribe in Idaho has declared a bloodless
   war with the United States Government over land.
   Houston Post, June 4, 1975, Pg. 10 AA, A. P. Date-
   line from Bonners Ferry, Idaho.

3. The New York Times, Vol. CXXVI #43,422, December 12,
   1976.

4. Smithsonian, Vol. 5, # 7, October, 1974, pg. 47.

5. Business Week, Number 2397, September 8, 1975, p. 76.

6. Pittsburgh Post-Gazette, August 1, 1973.

7. Business Week, Number 2320, March 2, 1974, pg. 38.

8. Independent, Gallup, New Mexico, August 7, 1976, pg. 1.

9. United States Commission on Civil Rights, May, 1973.

10. Bureau of Indian Affairs, 1970.

11. Independent, Gallup, New Mexico, August 20, 1974, pg. 1.

CHAPTER VIII

Spanish Speaking Americans

Our second largest minority in this country is made up
of the Spanish speaking Americans. The Spanish speaking
Americans are classified as those citizens of Mexican origin,
Central or South American origin, Puerto Ricans and Cuban origin. The table shows the ethnic class and number of Spanish
speaking Americans in this country.

Table XI

Ethnic Origin	Number
Mexican-American	6,300,000
Central or South American	2,000,000
Puerto Rican	1,500,000
Cuban	700,000
Total	10,500,000

Source: Census Bureau, 1974

The Census Data show there are 10,500,000 Spanish speaking
Americans in this country. This estimate appears to be too low.[1]
If the illegal aliens are counted, there are 16,000,000 or more
Spanish speaking Americans in this country.

However, if the definition of "American" as defined by
the Census Bureau excludes alien then their data could be
correct. But from a broader context, and from the impact which

aliens have on the economy in certain states, then we must count these aliens. Our analysis of the alien problem will be covered subsequently in this chapter beginning with a discussion of the economics of the group above.

The median income for Mexican-American families in 1972 was $7,910. Puerto Rican families had a lower median family income of $7,160. No data were available for Cubans or the Spanish speaking persons of South and Central American origins. Median income for all families in the United States for 1972 was $11,120. This was the high-water mark. The severe recession of 1973-75 pulled the median income in this country down to $10,500 for all United States families. In 1972, Mexican-Americans were earning seventy-one percent of the income of United States families; Puerto Ricans were earning only sixty-four percent.

Economic data supporting the Census findings, came from a report published by the United States Department of Labor Statistics in December,1973. The Labor Department report showed that the Spanish speaking Americans, or Latinos, or Chicanos have few marketable skills and the language barrier further hinders them from jobs that pay more than the median income. However, although the Chicanos fared worse than the average American family, they were above the average black family in income. They were about $3,100 below the average income of the white family, but $300 above the average black family. It was estimated that twenty percent of Spanish speaking families were earning below the poverty level. The government's definition of poverty level income in 1970 was $3,745 for a family of four, but for the same family of four, in 1973 it was $4,275. This twenty percent of Spanish speaking families compared with ten percent of white families and thirty percent of black families.

The Mexican-American family income is diluted somewhat because of family size and lower educational attainment. In 1973, there were four or more members in the average Mexican-American family. In educational achievement, only fifty percent of young adults twenty to twenty-nine years were high school graduates. Of those adults who were forty-five to sixty-four only one fourth had completed high school. Mexican-Americans live mostly in the Southwest. The states of California, Texas, Arizona, New Mexico and Colorado claim ninety percent of Mexican-Americans. Urban areas claim more than eighty percent of these Mexican-Americans in the southwest and California.

Puerto Ricans have largely migrated to New York City where they are located mainly in Manhattan Island. Others live in Florida.

Cubans as a branch of Spanish speaking Americans were mainly political refugees and of the professional class. Cubans, mainly located in the Miami area and Dade County Florida, left Cuba when Castro seized power more than fifteen years ago. They are mainly middle class and have moved into the mainstream of economic life in the Florida region.

The occupational patterns of Spanish speaking Americans
are reflected in their incomes. Mexican-Americans are generally
employed as farm and railroad workers, but by 1970, they were
also found among skilled craftsmen, holding out of five jobs.
They were heavily employed in construction work as bricklayers,
cement finishers, carpenters, pipe fitters and other allied
construction jobs. In the white collar category, Spanish
speaking men were employed as salesmen and in professional and
and managerial occupations. But even in these categories, their
salaries were below those of white males in similar job categories.

Urban Conditions Among Mexican-Americans

Two reports dealing with Mexican-Americans in an urban
setting came out of Houston, and Dallas, Texas in 1975. The
Houston report was a summary of differentials in pay scales
among the ethnic and sex groups for equal pay. These dispari-
ties in pay scales were a throw-back to the hoary past by
whites in Houston, when they thought a black, a woman or a Chicano
did not have to live like a white person, so ergo, they did not
have to have as much pay as a white person. Of course, this
was the zenith of white paternalism in Houston, Texas. Table
XII shows these differences, based on ethnic origin and sex.

Poppy Northcutt, former women's advocate for the office
of Mayor Fred Hofheinz, is seeking to identify these salary

Table XII

City of Houston, Texas

Average Salary For Fulltime City Employees

Class	1974	Annual Salary
1. White Males		$11,900
2. Mexican-American Males		9,000
3. Black Males		8,400
4. White Females		7,700
5. Black Females		6,600
6. Mexican-American Females		6,600

Source: City of Houston, Texas, Civil Service Department, 1975.

differentials. The above table shows that the Mexican-American males are in second position, although the Mexican-American population is only twelve percent of the population while blacks make up twenty-eight percent of the population of Houston, Texas. These data show that the Mexican-American population are more highly politically oriented than the blacks. The data also show that the old folk myth of Texas being hard on horses, women and minorities is somewhat apropos judging from the data.

In 1975, the total male employment in the city of Houston was 9,573. In city government, white males held 6,454 of the jobs or sixty-seven percent. Black males held 2,317 of the jobs, or twenty-four percent. Mexican-American males held 802 jobs for males, or eight percent.[2]

Total female employment in Houston in 1975 was 1,988. White females held 1,404 jobs or seventy-one percent. Black

females held 411, or twenty percent. Mexican-American females
held 173 jobs, or nine percent. The percentages of female jobs
closely parallels those of the males for ethnic and sex groups.
But the significant inequality is in the types of employment.
Mexican-Americans are heavily employed in cleaning and repairing
sewers and sweeping the streets. Blacks are heavily employed in
garbage and trash collection. These are the lowest paying jobs.
Thus, in the entire job spectrum in the city of Houston, Texas,
in the total of 11,561 jobs, Mexican-American, Blacks and females
are low on the totem pole. The white male dominates, not by
right of competency, but by right of conquest.

Time of Change

John Butler, a former postal offical, and head of the
city's Affirmative Action division in 1975, requested hiring
goals for minorities and females from each division in city
government. Mr. Butler let it be known that the city was checking the hiring policies for minorities and women with each firm
doing business with the city.

Other appointments by Mayor Fred Hofheinz have been Dr.
Hortense Dixon as the city's first black woman executive assistant
to the mayor. Mr. Palmer Bowser, a local black businessman, headed
Houston's Manpower Program and Mr. John Castillo, a Mexican-
American, headed the new program on community development. Another
Mexican-American, Mr. Lionel Castillo, was elected Comptroller of
the city of Houston in 1971 and reelected in 1973.

A second report, out of Dallas, shows that Mexican-Americans occupy some of the worst housing in that city. Sub-standard housing was occupied by twenty-seven percent of Mexican-Americans, while one-fifth of the blacks and four percent of whites were in similar housing.

Average incomes in Dallas for 1975, showed that Mexican-Americans earned $9,232. This amount was above blacks which was $7,080 and far below whites which was $14,615.[3]

In educational achievement the average Mexican-American was about on the ninth grade. The reason why Mexican-Americans have in general higher incomes than blacks is that there is a heavy concentration of Mexican-Americans in the trades and skilled crafts. Blacks were on the 11th grade level. Whites were on the 12th grade level. The educational problems of Mexican-Americans in Dallas were brought by the increase in population from a low of 29,464 in 1960 to 67,902 by 1970. By mid-1975, an increase of 10,000 brought the population to 77,000. These immigrants came from the Rio Grande Valley and small towns, and lacked the skills as well as the educational background necessary to hold better-paying jobs in Dallas.

Migratory Workers, Braceros, Wetbacks and Illegal Aliens

Migratory workers can be citizens of this country, be aliens with temporary permits to work in this country, or be illegal aliens such as wetbacks. Migratory workers are mainly employed in agriculture. Members of the National Advisory Council on Economic Opportunity have investigated this problem on migratory care and have found that, in trips to New York State, such workers live under very poor conditions and are paid low wages. Employers often cloak the hiring of illegal aliens as migratory workers by stating that United States citizens will not do agricultural work. However, one of the main reasons for hiring migratory workers is that they provide cheap labor, and, in the case of the illegal entrant, the employer keeps a club over his head through threats. He will be sent back to his homeland if he complains.

Migratory workers are needed to harvest specialized crops in various areas such as sugar beets in Colorado, cash vegetable crops in Maryland, Pennsylvania, New Jersey, and New York; and fruit in Washington, California and Oregon. In Texas, Arizona, New Mexico and California migratory workers are used to harvest citrus, leguminous crops and grapes.

The Migratory Stream

The migratory stream flows northward from Florida, Texas and California. The Florida stream is mainly composed of blacks from Florida and other parts of the South as well as come illegal migrants from the Carribean and Puerto Ricans. The Texas stream is composed mainly of Mexican-Americans and illegal aliens from Mexico. The California stream is composed mainly of Mexican-Americans, illegal aliens and Orientals.

The Atlantic coast stream covers the states of Florida, Georgia, South Carolina, Virginia, Delaware, New Jersey, Pennsylvania and New York. These migrants pick vegetables, potatoes and fruit. The racial composition on the eastern coast is made up of seventy-five percent blacks, twenty percent Spanish speaking Americans and five percent white. This is the mainstream of migrants moving up through the Atlantic Seaboard states. There is a sub-stream that moves up into the mid-west through Ohio, Illinois, Wisconsin, and Michigan. This process is reversed in October and November when the migrants move back into Florida for the winter.

Investigations and research on migratory workers show that forty percent live in the South. Sixty percent are divided between the North and West. Migratory workers usually have one employer and travel 1,000 miles from home although some travel less than seventy-five miles from home. The usual work year is eighty-two days. From 1946 through 1965, the number of migratory workers fluctuated around 400,000. In 1972, this number was down to 310,000. This decline was caused by mechanization and a reduction in the number of children employed as workers.[4]

Wages of Migratory Workers

Migrant programs in California, covering forty-one counties, reported on products, population, harvest work period, wages and migrant labor demand. Twenty-one counties were selected from the forty-one to determine the minimum and maximum wages paid. Wages ranged from $1.65 per hour to $3.50 per hour.

Wages paid in Florida for twenty counties of a total of twenty-eight covered by the Migrant Program in Florida show that wages ranged from a low of $1.45 per hour to $2.50 per hour. Wages paid migratory workers in Florida average about eighty-seven percent when compared with those in California.

In Texas, wages ranged from a low $1.25 per hour up to $2.35. Forty-two counties using migratory labor were selected from a total of eighty-five covered in the report on Migrant Programs in Texas. Twenty of the forty-two counties did not make wages available to the researchers in Austin, Texas. From the base of $1.25, wages for migratory workers in Texas were only seventy-five percent of those paid in California and eighty-nine percent of those in Florida. The Lone Star State thus pays its migratory workers the lowest wages of the states using migratory workers. With such a great use of migratory workers in a heavy agricultural and ranching state, these low wages are the basic reason Texas has more people on the poverty level than any other state in the nation.

Health and Housing of Migratory Workers

It is not only that wages for migratory workers are the lowest of the lowest kind, but it is also possible that migratory workers remain migratory because of lack of education and health facilities. In California, Florida and Texas, the three states which have the largest number of migratory workers, health care for these people is also far from adequate. Since it is also inadequate for middle income and affluent Americans, can we expect much more for the migratory workers in this country? Yes, we should expect more, because agricultural pay, in and of itself, is low pay. Stoop labor does not call for skills that are needed in industry or in the profession. Although this is a maxim in the agricultural world, it is one of the perennial questions hammered on by Cesar Chavez, the champion of the farm workers in California. Because wages are low, this does not mean that health care should be lacking.

Since work by the migratory workers is akin to regimented labor and they are usually employed by one employer, then there should be some kind of sick call or medical check-up scheduled periodically by the employer. This is not done. Research has shown that few counties in the three states named above provide medical services for the workers. However, educational services for the workers are provided, with few exceptions, in all the counties.

Exposure to Pesticides

Pesticides are a hazard to the health of migratory workers. Researchers at the University of Houston, through a research grant from the government found that migratory workers moving

up the Atlantic Seaboard stream were exposed to numerous pesticides while picking vegetables and fruits. Pesticides used
included parathion, guthion, sevin, toxaphene, endrin, thiodan,
prolon, systox, solone, lannate, lindane, methoxychlor, thio-
dene, malathion, imidan, zolone, lear arsenate, tepp, fervan,
captan, meta-systox, and dieldren among others. Investigators
found from data collected from the East Coast Migrant Stream
that the higher the exposure to these pesticides, the greater
the susceptibility to toxic effects.

Housing

Housing for migratory workers is of the worst kind. Such
housing could be equivalent to urban slums, or worse. Sanitary
facilities for rest rooms and bathing in a bathtub were rare.
Showers were available and outhouses were the usual facilities
provided. At one migratory camp visited by members of the
National Advisory Council, one of the members asked the employer
whether he had running water for the migrants. The employer
replied that they did have running water. The people run for
their water from the stream back to their living quarters with
buckets! Housing is usually located within the perimeter of the
working area. If an orchard is being worked, the the housing of
the migrants is within the orchard. Living and working conditions
are co-terminous. Therefore, the workers have a double exposure
to pesticides while working and while living. Since clothes worn

while working are exchanged in the living quarters and stay in
the living quarters until washed, then the workers are exposed
both on the job and off. Also, wives and children of the
workers are exposed to this contaminated clothing.

Alien Workers and Illegal Aliens

How many alien workers and illegal aliens have slipped
into the migratory stream is not known. But it is known that
a steady flow of alien workers has crossed the United States
borders in ever-increasing numbers over the past six years.

The first organized attempt to import an alien labor
force was during World War II. An agreement was entered into
by the United States Government and Mexico to use Mexican
farm laborers on farms and ranches in California and in the
Southwest because of a shortage of man-power during the war.
Of course, under our present laws, the child born of foreign
parents in this country, becomes a United States citizen. This
program flourished until 1965, when the United Farm Workers and
the AFL-CIO in Texas objected to the importation of Mexican
farm workers. Notwithstanding the ban on alien workers, Mexicans
and other aliens have found that they could cross the Rio Grande,
and also the long border in the Southwest running from Browns-
ville, Texas, to Tia Juana in the Mexico-California area. The
workers who braved such crossings were called wetbacks, and those
who held twenty-four hour cards, green card holders. As late as
August 17, 1973, the United States Immigration Naturalization

Service was permitting aliens to work in the United States under
the guise of "returning resident aliens," who had never maintained
a residence here and only worked in Texas or the Southwest for
a few months a year. The Immigration Service was seeking to
classify the migrant workers as returning resident aliens. Visas
are not required of "returning resident aliens." The United
States Court of Appeals agreed with the Farm Workers Union and
the AFL-CIO. However, it is strange that a United States Government agency will try to circumvent the will of the Congress in
permitting alien workers to enter the country to work at jobs
that could be manned by its own citizens.

One year later, in 1974, the Mexican government proposed
a new agreement for migrant workers but the United States Embassy
in Mexico City did not accept it. With a burgeoning population
of more than 30,000,000 and most of its citizens earning incomes
far below the poverty income of this country, it is no wonder
that the Mexican government would like to export manpower to
the United States. The Embassy could not go along with the
proposal because of high unemployment in this country.

The Mexican government retaliated by declaring that
those Mexican migrants who were working in the United States
were not being given neither humane nor civil treatment. In
1973, the United States had deported 600,000 of these illegal
entrants. Lack of funds increased the problem of deporting
aliens in many of the cities of this country and especially

in the Southwest where many aliens are discovered. Aliens are
not hard to locate. They usually cannot speak the English
language wel. But even after they are located, if there is no
money to deport them, they are left on the streets to shift for
themselves. Police officers in these cities are apt to arrest
the aliens for more serious offenses and they are then carted
off to jail, stand trial, are convicted and sent to the state
prisons. Such action is tantamount to operating a slave labor
force under the cover of prison reform. [5]

One of the most serious problems embedded within a problem is the illegal entry of the Mexican wetback across the Rio
Grande into Texas and from the northern most states of Mexico,
Leon, Chihuahua, Sonoro and Baja, California.* Upon investi-
gating smuggling along the long Mexican-United States border,
the Border Patrol and Immigration Service frequently discover
corpses of wetbacks or braceros in the Rio Grande or in the
brasada. It works usually like this: - poor wetback gives money
to a contrabandista. The contrabandista promises to transport
the wetback across the border. Jobs will be waiting for them.
A small truck or covered wagon will take them across the border.
On the trip they will not have food nor water. Told that the
Rio Grande may lie over the next arroyo, the unsuspecting
wetback may plod into a trap. Or the bandista may shoot the
wetback to avoid identification. This kind of smuggling is
one of the most vicious; it is difficult to stop because it is
done in small bands or ones or twos.

*During 1975 there was a veritable outpouring of
articles in newspapers and magazines bringing attention to the influx of illegal migrants coming into
the United States. While Attorney General William
B. Saxbe was over the Justice Department, he called
for deporting 1,000,000 aliens. He recommended a
$50,000,000 increase in the United States Immigra-
tion and Naturalization budget to do this. In 1973,
the Border Patrol caught a record number of 156,886
illegal aliens. This was an increase of 62,666 over
1972. Mexican-Americans in Texas raised questions
on what can be done about the 1,000,000 illegal Mexican
nationals in Texas. Labor unions sided with the Mexican-Americans. However, it was found that Mexican-
Americans were ambivalent on this issue. In San Diego
in November, 1974, an "Ad Hoc Committee of Chicano
Rights" called a news conference challenging Saxbe's call
for deporting 1,000,000 aliens. The Committee thought
this was a call for racial suppression of the Chicano-
Latino community in the United States. Addressing the
Border Patrol Academy in Los Fresnos, Commissioner
Leonard Chapman, Jr. was aghast at the illegal aliens
flooding the United States. He said they were displacing
American job holders making as much as $4.50 to $6.00
per hour. In San Pedro, California, 47,000 deportable
aliens were arrested in three weeks. Law enforcement
officials seized marihuana and other drugs during these
roundups. Michael Satchell wrote a series of articles
for the Washington Star News on the illegal migrants in
the San Pedro area in California.

Working Illegal Immigrants

As the recession of 1973-75 deepened in the winter of

74-75, increasing attention was given to illegal immigrants in

the United States. The problem has exacerbated because the

aliens had taken jobs from United States citizens. The argu-

ment for years has run that the illegal immigrant is doing

work that United States citizens would not do. These jobs have

been stoop labor, mainly agricultural work in California, and

along the Texas, New Mexico, Arizona border.

During fiscal 1974, the limit on aliens immigrating into the United States was 394,000. Congress set this limitation for keeping families together, admitting needed workers and hardship cases. The term "needed workers" is euphemistic. With a recession there is really no need for additional workers. In the Southwest these illegal immigrants are wanted for working on ranches, as domestics, in manufacturing, and in service capacities. There is no question that the illegal immigrant is exploited by the employer. His wages are lower than the United States workers. He may or may not receive Social Security. If the illegal worker complains, the employer can send him back to his native country, or have him deported by the immigration service. Nobody really knows how many illegal aliens are in this country. In 1974, the Immigration and Naturalization Service deported 788,000. It is estimated that there are between 4,000,000 to 12,000,000 in this country. Notwithstanding all of the humanitarian reasons for amnesty for these aliens, the imposition on social services may far outweigh the labor contributions. The term social services includes education of the children of these aliens, medical services, welfare, crime, and cost of police work. Where do these illegal immigrants come from? The main spawning grounds are Mexico, the Dominican Republic, Haiti and El Salvador.

Working Illegal Immigrants

In other parts of the world, the sources of illegal immigrants are Hong Kong and the Phillippines. Based on research by Laurence H. Silberman of the United States Justice Department illegally working aliens have a decided impact on present employment practices in this country. Silberman has found that illegal immigrants are not only taking agricultural jobs, but also high-paying jobs in the large metropolitan areas in this country; they are competing with ethnic and minority groups and lawfully admitted resident aliens; they act as labor supply for the employer without benefit of analysis by the Department of Labor and send money out of the country to relatives, thus acting as a negative influence on our balance of payments problem, yet make small or no contributions to the income tax system.

Peter Rodino, the pudgy Congressman from New Jersey who became known from his televison appearances during the House Judiciary Committee's impeachment proceedings of President Nixon, has introduced in Congress a bill designed to slow down the entrance of illegal immigrants coming into this country. Rodino's bill would make the employers responsible for hiring the illegal immigrants. On first warning a citation would be given to the employer. On the second violation the employer would be fined $500 for each illegal immigrant hired. On the third violation, the employer, in addition to paying $1,000 for each alien hired, would also serve a year in jail.

---

1. Houston Chronicle, January 16, 1974. pg. 12, Section 3 from an article by Robert Waiters in the Washington Star News.

2. Houston Chronicle, May 18, 1975, pp. 1-8, Sectional.

3. Dallas Morning News, December 14, 1974, Section D.

4. There are three excellent reports on migrant workers available to the reader. Migrant Programs in California, Migrant Programs in Texas and Migrant Programs in Florida all published by the Juarez-Lincoln Center, National Migrant Information Clearinghouse, 3001 South Congress Avenue, Austin, Texas 78704.

5. In Albuquerque, New Mexico, in January, 1975, illegal aliens were incarcerated in the local jail. Mariano Islas, the Director, stated that the cost of housing these aliens was six dollars per day, which the county could not afford. These were immigration violations. Lucas Powell, deputy police chief, went on arresting aliens mainly from Mexico. Most of them were booked on charges not involving immigration laws.

CHAPTER IX

Equal Employment Opportunity

In the first part of this work we have covered the elderly,
the American Indian and the Mexican-American. We now turn our
attention to the American blacks, the fourth and the largest ethnic
minority in the United States. To the credit of the blacks must be
given the assault on civil rights. Books in themselves could be
written on this subject. Historical precedents on civil rights
were started prior to the Civil War. The most recent assault on
civil rights was the enactment of the Civil Rights Act of 1964. But
even prior to this act, a Fair Employment Practices Act, or rather
executive order proclaiming a FEPC were issued as early as 1941.

Jobs and equal employment opportunity are the bedrock of
all civil rights legislation passed and executive orders issued
by various presidents of this country. Behind these two measures
lie equality of opportunity, but knowing that racism has been
institutionalized in this country, the insidious fight goes on and
on by blacks seeking to overcome.

Historically, we shall cover the period of equal opportunity,
and then move into Affirmative Action programs, employment and unemployment on various levels of government.

Following in the lead of the blacks on civil rights are the
women's lib movement and the Gay movement. But these are non
sequiturs. These two movements are diametrically opposed to the

deep problems of blacks on getting equal opportunities in this
nation. The women's lib movement is dealing with sex discrimination and the Gay movement is seeking to obtain moral acceptance
of homosexuality. However, if they can "piggy back" on the civil
rights movement, this may be an off-handed manner of gaining
acceptance of their causes. But we now turn to the struggle of
the blacks in obtaining jobs. Having a job is the answer to
welfare, economic crimes, self esteem and playing a significant
part in the unfolding of the human drama from day to day.

Equal Employment Opportunity

Equal employment opportunity in the Federal Government
began as early as 1883 with the enactment of the Civil Service
Act of 1883. The act was later expanded to include prohibitions
on discrimination because of religion. In 1940, the act was
amended to include race, creed or color.[1] Also, during the
depression of the thirties, the National Industry Recovery Act
had banned discrimination. But since the ploys omitted a
definition of discrimination, enforcement of the non-discrimina-
tion clause in the act was mute.

Between 1941 and 1963, more than 200 fair employment practice proposals were brought before the United States Congress.
Besides proposals from Congress, Executive Orders were issued
by every president up to the passage of the Equal Employment
Opportunity Act in 1964. President Roosevelt issued EO 8802 in

1941. This order established a Fair Employment Practices Commission. Because the Commission lacked enforcement powers, its rulings could not be enforced. This first Commission suspended operations in 1943. A second EO, 9346 was issued in 1942 which embraced total employment by Federal Government contractors as well as recruitment and training for war production. The southern bloc in Congress as well as private contractors lobbied against the order. Again the EO lacked enforcement powers. The commission was dissolved in 1946. The war was now over, and the country could get back to business as usual.

But what A. Philip Randolph had urged President Franklin D. Roosevelt to do in 1941 would not die. President Harry S. Truman during his tenure of office created a Fair Employment Practices Commission but it lacked enforcement powers.

President Dwight Eisenhower on August 13, 1953 created a fifteen-member committee on government contracts. Executive Order 10479 established the committee. Again, the committee had no teeth in its ruling. But Eisenhower would not stop. He issued EO 10577 on November 22, 1954. Section 4.2 of the order prohibited racial, political, or religious discrimination. A subsequent EO 10590 was issued on January 18, 1955. This order created for the first time the President's Committee on Government Employment Policy. The EO 11246 of September 24, 1965, ordered by President Johnson set up the present Equal Employment Office and gave the enforcement powers which the others were

denied. Affirmative action was included in this order. But prior
to Johnson's assuming office , President John F. Kennedy had
issued EO 10925, which set up the President's Committee on Equal
Employment Opportunity. Unlike the other EO's this one issued
by Kennedy required contractors to take affirmative action to
actualize anti-discrimination policy. If companies did not comply,
the committee could refer the cease and desist order to the Justice Department or terminate the contract. This order covered
all federally assisted construction. A contractor also could not
bar employment based on age. As Vice-President, Johnson chaired
the Committee on Equal Employment Opportunity. The Committee was
abolished in 1965. The Department of Labor phased it into the
Office of Federal Contract Compliance to deal with federal contractors.[2]

The three years in which Johnson was Vice-President found
him championing EEOC. In 1961, he spoke four times before various groups seeking to overcome hoary headed myths on hiring
minorities by companies which had government contracts. In 1962
he addressed himself to these issues six times. In one of his
meetings with the Equal Employment Office, Johnson cited specific
achievements of blacks in obtaining jobs in areas which had previously been denied to them. A tobacco plant in North Carolina
hired its first production workers. For the first time an oil
refinery in Illinois, and oil and chemical plants in Louisiana
hired black production workers. A metal fabricator plant in

Missouri began hiring blacks. Aircraft plants in Georgia and North Carolina began complying with EEOC policy as well as electronic plants in Georgia, North Carolina, Connecticut and Tennessee.

The Johnson Committee conducted surveys in the Federal Government. It was disclosed that employment of Negroes in Civil Service grades five (5) through eleven (11) had increased by seven percent. Over-all employment in the same grades had increased by five percent. Negro employment as of November 15, 1962, was triple the normal rate. An increase of 10,270 was added to payrolls. There was a projected increase of 3,772. While Johnson was over EEOC in 1962, 4,491 blacks enjoyed upward mobility by moving into middle management positions in the Federal Government and 343 were moved into executive positions.

In 1963, pressure was being exerted by the Civil Rigts acti- vists for a bill that would guarantee Equal Employment Opportunity. In the summer of 1963, Martin Luther King led a march on Washington. A bill was being readied in Congress on Civil Rights, sponsored by the House Committee on Education, chaired by the late Adam Clayton Powell, and by Labor. On November 23, 1963, Kennedy was assassinated. Early in 1964, The Civil Rights Act was passed which included Equal Employment Opportunity in Title VII. Com- mittees in both the House and Senate had tried to black passage of the Act. The House Judiciary Committee never held hearings on the bill. Over a twenty-year period, House Committees had detailed the need for such legislation. In the House, Representative Emmanuel Celler, (D-New York) and William McCulloch, (R-Ohio) were the helmsmen. In the Senate, Hubert Humphrey, (D-Minnesota) and Thomas Kuchel, (D-California) were the floor managers for the bill. Joseph Clark, (D-Pennsylvania) and Clifford Case, (R-New Jersey) led the floor fight for Title VII. All during the intense House debate, eighteen amendments were tacked onto the bill. In the Senate there were eighty-seven amendments in eighty-three days. Senator Dirksen, from Illinois, and Mike Mansfield from Montana, offered a substitute bill. This substitute was finally adopted. It was a far different bill from the version passed by the House. Along with Dirksen and Mansfield, Humphrey and Kuchel in constant contact with the Justice Department, developed the bill.[3]

With the passage of the Civil Rights Act in 1964, there was a lull on the domestic front. The War in Vietnam was heating up and Johnson asked and got from Congress the Gulf of Tonkin Resolution. This resolution gave the president almost a free hand to pursue the North Vietnamese wherever necessary when American troops were threatened. This resolution actually gave carte blanche to the president to step up the war in Vietnam.

Recognizing that Civil Rights was the major domestic issue at this time, Johnson issued Executive Order 11246 on September 24, 1965. Again, this was the innovation of affirmative

action within the Civil Service system itself to upgrade blacks
into more white collar, middle management, and executive positions. Johnson remarked before the Commission:

> As of June, 1965, the Government has about 375,000
> members of minority groups on its rolls, of which
> 308,657 were Negroes. Negroes accounted for 13.5
> percent of the Federal Work force, while they
> actually made up approximately 10 percent of our
> overall population. Negro employment has increased
> during the three years ending June, 1965, by 5.3
> percent while the total Federal employment increased
> only 1.6 percent during the same period.[4]

In September, 1966, Stephen Shulman became the first
Chairman of EEOC. Now that the Commission had a quasi-judicial
status, complaints began pouring in on job discrimination. In
the 1965-66 period, the Commission received 9,000 complaints.
Most of these complaints came from blacks. During this time
frame, unemployment among blacks was eight and two-tenths percent, about double the white rate.

Job Discrimination

In the center of these vast controversies of equal opportunity was John K. Powell, Jr., Chairman of the Federal EEOC.
Powell is a black lawyer from the Harvard Law School. His predecessor was William H. Brown, III, from Philadelphia. Brown's
predecessor was Clifford Alexander. Brown was so diligent in
the pursuit of implementation of EEOC, that he was booted out
under pressure from labor and big business. Brown was caught
up in the Nixon maelstrom of 1973. It is an understatement that

the EEOC is the most beleagured agency in the vast maze of the
Federal Government. In its development the EEOC was a concilia-
tion agency. In 1972, it was given authority to sue. At the
end of September, 1974, the EEOC had 100,000 cases on its calen-
dar. By 1976 this list had increased to 150,000.

Under the prodding of the Equal Employment Office of
Economic Opportunity, in 1974, the steel industry and the union
(USW) entered into an agreement with the Federal Government that
for all intents and purposes was to end discrimination in employment and hiring against minorities. The agreement also covered
the end of sex discrimination differences in pay practices.

The plan is designed to give back pay to all individuals
who prior to 1968 were discriminated against in hiring practices,
upgrading and underemployment in the steel industry. The plan
also will end the hiring practices which in the past kept minorities in low paying menial jobs. The plan will affect about
70,000 blacks, Spanish speaking persons and women workers in the
steel industry who were hired prior to 1968. Even before the
plan got underway, Herbert Hill, long time civil rights worker in
the employment field for the NAACP, attacked it. The provision
Hill disliked relieves the company and the union from any court
action on the signing of a waiver by the employee for back pay
or for infringement of employee's civil rights. In case a suit
was brought by an employee who thought he had been wronged by
the company, the government would defend the company against the
employee.

Mr. Hill contends that such action, in-concert by the government, company and the union, actually nullifies the Title VII of the Civil Rights Act of 1964, which gave the right to individuals to sue under discriminatory acts in employment. Hill reacted sharply to the settlements in the steel-USW settlement. Most of the individuals received only about $350,000. He thinks that the settlement should be in the thousands for each individual affected.[5]

Of all of these cases only one percent is called reverse discrimination, being filed by white males. It is felt that these cases will increase as the recession deepens. But for minorities seeking equality in jobs, upgrading, and increases in pay, along with their fellow workers, EEOC has successfully won cases against some of the giants in the corporate world. Among them have been American Telephone and Telegraph Company, United States Steel, eight other steel companies, and Standard Oil Company of California. These cases have been settled for more than $82,000,000 for employees who have been discriminated against. Settlements are pending in the aluminum, copper and automobile industries.

In one of the significant suits brought under the outright malicious job discrimination in Detroit, Judge Damon Keith ruled that the giant utility, Detroit Edison Company, was guilty of discrimination against blacks. The ruling carried $4 million in damages against the company. To add salt to the wounds, it was found that one of the unions representing the employees also was guilty of discrimination against blacks. Local 223 of the Utility Workers of America was ordered to pay $250,000 in damages. It was found that the Local 223 and the company had repeatedly rejected demands by the blacks for promotion and upgrading on the job.

Within the ruling handed down by Judge Keith, Edison was instructed to bring its work force up to thirty percent blacks and in promotion policy extend equal representation to blacks on various job levels until at least twenty-five percent of the jobs were held by blacks. The company was ordered to discontinue intelligence and aptitude tests.[6]

The corporate structure will be the main emphasis on affirmative action. Prodding can be done by the government and suits can be filed, but ultimately the corporations, who are the main sources of employment, must implement Affirmative Action. One of the large corporations which is emphatically implementing Affirmative Action is Consolidated Edison, the big public utility in New York City. A release of their 1975 Annual Report, shows that the number of female employees was up thirteen percent from just five years ago. Women make up twelve percent of Con Ed's labor force. Supervisory positions held by women, now about 506, are a gain of more than fifty percent since 1970. Professionals among women are twice the number in 1970, now numbering 164. Women performing technical jobs, such as line workers and repairs, have moved up from 58 to 133. There are two female officers, and one woman is a member of the Board of Directors.

Among blacks, it is estimated that Con Ed has an improving record. Purchase from minority firms in 1975 totaled $2,658,287. This was an enormous increase from 1969, the first year of the program when it was only $81,000. Serving on the board of Con Ed is a black in Franklin H. Williams, President of Phelps-Stokes Fund, and the secretary is Archie N. Bankston.

Minorities seeking employment in jobs where they are the first to open such doors have had the onus of being fired or let out first when business declines The Supreme Court sought to correct this on March 24, 1976, when it ruled that people denied a job solely on the basis of race or sex, can, upon reapplying, be given seniority by court order. Five of the Justices, Potter Stewart, Byron White, Jr., Thurgood Marshall, Harry Blackmun, and William Brennan, Jr. ruled in favor of the measure. Justices Lewis Powell, Jr., Warren Burger, and William Rehnquist dissented. This ruling is another milestone in the long ardous path of minorities and women seeking justice under the Civil Rights Act of 1964.

Another government agency that has great clout, but has not used it as a force of good in this democracy, is the Department of Labor's Office of Federal Contracts Compliance. After being dormant for years, this office, according to Business

Week, is stirring again.[7] The main reason is that there are expected returns in employment. A second reason is that Lawrence Z. Lorber, a youngish, ambitious administrator, is seeking to make a mark. Lorber is a former executive assistant to Labor Department solicitor William J. Kilbert. In the latter part of March, 1976, Lorber assumed his duties with the Office of Federal Contract Compliance. Immediately he issued a directive forbid

Timkin Company from bidding on federal contracts because of discrimination in the hiring practices at a plant in Ohio. This was the first such order issued by OFCC in more than a year.[8]

Affirmative Action offers the greatest promise, according to John Kenneth Galbraith, for bringing women and minorities into the decision-making suite of American corporations.[9] Galbraith is after full integration. However, with the implementation of integration in this society, it must not be done at the expense of identification. Of course blacks want integration, but they also want independence within integration.

The whole concept of Affirmative Action, a program designed to give preferential treatment to blacks and other minorities for the sins of past discrimination, has been challenged in the DeFunis case, known as DeFunis vs Odegaard. DeFunis, a Jew, sued the University for admittance on the basis of his high test scores which were better than three of the black students who were tested. Although blacks were given preferential treatment on admittance over DeFunis, DeFunis was subsequently admitted, and the case became moot.

The pro DeFunis forces are some of the Civil Rights organizations who were aligned with blacks in their civil rights struggle in the fifties and sixties. These organizations are B'nai B'rith, Anti-Defamation League, National Association of Manu acturers, United States Chamber of Commere, A. F. L./C. I. O. They are a few of the approximately 100 organizations on DeFunis's side. The forces against DeFunis were of course, the old line NAACP, Chicanos, Women's Rights group, American Bar Association of American Law Schools, to name a few of the more than 100 organizations. These two lineups show that a mixed bag of organizations are for Affirmative Action and against it. The WASP's are breaking bread with Jews seeking to promote so-called merit over justice. Even the A. F. L./C. I. O., which has had a dismal record on improving the lot of blacks in hiring and upgrading, were pro-DeFunis. Along with labor are the NAM and Chamber of Commerce. Very seldom, if ever, does one see these organizations agreeing on what is good for this country. But when it comes to minorities and blacks we have agreement.[10]

Since the DeFunis case became moot, there has arisen the Allen Bakke case, a white engineer who wanted to become a physician. The University of California at Davis refused him admission on the grounds that a certain number of minority students had to be admitted, hence there was no room for him. Bakke sued on the ground that his test scores were higher than the minorities who were black. The California Sumpreme Court ruled in his favor and the case has found its way to the United

States Supreme Court. The issues are the same as with DeFunis. The forces that were for DeFunis are for Bakke.

Nina Totenberge, writing in the New York Times Magazine, feels that the issue is so disruptive that it has split the old liberal alliance of labor, Jewish and Civil Rights groups. However, it is questionable as to whether this liberal alliance was ever valid, if it is being sundered over the DeFunis case. These organizations were seeking their own self-interest and using blacks and Civil Rights as a foil. This country has never had a real merit system. Discrimination has been practiced for more than 200 years, and, with all the vested interest groups fighting for advantage with the spurious notion that the so-called white race was superior to the blacks, browns, and red, how could merit be a matter of policy? Merit has meant that it was practiced for the most part, only among whites. Certainly not for blacks, browns and Indians. Now Affirmative Action is a part of our law endorsing preferential treatment to blacks, Chicanos and Indians. This is being challenged by the same vested interets that have traditionally been against blacks, browns and Indians in their search for justice and equal rights in this country. Affirmative Action is not against whites, Jews, Polish or any other ethnic group in this country. Affirmative Action is designed to redress past wrongs which were conceived to stunt and curtail the normal growth of the black minorities in our democracy. When, in the politico-economic process of a party in power or decisions of the

Supreme Court take action to correct old wrongs, the ethnic groups
which feel they are omitted from such action, take offense against
the ethnic group which is temporarily favored. This form of
inculpation is a distant throwback to the Luddites in England
who took sledgehammers and broke up the machinery because they
thought the machinery was taking their jobs.

Conclusion

The aftermath of the John F. Kennedy assassignation on
on November 23, 1964, and the ascendance of Lyndon B. Johnson
to the presidency, brought on a wave of Civil Rights legislation
enacted by Congress, unknown to any other administration in the
history of this country. The kernel of this legislation was the
outlawing of job discrimination based on race and sex. Has the
law accomplished its purpose over the past twelve years? Is
there a need of improvements in the law? Can an economic recession blunt or hinder equal employment opportunity?

To answer the first question is yes, the law has accomplished its purpose. The intent of the law was to outlaw racial
and sex discrimination. It was explicit. Title VII of the
Civil Rights Act of 1964 was clear in this respect. Improvements in the law can be made in its enforcement. Every second
of the delay in enforcement affects a minority person or a
woman who is in the process of applying for such a job in conflict or a promotion. The developing question on improvement

is the rising clamor from white males, who, having previously enjoyed a preferred status in the job market, are protesting that they are being discriminated against. Nothing, of course, could be further the truth. For decades and decades the white male has harbored in his thoughts the castration of the black male and the complete subjugation of the white female. The ascendancy of the black male and the rejuvenation of white and black females in the liberation movements have cast a shadow over the white male. His preferential status has been challenged. The big question is, are quotas for hiring and firing reducing the employment of white male? Of course not. Quotas do not mean that a black or a woman will take a white male's place. Quotas, where they can be administered, mean that equality is being established among minorities and women. White males have long hidden behind job sinecures of slothfulness and indifference. By requiring that qualified black men and women be hired only makes for greater competition in job placement. No longer should there be a preferential position for the white male. However, in times of recession and business downturn, there will be a clamor for release from laws on job discrimination. Lawyers and personnel administrators will look for signs from Washington for relaxing stringent requirements of the law. The recession or business downturn is not a reason for relaxing the laws. In the recession of 1974-75, there was a surfacing of who would be affected in layoffs. Heretofore, the person with seniority would be laid off last. The newly hired man would be laid off first. Extremely conservative union rules and regulations built in this safeguard to protect union workers. Seniority can mask incompetence. There is no assurance that every individual in a seniority position is more competent than a newly hired individual.

The present contract provisions between a company and the Equal Employment Opportunity Commission specify that a certain percentage of employees be black and women. Such a contract is on a collision course with union seniority rules. This issue was brought to a head when women were laid off in a General Motors plant in Fresno, California. A suit was brought against the company on the grounds that seniority perpetuates discrimination. A pending court decision on seniority is the case of Charles Watkins, et al vs the Continental Can Company and the Steel Workers Union. This case, according to observers, placed in context the issue of reverse discrimination. In the DeFunis case the issues of Affirmative Action complement Title VII of the Civil Rights Act of 1964.

---

1. Lyndon B. Johnson Library, Administrative History of the Civil Rights Act, Vol. 1, Austin, Texas.

2. Administrative History of the Civil Rights Act, The Johnson Years, November 1963-1969, Vol. 1, Lyndon B. Johnson Library, Austin, Texas.

3. Public Papers of the President, Lyndon B. Johnson Library, 1966.

4. Public Papers of the President, Remarks on Equal
    Employment Opportunity in the Federal Government,
    March 17, 1966, Lyndon B. Johnson Library, Austin,
    Texas, p. 332.

5. The New York Times, Vol. CXXIII, No. 42,449, April
    14, 1974, pp. 1-21.

6. William Grant, Jude On The Firing Line, pg. 684. The
    Nation, Vol 217 #22, December 24, 1973.

7. Business Week, Number 2426, April 5, 1976, pg. 113.

8. Ibid.

9. Black Enterprise, Vol. 4, No. 11, June, 1974, pg. 111.

10. The New York Times Magazine, April 14, 1974, pg. 9.

11. Ibid.

CHAPTER X

Employment and Unemployment

The Full Employment Act of 1964, which ushered in the
Council of Economic Advisers, was supposed to work towards a
full employment work force. But only in times of war--the
latest being the Vietnam War, did we really have full employ-
ment--a work force that was ninety-seven percent employed and
only three percent unemployed. In some countries such as
Germany and Japan, unemployment has been reduced to as low as
one percent. However the reader must realize that definitions
of unemployment vary from country to country.

With the end of the Vietnam War in 1973, a devastating
recession hit the United States as we approached 1974. This
was the worst recession since the great crash of 1929. In
1974, the unemployment rate went as high as ten percent. Thousands of construction workers were laid off in the Northeast,
and auto production in Detroit was almost halved from the previous year.

In mid-1976, unemployment had been reduced to seven and
one-half percent and employment had increased to 87,400,000,
an all time high. But the reader must realize that our total
labor force in this country stands at 94,486,464. Thus, our
work force is about forty-four percent of our total population
of about 215 million. But the employed force is only forty
percent of our population. Startlingly , this is one of the

lowest rates of national employment in the western world. So, really we are an unemployed nation. The punitive effects of an underemployed force fall heavily on minorities. The following analysis concerns this aspect of employment and unemployment.

Basically because of the greater educational achievement which young blacks, over the past generation, have been encouraged to make, there was a decided improvement in the employment of blacks in managerial and white collar jobs between 1960-70. It has been found that in the black community there is a high correlation between earnings and education. The higher the education, the higher the earnings. We are speaking of earnings over a life time, not for a three-or five-year period.

Notwithstanding education, black workers have been moving up the occupational scale because of the great Civil Rights Acts of the sixties, Affirmative Action and the Equal Employment Opportunity Office. These government agencies have done as much or more than private business in initiating action for white-collar employment of blacks.

In 1960, according to the Department of Labor, two of every five black workers were in white-collar, skilled or operative jobs. In ten years the number had increased to fifty percent. Managerial and white collar jobs do not have as high a cyclical rate of unemployment as semi-skilled jobs. Under prodding of the EEOC, blacks and other minorities have entered white-collar jobs and technical fields at a rate greater than

whites, but their up-grading on these jobs has been only slight.
White-collar jobs are not the "top-of-the-mountain" desired
jobs that they are alleged to be. Most white-collar jobs
are in the clerical category.

General Electric

General Electric reported in December, 1974, that hiring
of blacks had increased fixty-four percent since 1968. From an
analysis of this report, it was found that only after prodding
by the Equal Employment Opportunity Commission did GE make a
concerted stir towards hiring greater numbers of blacks. Just
about five years ago, in 1973 , EEOC found that in 200 domestic
branches of GE, discrimination was rampant based on race, sex,
and national origin.

In the December, 1974 report, GE issued figures showing
its employment pattern. In its 315,500 employment work force,
there were 28,665 blacks. These blacks represented 9.1 percent
of labor force. Among professional personnel, blacks were only
2.7 percent, or 1,200, and only two percent, or 550, of the
managers and senior officials of the company.

As early as the late 1930's GE became one of the first
major companies to take a stand against discrimination. Gerald
F. Swope, the president at that time, called for no discrimination because of race and color, but these mandates were never
carried out. During World War I, when A. Philip Randolph urged

President Roosevelt to issue a Fair Employment Practice Commission Executive Order, GE again called for equal-employment laws. But these calls for equal employment opportunity were meaningless unless implemented by top management and really enforced. Only since 1966, when GE put forward its Affirmative Action program, did the giant electrical equipment and appliance firm really begin enforcing equal employment.

As usual, in cases where minority employment has lagged it is a common excuse that the problem is not discrimination, but a supply of eligible blacks. Since GE employed numerous engineers they just could not find enough blacks. However, when there were black engineers looking for jobs, the large plants like GE would not hire them. Seeking to do something about this problem of a shortage of black engineers, GE gave to Prairie View A & M University a grant of $150,000 to train black engineers.[1] Dean A. E. Greaux, the dean of PV's School of Engineering received his degree in engineering in 1952. At that time, Dean Greaux could not even get an interview with any official in order to be hired as an engineer.

General Motors

One of the major manufacturing firms in this country, General Motors, is taking Affirmative Action to integrate minorities and women into their employment program. In 1973 at their General Motors Institute there were 88 minority students and 31 women in the pre-freshman program. In 1965 there were only 13 minority students at General Motors Institute. Only two years ago there were 167. In 1973 there were 412 enrolled.

Employment of minorities at GE has grown from 11.2 percent of the corporation's United States work force in 1965, to 16.7 percent at the end of 1972, and over 17 percent at the end of 1973. In white-collar jobs at GM, progress among minorities has grown from about two percent in 1964, to be about five percent in 1971, and at the end of 1973, to more than eight percent.

When these percentages are converted into people, it is found that GM today employs about 113,000 minorities and 97,000 women. Since GM is the premier manufacturing corporation in this country,[*] they pay their employees premier wages. Whether the job is white-collar, or blue collar, the average salary is more than $12,500 annually.

The two cases cited, General Electric and General Motors, have gone far in helping to create a black middle class with a level of earnings upwards of $10,000 per year. Those black families which earn $6,000 or less are far greater in number and will be dealt with subsequently to show their plight. But the black middle income family has shown phenomenal increase. The CBS program "Four Portraits in Black" pointed up this increase through four case studies. The increase has been enjoyable but grueling.

This program "Four Portraits in Black" was telecast by CBS on Friday, April 26, 1974. Hal Walker, a CBS news correspondent, narrated the program which was designed to show four case studies portraying the black middle class. Usually what the TV viewer sees is the polarization of blacks: the well-to-do blacks who are living on an affluent scale, and the poverty-stricken blacks eking out a living as was depicted in the film "Sounder." The CBS program showed the black middle class and demonstrated how they had escaped from poverty.

Census data, used in the narration, showed that, in 1951, 89 percent of black families had an income less than $7,000 per year, not very high. During the same period, white family income went up at a much faster rate. Middle class black family income appears spectacular because their income was so much lower than white twenty years ago. With the black women working and in numerous cases earning more than their husbands, the average black family income is $11,000 per year.

In clerical work alone there are more than 800,000 black females. More than 1,500,000 black females head families. Whereas black females finishing college earn $7,100 per year, they are only $200 short of the earnings of white women graduates. A somewhat oblong comparison of black and white men shows that black men with four years of college earn $9,000, but the white man has only to finish high school to earn $9,000. So, the comparison here is glaring. Black college women earn proportionally much more than black college men. Black college women are increasingly moving into law and medicine. However, it has been in the accounting profession, that bastion of white puritanism, that black women are beginning to make in-roads. Peat, Marwick and Mitchell in its Houston office is now hiring black women accountants.

Hiring of black women and blacks in accounting firms has been spurred by EEOC order number four. This order, from the Executive Office of the President, required personnel statistics in Affirmative Action from employers with fifty or more employees. The number was lowered to twenty-five or more employees in March, 1973, and with a government contract of at least $50,000. The order required that employers notify their employees of equal hiring, promotion and training of minorities and women. Black women are not too optimistic that private accounting firms will be hiring many blacks.

Accounting firms are blood brothers to the executive suite and the hidebound attitude of the private accounting firm still results in treating women as interlopers in their profession. Even black males do not look favorably on black women in the profession of accountancy.[2] Penetration of the profession of accountancy in private industry will be the main opportunity for employment of black women. There are 100,000 accountants in this country. The market for accounting is growing. This is the major area of employment. The second area is institutional, and the third area is government. The General Accounting Office is probably the equivalent of a public accounting firm. Through October 31, 1974, the GAO employed in its Washington office and regional office 319 women. Of this number fifty-nine were black women. Some of these are lawyers. Four of these black women are in class GS 13, earning between $20,677 and $26,878 annually.[3] As a counterpart to the GAO, a sister government agency which relies heavily on accountants is the Internal Revenue Service.

Although the black women have found that employment in the Big Eight accounting firms is difficult to secure, they have found a welcome opportunity in the Internal Revenue Service.

Under the pressure of Civil Rights advocates, Affirmative Action and the feminist movement, a company that hires a competent black woman in any capacity has met the requirements of these two groups. They have hired a woman. This will satisfy the women 's lib. They have hired a black. This will satisfy the Civil Rights advocates and Affirmative Action. In these instances, the black male can be discriminated against. The citation above is exceptional, it is not common. Black women as well as white women are not hired in the market place as much as white men and black men. In looking for competency, the recruiter will invariably, subconsciously look for the male first. As Simone Beauvoir, the French writer, maintains, the feminist movement will overcome capitalism long before it overcomes paternalism. Notwithstanding the women's lib movement and the tigerish feminist movement, men still look upon women as love objects. Men want to love women, protect them and marry them. Women want to rid themselves of paternalism or as love objects. Betty Friedan, who is given much credit for the start of the women's liberation movement, feels that women are necessary to help men and families to maintain living standards that American families are accustomed to. The thirty-five million working women today will not go back home again. Even in a recession there are demands that layoffs be in proportion to men and women, not based on seniority. Women are now sharing the economic responsibilities of the home. This will continue for all age groups--the young married couples, the middle aged and the aged. The proportion of black females working is far greater than the proportion of white females working though this gap is closing. White women are seeking work and getting work much faster than black women.

Black Males In Management

Black males in professional, technical and managerial positions almost doubled in the 1960's from seven percent of all employed Negro men in 1959 to 13 percent in 1971. Gains are in large companies. In firms with 100 or more employees the proportions of black men in professional, technical and managerial positions almost doubled between 1966 and 1970. The percent of change went from 3.7 to 7.1 percent.

In releasing these data, the Department of Labor based its findings on a study by Recruiting Management Consultants, Inc. This is a minority owned firm with headquarters in New York. The survey queried 500 black men. All but sixteen had college degrees in business administration, science, engineering or law. Two-thirds were under thirty-five years of age. Few of them had had other work experience. An average of 6.5 years was spent by the group in private industry.

The survey covered a broad range of business and industrial activities. Forty percent were engaged in services at the corporate level. These men were in personnel, legal, industrial relations and public relations. Only 27 percent held managerial posts. The median salary in 1971 was $14,389 annually. Although the respondents thought they had done as well as whites on a comparable level, they also felt that as professionals, they did not have the same opportunities as whites had in their firms. The respondents felt that they had gone about as far as they could. There was a ceiling above which they could not go.

And why cannot the black males in management reach about $51,000 and stop having difficulty going higher? Galbraith in his research has observed the same findings. It is basically the intransigence of the white establishment in the executive suite. This is the last outpost of the conservative, the WASP.

But it must be breached if this free enterprise, democratic system is to become viable. The door of the executive suite should not be closed to Jews, blacks, browns, the foreign-born and Orientals. The glimmer of light here is in the multinational corporation. As it extends its branches world-wide, to continents all over the world, then the ultra conservatism that hangs over the executive suite will be lifted and meritocracy will prevail over plutocracy and nepotism.

The table below shows the percent of black officials and managers in some of the major companies in this country.

TABLE XIII

American Companies Percentages of Black Officials and Managers
1973-74

Rank	Name of Company	Percentage of Black Officials and Managers
1	Greyhound	11
2	Bank of America	9.9
3	Bankers Trust of New York	9
4	First Penn Bank	8.6
5	Brown and Williamson (Tobacco)	8.2
6	Xerox	6.7
7	Chase Manhattan Bank	6
8	Ford Motor Company	5.6
8	American Airlines	5.6
9	Citizens and Southern Bank	5.4
10	Honeywell	5.3
11	General Motors	5.2
12	American Motors	5.1
13	General Foods	5.0
14	Con Edison (Utility)	4.7
15	A. T. & T. (Communication)	4.3
15	First National City Bank (N. Y.)	4.3
16	Metropolitan Life (Insurance)	4.2
17	Bethleham Steel	4.1
18	Ralston Purina	4.0
18	United Airlines	4.0
19	Trans World Airlines	3.8

XIII (Continued

Rank	Name of Company	Percentage of Black Officials and Managers
20	American Can	3.4
21	Scott Paper	3.3
22	Connecticut General (Insurance)	3.0
22	Goodyear	3.0
23	Montgomery Ward	2.9
23	J. C. Penney	2.9
24	National Homes	2.8
24	Western Electric	2.8
25	Eastern Electric	2.4
26	Grumman (Aircraft	2.2
26	Kraft (Foods)	2.2
26	Liggett Group (Tobacco)	2.2

1973-75

Rank	Name of Company	Percentage
27	Southern Pacific	2.1
28	Standard Oil (Indiana)	2.1
29	Bendix	2.0
29	Pitney Bowes	2.0
30	Owens Illinois (Glass)	1.8
31	Prudential (Insurance)	1.4
31	Shell Oil	1.4
32	Delta Airlines	1.2
33	Aetna Life & Casualty (Insurance)	.9
34	Gulf Oil	.8

In the period 1970-75, there were three distinct occupational groups among blacks: professional, technical and managerial; clerical sales, craftsmen and foremen; semi-skilled and service workers. The highest paid were those in the professional-technical-managerial category. Earnings were about $200 per week. The middle income category earned about $150 per week and the lower paid workers among blacks were earning $100-$125 per week.

In the unskilled and service categories blacks have a disproportionate share of the workers. Other minorities are far less. White employment is just the reverse. High employment of whites is observed in the managerial, technical, sales and clerical categories, with low employment in semi-skilled, unskilled and service workers.

In the ten-year period between 1960-70, the increase in professional, technical, and managerial categories increased by more than 100 percent. On the middle level, the increase was sixty-four percent and on the lower paid level there was a decrease of fifteen percent. About 8,000,000 blacks were employed in these three large categories at the end of 1970. The charts following show comparisons between black workers and white workers. As the largest minority in this country, blacks have shown tremendous gains, but are still proportionately far behind the absolute growth. The black professional and managerial class is growing at an enormous rate. The black middle class is showing tremendous gains. It is in the lower paid level where blacks show a dismal record. In fact this class is really increasing in absolute terms.

The two charts on education show why there is a disproportionate number of blacks in lower paid jobs. Almost fifty percent of these black workers are without a high school diploma. Although the educational gap has been closing for those between 25-29 years of age, the breach is still wide in employment and in the earnings

OPPORTUNITIES FOR
OCCUPATIONAL ADVANCEMENT OF BLACK WORKERS
HAVE BEEN IMPROVING . . .

BETWEEN 1960 AND 1970, THE NUMBER OF BLACK WORKERS IN HIGHER-
PAID AND MIDDLE LEVEL OCCUPATIONS¹ INCREASED SHARPLY . . .

Chart 1a.
BLACK WORKERS

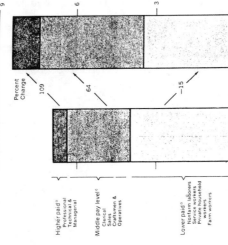

Millions of employed

Percent
Change

109

64

−15

1960   1970

Higher paid°
    Professional
    Technical &
    Managerial

Middle pay level°
    Clerical
    Sales
    Craftsmen &
    Operatives

Lower paid°
    Nonfarm laborers
    Service workers
    Private household
        workers
    Farm workers

. . . while the number of black workers in lower-paid occupations decreased.

See Introduction, page 1, for occupational pay level definition.

2

. . . WORKERS WERE SMALLER, PROPORTIONATELY . . .

Chart 1b.
WHITE WORKERS

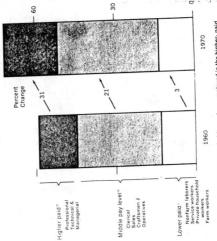

Millions of employed

Percent
Change

31

21

3

1960   1970

Higher paid°
    Professional
    Technical &
    Managerial

Middle pay level°
    Clerical
    Sales
    Craftsmen &
    Operatives

Lower paid·
    Nonfarm laborers
    Service workers
    Private household
        workers
    Farm workers

. . . but the share and number of white workers employed in the higher- paid
occupations continued to be much larger than for black workers.

3

of the black-white syndrone. Whites with a high school education
in the crafts earn as much as blacks with college degrees. It is
only in the professional groups that blacks match or earn more
than whites.

Government Employment

The biggest employer in this country is government. This
appears to be an analogous situation in a free enterprise economy.
About 14,000,000 people are employed in all levels of government
in the United States. The two leading states in government
employment are New York and California with more than 1,000,000
workers each. The Federal Government is the largest employer--
moving from 2,002,000 in 1972 to 2,795,000 in 1974. About 21
percent of minorities are in the Federal Government work force.
However, growth in government employment is increasing on the
state and municipal level. Proportionally, employment on the federal level has declined. The total number of blacks in federal
civilian employment is about 500,000. This decline has been
absorbed by the state and local government through a decentralization process of subsidies, grants, and revenue sharing plans.
State government work forces grew from 909,000 to just about
3,000,000 from 1974 to 1972.**

As we analyze employment of minorities by the layers of
government it is evident that the Federal Government has been
very laggard even in carrying out their responsibilities in
Affirmative Action.

Although blacks in the post office number 130,000, or about twenty-five percent, in a report from the United States Civil Service Commission,[5] minorities have made little progress in upgrading in Federal Government employment. The report showed that forty-one percent of minority workers employed by the Federal Government are caged in low earning categories--grades one through four--while in the managerial and supervisory positions there are only three percent in grades sixteen to eighteen of the General Schedule.

Blacks In Government Super Grades

In early 1974, Black Enterprise compiled a survey on the number of blacks in executive positions in the Federal Government. Their findings show that 239 blacks at this time held top echelon jobs in the executive branch of the Federal Government. These jobs are appointments by the President. They are not necessarily civil service jobs. As noted by the article, the list appears impressive, but there are 11,000 such jobs in the Federal bureaucracy. These top jobs held by blacks barely exceed two percent.

Blacks holding positions in the GS-16 category are on the bottom rung of the super grade ladder. It is known that the White House reviews appointments on grade scales as they move up the ladder beyond grades 15 and 16. Even during the Nixon administration sixteen black generals were appointed and the first black admiral and the first black assistant secretary of the Navy. Besides these appointments, Nixon appointed the first black general counsel of the treasury, as well as a black to the Federal Communication Commission. In the first year of the Ford Administration the first black was appointed as head of the Transportation Agency.

Earnings of blacks in GS grades 16 and above range from $25,000 to more than $30,000 annually. There were 192 blacks at this supergrade level. Twenty-nine blacks were in jobs paying $30,000 and above. These positions do not include the sixteen black generals and admirals serving in the armed forces.

Federal Bureau of Investigation and Central Intelligence Agency

Periodic reports from the Civil Service Commission reveal the difficulty of cracking a Federal Government bureaucracy. It has often been said that it is not the government that is derelict, but the people who are running it. Bureaucrats in our time seek to perpetuate themselves, not an on-going government program. Two of the hardened Federal Government Agencies that have been hard on minorities are the Federal Bureau of Investigation and Central Intelligence Agency. The FBI had about 72 black agents in 1972, 81 in 1973, in 1977 there are 113. Other minorities in the FBI are 122 Spanish speaking agents, 17 American Indians and 22 Oriental Americans.[6] Since Kelley took over the FBI he has shown great empathy for hiring minorities. The late J. Edgar Hoover was hard on blacks and minorities. But the CIA, when it came under intense criticism, was revealed as having one of the smallest percentages of minority employment of any federal agency. In 1967, a local Washington black activist wrote to the CIA about their discriminatory hiring practices. At this time the highest ranking black was GS-13, the equivalent of $15,000 annual earnings. Recently, among the 12,000 CIA non-clerical employees there were less than twenty blacks. Among the security forces in Washington and the custodian personnel, blacks were well represented. Of course, it is a violation of national security for the CIA to reveal the number of blacks engaging in espionage or staff work on economic intelligence.[7]

The CIA grew out of the old OSS of World War II days. The OSS meant Office of Strategic Services. President Roosevelt appointed William Donovan to head this office as an overview of all the intelligence gathering agencies of the Federal Government. Each of the services had its own intelligence section--the Army, Navy, Air Force and the Marines. Since espionage had taken on an added dimension in World War II, the CIA which stands for Central Intelligence Agency would transcend these separate agencies in foreign affairs.

Under the World War II leadership of Donovan and Foster Dulles, the CIA under General Bedell Smith, Richard Helms and William Colby, took on a clubby atmosphere and recruited mainly in the Ivy League and the Big Ten schools. Also, under the tenure of Helms and Colby, the CIA came under a withering scrutiny by the public and former employees of the agency. Lists of agents were revealed and it is alleged that one agent was murdered in a foreign country because his cover was lifted. When President Ford assumed office, he appointed George Bush, former Congressman, and Special Envoy to China to head the CIA. Under Bush's tenure the CIA was cast in a new light. Only two percent of its budget went for the old "cloak and dagger" activities.[8]

The main function of the CIA is to collect data, researching the entire spectrum of life abroad as it affects this country. Notwithstanding weaponry research, the CIA employs scientists and scholars in economics, geography, political science, history, psychology, languages, engineering, mathematics and other technical fields. Student interns are also accepted for the above fields.

How do minorities fare in the CIA employment structure? At the present time 10 to 12 percent of CIA personnel are black. However, it is estimated that 90 percent of these positions are in GS classifications from one to 10, or range in salary from $5,559 to $14,824. Salaries for GS 11 to GS 18 range from $16,255 to $48,554 annually.

It must be remembered that these are the pay scales of managerial and white-collar employees.

Obtaining enough qualified, competent personnel for its far-flung activities is a difficult task for the CIA. And it is doubly difficult to do this among minorities because the minorities have never related to the CIA. Minorities have been estranged from the CIA because of its highly classified nature, and its former record of break-ins. But during the period 1975-1977, vigorous recruiting of minorities has been undertaken by the CIA. The Agency is looking for qualified graduate students and personnel as previously mentioned.

The CIA has a poor record among minorities. About ten years ago, the Inspector General of the agency made a survey of the Office of National Estimates. There were no blacks, Jewish or women professionals in the agency. There were only a few Catholics.

The CIA grew out of the Office of Special Services of World War II. Since its founding it has been a presevre of the Ivy League and heavily larded with the White Anglo-Saxon Protestant. Since heavy criticism has been leveled at the agency for its discrimination, the CIA has turned to the Midwest and Southwest for recruiting.

Federal Reserve Report

The Federal Reserve System made a study on the employment of blacks in business and found that 25 percent of businesses have not employed any blacks. The report showed that businesses with fifteen or more employees--25 percent--have no black employees. In the commodities and security industry, half of these companies had no black employees. Companies that had to make reports to EEOC showed greater employment of blacks than companies which did not have to make reports. There was a 21 percent increase in the employment of blacks in reporting companies and 15 percent in non-reporting companies.

Government Diplomats

Representing this country abroad as ambassadors and operating on the highest level of diplomacy, are men and women who are the alter egos of the administration in power and the cross section of the population of this country, and who have the skill of a tight rope walker crossing a chasm. These men and women in the touch and go of international diplomacy are often just skirting the razor's edge in diplomatic maneuvers.

There are 120 of these people. Some of them have bought their positions through large contributions; others have earned their positions through an affinity for the people where they are stationed. However, the shocking fact is that there are only five blacks among these 120 people in the diplomatic service of this country. Here we have the world's leading democracy not giving representation to their blacks in the foreign diplomacy. This is a shocking neglect. To say they are not available is an untruth. They just have not been utilized because of the racist attitude of our state department.

Table XIV reveals that white males have a decided edge on black and Spanish speaking males in securing employment in

TABLE XIV

Comparisons of Minority Groups With White State Employees
Texas   1973

Racial Designation	Employed	Percent	Annual Pay Scales Males	Females
White	94,353	80	$8,532	$ 5,537
Black	11,911	10	4,855	4,518
Spanish Surnames	10,653	9	5,930	4,682
Other	1,138	1	NA	NA
Total	118,055	100		

Source: Texas Legislative Council, April 10, 1973

the state government.   The increase over black males is 75

percent and over Spanish speaking males is 44 percent. Although

whites are 70 percent of the population in the state of Texas,

they hold 80 percent of the state jobs.   Blacks are 12 percent

of the population and hold 10 percent of state jobs; Spanish

speaking persons or Chicanos, are 18 percent of the population

yet they hold only nine percent of state jobs.

Sex differences are revealed in that white females on

the average earn only 65 percent of the pay of white males.

Black females, similar to their black male counterparts, have

only 82 percent of the white females'income.   The Chicano

female is running slightly ahead of the black females with 85

percent of the white females' income.

The data, researched by the Texas Legislative Council,

showed that only nine percent of all state employees earned

more than $14,147 annually. Of all the white males, 16 percent

earn more than $14,147, but only about four percent of all

blacks are in this category. Since most of the state employees

are located in Austin, the capital   employment is heavily

weighed in favor of the whites because of historic racial

discrimination in Austin, and state employment is usually

the reservoir of the political hack who has lost in a poli-

tical race. About half of the service jobs, or 5,753, are

held by blacks. These are janitorial and maintenance and they

are usually based in Austin. In these same jobs, only about

28.5 percent are whites.

Municipal Employment

There has been a decided increase in municipal employ-

ment because of the increasing urbanization of the services

that the city offers in contrast to the rural areas. Nation-

wide, the number of city employees has increased from 1,700,000

in 1967 to 2,000,000 on 1972. Because of the influx of people

into   the cities, an increase in city employment has also

been attributed to the unionization. The zeal to catch up

with an increase in pay scales in private industry and the

pernicious rate of inflation has caused an intensification of

unionization. In New York City, the number of employees went

up from 250,000 in 1967 to 280,000 in 1972. In 1975, the

number reached 330,000. Seeking to be all things to all

people, New York City, through the use of city employees,
has caused some of New York City's severe fiscal problems.

Where do minorities fit into the employment picture
in New York City? As late as 1973, blacks occupied 25 percent
of city jobs, but were only 21 percent of the population.

Puerto Ricans were holding six percent of the city
jobs, but were 10 percent of the population. The New York
Commission on Human Rights for 1971, reported that the black
employment in federal jobs was 26 percent, just about the
same as city employment, but below the 36 percent employment
of blacks in state jobs.

Class	Number	Percent
Hospitals and Sanitariums	22,022	54
Education	16,303	18
Public Welfare	10,304	44
Police Protection	3,332	9
Fire Protection	614	4

Data for Puerto Ricans for the 1971 period show

Education	5,101	6
Housing Services	2,500	16
Police Protection	923	3
Fire Protection	91	1

Source: Commission on Human Rights, New York City, October,
1973.

In what capacity are these blacks employed in New York City? The data in the previous table show the class of employment, number and percent of blacks and Puerto Ricans for 1971.

The report shows the heavy concentration of blacks and Puerto Ricans in the service forces. This pattern of minorities in the service forces where pay scales are low is rampant whether in New York, Atlanta or Houston, Texas. Women employees in New York represented 42 percent of the work force, but were 53 percent of the population. There were heavy concentrations of women in education and public welfare jobs, or 65 percent, and in hospital and sanitarium functions, 62 percent.

About two-thirds of the Puerto Ricans earned less than $7,300 annually and about half of the blacks. Only 11 percent of the whites earned less than this $7,300 annually. Among females, 41 percent in New York City earned less than $7,300 but only 13 percent of males earned less than this amount.

Unemployment

The greatest economic catastrophe that can befall a worker is his loss of job. Unemployment haunts him. To the wealthy and those on fixed incomes, inflation is the devil. But to the worker, if he has a choice between inflation or unemployment he would opt for inflation. Some money to spend, although it is losing purchasing power, is better than

not having money to spend. At a job rally in Washington in
May, 1975, this was clearly shown. Unemployment in March,
1975, rose to 8.9 percent. Of these unemployed, more than
half, or about 55 percent, were blue-collar workers. Cabinet
members in the Ford Administration were predicting unemployment rates as high as nine percent. Such figures frighten
workers. A long-time period of high unemployment generates
the possibility of social unrest. Such social unrest is
unlikely in a presidential election year. If such unemployment persists indefinitely then social unrest will surely
follow.

Teenage Unemployment

Black teenagers as well as Mexican Americans and Puerto
Ricans have one of the highest unemployment rates of any group
in this nation. The recession of 1974-75 showed that in the
South Bronx section in New York City unemployment among these
teenagers was 40 percent. The rate of black men 20 - 25 years
old was 25 percent. The same rate held for Puerto Ricans.
The Bureau of Labor Statistics, which covers New York and New
Jersey, estimates that minority unemployment in this region is
higher than the national average. Lack of such employment
for teenagers and minorities exacerbates social problems.

Joining the chorus for really full employment for
those who want to work, are able to work, and are looking for

work is the American Assembly on Manpower Goals. This group is made up of businessmen, labor leaders, economists and government officials. The unemployment rate of seven and one-half percent during 1976 would have to be reduced gradually to three percent to avoid incurring a high rate of inflation. Some of the proposals of this group are:

1. Establishment of a National Youth Service which would help unprepared youth become productively employed.

2. Creating and expanding work-study programs and effectuating a transition of youth from school to work.

3. Subsidizing employers for hiring youth.

The Assembly meeting at Arden House in Harriman, New York, was sponsored by the American Assembly of Columbia University along with the National Commission for Manpower Policy and the Ford Foundation. Dr. Eli Ginsberg, an old hand at helping minorities, directed the project.[8]

High unemployment is the bane of a free enterprise system. From a historical context it appears that, because of the business cycle, it cannot be avoided. Because of people changing jobs, students entering the job market, new inventions and discoveries, there will always be some unemployment. Economists have four types of unemployment: frictional, seasonal, cyclical and secular.

Frictional means temporary unemployment because of changes in job orders, firing, quitting, displacements, temporary shutdowns, model changeovers, jurisdictional disputes, strikes, suspensions, insubordination and layoffs. Seasonal unemployment means loss of job because of the seasonal nature of the product. Straw hats do not sell well in winter. Florida hotels are not crowded in summer. The construction industry does not build as many buildings in winter as they do in spring, summer and fall. Cyclical unemployment is the result of the business cycle. The auto industry has gone through this phenomenon many times. The most recent is the 1973-75 recession when more than 200,000 were laid off, some for more than six months. The steel industry has had its feast and famine periods. Cyclical unemployment can lead to secular unemployment. Unemployment of this kind is long term when an industry is declining and significant product shifting is taking place in the economy. Railroading is a secular industry. The coal industry went through secular unemployment after World War II when public utilities switched to gas for generating electricity. With the energy crisis upon us, it is possible that utilities will shift back to burning coal, and we will see a resurgence in coal mining and a boom in coal-producing states. The long period of unemployment, fifteen weeks or more, shakes the faith of a person not only in himself, but in the system.

Since individuals are not inclined to blame themselves, but tne system, then it is the system which is lambasted. Hence, this is why,basically, critics of this system, and especially poor whites, browns, women and blacks, hammer at the flaws in this system. The free enterprise system is vicariously flawed by not providing a job for those who want to work. Serious challenges are now being pointed at the system not only by economists and social scientists, but also politicians and those in the natural sciences. Profits for the sake of profits is inherently biased against the unemployed and the poor. There must be a better way. That way will have to be battle-tested and weighed. The profit motive must yield to corporate social responsibility.

Is it cast in the stars or in the poor themselves that they are underlings? Will the poor or the unemployed be with us always? Yes, in the spirit, but not necessarily in the physical goods of life where middle income living standards are prevalent. In a society where great wealth ranges from thousandaires to millionaires hence to billionaires, there is a studied design of built-in poverty. Of course, it would be almost impossible to get a confession from the affluent that this was so. It would no doubt be denied. But the price system in and of itself does have this result. It is obvious that, within the price system itself, those who cannot pay the price cannot purchase. But criticism of a system is not enough, nor is pointing out its flaws. A better system can be found. This is where new discoveries will come forth. In the recession period of 1973-75, the unemployment rate crept up to almost nine percent for a national average. Among blacks the unemployment rate was double. For black teenagers the rate was as high as 40 percent. This was the highest since the great, baleful, depression of the 1930's. Again, this high unemployment rate not only hit the middle income group, but the poorest of the poor.

In the olden days, those days of centuries ago, the rich few, the opulent, had to protect themselves from the so-called barbarians. Witness the castles built on hills and mountains in Europe. Witness, also, the Chinese Wall. Today, the poor seek to protect themselves from the wealthy. Since we live in a money economy, we need money to buy the goods and services we need and want. Basically, the unemployed have been denied money or access to money through unemployment.

Overcoming the unemployment is not easy in a free enter-prise system. Hence, the free enterprise system will have to be complemented through government action on all levels. This is now being done. The Black News Digest shows what was done for the years 1971-73. Administrator Robert J. Brown reported that in job placements as of April 2, 1973, 62.8 percent of poor people were placed and placement of minorities was increased by 37.4 percent. The "turnaround" in job employment which began in 1971 is still continuing.

In the first half of fiscal 1972, placements of the poor went up 39.1 percent. Minority placements went up by 20.5 percent. During the first half of 1972, 1,309,000 persons were placed. This was a 21.5 percent increase over the 1971 half-year figure.

The table below shows the placement of minorities and the poor.

TABLE XV

Placement of Minorities and the Poor by the Employment Service
1971-1973

Individuals Placed	1st Half FY 1971	1st Half FY 1972	Percent Increase	1st Half FY 1973	% Increase over '71
Minorities*	1,007,000	1,309,000	21.5	1,610,000	49.5
Poor*	261,000	363,000	39.1	425,000	62.8

Source: Black News Digest, April 2, 1973

* The figures above show an overlapping of poor and minorities. One may be both a minority person and poor. However, all minorities are not poor.

Unemployment over this same thirty year period has ranged between three and nine percent. From examination, it has been found that political parties in power have done a better job in controlling inflation than in controlling unemployment. The pollsters previously mentioned found that the Republican Party has been considered as being more responsible for unemployment than the Democratic Party. It is an anomaly, however, that when this country is committed to a work ethic, yet the

percentage of this country's population which is working is
far less than in countries such as Japan, West Germany and
France. In these countries, the ratio of employment to population runs as high as 70 percent. It is also ironical that our
system has a built-in unemployment rate in the minimum wage.
Such a minimum screens out thousands of youths or teenagers
from working. It is further found that with a national
unemployment rate running as high as six or eight percent,
almost every time, the rate is double for blacks and minorities. It is suspect that our so-called work ethic does not
extend to blacks, but instead there is a constant welfare or
subsidy syndrome for a large percentage of the black population.

During periods of inflation, the value of the monetary
unit, our dollar , is reduced relative to prices. More money
is needed to buy less and less. When rates of inflation are
in double digits, people feel that this is the number one
economics problem. There is a tendency for the population to
make the Democrats responsible for inflation. Over the three-
year period, 1974-1976, inflation went from a high of 14 percent
down to a low of 6.5 percent. As inflation subsided unemployment
became the prime problem in 1975-1976. From a high of about nine
percent in 1974, unemployment went down to about 7.5 percent in
1976. The poll-takers in this country reported as of February,
1976, that the American people felt that unemployment was

the number one problem.[9] During 1976, President Ford was still focusing on inflation to a greater degree than unemployment. Fighting the wrong dragon can bode ill for an administration in power.

In the nuances of politics and economics in this country, the public (according to the pollsters) feels that the Democratic Party can handle economic affairs better than the Republicans. When economic issues are uppermost in the peoples' minds, such beliefs can benefit the Democratic Party far more than the Republican Party. By the same token, people feel that the Republicans can handle foreign affairs better than the Democrats. But people living in foreign countries do not vote in American elections.

As 1976 began, the employment to population ratio stood at 56.4 percent. In 1977 the ratio had dropped to 42 percent. For a period of about 30 years, the percentage of working population in this country has averaged about 55 percent.[10]

The above data were collected by the Employment Service. This service is a joint operation by the Federal Government and the states. It is financed through the Department of Labor. Funds are derived from an employer tax on payrolls. Each fiscal year from 1971 to 1973 shows hefty increases. Administrator Brown states that:

> We are proceeding on the theory that the more job listings we have, the better we can serve the work needs of the poor, the disadvantaged, and the

minorities. While emphasizing our services to
employers so we can list a maximum number of
jobs, we are continuing to stress the placement of those who are disadvantaged.[11]

But notwithstanding the number of employers who work

for the government through the United States Department of Labor,

Community Services Administration, HEW, Department of the

Defense and the other myriad government agencies, the private

sector employs 85 percent of the work force in this country.

So, it is in the private sector where the great majority of the

work in planning and implementation will have to be done. If

we may consider cybernetics, data processing or computer

science, these are exacting a great toll from those persons on

low incomes. As factory, dock and mine operations are gradually

automated and computer controlled, employment is further eroded.

These are the areas that employ large numbers of blacks and other

minorities.

In the cybernetic transition that is now taking place

in this country, it will be the low income workers who will be

hardest hit. The computer programmer has learned already that

his machines have the greatest appeal in government and industry

where the task is routine and repetitive.[12] These routine and

repetitive tasks are where the low income people work. These

are where the minorities work.

As automation and data processing become more pronounced,

minorities in employment are caught between two forces.

Automation reduces job opportunity in the routinized, repetitive tasks and these are generally in the low income groups. Now, when these people are replaced by machines, such as with container-ized cargoes, the jobs increase for those who make the machines. Here we have an expansion of employment in machine production, but a reduction of employment in the area replaced by the machine. Since most of the minorities are hired in low paying menial jobs, their employment is taken away and there is no substitute because they lack the skills to make the machines where employ-ment is expanding. Because of job bias and racism they are fur-ther locked out.

In order to reduce unemployment, planning must be done by private industry. Involuntary unemployment compensation can be reduced through planning. Notwithstanding unemployment compensation, about 30 percent of the working population are not covered. This group suffers far out or proportion to their numbers. The working poor and the unemployed want to improve their job classifications and upgrade themselves. The Poverty Institute at the University of Wisconsin has conducted research which shows that, with the proper incentives, people will con-tinue to seek to upgrade themselves and earn higher wages. The negative income tax offers great promise. Also, there is need of a complete overhaul of the welfare system along with the entire social insurance program. Those who are looking for work, but cannot find work, should be provided with a minimum cash income.

Most of the other palliatives, such as food stamps, have not provided the incentives for which they are intended. Commitments by
the Federal, state and local governments, as well as private
industry, through proper planning will ameliorate the unemployment problem. Such solutions will prevent the rise of a vast
underclass of all races, but mostly of the black people. Vast
numbers of blacks, browns and Indians feel already that they cannot make it in this society. They feel that this society has
ignored them and bypassed them. These notions should not be
reinforced by a system based mainly on profits, but one with
profits along with social responsibility.

Jobs in State Government Held by Minorities

Near the end of 1976, a report released on December 24,
by the New York State Civil Service Commission, showed that
blacks held 19 percent of the jobs in state agencies excluding
the state university system. This report,which included data
as of the summer of 1975, was the first report since 1967 on
Minority employment in New York State agencies. This new report
covered 156,812 employees in state government. About sixty-eight
agencies were included in the executive branch. Blacks make up
about 15 percent of the New York State labor force. Listed in
Table XVI are some of the agencies showing black representation
and the percent of the total agency.

TABLE XVI

Selected List of State Reporting Agencies
New York Civil Service System

Authority or Department	Minority Employees	Total Employees	Percent
1. Bridge Authority	0	114	0
2. State Police	51	3,971	1.3
3. Transportation Dept.	322	14,020	2.3
4. Dept. of Environ- mental Conservation	43	3,117	1.4
5. Thruway Authority	81	2,901	2.8
6. Agriculture	46	1,107	4.2
7. Drug Abuse Services	1,641	3,880	42.3
8. Mental Hygiene	19,698	63,955	30.8
9. Division of Youth	584	2,180	26.8
10. Human Rights Division	90	226	39.8

Source: New York State Civil Service Commission, December, 1976.
Data reported in article in New York Times, Vol. CXXVI
#43,436 Section 5, pg. 43, December 26, 1976.

Blacks numbered 24,371, whites 126,809, Spanish surnames

4,264, Asian Americans 893, American Indians 248, and others

227. Males totaled 87,442 or about 56 percent of the total.

From the table it can be seen that blacks were heavily represented

as well as other minorities in the Drug Abuse Services, Mental

Hygiene, Youth and Human Rights areas of the state government.

These jobs were in the paraprofessional category and from

the following table ranged in the pay scale from about $4,000

per year to about $25,000 plus.

Examination of the higher paying positions among state

employees in New York, reveals that minorities represent only

about three percent of those officials earning $15,000 and above.

TABLE XVII

Salary Groupings of State Employees
and Percentage in Groups, 1975

Salary	Total	White	Black	Spanish Surnamed
1. $ 3,999 or less	3.0	3.4	1.4	1.2
2. 4,000 - 5,999	2.4	2.2	3.3	4.2
3. 6,000 - 7,999	18.0	16.4	23.8	32.2
4. 8,000 - 9,999	24.5	23.5	29.6	27.9
5. 10.000 -12,999	27.4	26.6	32.2	24.2
6. 13,000 -15,999	13.1	14.6	6.6	5.5
7. 16,000 -24,999	8.9	10.2	2.6	2.4
8. 25,000 plus	2.8	3.0	0.6	2.4

Source: Ibid.

Government Employment

Only four percent of the employees in NASA are black.
Only three percent are Mexican-American out of a total work
force of 4,000.

Nonwhites and Spanish-speaking persons now comprise 17
percent of this country's labor force from age 16 to 64.   Blacks
make up 10.5 percent of the total.   There has been a 14 percent
increase during 1976 of blacks holding high echelon federal
white-collar jobs and a decline in blue-collar and postal
service jobs.

In Civil Service blacks still comprise 20.1 percent of
workers in GS grades one through 4, earning $5,800 to $10,800
a year, compared to only 3.4 percent in the super grades
earning from $20,000 to $54,410.   In 1973 blacks made up only
2.5 percent of the super grades.

TABLE XVIII

Minorities Employment in Federal
Civilian Jobs - 1976

Minority	Number of Jobs	Percent
Blacks	387,964	16
Spanish Speaking	82,442	3.4
American Indian and Oriental	48,495	2.4
Total	518,901	21.4

Source: United States Civil Service Commission, 1977.

In 1976 there were 2,424,777 Federal Civil Service workers. Minority group people increased by 2,801 to 21.1 percent. Minorities held 7.1 percent of the top Civil Service jobs in GS-12 as compared to 5.5 percent in 1973 and only 2.8 percent in 1970. Total Federal employees in 1976 reached 4,238,650 with 84,763 in Federal regulation.[13]

In the top four management levels of the Federal Government there are 20,365 employees. All of these officials draw the same salary which is $39,600, annually.[14] Minorities occupying some of these top positions are estimated to be two percent, or 407. Of these minorities, blacks within comprise about one percent.

Pay scales for the 22,800 persons employed in the Federal Government range from $39,000 to $65,000. Of these 22,800 individuals, 2,400 are members of Congress, judges and cabinet officers. Their salaries range up to $65,000. However, there are 20,400 others who have a ceiling of $39,000. It is estimated that blacks are about one percent of the total of 22,800, who are in these upper pay brackets of the Federal Government. Thus, there are only about 228 blacks who are in these top pay groups. These include the seventeen in the Congress, one in the Senate, and five black ambassadors.

A recent study by the Joint Council 16 of the International Brotherhood of Teamsters, found that, of the 2,091,000 United States citizens who started jobs since we drifted into the recession of 1973-75, 1,325,000 of these workers were hired on government payrolls and 766,000 in private employment. Most of the government workers went into local and county government employment. There was a gain in local and county jobs of 855,000, or 11 percent; state government increased by 371,000, or 13 percent, and Federal Government increased by 96,000 workers, or 3.6 percent.[15]

In selected areas of Civil Service and Federal employment it has been found that only four percent of State Department officers are black and only nine percent are women.

In 1961 it was found that of 5,873 jobs in the FBI, blacks held only 11. In 1970, ten years later, the number of jobs in the FBI had increased to 7,689, but the number of blacks had only grown to 51. In 1976, when the number of FBI jobs had increased to 8,617, the number of blacks had increased only to 131. In this same year Spanish speaking employees had increased to 141, Indians 17 and Asians to 25.

During 1976, the Congressional Black Caucus discovered that of the 17,000 positions opened to employment by Congress, only 600, or only 35 percent, of these jobs were held by blacks. The Caucus, recognizing the small number of blacks in such positions as stenographers, secretaries, messengers and administrative assistants, began a campaign to have internships in political science to train young blacks in these positions.

In the Department of Transportation, under Secretary Coleman, black employment increased to 13 percent, but among the 24,000 air controllers in this country, only five percent are black and only four percent of the total are women.

In the first year of the Carter Administration, out of 300 White House appointments, only 32, or 11 percent, were black.[16]

---

1. Wall Street Journal, Vol. LIV, No. 114, December 10, 1974, pp. 1, 29.

* Exxon has more assets than GM. The Fortune lists Exxon as the largest corporation in the world.

2. MBA (Master in Business Administration),February, 1975, Vol. 9.

3. Ibid.

4. The New York Times, Vol. CXXV, No. 42,981, September 28, 1975, pg. 53.

5. Money, Vol. 2, No. 11, November, 1973.

6. Federal Bureau of Investigation, March 17, 1976.
    Also quoted in the Houston Chronicle, March 17,
    1976, Section 3, pg. 5.

7. Ramparts, Vol. 12, July, 1974, pg. 25.

8. Wall Street Journal, Vol. LVIII, # 60, September
    24, 1976, pg. 1.

9. The New York Times, Vol. CXXV, No. 43226, May 30,
    1976, pg. 32.

10. Wall Street Journal, Vol. XLVII, No. 35, February
    20, 1976, pg. 6. Faulty Clippers for the Economy,
    by Alfred L. Malabre, Jr., News editor of the
    Wall Street Journal.

11. Black News Digest, U. S. Department of Labor, April
    2, 1973.

12. From the Center Magazine, Vol. VI, #4, July-August,
    1973, James F. Ahern former police chief, New Haven,
    Conn., pp. 51-57. See above, in the cybernetic
    change-over low income workers will then become
    the leisure class, p. 55.

13. Donald N. Michael, Projections and predictions for
    the technological society made more than a decade
    ago. Reprinted from a 1962 Center pamphlet.

14. Business Week, Number 2464, December 27, 1976, pg. 29.

15. The New York Times, Vol. CXXVI, No. 43,359, pg. 29.

16. The Washington Post, July 20, 1977, pg. B-7.

Chapter XI

Business and Entrepreneurship

Calvin Coolidge, a dour and taciturn politician, and
the 28th President of these United States, said more than a
generation ago that the business of America was business.
Coolidge did not make many statements and when he did he was
heard.

The business of America is truly business. There are
more than 10,000,000 businesses in this country. By far 90
percent of them are sole proprietorship, "mom and pop" grocery
stores, barber and beauty shops, service stations, drug stores,
lawyers, doctors, engineers, dentists, small contractors,
roofers, auto mechanics, repairmen, consultants, real estate
and insurance brokers, painters, accountants and a myriad of
other small manufacturers, retailers and shop keepers.

Where do minorities stand in the hectic, hurly burly,
uncertain world of business? Minority businesses number
320,000 at the end of 1974. Black businesses number 195,000,
or 60 percent, of the minority businesses. Spanish speaking
businesses number 120,000, or 39 percent, and Oriental and
Indian business numbers 5,000, or almost two percent.

The basic problem among minority businesses and black
businesses is lack of managerial talent and marketing skills.
There is not a decided lack of technical skills as to

craftsmen and small contractors. Managerial talent implies
entrepreneurship. How to run a successful business is enough
to stretch the talents of any gifted entrepreneur in a free
enterprise, competitive society. It is much more difficult,
if the person is a brown, black, Indian or Oriental. Invariably,
minorities think of marketing to minorities in lieu of market
to the total market. Another basic problem is overcoming hostility on the part of fellow ethnics. There is still a myth
among blacks that the white man's ice is colder than the
black man's ice. And there is still an underclass of blacks
who through self immolation seeks to pull successful blacks
down to their own level. In 1973, a federal advisory panel
recommended the creation of a national education and training
curriculum to help blacks and other minorities to become better business managers.[1]

Flowing from lack of management are these shortcomings
in minority entrepreneurship.

1. Lack of surveys and researching business (marketing)
2. Poor locations (marketing)
3. Poor record keeping
4. Non-payment of taxes
5. Little or no advertising, (Federal Unemployment
   Tax Act, Social Security, Sales and Income)
6. Lack of working capital
7. Non-use of lawyers on leases and contracts
8. Rugged individualism (all decision making centered
   in one person, brooking no suggestions from outsiders on his operations)
9. Poor personal practices
10. Lack of punctuality

The shortcomings of management deficiencies could be listed ad nauseum. Deficiency does not solve anything. Efficiency and productivity meshing with a sense of the profit motive will solve the management problem. Seeking to help the minority business men are these organizations: ACE, SCORE, B'nai-B'rith, RAMP, Chamber of Commerce, SBA, OMBE, National Business League, VITA (Volunteers in Technical Assistance). Through workshops, seminars, conferences and conventions, the organizations named above are helping to improve minority management. But the end of the tunnel is not in sight yet. The naivete of a black entrepreneur can be seen in the following real life example.

> In a southern city some years ago, a funeral director and eight local businessmen were able to wangle a state banking charter out of a state Banking Commission on the grounds that said city needed a black bank. At this time there was a moratorium on state banks because of a recent bank scandal. This businessman was able to pull this off with the help of a local white man. The local white businessman furnished the great majority of the initial capital and blacks the minority interest. However, the majority interest was given to the whites on the grounds that blacks would have an opportunity to buy back the majority interest. The bank was located in a predominantly black area. However, after the bank was started the employees who were mostly black were gradually changed to white and the bank moved downtown. After duping the blacks, the whites never sold back their interest. The moral here is that if you are going to start a business be sure that the original organizers get control at the outset and maintain control.

Possibly, the greatest contribution blacks are making in the world of business is in the financial arena. Since the chartering of the Riverside National Bank of Houston, Texas in 1962, the first black bank chartered in the United States in forty years, there has been an increase of twenty minority banks in this country. In subsequent pages we cover the progress of the minority banks in this country.

The leading business city for blacks in this country is Durham, North Carolina. Since Durham is the home of the North Carolina Mutual Insurance, the largest black business in the United States, a firm foundation has been laid. Clustered around Mutual are its sister financial institutions such as Mutual Savings and Loan and the Mechanics and Farmers Bank which was founded in 1898.

The largest black owned manufacturing concern in the United States is Johnson Products Company. It is alleged that Johnson founded his company in 1954. He early sensed that black beauty products for black women was a growth industry. He started mixing hair straightening tonic in the rear of a beauty supply shop in Chicago. Madame C. J. Walker was the original discoverer of black beautiful women and how their beauty could be enhanced by products manufactured specifically for them. This is just another clear example of closing a gap in the market.

Starting with just $250, within the month, Johnson had banked almost $1,000. At the end of 1960, Johnson had grossed about $450,000. As the Civil Rights movement gained momentum, and blacks were seeking greater identity, by 1964, Johnson's company had reached $1,000,000 in sales. Within five years

his business had increased ten fold to $10 million. At the
end of 1975, Johnson Products Company had reached $39 million
in sales. The company's stock was quoted on the American
Stock Exchange at $18-5/8. During 1975 the stock had reached
a high of $28 per share.

Need of More Black Capitalists

Writing in the New York Times for Sunday, April 21, 1974,
John H. Johnson, publisher of Ebony Magazine, says there is
a need of more black capitalists. Given the grants and loan
guarantees made by SBA and OMBE, Johnson feels that there are
two specific reasons why there has not been more emphasis on
black entrepreneurs, lack of commitment on the part of blacks
themselves and lack of commitment on the part of the government. The government has moved all too slowly in the age-old
problem of black exclusion. The diaspora of American blacks
still stalks the black businessman as he goes about his daily
tasks seeking to make a profit. Theodore L. Cross, author
of Black Capitalism, implies that just jobs in themselves will
not correct the great imbalance of discrimination and inequality.
There is a need of not only 50 black millionaires, but 25,000
black millionaires and more than 50,000 blacks serving on the
great corporations' boards of directors and executives earning
$50,000 to $100,000 a year. Black working wives contribute 32
percent of family income, white working wives contribute only

26 percent. Money spent has not produced the desired results. A basic reason for this omission is the maxim that entrepreneurs are made not born. Government programs, in their haste, and at times their political overtones, have sought to take a fledging would-be entrepreneur and set him up to create a going business. Recent emphasis has been directed towards helping to make greater successes out of successful business- men than creating new ones. A creative entrepreneur knows that to get a business going entails hard work, long hours, some money or collateral, plenty of risk taking and a strong desire. Linking this entire spectrum requires imagination. Imagination carries with it the elan and the cran. These are ingredients which the entrepreneur must possess. They must become an obsession with him if he is to succeed. The rules of the entrepreneurial game are simple. He not only must know the rules and know them well, but must also know how to apply them.

Another factor which has made it difficult for the black entrepreneur is the problem of overcoming his ghetto mentality. The black businessman must do business not only in the black areas but in the white ones also. In a free enterprise economy such as exists in this country, people want quality and service. Race,only in the extreme sense, will offset these two basic factors.

Government Aids to Minority Business

Hardly any United States Government program, enacted to aid the economy through defense spending or agricultural subsidies, fails to aid the small businessman as well as the minority businessman.* The specific government programs which are now aiding the minorities are the Small Business Administration and the Office of Minority Business Enterprise.

The SBA

Growing out of the War Plants Administration of World War II, the SBA was legislated into existence in 1953, during the first Eisenhower Administration. Heavy emphasis was placed on small business and minority business during the tenure of Eugene P. Foley. Foley started the six by six program which made small loans to minority businesses for $6,000 for six years.

From 1968 through 1973, there was a decided increase in loans or guarantees made to minority businesses. However, in 1972-73, there was a tapering off of increases in loans. This was the result of the recession which began in 1973. Table XIX shows the number of loans, increase, and percent of increase for six selected years, from 1968 through 1973.

Backing up the number of loans made to minority businesses has been the amount of money. SBA has funneled $300 million into minority businesses with no competitive bidding. During the

TABLE XIX

SBA Direct Loans or Guarantees to Minorities

Year	Number	Increase	Percent of Increase
1968	2,335		
1969	4,654	2,319	99
1970	6,262	1,608	35
1971	7,776	1,514	24
1972	9,016	1,240	16
1973	9,074	48	1

Source: Small Business Administration, 1974. See Black
Enterprise, Vol. 5, No. 6, January, 1975, pg. 27.

recession of 1973-75, loans to minority businesses declined

from $262.9 million in the first half of 1973 to 94.4

million in the second half.

Office of Minority Business Enterprise

Since the organization of the Office of Minority Busi-

ness Enterprise in 1969, this government agency, working with

the Department of Commerce has aided immeasurably in helping

the minority businessman.[2]

As 1974 closed, OMBE had funded:

1. Business Resource Development Center   20

2. Construction Contractors Assistance

    Centers   16

3. Local Business Development Organiza-

    tions   149

4.	Minority Trade Associations	21
5.	State OMBE Organizations	13
	Total	199

Source: Office of Minority Business Enterprise, Access, November/December, 1974.

The private sector has initiated actions through Affirmative Action Program to help minority businessmen. The Small Business Administration and the Office of Minority Business Enterprise are limited as to what they can do to help minority businessmen. Grants, loans and counseling are fine. But these government agencies can neither manufacture nor order service products from the minority businessmen. Private industry can do this, and they have been doing this. Prodded by Affirmative Action since 1971, members of the Fortune 500 (Sears, U. S. Steel, General Motors, International Harvester Company, Western Electric, A T & T, Standard Oil of Indiana, Rockwell and Honeywell, et al) have purchased products from minority-owned enterprises. The National Minority Purchasing Council lists more than 600 companies in American Industry which are purchasing from minority businesses. The Wall Street Journal states that the Chicago Purchasing Council records $360 million worth of products purchased by 260 large companies from minorities.[3]

Dr. Randolph T. Blackwell was appointed to the office of Director of the Office of Minority Business Enterprise in the fall quarter of 1977. Dr. Blackwell was formerly Executive Director of Southern Rural Action, Incorporated, based in Atlanta, Georgia. Dr. Blackwell's responsibility has been stated to implement the Carter Administration's avowed purpose in improving minority business development.

Franchising

Franchising among blacks has shown remarkable growth. A new Commerce Department survey shows that minorities are continuing to move into franchising. However, the survey shows that only 1.5 percent of the non-traditional franchises were owned by minorities.

Based on "Franchising in the Economy 1973-75," the findings from 1,005 respondents show that from 326 franchisers there was a total of 2,453 minority-owned franchises in 1973. Two-thirds of the franchisers stated that they had no minority franchises, and 42 firms, which were by far the largest franchisers, showed no evidence that they had any minority franchises.

The data below show minority ownership of franchises:

Ethnic Group	Franchises Owned
Blacks	1,190
Spanish Surnames	1,015
Orientals	211
American Indians	31
Total	2,447

Source: United States Department of Commerce, Office of Minority Business Enterprise, Access Magazine, March/April, 1975.
Access is a house organ of the OMBE.

A comparison of previous years which are far more comparable, shows in 1972, based on data from 909 respondents, that 291 franchisors reported 2,101 minority-owned franchises. In 1971, 173 franchisors reported 1,186 owned by minorities.

Minority ownership of franchised businesses in Table XX shows that there are heavy concentrations of ownership in automotive products and services and fast food franchises. Retailing and service establishments are well represented. Construction and manufacturing are among the least represented.

Business Owners of Spanish Origin[4]

Since the last survey of businesses of Spanish origin by the Commerce Department in 1969, it was found that the volume of businesses of Spanish origin increased by 58 percent to an approximate total of $5.3 billion in 1972 from only $3.4 billion in 1969. The number of businesses owned by Spanish speaking individuals increased from 96,086 in 1969 to 120,108 in 1972. Two states dominated Spanish speaking businesses. They were California and Texas.

State	Businesses	Receipts
California	28,166	$1.3 billion
Texas	23,651	1.0 billion

Areas of concentration of Spanish origin firms were in manufacturing, construction and retailing. Increase in the retail firms went up by 8,932 and the construction firms 6,656.

TABLE XX

Minority Ownership: 1974 Number of Establishments

Kinds of Franchised Business	Total	Minority Groups			
		Black	Spanish Surname	American Indians	Oriental
TOTAL--ALL FRANCHISING	3,072	1,325	1,348	64	335
Automotive Products and Services	734	433	264	18	19
Business Aids and Services	185	57	106	5	17
Construction, Home Improvement, Maintenance and Cleaning Services	162	37	101	7	17
Convenience Stores	204	39	92	4	69
Educational Products and Services	51	25	26	0	0
Fast Food Restaurants (All Types)	720	258	343	18	101
Hotels and Motels	42	7	19	1	15
Campgrounds	8	2	5	1	0
Laundry and Drycleaning Services	138	84	43	2	9
Recreation, Entertainment and Travel	49	20	20	0	9
Rental Services(Auto-Truck)	38	13	24	0	1
Rental Services(Equipment)	12	5	5	0	2
Retailing (Non-Food)	176	59	86	4	25
Retailing (Food Other Than Convenience Stores)	518	272	193	3	50
Miscellaneous	35	14	19	1	1

Source: Office of Minority Business Enterprise, 1976.

Revenues for these two categories went up to $732 million and $375 million.

Alex Armendaris, former director of OMBE reported in Access that the most popular franchise areas with minorities are:

Class	Number
Automotive Products and Services	627
Fast Food Restaurants	524
Food Retailing	348
Non-food Retailing	162
Laundry and Dry Cleaning	157
Total	1,191

Source: Department of Commerce, Office of Minority Business Enterprise, Access Magazine, March/ April, 1975.

In the traditional franchises such as gas stations and auto dealerships, there was a decrease among minorities. The recession in auto sales as well as the energy shortage has been the main cause of a decline in gas station and auto dealerships.

Gains in the non-traditional area were in fast food franchises and auto parts. Fast food franchises appear to be indigenous to blacks, especially in the South. These gains in fast food franchising also reflect the internal mobility of the black population, the number of black women working, and the reasonable cost of fast food service.

Besides moving into franchising, blacks have finally begun to move into manufacturing. These areas have been in machine tools, textiles, jewelry, ceramics, and food processing. Recently in hotel-motel management we find a movement toward black management. These are usually franchises, or black managers are employed by the owners. Dr. Randolph Blackwell, director of the Southern Rural Action Conference sponsored a conference for minority manufacturers of eight southeastern states in Atlanta, Georgia on October 9 and 10, 1975. The meeting was a working conference on economic development.

Black Hotelmen

At the turn of the century it was found in this country that black hotelmen dominated the various places of public accommodation. As the hotel business began to expand after World War I, black waiters, bellhops, doormen, and greeters were quite prolific. As more whites returned after World War I to the North, they came to replace blacks in these various capacities. Since the end of World War II more and more we find that blacks are moving back into the hotel-motel business. Tuskegee Institute has for years placed in their curriculum courses in hotel-motel management. Not only are blacks now developing their ownership of hotel-motels but they are also becoming managers and administrative personnel of chain hotel-motels in this country. Some of these chains which have employed blacks as managers are Sheraton, Hilton, Marriott, Chicago Regency Hyatt House and the Holiday Inn.[5] As this country continues to grow it is believed that blacks will play a greater role in hotel-motel management over the next twenty-five years.

Security Businesses

The security business is gaining attention from minorities. Social Security Insurance Company handles the collecting of tickets and providing security for the Superdome in New Orleans. In Pittsburgh, Pennsylvania, A & S Security Systems, Inc. employs sixty full-time and 20 part-time employees. They have a payroll of $6,000 per week. The problem plaguing A & S is the high, high turnover of personnel. Harvey Adams is president of this company. Smaller black outfits--one, two and three man companies are providing security for banks, insurance companies and supermarkets. Some of these small entrepreneurs, one and two man companies, work part-time. Pay in the security business is still modest. Guards doing off-duty assignments receive from $3 to $6 per hour. Pay for one night can reach as much as $50. This kind of pay can really supplement a modest weekly pay of $150. Because of an increase in the rate of crime and the need to guard company secrets such as blue prints, research, surveys and records, security has taken on a new dimension in this country.

Personnel Placement

Since the emphasis on equal opportunity employment, companies have been contracting with black personnel placement companies to go out on headhunting expeditions. These black personnel companies are specialists in psychology, sociology, and the behavioral sciences. They usually have master's degrees. They contract with companies on locating specialized personnel to fill positions such as engineers, data processors, accountants, lawyers, and technicians. The personnel placement practitioners are paid a flat commission of 10 or 15 percent of the annual salary of the black minority member that they place in a position.

National Minority Purchasing Council

National Minority Purchasing Council is a young organization, only four years old. Its basic purpose is to aid the small minority-owned firms in their sales.

In the first year of operation the NMPC had a goal of $86 million. The table below shows the progressive increase and sales made by the NMPC to minority firms.

Year	Amount
1972	$ 86 million
1973	237 million
1974	360 million

Figures for 1975 are not yet in, but it is expected that purchases will amount to $500 million, and for 1976, they reach $750 million. One must remember that the figures cited above has been reported by the 30 NMPC regional councils. About 40 percent of the membership in the fail to report their purchases from minority-owned firms.

Because these corporations engaged in an experiment, many of them are reluctant to report this data because of a possible backlash if it is successful. The executive director, Phillip A. Duffy, says the council is still proving itself. In the coming years the council expects to place $1 billion in services and goods from minority firms in the areas of printing, janitorial supplies, office supplies, office furniture, carpeting, security service, light construction, roofing, plumbing, landscaping, painting, and others.

Research has shown that the minority business person must seek giant corporations which need the supplies which are available. When more is done and members of Fortune 500 continue to show a willingness to do business with the minority firms, there will no longer be a need for the NMPC.

The Education of Minorities in the World of Business

The formal education of blacks in the world of business has been given capsule treatment in departments of economics and in the few predominantly black schools of business administration. It was not until the mid-sixties that attention began to be focused on upgrading and emphasizing blacks in business.

The Civil Rights movement was the catharsis for this development. A survey taken in 1966, showed that there were only
50 blacks enrolled in the white schools of business administration in this country. At the end of the academic year in
1974, there were 1,000, or two percent. Although this is
only a small percentage of the 50,000 students enrolled in
schools of business administration, it is a decided increase
in ten years.[6] The data above do not include the enrollment
of minorities in the three predominantly black schools of
business administration in this country, Texas Southern University, Howard University, and Atlanta University. In these
three schools alone, there are more than 2,000 students enrolled
in business administration. During 1974, Texas Southern University and Howard University each received a grant of $500,000
from the American Banking Association to create banking departments, specifically to educate minorities in the art and concept of banking. These grants, which will be expended at the
rate of approximately $100,000 per year, will aid greatly in
turning out about fifty students per year in banking.

The present approach to recruiting minorities into the
business school is through the consortium approach. In 1974,
the first group, which was one of the most successful programs
which was sponsored by the University of Wisconsin, involved
the University of Southern California, Indiana, Wisconsin,
Rochester, North Carolina and Washington University of St.
Louis.

This six-school grouping was launched in 1966, on a
Ford Foundation grant. Head of the grant was Dr. Sterling
Schoen, a live wire professor at Washington University. He
was attempting with missionary zeal, to get minorities into
the power structure of the business world. He felt that
Chicanos, Puerto Ricans, blacks, Cubans and American Indians
must be included in the mainstream for survival for these
minorities and for the system itself.

Business Week stated that Schoen was such a persistent
fund raiser that "134 companies including IBM, GM and many
other giants provide $475,000 of the consortium's $750,000
budget this academic year."

Two other groups are also hard at work recruiting
minorities into the business world. One is COGME--Council for
Opportunity in Graduate Management Education. This grouping
includes Harvard, MIT, Wharton, Stanford, Columbia, Chicago,
Carnegie-Mellon, Cornell, Berkely and Tuck. The Alfred P.
Sloan Foundation bank-rolled COGME to the tune of $700,000 for
1974. This money composed 84 percent of its budget. Some
individuals in business administration thought that they had
properly addressed themselves to fulfilling the needs of
minorities in business. Not so, says Bert King, director of
the COGME project. Stipends to students now account for 55
percent of student costs. Formerly such stipends paid 75
percent of student costs. A third group, which operates

similarly to COGME, is composed of the business schools of
New York University, Syracuse, University of Massachusetts,
Howard, Atlanta, and Arizona State.

Besides these consortiums, individual business schools
are recruiting. At Harvard, under the MBA program, in 1974,
there were 124 minority students and 146 women. These 270
minorities and women make up percent of the total students in
the MBA program at Harvard. The minorities alone make up
eight percent. Harvard's start is not auspicious, but is
an encouraging one. Dr. Stuart Taylor, a black professor at
Harvard's Business School has caustically criticized Harvard's
recruiting efforts. The high failure rate at Harvard has
discouraged some blacks.

With the tenor and tone set now for minorities in business
which begins with education--formal and informal--what happens
when the black boy, the Chicano, the Puerto-Rican and the
other minorities, including Italians, Poles, get their degrees
and seek employment, upgrading and salary increases in the
great-great-great world of business?

Each spring, from about February and through June gradu-
ations, the corporated lords of this country send their minions
and personnel recruiters into the placement centers of the black
and white colleges seeking young blacks for positions in line
and staff positions in the corporate structre. What are the

results of this recruiting and where does the graduate go? We
are here speaking of the MBA, not the B. A. Graduate. From
a survey by Dr. John Hemphill and Marshall Reddick,[7] it was
found that the black respondents stated that "being black"
was a primary reason for obtaining their present positions.
It was reiterated that hiring of blacks was also done because
of government pressure. Table XXI shows changes in job positions as a result of obtaining an MBA degree. There is a
decided movement up the ladder once the MBA is obtained. The
first column in Table XXI is greater than 100 because of the
multiple answers. Obtaining the MBA was highly gratifying to
those who held staff positions as well as to those in management.

TABLE XXI

Changes in Job Positions as a Result of Obtaining an MBA

	Position Held Before MBA (Percent)	Position Held By Recent Graduates Percent
Staff	38	43
Technical	33	10
Unskilled	29	--
Managerial	24	43
Clerical	19	--
Sales	10	4
Skilled	10	--
No previous Work Experience	10	--

*Note Percentages add to more than 100% because of multiple
  answers.

Table XXII shows the broad spectrum of industry which attracted the MBA graduates. The ten classes represented by the researchers show that the top four were foods, petroleum, banking and industrial. Over half entered manufacturing while the remainder went into service industries. There is a noticeable lack of the MBAs entering advertising and the entertainment markets.

TABLE XXII

Industries in Which Consortium Graduates Have Jobs

Industry	Percentage of Graduates Taking Jobs, by Industry
Foods	14
Petroleum	14
Banking; Finance	14
Industrial	14
Computers	10
Pharmaceuticals	10
Health, beauty aids, soaps	10
Consumer Goods (Unspecified)	10
Services (Unspecified)	4

Over half (57%) of the respondents entered manufacturing indus-tries while the remainder entered the services industry.

This was in the period from September 1, 1971 to March 27, 1972. These figures are from the College Placement Council. Minority MBA's, about 66 percent, reported that their starting salaries ranged from $14,000 to $16,000.

It is possible that a black MBA or minority MBA will start off at a higher salary than a white MBA. The rationale for this is the intensity of effort on the part of the business to say that they are an equal employment opportunity employer. With a black on the staff they are in the ball game. But, according to black MBA's, once this is done, the white MBA may be promoted over his head for many reasons,* institutionalized racism, black complacency, black over-employment, under-employment of poor whites, guidance on the part of management for its black-management personnel, isolation of blacks by management, lack of job requirements as well as lack of orientation.

As late as June, 1974, Black Enterprise, the slick, black publication on business entrepreneurship, which is a cross between Forbes, Business Week, and Fortune, held an interview with John Kenneth Galbraith, the former Harvard economist. Galbraith stated that earnings above $15,000 per year were almost the exclusive preserve of a white male society. Although these data were about five years old, they are still valid in our present day research on the American corporation.[8]

---

[1]Houston Chronicle, January 10, 1973, pg. 2.

*Representative Parren J. Mitchell from Baltimore, Md., a champion of minority business has introduced a bill in Congress which will give to minority contractors two percent of federal contracts that is worth $1,000,000 or more. Minorities now get less than seven-tenths of one percent of these contracts.

[2]Business Week, #287, June 30, 1975, pg. 101.

[3]Wall Street Journal, Vol. LVII, No. 4, January 7, 1976, pg. 1-7.

[4]Access, Office of Minority Business Enterprise, May/June, 1975, pg. 2.

[5]Black Enterprise, Vol. 5, No. 9, April, 1975, pp. 33-36.

[6]Business Week, Number 2338, July 6, 1974, pg. 58.

[7]MBA, Vol. 7, Number 6, June-July, 1973, pg. 4.

*In a recent study by David L. Ford, Jr., of the School of Management and Administration, The University of Texas, it was found that eighteen of twenty-six black MBA graduates after five years of employment were still in first year supervisory positions.

[8]Black Enterprise, Vol 4, No. 11, June, 1976, pg. 111.

CHAPTER XII

Minority Financial Institutions

An analysis of minority financial institutions will begin
with the commercial banks, savings and loan associations and
insurance companies.

Aiding in the development of these institutions, in
addition to the stockholders and depositors, are government
agencies such as the Office of Minority Business Enterprise,
Small Business Administration, Department of Commerce, Treasury
Department, Securities and Exchange Commission, Office of
Economic Opportunity and the Comptroller of the Currency.

In 1955, there were only fifteen minority banks in this
country. In 1969 there were only thirty-one minority owned
banks. Deposits at that time were $396.5 million. By 1975,
there were seventy-eight. In 1977 there were eighty-five.
Fifty-three of these banks were black controlled, three were
Indian, twenty-five were Spanish speaking, three were Chinese-
American and one women's. Even the fifty-three which were
black controlled may have had white and Mexican-Americans on
their board of directors. The same conditions may apply to
the Mexican-American controlled banks. The dramatic quin-
tupling of these minority banks over a twenty-year span can
attest to the emphasis placed on minorities getting into the
economic mainstream. Of the fifty-three black-owned banks,

deposits in 1975 were $663 million. Spanish-speaking American banks have $619 million, American Indian, $11 million, and Chinese-American, $75.3 million. The three largest banks are controlled by Spanish-speaking American and Cubans in exile. They are the Republic National Bank of Miami with $127 million, Ranco de Ponce in New York City with deposits of $120 million and the Bank of Miami with deposits of $114.5 million. Independence Bank in Chicago is the largest black-owned bank with deposits of $55.4 and assets of 61.8 million at the end of 1975. Albeit such participation is small in comparison with the giants in the industry. Needless to say, it is an advancement over what existed prior to the Civil Rights Act of 1964, and the War on Poverty which began in 1965.

Of the 14,000 commercial banks in this country, minority-owned banks comprise one-tenth of one percent. Assets of these minority-owned banks approximate a little more than $1 billion, which is about one-tenth of one percent of the total assets of all commercial banks in the United States. Deposits in minority banks in 1977 reached $1,500,000,000 billion billion. The ratio of assets to deposits is 1.14:1. If rankings were listed, minority banks would rank 247th among the nation's banks.

What are the problem areas of minority banks? Profits! But this is an oversimplification. The bottom line on the balance sheet or income statement, does not necessarily test performance, but it does show the results of operations. Profits of banks must show a degree of efficiency for their own perpetuation.

In a study of <u>Performance Characteristics of High-Earning Minority Banks</u>,[1] Jim Tucker and Bruce J. Summers found that eleven of the forty-five banks which they analyzed had a consolidated return on investment of 12.6 percent. Most studies of minority banks have compared minority banks with the large banks in relationship to assets, liabilities, deposits, earnings and losses. Dr. Tucker and Dr. Summers compared the leading minority banks and those they called the residuals. The significance of their findings shows that minority banks can be as successful and profit oriented as the large banks given the same environment in which these large banks operate.

One of the main problem areas of minority banks is personnel. Some of the minority banks have had five presidents in five years. Minority banks find it difficult to retain vice-presidents, cashiers and tellers. One of the reasons for such non-retention is that, once the employees obtains sufficient training, he begins looking for another job in banking. Since minority banks cannot pay him what he thinks his services are worth, he offers himself as prime bait for the large downtown banks. Furthermore, since the large white-controlled banks are under pressure to hire more blacks, Mexican-Americans, and Indian, the young black banker can be ardently courted by the downtown banks, and at asking prices ranging from $2,000 to $5,000 above what he was making in the minority bank. It appears that the minority banks should be paid for training bank personnel for the downtown banks.

A second problem is lack of capital. If a minority bank is capitalized at $500,000, and deposits cannot exceed its capital structure more than ten to one, the, deposits cannot be greater than $5 million. If the loan ratio is about sixty percent of deposits, then about $3 million will be out in loans. Some of the minority banks have fifteen to twenty times more deposits than capital. For a small minority bank to grow, it must always seek more deposits, increase capital, make judicious loans and service the accounts of its customers well.

A third problem is management. The problems mentioned above are the personnel problem and profit making. Management is the bridge between the two. Minority banks run abreast of untold management problems. This is not to say that minority banks are not managed as well as the large banks, but it does say that poor management which begets losses cannot be averaged out in a small minority bank. In many minority banks, the president or chairman of the board may have a nonpaying job. He must rely heavily on his executive vice-president and other loan officers for records and accurate accounting procedure. If

this president or chairman of the board is not on top of the
situation at all times, the bank can be washed from under him
and his board of directors. Usually such causes of failure
in most banks are bad loans, or downright collusion between
the bank officers and borrowers. The Board of Directors is
responsible for directing the bank. They are responsible to
stockholders, customers, and banking authorities in the Federal
Reserve System, Comptroller of the Currency and Federal Deposit
Insurance Corporation.

A fourth problem is lack of, or non-financial counseling. A full-servcie bank as the name implies should be a
full-service bank. The minority bank is in a unique position
to offer financial counseling to its customers, charge them
for it, and make a profit from this service. The service
charge itself for drawing checks is not necessarily financial
counseling. It is a bookkeeping entry for service. Financial
counseling implies having the check sent to the bank which
then handles all payments for the customer. Payroll accounting
is a similar activity usually performed by large banks that
could be assumed by minority banks for businesses in their
market area. Customers who borrow from minority banks for
consumer loans, may deposit the check in another bank. They
do not open their account in the minority bank from whom they
are borrowing. It is the exception rather than the rule that

the minority bank is a conduit through which checks drawn on it are paid to customers at downtown banks. In instances of this kind, and they are the great majority, the minority banks are acting as tellers for the large downtown bank. It is the exception when a check drawn on a minority bank is debited to the customer's account and credited to another in the same bank.

A fifth problem area is marketing. Minority bankers apparently are not tuned to selling their product in the area where they are located. Blacks do not come to a black bank because it is black. Mexican-Americans do not come to a Chicano bank because it is run by Chicanos, nor do Indians patronize an Indian bank because Indians run it. It is patently understood that Americans go where they get the best service. It is suggested that minority bankers must move through their communities to obtain the accounts of individuals living within a radius of at least two square miles of their banks. They must service the small businessman, professional man/woman and retiree. Most minority banks plateau after a few years growth, but do not grow at the rate of industry.

To offset some of the problems of these minority banks, a program of increasing the deposits for minority banks has been underway for five years. At the end of 1973, the Office of Minority Business Enterprise reported in it house organ Access, that $150 million in new deposits had been generated

for minority banks. Working through the National Bankers
Association, the trade group for minority bankers, the Treasury
Department coordinated deposits from the Government sector and
the OMBE to solicit deposits from the private sector.

More than five hundred companies participated in the
drive. Included in this number were companies like General
Motors, A. T. & T., Xerox, Atlantic Richfield, Mobil Oil, IBM
and Prudential Insurance. Another move is underway to encourage
the minority banks to increase their capital structure. The
minority banks must sell more stock to minorities in their
own market areas.

One of the minority banks that has a good record on selling stock in its own market is Independence Bank of Chicago.
In the past five years Independence has had three stock offer-
ings. Its most recent one raised $1 million in capital to
maintain pace with its assets. Alvin J. Boutte, the boyish
looking president assumed the presidency in 1970, when the
bank had a multiplicity of problems: poor customer relations,
inability to attract or hold experienced officers, a loan
ledger with numerous low quality loans. Under Boutte's
guidance, deposits have moved from $17 million to $60 million.
It is the second largest of all minority banks. The largest
minority bank is Republic National Bank of Miami. In 1970
Republic had deposits of $20 million. By 1974, deposits had
reached $80 million.

Other levels of government such as local municipalities
and state governments have not seen fit to deposit in minority
banks on the scale of the Federal Government and private business. Tax payments could be deposited in minority banks without interest paid to municipality or state to enable these
minority banks to make loans to the people in their market
areas. Governments have a duty to help minority banks, just
as they make deposits in the billion dollar banks.

Another way of raising capital is selling debentures. A
debenture is a form of security issued by a carrier on full
faith and credit. No kind of collateral is required as security
for the debenture. This type of security usually carries a
return of six or seven percent. Debentures are a form of lever-
aging. It is a form of financing through debt. Between these
two forms of raising capital--equity and debt, which is best?
Raising capital through equity or selling stock in the community
is preferred. Raising capital through debentures or debt nar-
rows the base. Return on debentures are fixed at six or seven
percent. Similar to bondholders, debenture holders are paid
first. Financing through equity means that any share holder
can have a piece of the action. Such financing broadens the
base of the minority bank and increases its credibility in the
community.

Table XXIII shows the location of the various minority banks. It further shows that these minority banks are located mainly in the South. The largest northern city that has more than one minority bank is Chicago.

As noted from date of origin, most of the minority banks have started since 1964. Again, the advent of so many minority banks is an emphasis on economic development among minorities. The prospect for additional minority banks is promising. James H. Marx, director of OMBE's capital development program, feels that there are twenty-three more minority banks in process or organization. The cities where these minorities are seeking to strive for improvement of their economic conditions are Mobile, Alabama; Jackson, Mississippi; Columbus, Ohio; Houston, Texas; Dallas, Texas; and Shreveport, Louisiana. Marx feels that the increasing growth of minority banks is a good omen. Although their combined deposits are now slightly more than $1.5 billion, all of them together would rank 247th in size of the nation's banks. Growth means problems. It is incumbent that the banks now in existence be strengthened and that the new ones being organized have directors with a business-like attitude who bend all of their efforts towards making their banks profitable.

Bank Failures

When a minority-owned bank fails, rumbling and reverberations echo throughout the minority community. In the spring of

TABLE XXIII

Minority Banks In The United States, 1976

Name	City	State	Chief Officer	Date Opened	June 30, 1975 Deposits (000 omitted)	Assets	Dec. 31, 1975 Deposits (000 omitted)	Assets	Emp
1. Bank of Miami	Miami	Florida		4/30/56	114,510	127.037	55,697	61,565	80
2. Independence Bank	Chicago	Ill.	Alvin J. Boute	12/14/64	55,447	61,804	45,933	49,359	120
3. Seaway Nat'l Bank	Chicago	Ill.	R. J. Pearson	1/ 6/65	46,294	50,823	36,618	40,092	78
4. Cathay Bank	Los Angeles	Ca.		4/19/62	46,294	52,014	36,836	40,687	66
5. Industrial	Washington	D. C.	B. D. Mitchell	8/18/34	37,758	41,011	26,798	34,806	68
6. Mechanics & Farmers	Durham	N. C.	John H. Wheeler	8/ 1/08	34,695	38,812	36,115	38,147	65
7. Citizens Trust	Atlanta	Ga.	I. O. Funderburg	6/18/21	30,585	38,817	34,793	37,868	60
8. Bank of Finance	Los Angeles	Ca.	L. C. Squires	11/16/64	30,819	36,698	39,863	42,290	55
9. Bank of the Orient	San Francisco	Ca.		3/17/71	26,624	35,491			
10. Freedom Nat'l	New York	N. Y.	H. F. Fierce	12/18/64	32,865	33,033			
11. First Independent Bank	Detroit	Mich.	D. B. Harper	5/14/70	26,946	29,097			
12. Consolidated Bank and Trust	Richmond	Va.	V. W. Henlry	7/ 3/31	22,994	25,395			
13. United Nat'l Bank of Washington, D. C.	Washington	D. C.	Samuel Foggie	8/31/64	22,355	24,754	24,011	36,396	47
14. Tri-State Bank	Markham	Ill.		4/27/62	21,872	24,499			
15. Tri-State Bank	Memphis	Tenn.	Jesse H. Turner	12/16/46	22,825	24,539	20,075	22,564	60
16. Highland Comm. Bank	Chicago	Ill.	G. H. Brokemond	11/ 9/70	21,342	24,493	19,467	20,591	53
17. Douglas State	Kansas City	Ks.	Sharnia Buford	8/25/47	19,528	23,355	18,316	20,454	36
18. Southside Bank	Chicago	Ill.	T. P. Lewis	5/ 1/72	18,168	20,911	18,707	20,017	44
19. Gateway Nat'l Bank	St. Louis	Mo.	J. B. Mickie	6/18/65	17,917	19,991	17,503	19,349	44
20. Pan-Am. Nat'l Bank of E. Los Angeles	Los Angeles	Ca.		4/27/65	11,367	19,891			
21. First Enterprise	Oakland	Ca.	L. A. Edwards	6/ 5/72		16,600			
22. Gateway Nat'l of Chicago	Chicago	Ill.	J. G. Bertrand	1/11/57	15,218	18,679	12,363	17,519	47
23. Midwest Nat'l	Indianapolis	Ind.	John P. Kelly	10/ 3/72	14,449	18,533	13,569	17,016	35
24. City Nat'l of New Jersey	Newark	N. J.	C. L. Whigham	6/11/73	14,822	16,254	14,412	15,693	22

TABLE XXIII (continued)

Name	City	State	Chief Officer	Date Opened	June 30, 1975 Deposits (000 omitted)	June 30, 1975 Assets (000 omitted)	Dec. 31, 1975 Deposits (000 omitted)	Dec. 31, 1975 Assets (000 omitted)	Emp
25. Liberty Bank and Trust	New Orleans	La.	A. J. McDonald	11/16/72	11,239	14,406	13,299	16.475	38
26. First Plymouth Nat'l Bank	Minneapolis	Mn.	J. M. Warder	2/14/69	12,862	14,087	11,729	15,025	25
27. Popular Bank of Hialeah	Hialeah	Fla.		10/12/73	12,108	13,625			
28. Continental Nat'l Bank of Miami	Miami	Fla.		5/10/74	11,176	13,476			
29. Unity Bank & Trust Co.	Boston	Mass.	M. J. Peak	6/24/68	11,317	13,378	10,220	12,068	
30. Riverside Nat'l Bank	Houston	Tx.	Carl Carroll	8/16/63	10,531	12,077	11,466	12,975	
31. Pan American Nat'l Bank	Union City	N. J.		7/30/71	10,556	11,900			
32. North Milwaukee State Bank	Milwaukee	Wis.	C. M. Wilson	2/12/71	10,096	11,671			
33. Guarantee Bank and Trust	Chicago	Ill.	O. S. Williams	4/13/46	10,146	11,475	9,259	10,399	28
34. Vanguard Nat's Bank	Hempstead	N. Y.		5/13/72	9,558	11,239			
35. Pan American at'l Bank	Houston	Tx		6/17/70	8,845	10,377			
36. First Bank & Trust	Cleveland	Ohio	J. Bustamente	6/17/74	8,202	10,949	12,611	12,213	17
37. Carver State Bank	Savannah	Ga.	R. E. Jones	1/ 1/27	7,707	10,508	8,057	10,437	21
38. Unity State Bank	Dayton	Ohio	Milton Bledsoe	8/10/70	9,236	10,503	7,104	7,626	
39. Centinel Bank	Taos	N. M.		3/ 1/69	8,675	10,000			
40. Citizens Savings Bank & Trust	Bashville	Tenn.	M. G. Ferguson	1/ 4/04	9,099	9,989			
41. Metropolitan Nat'l Bank	McAllen	Tx		11.17/72	8,045	9,343			
42. Liberty Bank of Seattle	Seattle	Wash.	J. C. Purnell	5/31/68	7,863	8,729	9,560	10,485	16
43. First State Bank of Danville	Danville	Va.	L. Wilson York	9/18/19	7,299	8,338	7,259	8,338	14

TABLE XXIII (continued)

Name	City	State	Chief Officer	Date Opened	June 30, 1975 Deposits (000 omitted)	June 30, 1975 Assets (000 omitted)	Dec. 31, 1975 Deposits (000 omitted)	Dec. 31, 1975 Assets (000 omitted)	Emp.
44. American Indian Nat'l Bank	Washington	D. C.		11/15/73	7,094	8,638			
45. Los Angeles Nat'l Bank	Los Angeles	Ca.		12/18/73	5,415	8,250			
46. Continental Nat'l Bank	El Paso	Tx		9/16/74	6,693	7,751			
47. Banco Del Pueblo Cuml.	Santa Ana	Ca		7/ 1/71	6,992	7,548			
48. United SW Nat'l Bank of Santa Fe	Santa Fe	N. M.		12/17/73	6,367	7,484			
49. Atlantic Nat'l Bank	Norfolk	Va.	C. M. Reynolds	9/ 8/71	6,201	7,115	6,935	7,784	17
50. Hemisphere Nat'l Bank	Washington	D. C.		6/18/74	5,221	6,830			
51. American State Bank	Tulsa	Okla.	Leroy Thomas, Sr.	11/19/70	4,953	6,280	5,357	6,303	17
52. Banco Int'l Bank of De Arizona	Tucson	Ariz.		8/18/72	5,288	6,280			
53. Peoples Nat'l Bank of Springfield	Springfield	Ill.	Richard Rush	/70	5,224	6,027	2,224	6,027	11
54. Brownsville Nat'l Bank	Brownsville	Tx		8/23/74	4,782	5,940			
55. Plaza Nat'l Bank	Harlingen	Tx		2/19/74	4,272	5,373			
56. Republic Nat'l Bank of New Orleans	New Orleans	La.		6/18/74	5,057	6,000			
57. Banco De San Jose San Diego	San Diego	Ca.		11/ 8/73	3,974	4,466	5,717		
58. Pacific Coast Bank	San Diego	Ca.	Robert Stevens	3/ 9/73	3,974	5,346	4,928	5,823	21
59. Greensboro Nat'l Bank	Greensboro	N. C.	William Pickens	11/ 2/71	4,243	5,235	4,337	5,205	
60. Victory Savings Bank	Columbia	S. C.	H. D. Montieth	10/31/21	4,438	5,146	4,447	5,124	

TABLE XXIII (continued)

Name	City	State	Chief Officer	Date Opened	June 30, 1975 Deposits (000 omitted)	June 30, 1975 Assets (000 omitted)	Dec. 31, 1975 Deposits (000 omitted)	Dec. 31, 1975 Assets (000 omitted)	Emp.
61. Popular Bank of Tampa	Tampa	Fla.	Elroy Venice	3/30/73	4,575	5,719			
62. Lumbee Bank	Pembroke	N. C.		12/22/71	4,103	5,028			
63. El Valle State Bank	Albuquerque	N. M.		7/ 9/74	3,977	4,919			
64. American State Bank	Portland	Ore.	V. F. Booker	8/ 4/69	3,728	4,392			
65. Medical State Bank	Oklahoma City	Okla.	D. E. Jacobs	2/ 7/73	4,164	4,703	4,500	4,986	14
66. Colorado Nat'l Bank	Denvee	Colo.		3/31/73	3,922	4,337			
67. Pan American Nat'l Bank of Dallas	Dallas	Tx		4/30/74	3,329	4,152			
68. Far East Bank of Los Angeles	Los Angeles	Ca		12/ 8/74	3,561	3,839			
69. Univ. State Bank of Wichita	Wichita	Ks.	Michael P. Young	3/18/74	2,561	3,839	4,090	4,999	17
70. New World Nat'l Bank	Pittsburgh	Pa.		3/ 1/75	1,988	2,671			
71. Community Bank of Nebraska	Omaha	Neb.	L. E. Evans, Jr.	4/16/73	1,874	2,431	3,096	3,675	14
72. El Pueblo State Bank	Espanola	N. M.		3/20/73	8,437	9,747			
73. King State Bank	Houston	Tx	Abraham Beaton	7/31/75			2,427	1,415	
74. Plaza Del Sol Nat'l Bank	Albuqueque	N. M.	In process of organization						
75. Continental Bank of San Antonio	San Antonio	Tx	In process of organization						
76. Nat'l Security Bank of Tyler	Tyler	Tx	In process of organization						
77. First Prudential Bank	W. Palm Beach	Fla.	D. L. Bowden	5/29/74	2,257	3,528	3,129	4,303	11

1973, Skyline National Bank in Denver, Colorado, was declared
insolvent by the FDIC. The bank opened in December, 1971, with
blacks and Mexican-Americans represented on the board of directors. The bank closed in the spring of 1973. After a short
two and a half years, the assets were assumed by the FDIC.
What were the causes of failure? Lewis L. Gaither, Jr.,
president of the bank at the time of closure, tried to entreat
the United States District Court in Denver to halt the take-
over. Judge Alfred A. Arraj rejected the request for a temporary restraining order sought by Gaither. Gaither, according
to reports at the court hearing, did not feel that the Federal
Government had reason for taking over the bank. The bank was
capitalized by a 350,000 share stock offering at $20 per share
or $7,000,000. After its first quarter of operation, the deposits
were $2,330,000. By June, 1972, the assets had reached $10,000,000.

More bank failures took place in 1975 than in any year
since 1942, the post-depression year. In that year, the crusade
against Hitler, twenty-three banks failed. In 1975, eleven
banks failed. Among these eleven was one minority bank, Swope
Parkway National Bank of Kansas City, Missouri. At its closing
on January 3, 1975, this bank had deposits of $7.7 million.
Disbursements of the Federal Deposits Insurance were $6 million.
A list of these bank failures appears below.

TABLE XXIV

Bank Failures in 1975

Date	Bank	Deposits	F.D.I.C. Disbursement
		(Millions of dollars)	
Jan. 3	Swope Parkway National Bank Kansas City, Mo.	$ 7.7	$ 6
Feb. 14	Northern Ohio Bank Cleveland, Ohio	95	85.9
Mar. 24	Franklin Bank Houston, Texas	18.2	12.4
May 9	Chicopee Bank and Trust Chicopee, Mass.	10.4	5
May 30	Algoma Bank Algoma, Wis.	4.8	3.3
June 18	Bank of Picayune Picayune, Miss	15.6	11.5
July 1	Bank of Chidester Chidester, Ark	2.3	1.6
July 12	State Bank of Clearing Chicago, Ill.	61	48.5
Oct. 16	Astro Bank Houston, Tx	5.2	3.8
Oct. 21	American City Bank and Trust Milwaukee, Wis.	104	94
Oct. 24	Peoples Bank of the Virgin Islands Charlotte Amalie	14.5	10

Source: Federal Deposit Insurance Corporation, 1975.

The biggest question in bank failure is the cause. The second is the effect. Causes of bank failures arise from making more bad loans or uncollectible loans than good loans or collectible loans. When the uncollectible loans exceed the capital structure of the bank, then the examiners will call for bank liquidation. Other extenuating causes of bank failures are low quality of loans, such as a real estate loan which is long term. It is a poor banker who makes a long term loan with short term money, or makes speculative real estate loans with deferred payments of interest and principal for a period of three or five years. Some bankers are guilty of this practice when they expect to make big profits from their own subsidiaries. There are legislative proposals being considered which will help to prevent directors from abusing their office.

The effects of bank failures are not as severe as they were prior to the establishment of FDIC. From the table it can be seen that FDIC was able to cover all deposits up to $40,000. No doubt there were some depositors who had accounts exceeding $40,000. These were not covered. The other effect is on stockholders. It is possible that the stockholders could lose all of their investments. Costs of liquidating a bank can absorb any difference in paying off depositors and creditors. Four of the eleven banks that failed had deposits under $10 million. It is also possible that these four small banks

had not been operating over a long period of time. It is always
necessary for would-be bankers to make judicious loans. This
maxim is more compelling for small bankers than for large ones.
A small bank cannot average its losses over capital or times as
well as a large bank. It is possible that the closing of the
American City Bank and Trust of Milwaukee was due to loans made
to real estate investment trusts. The large banks that set up
these trusts in the finance frenzy of the late sixties have
seen their real estate trusts run aground. The real estate
market is in the doldrums. How long it will be there is contingent
on government help, reduction of interest rates, land values and
construction costs.

Presumably the FDIC assumed operations or sales of the bank's
assets when its liabilities exceeded its assets, Federal banking
regulations were violated, its officers were guilty of embezzlement,
or directors violated banking regulations. Preventing failure is
the greatest need of minority banks. The National Banking Association, the American Banking Association, the American Institute of
Banking, the Office of Minority Business Enterprise, the Federal
Deposit Insurance Corporation, and the Federal Reserve System are
all committed to preventing failure. At the present time two
predominantly black universities, Howard University, Washington,
D. C., and Texas Southern University in Houston, Texas, have been
selected by the American Bankers Association to train black and
minority bankers.

Another aspect of preventing failure is for the minority banks to participate with the downtown banks in loans, data processing and customer servicing. Independence Bank in Chicago has already embarked on bank participating loans for large businesses. Vanguard National Bank in Hempstead, New York, has also joined in bank participation. These are just two of the minority banks which have engaged in participation with other banks.

Not only are these two universities committed to improving banking among minorities, but also the American Banking Association, and the American Institute of Banking, the Federal Reserve System, the Federal Deposit Insurance Corporation and the State Banking Commission are cooperating in this endeavor. _Sui Juris_ is the aim of minority banks.

New Minority Banks opening in 1975 were:

Bank	City
New World National Bank	Pittsburgh, Pa.
First Bank and Trust Co.	Cleveland, Ohio
King State Bank	Houston, Texas
Commonwealth Bank	Omaha, Neb.
Security National Bank	Tyler, Texas

It is recognized that the flow of capital in a community is like the flow of blood in a body. The interruption of such a flow of capital can kill a business or severely impair its operations. In a money economy, such as exists in this country, organization of capital is necessary to promote the advancement of minorities from conditions of poverty and near poor into better living standards and improvements in the quality of living. Cooperating with the Securities Industry in raising capital are the member banks of the American Banking Association. After raising capital, it must be put to good use to make a viable economy.

Minority Banking

In the fall of 1974, the American Banking Association announced that it had surpassed its goal of making $1 billion in loans to minority businessmen. Back in 1970, the ABA started a five-year loan program by which banks would lend $1 billion to the minority businessmen by 1975. The goal was achieved one year ahead of schedule. ABA made a survey of 410 major banks located in large metropolitan areas. Findings from the survey showed that loans totaling $1,133,682,000 were made by these banks. The number of new loans almost doubled, in 1973, from 9,529 to 18,189. Data furnished by the banks showed $50 million and more in the deposit category. Since the sample was only about three percent of the more than 14,000 commercial banks in this country, it is reasonable to assume that far more than 410 banks made loans to minority businesses, which could far exceed the $1,133,682,000 reported. The doubling of loans shows a marked sophistication of use capital by the minority businessmen for further improving the survival rate of minority businesses. The ghetto economy, which forms many of their operations, must be improved. Community

Development Associations can do this. Volumes of research over the past quarter of a century show that the ghetto economy is characterized by high unemployment, poor housing, numbers and narcotics rackets, exportation of capital, absentee ownership, low income, low education and high welfare. These are the disadvantages. What are the advantages? High population density, downtown accessibility, community of interest, stable population, job accessibility, supporters of transit systems are some of the advantages.

By a process of shading the disadvantages into advantages, the ghetto economy could be made highly viable. This must be done by the residents themselves, with assistance from local, state and federal governments and private business as well. Potential development of housing in the inner city is highly possible. With the energy shortage upon us and high cost housing in the suburbs, the inner city offers reasonable housing and high accessibility to all of the needs of the people.

Savings and Loan Associations

Similar to minority banks, minority savings and loan associations have shown steady growth. From forty-three in 1970, S & L's grew to sixty-one in 1974, and at the end of 1976, numbered seventy-three. Six or more are presently in the process of organization and should be in operation in 1977. There were

forty-one predominantly black S & L's, twenty-five or more
Spanish Speaking S & L's and the remainder Chinese-American,
Cuban and Puerto-Rican. Assets in these S& L's amounted to
approximately $700 million at the end of 1976. Assets in
the black-owned S & L's at the end of 1975 amounted to $510
million. Research has shown that assets increase about eight
percent per year. Savings accounts or deposits in black-owned
S & L's at the end of 1975 amounted to $444 million. Deposits
are about 87 percent of the assets. Loans made by an S & L
are mainly on first liens on homes. Although S & L's are of
a dual nature--state and federal--loans which are made follow
a pattern of mainly home ownership. These loans are on FHA
and conventional mortages. On conventional loans, the borrower
must satisfy the loan requirements of the lender. A conventional
loan is usually made on 60 to 80 percent of the appraised value
of the dwelling. Under FHA, the loan is made on about 90 percent
of the appraised value of the dwelling. Some are made as high as
95 percent of the appraised value of the dwelling.

California leads the nation with eighteen minority S & L's,
the largest number, Texas and Virginia have five each. The
largest S & L is Carver Federal Savings and Loan Association in
New York City, with assets of $65 million. The second largest
is Broadway Federal in Los Angeles, California, with assets of
$50 million. Recent research has shown that S & L's will in the
course of time perform in a manner similar to commercial banks.

The Hunt Commission has recommended to Congress that S & L's accept checking accounts, consumer loans and carry on the services of a full service bank. Table XXV shows the minority savings and loan associations in this country.

Black-Owned Life Insurance Companies in the United States

Of all the black-owned financial institutions, the black life insurance companies lead the list. The largest black-owned business in the Western Hemisphere is North Carolina Mutual Life Insurance Company of Durham, North Carolina. At the end of 1977, this company had assets of more than $160 million. Insurance in force is now approaching $3 billion.

Forty companies now compose the black insurance trade organization known as the National Insurance Association. At one time in their history these companies numbered seventy-six. Through mergers and combinations the number has now been reduced to forty. Since 1967, six companies have been merged or purchased outright by member companies of the NIA. Assets have grown from $400 million seven years ago to $590 million in 1976. Insurance in force has increased from $2,250 million five years ago and is now approaching $3 billion.

The oldest of the member companies in NIA are North Carolina Mutual and Pilgrim Health and Life. They were founded in 1898. The youngest is American Woodmen of Denver, reorganized

TABLE XXV

Minority Owned Savings and Loan Associations, 1975

Name	State	City	Head Officer	Year Opened	Millions Deposits	Millions Total Assets	Ethnic Origin
1. Citizens Federal	Alabama	Birmingham	H. J. Willis	1957	$ 18,640	$ 20,025	Black
2. Gulf Federal	Alabama	Mobile	H. Leroy Davis	1964	3,812	4,190	Black
3. Tuskegee Federal	Alabama	Tuskegee	Richard Harvey	1894	6,565	7,128	Black
4. Home Federal	Alaska	Anchorage	John K. Robertson	1973			
5. Pan American	Arizona	Tucson	Gilbert Gonzales	1973			
6. Broadway Federal	California	Los Angeles	Elbert T. Hudson	1946	43,124	49,935	Black
7. Camino Real Fed.	California	San Fernando	Edward J. Trujillo				M/A
8. Chinese American Federal	California	San Francisco	Ben L. Hom				Chinese
9. Chula Vista Fed.	California	Chula Vista	Thomas Cano				M/A
10. City Center Fed.	California	Fremont	Rufus Hernadez				M/A
11. East West Fed.	California	Los Angeles	F. Clow Chan				M/A
12. Enterprise	California	Compton	Cornell R. Kirkland	1962	8,527	11,448	Black
13. Family	California	Los Angeles	Robert Bowdoin	1948	29,982	36,463	Black
14. First Pueblo Fed.	California	San Jose	James Clarke				
15. Fulcrum	California	San Francisco	D. L. Kimbrough	1973			
16. Hacienda Fed.	California	Oxnard	George F. Rosch				
17. Merit	California	Los Angeles	Bruce T. Kaji				
18. Oakland Fed.	California	Oakland	Joseph L. Rebello				
19. Pacific Fed.	California	Fresno	Kurt F. Griese				
20. Pan American Fed.	California	San Francisco	John Parry				
21. Pan American	California	Burbank	Richard Garcia	1973			M/A
22. Chinatown Fed.	California	El Cerrito	Winfred Tom				China-Am.
23. Valley First Fed.	California	El Centro	Henry J. Monroy				
24. Equity	Colorado	Denver	Earl M. West	1954	1,552	2,088	Black
25. Connecticut	Connecticut	Hartford	Edmund Barlow	1968	6,883	8,004	Black
26. Community Fed.	D. C.	Washington	Orlando Darden	1974	5,326	5,812	Black

260

TABLE XXV (continued)

Name	State	City	Head Officer	Year Opened	Millions Deposits	Millions Total Assets	Ethnic Origin
27. Independence	D. C.	Washington	W. B. Fitsgerald	1968	23,673	28,852	Black
28. Community Fed.	Florida	Tampa	James T. Hargret	1967	3,500	3,830	Black
29. Washington Shores Fed.	Florida	Orlando	Char. J. Hawkins	1963	3,872	4,611	Black
30. Mutual Fed.	Georgia	Atlanta	Fletcher Coombs	1925	14,123	16,932	Black
31. Hyde Park Fed.	Illinois	Chicago	Paul H. Berger	1934	41,824	45,094	Black
32. Illinois Fed.	Illinois	Chicago	Louise Q. Lawson	1921	1,705	1,966	Black
33. Morgan Park	Illinois	Chicago	Hugh P. Simon				
34. Service Fed.	Illinois	Chicago	Harry M. Hardwick				
35. Coronado Fed.	Kansas	Kansas City	Reuben Marquez				
36. Louisville Mutual	Kentucky	Louisville	George Cordery	1956	8,850	9,701	Black
37. First Federal	Louisiana	Baton Rouge	L. L. Eames	1964	12,502	13,703	Black
38. United Federal	Louisiana	New Orleans	Samuel O'Neal	1967	13,035	14,153	Black
39. Advance Federal	Maryland	Baltimore	W. O. Bryson, Jr.				
40. Dona Ana	New Mexico	Las Cruces	Carlos Blanco	1958	13,234	15,146	Black
41. Allied Federal	New York	Jamaica	Frank Thompson	1948	57,952	65,393	Black
42. Carver Federal	New York	New York City	Richard T. Greene				Puerto-Rican
43. Ponce De Leon Fed.	New York	New York City	Erasto Torres				Black
44. American Federal	North Carolina	Greensboro	Albert S. Webb	1921	7,133	8,898	Black
45. Mutual	North Carolina	Durham	John S. Stewart		11,135	13,822	
46. Major Industrial	Ohio	Cincinnati	Pauline Strayhorne				
47. Quincy	Ohio	Cleveland	Roy E. Conley	1919	8,563	9,728	Black
48. Berean	Pennsylvania	Philadelphia	James A. Hughes	1888	7,142	8,916	Black
49. Cosmopolitan	Pennsylvania	Philadelphia	Robert Nelson				
50. Dwelling House	Pennsylvania	Pittsburgh	Robert Lavelle	1890	4,420	4,791	Black
51. Community Federal	Tennessee	Nashville	Albert C. Galloway	1961	5,341	5,948	Black
52. Magnolia Federal	Tennessee	Knoxville	Ralph Houston	1973	2,100	2,746	Black
53. Mutual Federal	Tennessee	Memphis	Lawrence Wade				
54. Security Federal	Tennessee	Chattanooga	Roy Carson Bobo	1971	2,088	2,168	Black

TABLE XXV (continued)

Name	State	City	Head Officer	Year Opened	Millions Deposits	Millions Total Assets	Ethnic Origin
55. El Centro Federal	Texas	Dallas	Rene Gutierrez				
56. Magic Valley	Texas	Weslaco	Reuben Hernadez				
57. Mission Federal	Texas	San Antonio	Rudolph Kirchner				
58. Padre Federal	Texas	Corpus Christi	Robert Dunn				
59. Standard	Texas	Houston	Shirley Bradford	1958	6,250	6,776	Black
60. Berkley Citizens Mutual	Virginia	Norfolk	Elbert Stewart	1913	5,738	6,512	Black
61. Community	Virginia	Newport News	Samuel Urquhart	1957	0.721	0.627	Black
62. Imperial	Virginia	Martinsville	W. B. Muse	1963	1,314	1,419	Black
63. Magic City Bldg. & Loan	Virginia	Hampton	Walker Atkinson	1889	7,018	8,438	Black
64. People Bldg. & Loan Assn.	Virginia	Hampton	Johnnie H. Sykes	1889	7,018	8,438	Black
65. Union Mutual	Virginia	Richmond	G. F. Childs	1961	2,990	3,394	Black
66. Columbia	Wisconsin	Milwaukee	Thalia B. Winfield	1924	4,427	5,037	Black
67. Home Federal	Michigan	Detroit	W. R. Phillips	1946	17,900	19,885	Black
68. Founders	California	Los Angeles	P. W. Dauterive	1974	11,200	13,900	Black
69. New Age Federal	Missouri	St. Louis	Henry Bentley	1915	9,885	11,141	Black
70. State Mutual	Mississippi	Jackson	James E. Davis	1955	3,337	4,007	Black
71. Ideal	Maryland	Baltimore	E. G. Lansey	1920	1,496	1,707	Black

in 1966. The great majority of these companies evolved from burial, assessment and fraternal companies into full-fledged legal reserve life insurance companies.

Table XXVI shows the location, chief executive, and ranking by assets and insurance in force for the years 1976 and 1977.

REFERENCE

1. Economic Review, Federal Reserve Bank of Richmond, Virginia, Volume 62, No. 6, November/December, 1976, pp. 3 - 12.

TABLE XXVI

Black-Owned Life Insurance Companies in the United States

Company	Location	Chief Executive	Year Started	Dec.31,1976 Rank by Tot. Ass'ts	Rank by Ins.In Force
North Carolina Life Insurance Company	Durham, N. C.	W. J. Kennedy,III	1898	152.265	2,742,439
Supreme Life Insurance Company of America	Chicago, Ill.	John H. Johnson	1919	48.022	2,087,401
Golden State Mutual Life Insurance Company	Los Angeles, Ca.	Ivan J. Houston	1925	62.681	1,782,961
Chicago Metropolitan Mutual Assurance Co.	Chicago, Ill.	Anderson M. Schweich	1927	35.380	770,032
Atlanta Life Ins. Co.	Atlanta, Ga.	Jesse Hill, Jr.	1905	91.985	747,474
Universal Life Ins. Co.	Memphis, Tenn.	A. M. Walker, Sr.	1923	50.154	333,373
Booker T. Washington Insurance Company	Birmingham, Ala.	A. G. Gaston, Sr.	1923	15.296	205,157
Mammoth Life Ins. Co.	Louisville, Ky.	Julius E. Price, Sr.	1915	24.124	187,210
Pilgrim Health and Life Ins. Company	Augusta, Georgia	W. S. Hornsby, Jr.	1898	14.682	131,637
American Woodmen's Life Insurance Company	Denver, Colorado	James H. Browne	1966	9.625	80,304
Afro-American Life Insurance Company	Jacksonville, Fla.	James L. Lewis, Jr.	1901	100.261	76,444
Winston Mutual Life Insurance Company	Winston-Salem, N. C.	Selena Hayes Hall	1906	4.700	61,000
United Mutual Life Insurance Company	New York, N. Y.	Nathaniel Gibbon, Jr.	1933	9.706	46,305
Winnfield Life Ins. Co.	Natchitoches, La.	Ben D. Johnson	1936	3.117	44,468
Southern Aid Life Protective Industrial Ins. Company	Richmond, Va.	E. S. Thomas,III	1893	4.370	38,787
Central Life Ins. Co. of Alabama	Birmingham, Ala.	Virgil L. Harris	1923	4.984	37,995
Peoples Life Ins. Co. of Florida	Tampa, Fla.	Edward D. Davis	1922	6.876	35,232
Purple Shield Life Ins. Company of Louisiana	New Orleans, La.	Jesse Hill, Jr.	1922	4.305	32,926
Unity Life Ins. Co.	Baton Rouge, La.	Homer J. Sheeler, Sr.	1949	1.613	31,135
	Mobile, Alabama	Roger E. Allen	1928	1.764	22,819

TABLE XXVI (continued)

Company	Location	Chief Executive	Year Started	Dec. 31, 1976 Rank by Total Assets	Rank by Ins. in Force
Virginia Mutual Benefit Life Insurance Company	Richmond, Va.	Richard W. Foster	1933	4.330	21,025
Union Protective Life Insurance Company	Memphis, Tenn.	C. A. Rawls	1933	3.800	19,560
Gertrude Geddes Willis Life Ins. Company	New Orleans, La.	J. O. Misshore, Jr.	1941	1.897	18,410
Golden Circle Life Insurance Company	Brownville, Tenn.	C. A. Rawls	1958	3.634	17,963
Reliable Life Ins. Co.	Monroe, La.	Joseph Miller, Jr.	1940	0.911	17,252
Wright Mutual Ins. Co.	Detroit, Mich.	Wardell C. Croft	1942	2.881	17,022
Christian Benevolent Ins. Company, Inc.	Mobile, Ala.	William Madison Cooper	1926	1.572	15,779
Mutual Benefit Society of Baltimore City	Baltimore, Maryland	Henry O. Wilson	1903	4.902	12,926
Benevolent Life Ins. Co.	Shreveport, La.	Granville L. Smith	1934	0.955	12,066
National Service Industrial Life Ins. Co.	New Orleans, La.	D. W. Rhodes	1948	1.366	11,523
Keystone Life In	New Orleans, La.	Jesse Hill, Jr.	1941	1.850	10,933
Security Life Ins. Co. of the South	Jackson, Miss.	W. H. Williams	1940	1.113	8,358
Bradford's Industrial Ins. Company	Birmingham, Ala.	Daniel Kennon	1932	1.304	6,519
Lighthouse Life Ins. Co.	Shreveport, La.	Bunyon Jacobs, Sr.	1932	0.452	6,375
Majestic Life Ins. Co.	New Orleans, La.	Adam R. Haydel	1947	0.682	6,310
Superior Life Ins. Co.	Baton Rouge, La.	J. K. Haynes	1954	0.397	5,615
Lovett's Life & Burial	Mobile, Ala.	L. M. Lovett	1950	0.487	5,322
United Fidelity Victory	New Orleans, La.	D. W. Rhodes	1971	0.449	3,175
Valley Life & Cas. Ins.	Phoenix, Arizonia	L. J. Ragsdale	1963	0.270	0,391
Progressive Ind. Life	New Orleans, La.	C. L. Dennis	1948	0.194	0.880

CHAPTER XIII

Housing

Even before the energy crisis in the fall of 1973, people began to return to the cities. Suburban life did not hold the enchantment it once did in attracting people to the periphery of the city. Old problems of the cities came out to the suburbs. Also, it was recognized by real estate development that costs were rising in the suburbs at a greater clip than costs in the cities. The advantages of the city were that right of ways, sewage, schools, police protection, fire protection, water, and utilities were already there. These adjuncts that would have to be installed in the suburbs would not have to be installed in the cities. It must also be said that the declining birth rates have slowed down the march to the suburbs because additional space is not necessary for fewer children. So, cities across the nation are more and more beginning to develop their core areas. Mass transportation has been given a boost by the Federal Government. Cities such as Oakland, California; Kansas City, Mo.; Indianapolis, Ind.; and Memphis, Tennessee are developing their downtown areas. Detroit, Cleveland and Pittsburgh are well on the way having been doing this for the past twenty years. Houston, Texas, through many of the giant corporations in this country, is developing core areas. Texas Eastern Transmission is on the way to developing Houston Center, an office and apartment complex in the heart of downtown Houston.

The revival of the cities can be seen more graphically in economic statistics than in any other sector. A comparison of retail sales in the cities with the suburbs shows that there has been a greater increase in retail sales in the cities than in the suburbs. New York City, the largest of the metropolitan complexes in this country, saw retail sales jump six percent over the suburbs surrounding New York in 1973.

Another new development in the cities is called urban homesteading or urban pioneering, which involves taking old, run-down homes and rehabilitating them into livable quarters. In Chicago, John Waner, regional director of HUD, auctioned off 526 abandoned properties for urban homesteading.

Baltimore, Maryland had an early success in urban homesteading. Housing officials in Baltimore placed 300 homes in the hands of families who have promised to repair and live in the homes. These homes were purchased for $1.00, with loans up to $17,000 at six percent interest. Real estate taxes were foregone for the first two years. Finance people estimated that it would take $20,000 to make these home livable. In Houston, Texas, there are more than 1,000 pieces of property which have been abandoned by former owners. These homes are no longer taxable. No revenue of any kind accrues from them. The regional director of HUD in Houston is contemplating action similar to that which took place in Chicago. Urban homesteading was started in New Jersey. It later came to Philadelphia, and now it is catching on throughout the country. However, it is still in its infancy, and is in the crawling stage because of the money crunch and adverse practices by savings and loan institutions as well as banks and insurance companies. These are the lenders. If the lenders do not see fit to lend in any particular area in any given city, then the area itself can become a rundown, dilapidated slum. This has been done through what is called redlining.

Redlining means that the area, section, or zone is off limits for loans. That is, any one who wants to purchase in that area cannot get a mortgage loan on a home, business, or commercial establishment. This practice on the part of real estate boards and lenders ha accelerated the increase in slum ridden sections of the urban areas in this country. For example, suppose a white person wanted to move into Harlem or Chicago's Southside, or Brooklyn's Stuyvesant. It is possible that the potential mortgagee will not assume their first mortgage because of the area. Of course, the area is black, or Puerto Rican or Latin American. The redliners never mention race, but area. In Houston, Texas, real estate men have by-passed the whole inner city within the 610 loop. That is, people moving to Houston from another city are not even exposed to the inner city. Real estate dealers through their handouts and advertisements only suggest "their" areas for living. The redliners still want to steer whites from blacks and blacks from whites. This is still subtle racism practiced in another form by the lending agencies in this country.

A recent case in Cincinnati held redlining illegal when it is applied to race. In 1974, Robert Laufman and his wife made application for a loan on a mortgage to Oakley Building and Loan Company. This couple desired to purchase a home in the Avondale section of Cincinnati. The lenders turned them down on the grounds that they did not make loans in this section because it is a racially transitory area. That is, the area is moving from white to black. So, because of this reason, Oakley refused to make the loan. The federal judge who ruled on the case used the Civil Rights Act of 1968, maintaining that redlining is illegal when based on race. Civil Rights activists hailed this decision. It was the first breakthrough in the courts on redlining. When a lender refuses to make a loan in a section of a city which is undergoing racial transition, such refusal brings in its train a self-fulfilling prophecy which accelerates the decline in property values of the particular area.

In the State of New York, sentiment is crystalizing on banks forming a pool to finance mortgages in low income areas. Percy Sutton, President of the Borough of Manhattan, testified before the State Banking Committee. In overcoming redlining,

a pool of $33,000,000 has already been established by the
banks for loans in low income areas. The procedure would
go something like this. The banking industry would contribute to an agency administered by the state, up to 15 percent
of their mortgage commitments. This money would be used to
make loans to mortgagees in low income areas at one percent
above prime. The banks would be guaranteed a return on par
with the prime rate.

Comments on this bill revealed that redlining is not
only confined to ghetto areas, but can be applied to middle
income and the suburbs.[1]

The basic idea behind urban homesteading is to reclaim
homes and houses in the city that have been foreclosed because
of mortgage defaults or non-payment of taxes, have little
value, and present an eyesore to the neighbors and actually
aid in the further erosion of values in the city. In order to
get the property back on the tax rolls, city fathers are
actually "raffling" the houses off, auctioning them off to
the highest bidder and selling them outright. No best method
has been established yet. The basic requirements are that the
individual purchasing the home rehabilitate it and live in
it for a minimum of three years. Cost of rehabilitation of
these homes varies from $1,500 to as much as $7,000,00. The
significant question is, where will the occupants find lenders
willing to lend such funds at nominal interest rates to repair

the houses if these houses are in redlined areas? Urban homesteading offers an alternative to public housing. When public
housing got its start in 1937, public officials thought of it
as helping the poor who had been the hardest hit during the
depression of the thirties. Robert Weaver, who became the
first secretary of Housing and Urban Development, felt that
housing projects no longer offered economic betterment, but
were economic deadends.[2]

At the 50th Convention of the National League of Cities,
meeting in Houston, Texas, December 1 - 5, 1974, Richard Hatcher,
Mayor of Gary, Indiana , observed that the present housing
policies encourage new residential development without
encouraging the rehabilitation of the inner city housing.
Housing in the post-war period had been built mainly for
upper income, middle income and the elderly. The poor have
been left with old, decayed housing. Weaver hit the mark,
when one reflects on what happened at the Pruitt-Ingoe
housing project in St. Louis. This project became such a
trap for its occupants, that, in the course of time, even
the tenants abandoned the project.

When the Pruitt-Igoe public housing project in St. Louis
was launched in the mid-fifties, it was the sine qua non in
public housing for blacks and minorities. But this project
which cost the taxpayers $40 million and housed about 10,000
people in thirty-three buildings, became a project of thorns

and anguish. The tenants hated Pruitt-Igoe. Vandalism was
rampant. Absentee ownership was insouciant. The project
became ashes. The big questions in public housing projects
are why the project demeans the individual, is poorly managed
and hazardous to children and families. An exception to this
is in Cookeville, Tennessee, and Xenia, Ohio. While the National
Council on Economic Opportunity was on a trip to Cookeville,
Tennessee, discussing the programs with the Upper Cumberland
Development District, it was found that the public housing
project in Cookeville was well managed, clean, and a joy to the
tenants. It was learned that management expected the tenants
to maintain the premises and these were the result of his
management. Similar conditions were found in Xenia, Ohio.[3]

The basic problem in providing decent housing for the
minorities lies in the flaws our economic system. When public
officials speak of ratios of white to blacks in housing of
60 - 40 or 70 - 30, and the same or similar ratios are applied
to Mexican-Americans or any other ethnic group, what these
public authorities really mean is the continued dominance of
whites over the minorities. This is what is called built-in
racism. A white majority in the cities to sustain a viable
tax base. With high minority unemployment rates, marginal
jobs and underemployment, poverty levels are built into a
minority group's economic base. Ratios must be forgotten
and minorities must be moved into the full economic system if
we are to overcome subsidized housing for ethnic groups.

With visions of Pruitt-Igoe dancing in their heads, public housing officials are beginning to adopt new tactics in public housing. Local tenant-managers are being used in project control. The tenant-manager is chosen by the tenants. Paid workers and volunteers are occupants of the project. Pride in the project is being instilled in the tenants. Crime is being reduced and drug traffic is coming under closer scrutiny.

Subtle racism is rampant throughout this country in housing discrimination patterns. Notwithstanding Supreme Court decisions and the Civil Rights Acts of 1964 - 65 and local laws, subtle racism is practiced covertly mainly by the real estate industry. In mid-1974, an apartment operator with 6,000 units in Houston, Texas was barred by a federal judge from refusing to rent to blacks.[4] A limited survey of housing practices by the Greater Housing Opportunity Center showed that the discriminatory practice by realtors could be major factors in resegregation of integrated neighborhoods.[5]

When selling housing in satellite cities or unimproved lots[6] the white real estate developer reinforces the black myth, by economically telling the prospective white home or land owner that "there is no welfare here."[7] It is a paradox and ironical that most welfare in this country is received by whites, not blacks or Mexican-Americans. Also, the great majority of people on welfare are not able-bodied people but the handicapped, lame and wounded, plus women with

pre-schoolers, who would like to work, but the cost of care
for children may be greater than their earnings on their job.
A Harper's Magazine article says that when questioned by a
white prospect on whether or not any blacks live in the
exclusive sub-division, it is appropriate to say that"I guess
black people just don't want to live here, for some reason."[8]

Cost of housing in this country jumped from $24,300 to
$37,300 from 1971 through 1974. This was a 53.5 percent increase
in the price of a "typical" house, according to the National
Association of Home Builders of the United States. In various
regions the price was much higher. The Federal Home Loan Bank
Board for the first quarter in 1975, states that the price of
a new home in Atlanta, the Dallas-Fort Worth area, Washington,
Detroit and Los Angeles was $50,000. In the New York City
area, the price of a new home reached $54,300. All of these
prices were inordinately higher than consumer income. What
happened to the housing market in these areas? Builders were
caught between rising material costs and escalating union wage
scales. These inflated housing costs and labor costs were
not matched by consumer income. The Joint Economic Committee
found that families able to afford the "typical" home in the
cities listed above were only 21 percent of the families in this
country. It was quite evident that the housing industry had
priced 80 percent of the American families out of the housing
market.

The housing market was made worse by the phasing out of Section 235, the subsidy program for home buyers in low income brackets. Prior to 1973, 121,000 homes were produced under this program. This was 85 percent of all new units sold for less than $25,000. In the year after the fade-out, less than 10,000 units were built.[9]

Over the past fifteen years blacks have been shifting from renting to homeowning. Census data for 1970 show black home ownership approaching 42 percent.

During the Nixon administration a concept was projected in the councils of the Department of Housing and Urban Development to create new towns, much after the concept which started in Europe. More than 175 new communities were started and as late as 1976, most of these were in some state of development. But the bloom as cooled on the new town concept. Initially, a new town, once it qualified as such under HUD guidelines, could obtain certificates of eligibility. These certificates qualified the developers for grants for sewers and roads in the development. But the developers did not foresee the huge costs of land acquisition and the high cost of borrowed money. Although, the developers went in on these deals with their own money and lost millions, selling costs (getting people to buy houses in the development), cost of land, servicing the debt was greater than revenues produced by the developers. Many of the projects have been reacquired by HUD. One of the largest developments

is located north of Houston, Texas. It is called Woodlands.
It is on an 18,000 acre preserve of lush woods, golf courses,
lakes and horse trails. It is alleged that the original money
on the development was sponsored by Mitchell Energy and Development Corporation, an oil and gas enclave headquartered in
Houston, at a cost of $100 million.[10]

In 1960, census data showed 38 percent of black families
owning their homes. The 1970 data represent about 2,568,000
black households and for 1960, 1,974,000 black households. At
the mid-seventies, in all probability there will be a decline
in black ownership. This period has been characterized by
severe housing shortages which were brought on by inordinately
high interest rates on mortgages and high land values.

Housing Costs

Not only did housing costs almost go through the roof in
1973-74, but interest rates on new homes followed. Interest
rates rose from the old six percent low up to as high as nine
percent. If we throw in the points which ranged from two points
to a high of five points, the interest rates rose as high as
10 percent in some regions in the United States. These rates
pushed the total cost of housing far, far out of the reach of
the average American family income of $15,000 notwithstanding
the lower middle income home owner. It was found that the key
to home ownership was the monthly payment.

A subtle factor which has been one of the causes in increasing costs is the land cost. Zoning and environmental requirements, enacted by municipal governments with the express intent of excluding minorities, have been used in Massachusetts, New Jersey and New York to maintain that a home had to be constructed on a lot size of 1600 or 1400 square feet, and that only a certain number of houses could be built on a lot this small. In the midwest, land costs went up 74 percent and construction financing costs went up 148 percent. In early March, 1974, it was found that no blacks lived in Lake Havasu City, Arizona. Only twenty-one lived in all of Mohave County. During 1973-74, white real estate developers were flying people from Boston and the east out to Arizona, seeking to sell lots in the semi-arid desert. They could not take any chances that blacks would reduce their sales. These bland statements by whites continue to place pressures on good housing for all minorities. The latest research on deprived housing comes from the Joint Center for Urban Studies of the Massachusetts Institute of Technology and Harvard University. Their two-year survey, which was available in the winter of 1973-74, showed that seven million poor families-- those families earning $5,000 or less per year--have physically inadequate homes. Some five and one-half million are over-charged for rent and 700,000 do not have an adequate number of square feet for decent living. The researchers are looking at about thirteen low and moderate income families. These families represent about fifty million people, which is about 25 percent of our population.

Shortages in good housing in the seventies have been caused by many factors. One of the most glaring is the high interest rates charged for loans for homes. Zoning restrictions and government mandates have also been instrumental in creating housing shortages.

Zoning Exclusions in Suburbia

It has always been a ploy of the establishment to protect themselves against those people who were called undesirables, to enact rules and regulations that would make it virtually impossible for those of a lower economic class to buy into the exclusive area, that is, to prevent the poor, blacks, Mexican-Americans or Jews from moving into the area. A high tax base is maintained, as well as housing ordinances setting the minimum size of the house such as square feet on an outsize lot, construction conditions and maintenance costs. The rationale for these exclusions by the establishment was to protect the character of the neighborhood and the general development of the area.

In a recent case in New Jersey, the New Jersey Supreme
Court ruled that suburbia cannot pass ordinances that exclude
the poor and modest income persons. The Court saw such
exclusions as racial because more blacks are less affluent
than white. The opinion of the Court upheld a lower court
which ruled invalid the zoning ordinances of the Mount
Laurel Township in Burlington County. This county Township
by-passed the housing needs of low and modest income families.

It is a certainty that this case will be appealed to
the United States Supreme Court.* But because it is not a
federal issue the court may remand the case back to its
local jurisdiction. However, overtones of the case are
serious enough to cause concern to the lily-white communities in North Jersey,Connecticut, Oyster Bay and some Long
Island Communities.[10]

Construction subsidies, which the government sponsored
in the sixties, proved disastrous to low-income housing. These
subsidies were breeding ground for fraud, bribery and
escalating home costs. Such subsidies did not produce adequate
housing for low-income people. A freeze was placed on such
subsidies in January, 1973. In mid-1974, a new approach to
overcoming housing shortages for the poor was suggested by
the administration. The Housing and Urban Development

Department was authorized to rent new and existing housing for use by poor families. Another suggestion has been made by the administration and that is direct income support to poor families for housing. This measure has not been tested yet. Will landlords raise rents so high that the net effect will still hinder low-income families from living in diversified housing throughout a metropolitan area? It is quite patent that as soon as the landlord finds out that his tenant is in a rent subsidy program, it could become common knowledge throughout the entire apartment or rental complex. Home ownership is the answer for minorities. This gives them a piece of the action. Subsidies should be made available here. The minorities need to own a piece of land. Ownership means that they become more of an integral part of the economy than renting. Although another government agency such as the Federal Home Loan Bank Board issued new guidelines for fair treatment in housing loans, such rules are ineffective if the applicant cannot pay the mortgage because of high interest and monthly mortgage payments. The ruling on fair treatment which would ameliorate discrimination in home lending affects about 5,000 saving and loan institutions which the board supervises.

Conclusion

Because of the 1973-74 energy crisis as well as high interest rates, housing starts for 1974-75 were not encouraging. In 1972, more houses were built than in any other year in history. Home completions in 1972 amounted to 2,378,500. In 1973, 2,046,000 were built, down by 14 percent. In 1974, 1,000,000 were estimated to be built, down to about 22 percent. The Housing Act of 1968 programmed twenty-six million housing units over a ten-year period. At the end of 1974, there were about 9,500,000 completions. With only three years to go, this country will have to complete about 5,000,000 units per year to fulfill the needs of this country. This is almost an impossible task. But there is a possibility that this can be done if we concentrate on rehabilitating abandoned homes and buildings in the inner city. To fulfill housing needs for the low-income groups it is imperative that such needs can only be implemented by the concerted action of the construction industry, financial institutions, government (local, state, and federal), labor unions in the crafts, Chamber of Commerce, and revitalized housing codes.

In large cities in this country, the median income as reported by the Census Bureau in mid-1975, was $14,475. This was an increase of six percent over 1973. For whites within the big city, working full-time the year round, income was $18,754. For blacks in large metropolitan centers the median income was $13,585, an increase from 1973 of 12 percent. The white increase was eight percent. In the large cities of this country, black family income is 80 percent of white family income. For the nation at large, white family income is $13,360 and black family income is only $7,810. This spread of $5,500 represents black family income as only 58 percent of white family income. In the nation as a whole, black family income, relative to white family income, has only moved up by four percentage points since 1970.

Since costs of all housing flow from the highest priced homes and these prices range from $26,684 to $34,263 on a nation-wide basis, it is difficult to program new housing for the poor. Prices of homes have gone up almost 30 percent over the past four years. Median income is now $12,300. It has only gone up 10 percent over the past three years. With income only going up about one-third of housing costs, such large differences not only bode ill for the middle income housing market, but places new low-income housing in double jeopardy.

Officials in HUD feel that, by combining direct cash assistance with a construction program, they can close some of the gap in housing for low-income groups. H. R. Crawford, formerly HUD's Assistant Secretary for Housing Management, and once upon a time a top black in HUD, along with Gloria E. A. Toote, HUD's black Assistant Secretary for Equal Opportunity, feels that not only does direct cash assistance offer great possibilities, but also that white families are gradually moving into neighborhoods in the inner city. It is apparent that whites are gradually overcoming their hostility to blacks who live in the same neighborhoods with them.

---

1. The New York Times, Vol. CXXVI, # 43,380, October 31, 1976.

2. Black Enterprise, February, 1974.

3. National Advisory Council on Economic Opportunity, Trip to Cookeville, Tennesse, February, 1974.

4. Houston Post, May 14, 1974, pg. 13-A.

5. Dallas Morning News, March 2, 1974, pg. 25-A.

6. Houston Chronicle, July 10, 1974, Section 1, pg. 24.

7. Harper's Magazine, Volume 248, #1468, March, 1974, pp. 39-40.

8. Ibid.

9. Business Week, Number 2385, June 16, 1975, pg. 17.

10. The New York Times, Vo. CXXIV, # 42,799, March 30, 1975, Section 4, p. 5.

* In 1976, the United States Supreme Court ruled that the suburbs cannot exclude minorities based on housing restrictions.

CHAPTER XIV

Land Ownership

What is the most precious commodity a person can own
in a free enterprise economy? Land, that's what. Land ownership is the sine qua non of being in a free enterprise economy. Land ownership is the ultimate of being. Land ownership means to have a "piece of the action." This ownership
includes raw land on the prairie, land abutting on the sea-
shore, land in the mountains, a home, an apartment, a duplex,
a piece of a cooperative dwelling or part ownership in a
condominium. All of these things mean taking part in decision making, and land is what the poor and the minorities
lack. They should not be poor because they do not own land,
but because they do not own some land they are that much
poorer.

Ownership of land in modern times stems from the
organization of western society. The breakup of the king-
ships, monarchies, and ruling by divine right of kings,
brought into focus entitlement by individuals, old English
Common Law and property rights. The right to private property is one of the bedrocks of a free enterprise system.

And private property in land is what the poor and
the minorities lack. All during the sixties, when riots
and skirmishes occurred, it was found that when activists

located in one area they were soon uprooted and moved on to another. Each time that their lease expired, these activists had to move on. They did not own any land. Land requests have long been a cry in the Third World. Most revolutions stem from the demand for land by peasants, tenants, the unpossessed.

The biggest landlord in the United States is the United States Government. Who owns the land in this country is increasingly coming up for question. The great land grab in this country was the giving to the railroads 150 million acres in the nineteenth century. As corporate giants continue to gobble up the land, the individual farmer and land owner continue to be replaced by agribusiness, timber cutting, leisure-recreation businesses. The Indians, who were the first Americans, have seen their land holdings decrease from one hundred fifty million acres to fifty million acres. Blacks whose ancestors were free as well as slave, have seen their land holdings drop from fifteen million down to six million acres today.[1] Black farm owners have dropped from 175,000 over this same period to 67,000. In the Southwest, Mexican-Americans have lost millions of acres of land by not being able to pay taxes on the land, through claim jumping by Anglos and by abandonment.

Only after the Civil War were blacks able to acquire land in large acreage. The Homestead Act of 1862 excluded them because, as slaves at that time, they were not citizens. Some free blacks did take advantage of the Homestead Act, but their numbers were minuscule. As the great migration of blacks to the North began during World War I, they began to lose their land holdings. Further, great losses of land holdings came through ignorance, speculation on the part of white developers and squatting on land by giant corporations.[2]

Ownership of land in this country by the government, railroads and corporations have exacerbated the poverty problem. Recent writers on the land question in The People's Land, state that forty million United States citizens have migrated from the land to the cities and to the areas surrounding the cities. Replacing these people have been the giant feeding operations of cattle operators, vegetable growing corporations, mining, lumber and energy corporations. In the land are great energy reserves: oil, gas, sulphur, timber, lead, copper, coal, shale, water, phosphorus. This is far from being a complete list of energy reserves. Although one-third of land resources is still publicly owned, a study by the Federal Power Commission shows that eight major corporations have already leased 74 percent of all oil and gas reserves on public land.[3,4]

Redistribution of land takes on the same aspect as redistribution of income. It has been suggested that the Federal government reacquire public lands from the railroads and sell them back to people. The need is for a modern Homestead Act. A second suggestion is for the Federal government to obtain better contracts on leasing public lands to the corporations for energy purposes. A third suggestion is for the Department of Agriculture to reduce or terminate all subsidies or "welfare" to farmers for not producing. Land that is held out of production should be sold to low income families who will farm the land and not be charges on public welfare.

The policy of subsidies to agriculture has not completely served the purpose of the intent of Congress. It is certainly not beneficial to help the farmer in this country and in so doing commit irreparable harm to low income groups through denying them the opportunity to purchase land. The great welfare problem in this country is a built-in device to deny the poor a chance to get off welfare. This is partially caused by our land policy.

Land Restriction and Zoning

Our judicial system in this country set the precedent, as far back as 1926, that the United States Supreme Court should not enter into contravening zoning restrictions based on economic and social conditions. Writing in the Center Magazine for November, 1975, Robert M. Hutchins, president of the Center for the Study of Democratic Institutions, and formerly president of the University of Chicago, felt that this policy should undergo review.

President Hutchins cites six cases, Warth v. Seldin,[1]
Village of Belle Terre v. Roraas,[2] James v. Valtierra,[3] South
Burlington NAACP v. Mt. Laurel,[4] Ybarra v. City of Town of
Los Altos Hills,[5] and Euclid v. Ambler Realty,[6] in which the
State or Federal Courts have not contravened zoning restrictions based on social and economic conditions. Inadequate
housing and land use have been the greatest complaints lodged
against the system by moderate and low income groups. Within
this band are the poor and the minorities. This policy of
containment has confined poor whites, poor blacks, Indians
and poor Mexican-Americans to slums--urban and rural, ghettoes
and inner cities.

In the case of Robert Warth, etc. et al., the petitioners
v. Ira Seldin et al., organization and residents of Rochester,
New York, entered suit against the zoning ordinance. Petitioners
held that the zoning ordinance excluded persons of low and
moderate earnings from purchasing property in the town. Such
exclusion was in violation of Civil Rights Laws and against
their constitutional rights. The United States District
Court in western New York dismissed the complaint for lack
of standing. A writ of certiorari was granted by the Court
of Appeals, Second Circuit, and the case came to the U. S.
Supreme Court. Writing the majority opinion, Justice Powell
held that in the rules of standing none of the petitioners
met the threshold requirements which would invoke a decision

for remedial action on the part of the court. The U. S. Supreme Court affirmed the lower court's decision. In this decision the Supreme Court ruled five to four. Four justices dissented, Douglas, Brennan, White and Marshall. In this split decision, it would appear that zoning restrictions based on economic and social conditions are being given a harder and harder overview. In the other cases that followed, it became apparent that white suburbia was seeking to restrict blacks and other minorities, as well as low income groups, to containment policy. This policy was sanctioned by the United States Supreme Court.

In the case of Belle Terre et al., appellants, v. Bruce Borras et al., the ordinance was challenged on the grounds that the constitutionality of individuals was jeopardized because occupancy was limited, with the exceptions of one-family dwellings or to groups of not more than two urelated persons. The United States District Court for the eastern District of New York held the ordinance to be constitutional. The Court of Appeals reversed this decision and an appeal was taken to the United States Supreme Court. Justice Douglas wrote the majority opinion holding that the ordinance was relative to a state responsibility and did not deprive any person of his constitutional rights, and that proper land-use laws were directed towards the needs of the community and the family. Justices Brennan and Marshall dissented. The ruling in this case was seven to two.

In a very unusual case in California, the people of that state, through its legislature, enacted a law requiring that any locality which desired low rent housing should vote on the matter. People who were eligible for low rent housing challenged this requirement under Art. XXXIV of the California Constitution which stated that low-rent housing projects could not be developed or built in the state until such move was approved by the majority of the voters at a community election. A District Court with three judges sitting enjoined the enforcement of the referendum on the grounds that the appellants were denied equal protection of the laws. Justice Black wrote the opinion on the court. Burger, Harlan, Stewart and White joined him. Justice Marshall filed a dissenting opinion. Brennan and Blackmun joined him. Justice Douglas did not take part in the consideration of this case. In this case the court ruled five to three.

In the case of James v. Valtierra, these suits were brought by residents of San Jose and Dan Mateo County in California. Housing authorities in these areas were not able to apply for funds to provide for low-cost housing because the proposals had been defeated in the referendum. Justice Thurgood Marshall wrote a biting, bitter dissent. It follows:

> By its very terms, the mandatory prior referendum provision of Article XXXIV applies solely to any development composed of urban or rural dwellings, apartments or other living accommodations for

persons of low income, financed in whole or part by the Federal government or a state public body extends assistance by supplying all or part of the labor, by guaranteeing the payment of liens, or otherwise.

Persons of low income are defined as "persons or families who lack the amount of income which is necessary...to enable them, without financial assistance, to live in decent, safe and sanitary dwellings, without overcrowding.

The article explicitly singles out low-income persons to bear its burdens. Publicly assisted housing developments, designed to accommodate the aged, veterans, state employees, persons of moderate income, or any class of citizens other than the poor, need not be approved by prior referenda.

In my view, Article XXXIV on its face constitutes invidious discrimination which the Equal Protection Clause of the Fourteenth Amendment plainly prohibits. The States, of course, are prohibited by the Equal Protection Clause from discriminating between "rich" and "poor" as such in the formulation and application of their laws. Douglas v. California, 372, U. S. 353, 361 (1963) (Harlan, J. dissenting). Article XXXIV is neither "a law of general applicability that may affect the poor more harshly than it does the rich," Ibid. It is rather an explicit classification on the basis of poverty--a suspect classification which demands exacting, judicial scrutiny, see McDonald v. Board of Election, 394, U. S. 802, 807 (1969); Harper v. Virginia Board of Election, 383, U. S. 663 (1966); Douglas v. California, supra.

The Court, however, chooses to subject the article to no scrutiny whatsoever and treats the provision as if it contained a totally benign, technically economic classification. Both the appellants and the Solicitor General of the United States as amicus curiae have strenuously argued, and the court below found, that Article XXXIV, by imposing a substantial burden solely on the poor, violates the Fourteenth Amendment. Yet after observing that the article does not discriminate on the basis of race, the Court's only response to the real questions in these cases is the unresponsive assertion that "referendums demonstrate devotion to democracy, not to bias, discrimination, or prejudice." It is far too late in the day to contend that the Fourteenth Amendment prohibits only racial discrimination, or prejudice; and to me, singling out the poor to bear a burden not placed on any other class of citizens, tramples the values that the Four-teenth Amendment was deigned to protect.

The case of Southern Burlington County NAACP et al, Plaintiffs-Respondents and Cross-Appellants, and Ethel Lawrence et al, Plantiffs-Respondents v. Township of Mount Laurel, Defendant Appellant and Cross-Respondent was decided by the Supreme Court of New Jersey. Justice Hall, writing the opinion of the New Jersey Supreme Court, held that plaintiffs who were representing the blacks and Hispanic speaking individuals who were actively seeking housing, were not the only ones barred from municipalities by land use restrictions. The elderly, young families, single persons, and large growing families were also limited to available housing because of land use restrictions, high prices, expensive apartments. Hall accepted the oral argument of the municipality counsel that Mount Laurel land use was not directed toward exclusion based on race or social incompatibility but in the area of income and resources of people living in the area.

The township did not contradict the evidence. It admitted that land use in Mount Laurel was intended to pro-duce economic discrimination and exclude large portions of the area population. Mount Laurel occupies about twenty-two square miles in an area abutting on the Delaware River with Camden on the south and is not more than ten miles from the Benjamin Franklin Bridge crossing the river to Philadelphia. This is patently a suburban area, a satellite or bedroom community. As late as 1950, the township had reached a stable growth. The population was 2,818. In the previous ten years it had grown by only six hundred people. After World War II, the population reached five thousand five hundred in 1960, and by 1970, had doubled again. Because of the interstate highway system and the New Jersey Turnpike, the Township is cut into sections. The local ordinance was enacted in 1964. It was declared invalid by the trial court.

The remedy of the court was not to invalidate the zoning ordinance, but to modify it. Affirmative action was advised. Also the municipality was advised, on the basis of moral obligation, to establish local housing for the poor now living in dilapidated, unsanitary quarters.

Ybarra v. Los Altos

Mexican-Americans in California have been for decades the persons most deprived in income equality and civil rights. The case of Ybarra v. the city of the Town of Los Altos Hills, again shows a form of exclusion based on size of lot and kind of housing to be constructed on such property.

The city of Los Altos Hills, situated on the lower end of the San Francisco peninsula, is one of fifteen cities in Santa Clara County. Los Altos Hills is a bedroom community, with its residents commuting to neighboring cities for employment, education, cultural activities, medical and dental services and recreational activities. The city is devoid of most of the amenities of small towns. There are no city transportation services and sewage disposal is provided by septic tanks. Little or no maintenance is provided by the city for streets. The roads are narrow and winding, highly adaptable to the winding and hilly terrain of this community.

Jack Ybarra and cohort Jose Vasquez, as well as members of the Confederacion de la Raza Unida, were of Mexican descent. The Confederacion held options to purchase land in Los Altos Hills. The options were contingent upon the Confederacion obtaining zoning for multifamily dwelling and getting the Housing and Urban Development Administration approval under Section 236 of the National Housing Act of 1937.

The zoning ordinance which prevents the Confederacion from exercising their option was the provision of Los Altos that no lot shall be less than one acre in size and that only a single family dwelling should be allowed on this lot. Multiunit housing or apartments were also prohibited. Plaintiffs in this case were low income recipients.

In the legalistic ruling against the Confederacion, Weigel, the District Judge referred to the "granddaddy" of zoning--Village of Euclid v. Ambler. This case is cited innumerable times in the cases of zoning that have come before the courts in this country. It is the earliest case in this country, going back to 1926, which held for economic discrimination. We now turn to this case to examine its impact on zoning in the system of jurisprudence in this country.

The Euclid Case

Zoning is the _sine qua non_ of economic discrimination. It is usually the extent of such discrimination which incurs the wrath of the wronged person. The Euclid case demonstrates the _obiter dictum_ of the courts of this land. _Stare decisis_ is another cliche which is used by courts not to overturn previous decisions which are relevant to their own conclusions. The Euclid case grew out of an appeal from the U. S. District Court for the northern district of Ohio on January 27, 1926, when the Ambler Realty Company enjoined the village of Euclid from enforcement of a zoning law which would bring economic discrimination on the realty company and produce a decline in property values because of limited land usage in the village of Euclid.

Strong arguments were presented to the court for the appellant on the grounds of a distinction between the power of eminent domain and the state's police power. Notwithstanding adequate compensation, the right of an individual to retain and use his own property should be protected against the pretenses of a public need to condemn it. Under the police power of the state, the appellant argued that such police power is not necessarily compensatory, because such police power is inherent in the ownership of the property.

Justice Sutherland handed down the opinion of the U. S. Supreme Court. Euclid is a small village and is practically a suburb of Cleveland. At the time of the decision, the population was between 5,000 and 10,000 people. As early as November 23, 1922, the Village Council enacted a comprehensive zoning regulation for industry, apartments, single and multi-family dwelling, lot area, size and height of buildings

Sutherland reiterated that zone laws were of recent vintage. They originated around the turn of the century. Until this country began to urbanize, zoning laws did not have any impact on land use. But, as the country began to grow urban complexes, and increasingly so during this century, zoning laws have increased the requirements on land usage. Land use must find its application in the police power and public welfare. The decision was reversed, which meant that it was in favor of the Village of Euclid.

This early case in zoning litigation was one in which a real estate company was seeking to enjoin a municipality. Recent cases on zoning are ones of blacks, Mexican-Americans and other minorities against municipalities on grounds of racial and economic discrimination. But the U. S. Supreme Court is loath to interfere in jurisdiction which they feel are state and local issues, and on land usage they feel this should remain as it is. However, there is an increasing challenge to these legal barriers which promote economic discrimination through zoning in this country.

REFERENCES

1. Supreme Court Reporter, West Publication Company, St. Paul, Minn. 55102. Volume 95, #18, July 15, 1975, pp. 2197-2220. (95 5 Ct. 2197 (1975)

2. Supreme Court Reporter, West Publication Company, St. Paul, Minn. 55102. Volume 94, #13, May 1, 1974, pp. 1537-1546.

3. James v. Voltierra, United States Reports 402, October Term, 1970, pp. 151-143.

4. Southern Burlington County NAACP et al, Plaintiffs-Respondents and Cross Appellant, and Ethel Lawrence et al, Plaintiffs-Respondents v. Township of Mount Laurel, Defendant-Appellant and Cross-Respondent (Cite as 336 A, 2nd 713.)

5. Jack Ybarra v. The City of the Town of Los Altos, (Cite as 370 F. Supp. 742 (1973).

6. Euclid v. Ambler Co., United States Reports, Vol. 272, October Term, 1926.

CHAPTER XV

The Minority Political Spectrum

It has been seventy-seven years since the last
black from the Reconstruction period made his departure
from the U. S. Congress. The time was 1901, a new century was just one year old and this country had come out
of the Spanish-American War with its hegemony over the
Phillippines and Cuba. It was 1901, when U. S. Representative George H. White from the state of North Carolina
made his farewell address before the House of Representatives. White was a sad, embittered man. He was the last
of the valiant black men who had served in Congress from
the South during the period after the Civil War. Now he
was leaving the halls of Congress. The man was grief
stricken. He had been bruised, insulted, heart-broken.
White spoke about black people. He said they were God-
fearing, faithful, industrious. White felt the potential
was there. He said that phoenix-like they would one day
rise again.

Well, they have risen. They are still rising, but
not fast enough. The Voter Education Project reports
that in the elections of November, 1974, The biggest gains
were in the state houses. Thirty new seats were gained.
Four senate seats were won. The biggest gain was a new

seat in the U. S. Congress. In Tennessee, Harold Ford,

of the Memphis 8th Congressional District, won over Bob

Kuykendal, a Republican.

At present there are three black members in Congress

from the South, Barbara Jordan, Andrew Young and Harold

Ford, and ten black state senators and eighty-four blacks

in state houses. Here is a state by state breakdown:

Alabama: Two blacks elected for the first time to the
state senate. Increase in the house.from three to
thirteen.

Florida: Three black incumbents reelected.

Georgia: Andrew Young,member of Congress, easily reelected.
Two blacks elected to the senate. Total unchanged.
Total seats in the house now number 20.

North Carolina: Two won for the first time in senate. One
new member in the house.

South Carolina: Representation increased in the house from
three to thirteen.

Tennessee: Harold Ford won a seat for the first time in
Congress. Two won seats in the senate for the
first time. State house seats increased from
seven to nine.

Texas: Barbara Jordan easily won reelection in the 18th
Congressional District which cuts across the
city of Houston. House seats increased from
eight to nine.

In mid-year 1977, there were 4500 black elected

officials in this country, and at the U. S. Conference of

Mayors in Tucson, Arizona, Helen G. Boorsalis of Lincoln,

Nebraska, became the first woman to head the resolutions

committee. At this meeting in Tucson, Kenneth Gibson,
Mayor of Newark, New Jersey, became the first black mayor
to head the U. S. Council of Mayors as president.

Northern Political Gains

Impressive gains were made by blacks and other
minorities in the North and West. Two black Democrats won
lieutenant governorships. State Senator George Brown was
elected in Colorado, and State Senator Mervyn Dymally in
California. William C. Riles was reelected in California
as Superintendent of Public Instruction. Richard Austin
won reelection as state treasurer in Michigan. Henry
Parker became a second treasurer-elect in Connecticut.

Chicano candidates, Raul Castro and Jerry Apodaca,
won gubernatorial races in Arizona and New Mexico. A
former U. S. Ambassador to Boliva and El Salvador, Castro
became Arizona's first Mexican-American governor winning
over Russell Williams, a Republican, by a narrow margin.
A race issue was injected into the campaign over the ethnic
background of Castro.

Apodaca, who won in New Mexico, was the first Chicano
Governor in New Mexico since 1918.

Raul Castro is a naturalized U. S. citizen born in
Sonora, Mexico. He earned his law degree at the University
of Arizona. His political background included serving as

a court attorney and as a judge in a Superior Court of Arizona for five years. One of Castro's major coups was obtaining the votes of the Navajos. In 1974, the Navajos Tribal Council influenced 20,000 Navajos to register. Castro received most of these votes.

Jerry Apodaca grew up in Las Cruces, New Mexico. He was an outstanding football player on the University of New Mexico's football team. Prior to his election as a state senator in 1966, Apodaca came into the governorship from a background as a football coach amd experience in insurance, real estate and the shoe business.

For the first time in the history of this country, we have an Oriental as governor of a state. In Hawaii, George Ariyoshi won by a wide margin over Randolph Crossley, a Republican. A second Oriental, March Kon Fong, a Californian of Chinese ancestry won the position of secretary of state.

The year 1974 was a great one for women candidates. In the Ninety-Fourth Congress that convened in January, 1975, eighteen women served. A woman became governor of Connecticut. Ella Grasso, who retired from the House of Representatives, won a stunning victory over Republican Robert Steele. Ms. Grasso became the fourth woman in the United States to serve as governor, and for the first time ever, elected to the position, instead of having inherited it from her husband. The previous chief state executives on the distaff

side were Mirian "Ma" Ferguson of Texas, Lurline Wallace
of Alabama and Nellie Ross of Wyoming. In the New York
lieutenant governor's race, Mary Ann Krupsak, Democrat,
soundly trounced Ralph G. Caso, a Republican.

In other state elections, Susie Sharp was elected
Chief Justice of the North Carolina Supreme Court. She
is the first woman to hold such office in American history. In George Wallace's state of Alabama, women were
elected to five state offices as secretary of state,
treasurer, auditor, public service commissioner and associate
justice of the State Supreme Court. High ranking positions
in state government were also won by women in Arkansas
(state treasurer); Connecticut (secretary of state);
Delaware (treasurer); Indiana (auditor); Kansas (secretary
of state); Minnesota (secretary of state); New Mexico
(secretary of state); Ohio (treasurer); Wyoming (secretary
of state). It was estimated by Betsy Wright, head of the
National Women's Education Fund, on the day following the
election, (1974)--that the number of women had more than
doubled the 465 state legislative seats which were held
in 1974 to as many as 1,000. Legislative seats in the fifty
states of this country number 7,581.[1]

Looking back on 1974, it can be said that it was
a tumultuous year in politics. The persistent revelation

of data from the Watergate scandals and the publication of the Presidential Transcripts led to the resignation of President Nixon and the assumption of the presidency by Gerald Ford. Nelson A. Rockefeller, former governor of New York was confirmed for the vice-presidency in December. It was obvious that the electorate were so fed up with the double talk of the politician that they wanted a change. The change came in the unprecedented election of women to public office and the notable increase of blacks and other minorities to public office for the first time.

Voter registration among minorities has always been a process of urging, cajoling, threatening, and the virtual usage of pressure tactics to get them to register. It has been suggested that possibly registration by mail would entice more people living in slums and ghettoes to vote. States that have already adopted mail registration forms are Alaska, Kentucky, Maryland, Minnesota, New Jersey, South Dakota, and Texas. In some instances voting has increased immediately in the succeeding elections. One instance has been Montgomery County, Maryland, which includes Baltimore. In 1974, blacks voted at a rate five times greater than in previous elections.[2] Years of intense voter registration throughout the South, citizenship education programs, and a constant drumbeat on participation paid off in the election of minorities and women in 1974. In 1974, there were 7,000,000

registered blacks. At mid-1976, The Census Bureau reported
that there were 150 million U.S. citizens of voting age as
compared to 140 million American voters in 1972, a 7 percent increase. However, figures show that black voters were
increasing faster than the national average with an increase
of 10 percent in eligible black voters since 1972. Of the
25 million blacks in this country, fifteen million are of
voting age. Decisions by the Supreme Court on one man-one
vote had had their effect. Redistricting has also had its
effects.

A three-judge federal court in Texas ruled that
seven counties should be divided into single-member House
districts. This ruling virtually assured more representation in the Texas legislature for Mexican-Americans and
blacks. The ruling came on January 28, 1974 in Austin, Texas.
The counties affected are Travis, McLennan, Jefferson, El
Paso, Lubbock, Tarrant and Nueces.

Early in January, 1974, a federal court order was
issued in New York City which brought legislature and Congressional districts under review on how racial voting patterns were affecting blacks and Puerto Ricans. Political
leaders in New York City are anticipating the decision
which will be handed down by the Justice Department on the
conditions which will satisfy the Justice Department. It is
possible that there will be created an additional black Congressional representative, one Puerto Rican, and four black

3
state senators as well as five other minority assemblymen.

The issue of racial balance in New York City came up in 1971. Increasingly, since the Civil Rights Acts of 1964-65, this problem of racial minority representation in the various state legislatures has come under examination by minorities as well as by the federal courts. In the olden days, when it came to gerrymandering, minorities were screened out so as to reduce their representation in state houses as well as in Congress. Now, under the aegis of the federal courts, when there is a definite racial imbalance favoring a group because of boundary lines, such lines can be redrawn to include races so as to bring about a better racial balance. Under the Civil Rights Act of 1970, litigants suing for such redress are increasingly getting more and more consideration.

Standards for racial representation must still be determined. Much better census taking is necessary to include all minorities so as to give proper representation. Updating of population counts is in order. How do you count the races? Are there definitions of blacks and Puerto Ricans as well as whites?

In New York, an Assembly District has about 12,000 people. A Senate District has 300,000 people. A Congressional
4
District has about 425,000 people.

The tempo of blacks and minorities and women in politics is increasing. Not alone has Watergate and redistricting   had its impact, but slowly the old order

changeth.

In a Louis Harris survey in Mid-November, 1974, it

was found that it is no longer possible for a candidate to

get elected to office by attempting to get votes from white

people by scaring them about integration with blacks. Eighty

percent of the respondents did not think such tactics today

would help the white candidates. Only 13 percent thought

such tactics were helpful. In the past, George Wallace used

such tactics as did Richard Nixon when the former president

took such a strong position against forced school busing.

In 1968 and 1972, George Wallace did well using the same

tour de force. Appeals to race prejudice will no longer

bring in the harvest of votes which it did in the past.

As the year 1974 closed and the Ninety-Fourth Con-

gress began to grapple with the grave problems of 1975-76,

Democrats had a commanding lead in the House and Senate as

well as in the governorships in this country. Watergate

was a disaster for the Republicans. In order to make a come-

back in 1978, the Republicans will have to perform a miracle.

Their politics must be of the cleanest kind. The Republicans

must embrace all ethnic groups and overcome their extreme

conservatism which tends to exclude minorities who are

fighting for their very survival.

The women's liberation has had its impact on the

electorate. In high state offices women prefer to control

the purse strings. They like the treasurer's job. Also,
they want to keep a watch over the brood, so they have an
affinity for the secretary of state's job. Not many women
seek the mayor's job. We need women mayors.

However, in spite of their over-whelming victories,
the Democrats are not out of the woods by any means.

Prior to the election in November, 1974, the Democrats held a meeting of the Charter Commission in August,
1974. The hectic life of politics can be seen in this con-
clave. Robert Strauss, Chairman of the Democratic National
Committee, could hardly get the meeting under way before
blacks, women and liberal members made a rapid exit. The
objective of the Charter meeting was to lay the foundation
for the party's interim convention in Kansas City in December, 1974.

The convention, held December 6-8, 1974, was attended
by 2,500 delegates. Delegates represented the usual ethnic
groups and the special interests including organized labor
which sought to dominate the meeting in order to secure a
unit vote whereby all the delegates from a state would cast
their vote as a unit. Such a request by organized labor in
August had prompted the walkout by the liberals, blacks
and women. There were also squabbles among the ethnic groups.
When the blacks threatened a second walkout in Kansas City
in December over the unit rule the Italians wanted them to
walk out.

This off-presidential election year saw old cleavages mending again. Intellectuals were coming together for the first time since 1964. The election of Governor Carey in New York over the Republican Wilson saw the old ethnic groups, blacks, Jews, Catholics, and labor coming together as a coalition. The problem of the Democrats was holding such coalitions together for 1976 and beyond into 1978 and 1980.

Generally, these coalitions are solicited on precinct level, but they are formed at the national conventions.

Party Politics

Black delegates attending the national party conventions in 1976 varied widely. The Democrats met in New York City at Madison Square Garden July 1976 and nominated Jimmy Carter and Fritz Mondale for President and Vice President. Democratic delegates numbered 3200. Black delegates from the various states in the Union numbered about 300. About 10 percent of the delegates were black or minorities.

At the Republican Convention, meeting in Kansas City, Missouri, August 16, 1976, black delegates numbered 76 out of a total 2,256. The black delegates amounted to 3 percent of the total delegates. The party of Abraham Lincoln, which was organized in Ripon, Wisconsin, in 1854 by whites and blacks who were opposed to slavery, lost the great bulk of the black votes in the depression of the thirties. The real shift came in 1936, when Roosevelt achieved such an overwhelming victory over Alf Landon. Because of the many

innovations of Roosevelt and the New Deal, blacks switched
their votes and they have voted overwhelmingly Democratic
over the past forty years in national elections. The
National Black Republican Council, the minority arm of the
Republican Party, is seeking to garner most of their votes
from the rising black middle class.

Addenda to Party Politics

The record of blacks voting in presidential elections
since World War II shows a decided preference for the Democratic candidate....

Table XXVII below shows how blacks voted for the party
of their choice over the past eight presidential elections.

Table XXVII

Voting Preference of Blacks for President
in Selected Years

Year	Democratic Candidate	Percent	Republican Candidate	Percent
1948	Truman	60	Dewey	38
1952	Stevenson	58	Eisenhower	42
1956	Stevenson	56	Eisenhower	42
1960	Kennedy	75	Nixon	25
1964	Johnson	92	Goldwater	8
1968	Humphrey	86	Nixon	14
1972	McGovern	87	Nixon	13
1976	Carter	94	Ford	6

It is estimated by the Joint Center for Political
Studies in Washington, D.C. that Jimmy Carter had the
overwhelming support of blacks in seven states with 107
electoral votes. Those states were Texas (26), Pennsylvania
(27), Ohio (25), Missouri (12), Maryland (10), Louisiana
(10), and Mississippi (7). The Center, in cooperation with
the Metropolican Applied Research Center of New York, found
that in the other three southern states: South Carolina,
North Carolina and Florida, blacks heavily supported Carter.
These states had a combined total of 38 electoral votes.

THE ELECTION OF JIMMY CARTER

From the beginning of the campaign of 1976, which
started in 1975, there were touches of the unusual candidate
in Jimmy Carter. Here was a former Georgia Governor who had
the audacity, the _elan_ and _cran_ to challenge the Democratic
Party establishment. Coming out of the deep South, from a
state that was known for its segregation and hatred of blacks
in by-gone generations, Jimmy Carter, the candidate, began
his campaign for the presidency at least 22 months before
his election on November 2, 1976. The _Man from Plains_ traveled
more than 500,000 miles up and down, crisscrossing this country shaking hands, with an ever grinning countenance, extolling his virtues of honesty, and his born again religion.
He entered every state primary, and in most of them came out
ahead of his opposition.

As the year of 1976 dawned, he was able in a method-
ical manner, to beat Henry "Scoop" Jackson, George Wallace,
Mo Udall, Birch Bayh, Lloyd Bentson, Terry Sanford, Milton
Shapp, Sergent Shriver, and Fred Harris and win the Democratic nomination for the presidency at the July Democratic
Convention in New York City. Coming out of this convention,
the polls had Carter with a 32 percent lead over Gerald
Ford who had yet to be nominated by the Republicans in Kansas City, Missouri.

After Ford was nominated by the Republicans in
Kansas City,following a hard-won victory over Ronald Reagan,
the polls showed that the wide gap Carter had in July was
reduced to a margin of 12 percent. After Labor Day, the
contest for the presidency began to heat up. A debate was
proposed by President Ford; Carter accepted. In the first
confrontation on September 23, 1976, the polls had Ford winning over Carter, but, in the second debate on domestic economic conditions, Carter bested Ford. In the third and final
debate on October 19, Carter again came out ahead of Ford.
However, prior to the debates and in the interim between the
debates, Carter had given an interview to Playboy Magazine.
This was cited by the opposition as poor judgement on the
part of the Democratic candidate. Other gaffes were made by
Carter on ethnic purity. But Andrew Young, the black Democratic Congressman from Atlanta came to his rescue and
immediately Carter beat a hasty retreat, and it appeared

that order was restored to his quest for the presidency.
On the eve of the election, Ford had narrowed the gap down
to two percent.

On Sunday October 31, 1976, a Reverend Clennon King
from Albany, Georgia, journeyed down to Plains, Georgia,
about 80 miles from Albany, to join Jimmy Carter's church.
Rev. King (no relations to the late Rev. Martin Luther King,
Jr.) brought four other blacks with him. The Rev. King, along
with his cohorts, were barred from joining the church. A
resolution had been enacted in 1965, barring "niggers and
civil rights activists" from joining the church. Immediately
the Plains Baptist Church gained the national spotlight. It
was subsequently revealed that King had a bizarre background.
He had once run for president in 1960 on an Afro-American
ticket. In 1972, he ran again for president of the United
States as an independent. He managed a gubernatorial campaign in 1970, when his brother ran against Jimmy Carter.
He quit his brother's campaign and ran for governor himself
as a Republican. King had also served a four-year prison
sentence for non-payment of child support in California.

His other runs for political office found King making
a bid for city council, county commission and the statehouse
in the 1976 Democratic primary. In his roamings about the
world, King was expelled from Kenya in 1965, and from Jamaica
in 1962 where he was seeking political asylum from persecu-
tion in the United States.

It is alleged that the Republican National Committee tried to make capital out of the King incident in Plains, Georgia. They wired 400 telegrams to black preachers across the country, intimating that Jimmy Carter, a born again Baptist, was not fit to be president since he could not control his own church. Carter later explained to the press that he had tried to persuade the church to drop the barriers against blacks. He was unsuccessful, but he would try again, once the elections were over.

But Carter's quest for the presidency had really begun four years earlier, in 1972, at the Democratic National Convention which nominated George McGovern. In a heated caucus, his aides, Gerald Rafshoon, his public relations chief and advertiser, and Hamilton Jordan, his campaign manager, suggested that Carter become McGovern's running mate. Nothing came of this long shot. But Carter had seen the possibility of making a successful run for the presidency. He marshalled his forces and began his odyssey into the countryside.

When the returns came in on Tuesday and early Wednesday morning, November 2nd and 3rd, 1976, Carter had carried 23 states with a popular vote of 40,276,040, and 49 percent of the total 82,196,000. Carter received 297 electoral votes and Ford 241. These data were based on returns from 99 percent of the precincts in this country.

The political pundits, in analyzing the election returns,credited Carter's victory to his ability to bring together minorities such as blacks, Chicanos and Spanish surnamed, blue-collar workers, poor whites and the large southern block of states in the Sun Belt, running from Florida to Texas. The solid base of Carter's support was in the South. Among blacks in the nation as a whole more than 80 percent voted for him. In some precincts of the South the black vote was 95 percent for Carter.

The Joint Center for Political Studies, based in Washington, D. C. estimated after a survey of the vote, that Carter received 90 percent of the total black voters in more than 500 predominantly black wards. It was further estimated that 70 percent of the eligible black voters turned out to vote which amounted to more than 6,000,000. This was a record turnout and 28 percent above the turnout in 1972. Blacks voted with a vengeance. It appears ironical that blacks in this country would vote for a man from the deep South.

The deep South, dating back to the slavery days was always a feared place. To be sold down South carried foreboding connotations. And once this was known it drove some slaves to suicide.

But blacks voted for Jimmy Carter almost en masse By their vote they appeared to trust Carter more than Gerald

R. Ford. It appears ironical to note what strange alliances politics make. It was in Racine, Wisconsin, in the year of 1854, that blacks and whites came together to create the Republican Party. The avowed purpose of the Republicans in those days was to rid the country of slavery. Once the great clash of philosophies was joined in the Civil War, and Lincoln became President and freed the slaves, for 72 years, from 1860 to 1932, blacks overwhelmingly voted Republican, but since the New Deal Days of Franklin Roosevelt, they have voted overwhelmingly for the Democrats. There has been a deep abiding fear of Republicans by blacks since the run for the presidency by Barry Goldwater in 1964. In this election the Republicans for the first time in this century went after the South. Although Johnson had defeated Goldwater handily in 1964, in the 1968 election, George Wallace, running on a third party ticket got 9,000,000 votes, but Nixon won the presidency. Hubert Humphrey lost this election by a narrow margin to Nixon because of Wallace's entry in the race. In this 1968 election the South went for Wallace as well as for Nixon; and here blacks saw an unusual alliance of southern whites and northern blue-collar workers voting for Nixon. Blacks were frightened at being ostracized in their own land. They always suspected that the South was against them. The voter disenfranchisement, the "old Grandfather clauses," Ku Klux Klanism, beatings, police brutality, bombings, and lynching had been their heritage. They indeed thought they were children of Ham. When Jimmy Carter championed the cause of righteousness, and invoked civil rights and fair treatment of the downtrodden, blacks began to listen. They became more attentive. They had not heard words such as this since the days of Lyndon Baines Johnson. The interest of the blacks began to quicken. The experts on political science said there would be a low turnout, but the reverse happened.

Blacks really turned out to vote for Carter because there were forebodings that the Republicans would further erode civil rights, that the ultra right wing of this country would deny them good education and equal job opportunities and would try to turn the clock back. Ford's anti-busing stand alarmed them as well as the jingoism of Reagan. Blacks preferred the days when Ronald Reagan narrated Death Valley Days and the GE Theater. They wished the former governor of California would return to these insouciant tasks. But Reagan felt that the country needed re-structuring. His platform at the Republican Convention in August was adopted by Ford.

Knowing that there had to be a counter move to blunt the thrust of affluent whites who always protect their interests and usually vote Republican, the labor unions, the Urban League and the NAACP with help from numerous civil

rights and non-partisan groups launched Operation Big Vote.
First, blacks had to be registered, then they had to vote.
This they did, the biggest vote they had ever launched
to put Jimmy Carter in the White House.

The culmination of blacks voting in the South was,
of course, the election of Jimmy Carter. The influence of
the black vote had been on a rising tide since 1960. This
was at least four years before the Civil Rights Act of
1964 and five years before the Voting Rights Act of 1965.
Table XXVIII below shows the increasing number of blacks
voting in the South.

Table XXVIII

Blacks Voting in Presidential Elections
in the South 1960-1976

Year	Voting	Percent Increase
1960	1,463,000	
1964	2,164,000	51
1968	3,112,000	44
1972	3,576,000	15
1976	4,000,000	12

Source: Voter Education Project, Atlanta, Georgia, 1976.

From a low voter turnout of 1,463,000 in 1960, the
high water mark was reached in 1976 with a voter turnout
of 4,000,000. There has been a steady percentage of increase

each year over the past sixteen years, but the remarkable voting record for blacks in the South has gone up to 173 percent since 1960.

Along with the increased voting there has been an increase in black elected officials in the South. From a low of fifty in 1960, today there are 2,000 black elected officials in the South. The South is here defined as states in the old Confederacy including Virginia, North Carolina, South Carolina, Georgia, Florida, Alabama, Tennessee, Mississippi, Louisiana, Arkansas, and Texas.

References

1. Houston Post, November 6, 1974, Pg. 6A.

2. New York Times, Vol. CXXIV, #42855, May 25, 1975, Section E-6.

3. New York Times, Vol. CXXIII, #42361, p. 131.

4. Ibid.

Chapter XVI

Congressional And State Office Holders

The Politics of Senator Edward Brooke

The election of Edward Brooke as Attorney General
of the State of Massachusetts in 1962 surprised not only
millions of blacks in this country, but whites as well. But
it was no surprise to Edward Brooke. Since he graduated
from Howard University in Washington, D.C. in 1939, the
present senator from Massachusetts has kept his eye on the
brass ring. He went into World War II as a Second Lieutenant
of Infantry. He had attended ROTC at Howard University, which
was only one of two predominantly black universities which
had ROTC prior to World War II. The other one was Wilberforce
University of Wilberforce, Ohio. Assigned to the 366th Infantry Regiment, one of the few all-black outfits in World
War II, Edward Brooke trained at Fort Devens, Massachussets,
then went overseas where the 266th became a reinforced regiment to the 92nd Division. This Division was one of the two
all-black divisions in World War II. The other one was the
93rd Division, which went to the South Pacific and fought
on Guadalcanal.

The 92nd Division was assigned to Italy as a part
of the 5th Army under General Mark Clark. The 366th, before
it went into the line in November 1944, guarded air bases
in Italy around Naples, Rome and Foggia Main. Brooke was
assigned to the partisans in Italy where they harassed the

troops of Kesselring. During his tour of duty in Italy, he
married a beautiful Italian girl and the couple had two
daughters. At the end of the War, Brooke went to Boston
College and studied law. At the end of his law studies he
passed the Massachusetts bar and began practice in Boston.
While so doing he studied the political structure in the
Bay State. Casting his lot with the Republicans, Senator
Brooke early cultivated the friendship and guidance of
Senator Leverett Saltonstall and Henry Cabot Lodge and other
powerful Republicans in Massachusetts. Because he was a
clean politician, and had no fences to mend, he ran for
Attorney General in 1966 and won easily. How was it that in
a state with only 3 percent of the population black, he could
win with an overwhelming white vote?

Edward Brooke ran as a peoples' candidate, and not
as a black candidate. He represented all of the people in
Massachusetts. His record as Attorney General was exceptional.
He sent more racketeers and thugs to Massachusetts prisons
than any other Attorney General preceding him. Whites were
charmed with this light-complexioned, dark-haired black, who
was hardly a black man, but seemed more white than black.

When the powerful Leverett Saltonstall retired from
the Senate in 1966, Edward ran for the Senate. He again won,
and became the first black Senator to be elected to an office
since the period of the Reconstruction. He easily won re-election in 1972. In a quiet unobtrusive manner, Senator Brooke

has been effective in the Senate. He has stood for upholding
the Supreme Court on busing. He has withstood the wrath of
the Bostonians who were against busing. Bills and amendments,
introduced by him in Congress, have ameliorated racial discrimination in housing. He has been mentioned as Vice-Presi-
dential timber by Republicans running for the presidency.

The Politics of Barbara Jordan

What can a country do for a person that the person
cannot do for himself? It can advance his purpose, advance
his cause. This can be done by playing the game, the game
of politics. One of the adept persons who has been playing
this game with an adroitness that could shame the old politicians is Barbara Jordan, a Houston, Texas, black woman.
Coming out of Houston's Fifth Ward, a run-down rugulose area
that borders on the downtown area, Barbara Jordan has tra-
versed a generation in less than ten years. As a politician
she is moving fast, so fast, that her own colleagues in Congress stand by in awe.

Born in Houston in 1936, Barbara graduated from
Phyllis Wheatley High School in 1952, and later completed
bachelor's studies at Texas Southern University in 1956,
magna cum laude. The child of Arlyne Phathie nee Patten and
the Rev. Benjamin Meredieth Jordan, Barbara was reared in
the Baptist Church and early cut her teeth on hard work.
Three years after leaving Texas Southern University she completed work on her law degree at Boston University. But it

was at Texas Southern University that Barbara became an outstanding orator and debater. In an environment that was still highly segregationist, the professors at Texas Southern University took the students where they were and brought them up to a level of their own aspirations. Barbara early came under the influence of Dr. Thomas Freeman, the debating coach. Freeman graduated from the University of Chicago in philosophy. In Houston he is known as a highly expressive dramatic speaker. Clarity of speech, good diction, how to perceive an idea and dissect it, these were the things Freeman drilled into his debating team Freeman often says now that in the behavorial sciences a person must know how to speak well and write well. These two features were absorbed by Barbara while on the debating team, and during her career at Texas Southern University.

Sensing sweeping changes which were about to be unleased in politics in this country, Barbara, only three years out of law school, ran for the Texas House of Representatives in 1962. During this three-year period she had practiced law with two other black lawyers in a ramshackle frame building on Lyons Avenue in the heart of Houston's Fifth Ward. Not only did a black lawyer in those days go through a starvation period, but he could stay starved all of his life, if he did not quickly develop a thriving reputation. One way to do this was go into criminal law where, however, the obstacles were enough to slow even the most ambitious lawyer. The young lawyer early found that the criminal he defended could not pay him, and, if the lawyer could delay his sentencing on appeal, and the accused was out on bail, the criminal might steal or rob to pay off his lawyer for defending him. Criminal law, except in rare instances, was counter productive for the black lawyer. Of course, there were other ways a lawyer could make a living. But to Barbara Jordan, the one way that had appeal, attraction, and high visibility, was politics.

The iceberg of Civil Rights was beginning to crack in this country with the 1954 Brown v School Board decision. Eight years later, Barbara decided to run for the Texas House. She lost, but in 1964, she ran again. She lost again. Lyndon B. Johnson, the first Texas President, was in office then, and he had a soft spot in his heart for Barbara. With the blessing of the Sage of the Pedernales, Barbara ran for the Texas Senate in 1966 and won. This was the first time a black woman had won an elective office in Texas for such a high position. She immediately became a celebrity and had more speaking engagements than she could handle. Always going about a task with the aggression what would compare with that of Vince Lombardi, Barbara endeared herself to the Texas Senate.

The Civil Rights Bill and the Voting Rights Act had cast a new glow over politics in the Lone Star State. In 1966, the breakthrough came when, not only Barbara, but also

Curtis Graves and others won seats in the Texas State Government in Austin. These blacks were the first in the state legislature since Reconstruction. In fact they were the first black Democrats for blacks who won election during the Reconstruction period were Republicans. In Texas politics it was political suicide for a black to be other than a black Democrat. The amazing thing about Barbara was that she was able to move into Texas politics in Austin with the grace of a feline. It was not only amazing to whites but to blacks as well, that almost like a lamb, she had come into the lion's den of Texas politics. Segregationists and racists still abounded in the Lone Star State. There were senators and legislators who had jumped to conclusions about her even before she was seated, but, like the lamb, she quickly made peace with the lions. Whereas, other black legislators grated on the conscience of the white legislature by constant reference to their past sins against blacks and minorities, Barbara did not do this. Whereas, other blacks severely criticized the white establishment of Gatesville and other discriminatory policies, Barbara kept her peace. Barbara did this because she had the backing of the AFL-CIO, one of the most prejudiced anti-minority groups in the State, but just as politics can make all kinds of bed fellows, it made this one for Barbara. Immediately she went to work and was able to raise the number of weeks for unemployment compensation for workers in the state. Other bills which she sponsored

and that became law were a Texas Fair Employment Practices
Act and a minimum wage law, the first one in the state.
Overcoming the hostility of a state dominated by males -
Texas has always been hard on horses and women - Barbara
soon had the Senate holding her in awe. She mesmerized
them. This was done by her superior intelligence, candor,
and the ability to look them in the eye and damn them. Her
"great god father" was LBJ. As a champion of labor in a
"right to work" state, Barbara was the darling of labor
unions. A third reason was the groundswell for Civil Rights.
The representative in Texas is up for election every two
years. During this period, the politician is highly sensitive to minorities. The legislature as a whole did not want
to be cast as bigoted or racist. A fourth reason for deferring to Barbara was that she was a woman. The American male
has always deferred to the female, especially those with a
high degree of intellect. A fifth reason was that Barbara
was a black woman. Most of these white males were only used
to black women as maids, housekeepers, mammys, or a black
prostitute. Most of them had never come across a black woman
who had finished college. Because of their bucolic nature,
they never had such exposure. As a further addition to her
credentials, Barbara as a black woman with a LL.B was bordering on the unthinkable. Seeking to overcome their guilt
complex, the Texas legislature accepted Barbara. She became
a hit, and the soundings were heard throughout the state.

Ambition, that force which grips the achiever, had
a half nelson on Barbara. She again was reaching for the
brass ring. Knowing that her days could only be numbered
as a state senator, and with new decisions on voting rights
coming from the U.S. Supreme Court, Barbara aspired to
national office. An opening was the case of Baker v. Carr
in Memphis, Tennessee: one man, one vote. The Supreme Court
ruled that no longer could gerrymandering take place that
would deny a voter from exercising his right to vote for the
candidate of his choice. The new law in fact provided a stim-
ulus to minorities to vote for the man of their choice and
not be manipulated by the establishment.

With the help of influencial whites in Austin and
Houston, Texas, Barbara had the 18th Congressional District carved out of two other districts that had been split
between Bob Casey and Bob Eckhardt. Casey's district covered
the Houston Ship Channel and the National Aeronautics and
Space Area, better known as the Johnson Space Center. [*] Bob Eckhardt's district covered northwest Houston. In this district
were blue collar whites and poor blacks. The new district
carved out for Barbara ran directly through Houston's north-
side, downtown to the south side of Houston. The new area
includes her old area of the Fifth Ward, Chicanos living in
the central city, blacks, Texas Southern University, the
University of Houston, and, further south through the Cullen
Drive-South Park Area. In this new district live the poorest

of the poor-Chicanos and blacks; it also includes the downtown business district, high income blacks in the Timber-
crest-McGregor Park area and thence to the outlying districts of Sunnyside where we have a large population of
modest income blacks. The 18th District is a cross section
of Houston. In the 1972 election Barbara won easily over
Curtis Graves in the Democratic primary and won again over
her Republican opponent in the November election.

Making her appearance in the Halls of Congress in
January, 1973, Barbara Jordan, looking at the venerable
chamber, stated that it appeared that she had been here
before. A group of her followers had flown up from Houston,
and something akin to a female Roman Gladiatress, Barbara
came to conquer Congress. And this she did.

Appointment to the House Judiciary Committee gave
Barbara a rare opportunity to show her in-depth interpretation of the U.S. Constitution. After the Erwin Committee
completed its investigation of the Watergate Affair, the
House Judiciary Committee started hearings on impeachment.
With the hearings being televised, Barbara became a nation-
wide hit with her statement on constitutional principles.
High visibility, her knowledge of the constitution, being
black and a woman gave her an audience greater than any man
of the Committee. The House Judiciary Committee, probably
more than any other investigative governmental body, was the
instrument which impelled Nixon to resign. Barbara C. Jordan

so enthralled local Houstonians with her grasp of constitutional principles that one of her admirers put up a bill-
board acknowledging his appreciation for her explanation
of the meaning of the Constitution.

In November, 1974, Barbara ran for re-election. She
beat her Republican opponent, winning 95 percent of the vote.
Basking in the national spotlight with the fall-out from
Watergate, Barbara Jordan, when the 94th Congress convened
in January, 1975, had taken another giant step that many
other lawmakers had not achieved in a lifetime. Her standing with the close-knit Texas delegations was assured. These
Texans, from the days of the late Sam Rayburn and Lyndon B.
Johnson, held some of the most important committee chairman-
ships in Congress, Agriculture, Appropriations, Science and
Astronautics, Government Operations and Veterans Affairs.
In the Congress, Jordan was on the Judiciary Committee, Steer-
ing Committee, and the Government Operations Committee. She
was on two panels. One had been set up by the Democrats to
revive the economy and the other a House Committee to adjust
House methods to prevent disruptive changes.

In the House of Representatives one of her main contributions was the expansion of the Voting Rights Act of 1965,
which aided Mexican-Americans in Texas. She was also instrumental in adding riders to anti-discrimination clauses of the
Law Enforcement Assistance Act and revenue-sharing laws and

in sponsoring legislation abolishing fair trade laws.

At the age of forty-one Barbara Jordan had achieved fame, fortune and prestige. What other worlds were there for her to conquer? In the black community, Jordan must still take stands on issues that were not popular with the establishment. She had never critized labor and its racist stand on preventing blacks from achieving progress under Affirmative Action. Her constitutents did not know her position on wealth diffusion and its impact on the stability of the economy and the eradication of poverty. Barbara's critics complained that she was always politicking. She considered politics as the sina qua non of life. In Washington she shunned the Black Caucus. This observation is not to be severe on her because the Black Caucus had not shown any significant achievement as yet. Nixon never met with the Black Caucus and neither had Ford.

In Texas, light soundings have been taken by Jordan on a possible Senate race against John Tower in 1978. If the Democrats win in 1978 there is the possibility of a Federal Judgeship in Texas. But the political arena is wide open. The hills to climb beckon. At the present pace and with her ability to rap with the establishment the only thing to deter Barbara would be her health or a deep switch in the body politic in this country.

Although impressive gains were made in black office

holders over the past twelve years, in 1975, there was a net reduction in the number of black mayors. Prior to the November election in 1975, there were 143 black mayors. After the elections there were 130. There was a net loss of thirteen.

The Table XXIX below which shows the gain in black office holders in the South includes gains in offices other than mayors.

Table XXIX

Selected States Showing
Black Officeholders In The South
1975

Office State	Number Office	Number
1. Alabama		193
2. Arkansas		212
3. Florida		79
4. Georgia		221
5. Louisiana		278
6. Mississippi		237
7. North Carolina		210
8. South Carolina		153
9. Tennessee		118
10. Texas		155
11. Virginia		88
Total		1,944

Source: Voter Education Project, Atlanta, Ga., May, 1976

Offices held by blacks in the South range from mayor to the Congress of the United States. Other than municipal officials, members of boards of education dominate with 445, and county officials are third with 294. Table XXX shows these officials.

Table XXX

Offices Held By Blacks
In The South, 1976

Office	Number
1. Municipal Officials other than Mayor	827
2. Education Officials	445
3. County Officials	294
4. Police Chiefs and Law Enforcement Officials	204
5. Members of State Legislatures	88
6. Mayors	68
7. U.S. House of Representatives	3
Total	1,927

Source: Voter Education Project, Atlanta, Ga., May, 1976

John Lewis, who heads the Voter Education Project, reports periodically on the achievement of blacks in politics in the South. Over the past fourteen years the increase in blacks winning elective office is much greater than in 1965. In 1965, only 71 blacks held elective office in the South.

But even with these newly won elective offices in 1976, they represent only 2½ percent of the elective offices in the South, which number 77,800. Blacks are still underrepresented by 13,616 offices. We arrive at these figures based on the facts that blacks are 20 percent of the population in the eleven states included above.

At present there are seventeen blacks serving in the Congress. All seventeen were reelected in the 1976 elections. They are listed below.

1. Edward W. Brooke-U.S. Senator, Massachusetts

2. Yvonne Brathwaite-U.S. Representative, California

3. Shirley Chisholm-U.S. Representative, New York

4. William Clay-U.S. Representative, Missouri

5. Cardis R. Collins-U.S. Representative, Illinois

6. John M Conyers, Jr.-U.S. Representative, Michigan

7. Ronald V. Dellums-U.S. Representative, California

8. Charles C. Diggs, Jr.-U.S. Representative, Michigan

9. Harold E. Ford-U.S. Representative, Tennessee

10. Augustus F. Hawkins-U.S. Representative, California

11. Barbara Jordan-U.S. Representative, Texas

12. Ralph H. Metcalfe-U.S. Representative, Illinois

13. Parren J. Mitchell-U.S. Representative, Maryland

14. Charles B. Rangel-U.S. Representative, New York

15. Louis Stokes-U.S. Representative, Ohio

16. Walter Fountroy-U.S. Representative, Washington D.C.

17. Robert Nix-U.S. Representative, Pennsylvania

On December 12, 1976, Parren J. Mitchell was elected
head of the Black Caucus in the House. Mitchell succeeded
Yvonne B. Burke of California. Shirley Chisholm was selected
as Vice Chairman.

Andrew Young

It was no accident that Andrew Young was selected
to be one of Jimmy Carter's inner circle when he began to
run for the presidency. Carter knew Young from the Civil
Rights Movement of the sixties. In this rhetoric and blister-
ing fray, Young proved his mettle. In Birmingham he braved
the slashing tactics of Bull Connor with his yapping dogs
baring their fangs at blacks; in St. Augustine, the integration of this oldest city in the United States; and in
Selma, the bastion of bigotry. These were the main areas of
violence, beatings and baiting by the police forces of these
cities and their vicious police dogs.

While these violent conflicts were in progress, Young
was the activist not only on the picket lines, but also in
the negotiations as well. In Birmingham, as Martin Luther
King's co-protestor, they by-passed the recalcitrant white
power structure of this city and sought to contact Roger
Blough, the head of U.S. Steel, who was the absentee owner
of the city of Birmingham. Young gained a seat at the bargaining table with the power structure of Birmingham where
his negotiating skills won significant gains for blacks in

Birmingham.

All during his crisscrossing the South in the search
for justice and freedom, Young also made trips to Plains,
Georgia. The Man from Plains stood for integration. Jimmy
Carter had advocated the acceptance of blacks into the main
stream of Georgia. Young noticed this in his sojourns into
Plains. He filed this discovery for future reference.

When Carter made his bid for the presidency in thirty
primaries in 1976, the most ever made by any seeker for his
party's nomination, Young came out early for Carter. Of
course at that time Carter was not a name figure in American
politics. Early in his quest for the nomination blacks were
wary of him, a former Georgia governor seeking the presidency.
But Young allayed the fears of the black establishment as
well as those of the rank and file. When, early in his campaign, Carter made one of his gaffes on ethnic purity, Young
was one of the first black politicians to implore Carter to
recant. This Carter did and since that moment has endeared
himself to blacks.

Young was born in New Orleans. He has a medium build
with a coffee-colored complexion and a calm baritone voice.
From a sinecure in the United Church of Christ and the position of one of the prime movers in the Southern Christian
Leadership Conference, and the Civil Rights Acts of 1964 and
1965, Young, with extraordinary prescience, suggested that the

protest movement move into a political movement and this it
did. In 1970 he ran for Congress from Georgia, in the Fifth
Congressional District. He lost to a Republican, but he ran
so well that in losing he won the leadership of the Democrats in his district. In 1972, he won over his Republican
opponent and was re-elected in 1974 and again in 1976.

Young's district was 62 percent white, but he won
with a majority of the white vote and virtually all of the
black vote. Often the white power structure was not <u>sure</u>
of their candidate. Young quickly doused these fears. Young
approached the issues with reason and their application to
all people. Without yielding his concern for minorities and
liberal issues such as national health care, Young kept the
respect of the white business establishment in Atlanta. Whites
in Atlanta feel that he is one of the few blacks who really
understands the Establishment. In each of the subsequent
elections since 1972, Young has broadened his base of support.
His appeal is to young whites, liberals, students and professional people. He has kept his solid base among blacks and
has dramatically increased his support among whites. He endeared himself to the Establishment by his unabashed plugging
of Atlanta.

One of the great coups accomplished by Carter in the
primaries was his ability to replace George Wallace as a
spokesman for the South, and simultaneously beat Wallace in

the Florida primary. Carter won overwhelmingly in Florida
with 75,000 black votes. It is possible that without these
votes he would have come in second. It was after the Florida
primary that Young came out for Carter.

Wallace had now been removed as a threat. Carter was
the voice of the New South. Young, in the midst of political
maneuverings, had early realized that the spirit of Wallace
was not the spirit of the New South. When Wallace garnered
13 percent of the vote in 1968, with about 13,000,000 votes,
the governor of Alabama had become the spokesman of the South.
No credible black politician would touch Wallace. When Carter
made his strong bid for the nomination, Young sensed that
here was a man who could replace Wallace, and, in the Florida
primary, the denouement of Wallace had begun. The political
curtain for George Wallace was now coming down.

Young's early backing of Carter was not followed by
black politicians, but as Carter gained momentum in Pennsylvania, New York, Michigan, and Ohio, black politicians jumped
on the bandwagon. Young is due as much credit for making Carter president as Carter is for recognizing Young as a sound
advisor to his entourage.[1]

References

*Bob Casey is now serving on the U. S. Maritine Commission.

1. "The Making of Andrew Young Toward a Politics of Trust,"
    by Roger M. Williams, Saturday Review, October 16, 1976,
    pp. 6-11, Vol. 4, #2.

Chapter XVII

Black Mayors and Their Cities

In a speech in Houston, Texas, at a NAACP Freedom Fund
Dinner in 1970, Kenneth Gibson, the former stocky engineer and
Mayor of Newark, New Jersey, stated that if everything that
was wrong with American cities could be lumped together into
one city, then Newark was that city. Also, at an Urban seminar
in December 1973, Carl Stokes, former mayor of Cleveland, Ohio,
and later the suave, debonair New York newscaster, stated that
after Addonizio had raped Newark, he left it for Gibson. These
strong statements coming from the present mayor of Newark
and the former mayor of Cleveland have been confirmed in
Newark.

But notwithstanding all of Newark's municipal problems, which are similar to most of other cities' municipal
problems, the U. S. Conference of Mayors, a predominantly
white group, elected Kenneth Gibson as its president for the
year, 1976-77 at the conference in Milwaukee. Gibson became
the first black Mayor to hold this post.

An article in Harper's Magazine for January, 1975, shows
Newark to be the worst city in the United States. The article
was written by Arthur M. Louis, an associate editor of Fortune.
Louis's article was a take-off on H. L. Mencken's study made
in 1931, to determine which state was the worst. After

examining numerous variables and averaging them, Mencken found that Mississippi was the worst state and Massachusetts, the best. Louis took fifty cities in the United States and from a base of twenty-four variables compared them. The writer used Census Bureau data of the U. S. Government, private data and unpublished material.

The twenty-four variables were:

1. Murder and non-negligent manslaughter per 100,000 residents.
2. Forcible rapes per 100,000 residents.
3. Robberies per 100,000 residents.
4. Deaths from influenza and pneumonia per 100,000 residents.
5. Infant deaths per 100,000 residents.
6. Ratio of people to medical practitioners.
7. Hospital beds per 10,000 residents.
8. Median income per capita.
9. Percentage of families below poverty-income level.
10. Black-family median income as a percentage of white family income.
11. Percentage of housing units owned by occupants.
12. Percentage of housing units with telephones available.
13. Median value of owner-occupied single-family dwelling (Estimated by Owner).
14. Percentage of housing units with 1.01 or more persons per room.
15. Percentage of housing units lacking some or all plumbing facilities.
16. Percentage of high school graduates, individuals 25 years and older.
17. Percentage of college graduates, individuals 25 and older.
18. Who's Who entries per 100,000 residents.
19. Residents per square mile.
20. Micrograms of particulate matter per cubic meter of air.
21. Park and recreational acreage per 10,000 residents.
22. Public-library volumes per 10,000 residents.
23. Hotel and Motel rooms per 100,000 residents.
24. Places of amusement and recreation per 100,000 residents.

Here is a list of these cities and their rankings based on the twenty-four variables below:

1. Seattle (average rank: 14.0)
2. Tulsa (14.8)
3. San Diego (14.9)
4. San Jose (15.6)
5. Honolulu (16.4)
6. Portland (17.8)
7. Denver (18.2)
8. Minneapolis (18.8)
9. Oklahoma City (19.1)
10. Omaha (19.3)
11. San Francisco (19.46)
12. Nashville (19.54)
13. St. Paul (19.6)
14. Columbus (19.75)
15. Toledo (19.79)
16. Indianapolis (20.6)
17. Long Beach (21.2)
18. Milwaukee (21.9)
19. Kansas City (22.6)
20. Dallas (23.25)
21. Phoenix (23.33)
22. Los Angeles (24.6)
23. Fort Worth (24.7)
24. Cincinnati (24.9)
25. Rochester (25.3)
26. Oakland (25.9)
27. Washington (26.5)
28. Houston (27.4)
29. Buffalo (28.2)
30. Louisville (28.2)
31. Pittsburg (28.4)
32. New York (28.5)
33. Memphis (29.3)
34. Boston (29.6)
35. Miami (29.9)
36. Atlanta (30.0)
37. El Paso (30.7)
38. New Orleans (30.7)
39. Philadelphia (31.0)
40. Tampa (31.1)
41. San Antonio (31.7)
42. Norfolk (31.9)
43. Cleveland (32.0)
44. Jacksonville (32.2)
45. Birmingham (32.5)
46. Baltimore (32.7)
47. Detroit (33.0)

48. Chicago (33.7)
49. St. Louis (35.3)
50. Newark (41.6)

Trying to make his data meaningful, the writer
divided the cities into the five best and the five worst.
Among the twenty-four variables listed above, Newark was
listed among the worst in nineteen categories. These are
number 1, 2, 3, 4, 5, 6, 7, 8, 9, 11, 12, 14, 15, 16, 17,
18, 19, 21, 23, 25. Only in one category, public-library
volumes per 10,000 residents, was Newark listed among the
best. Why is it that Newark is one of the worst cities in
America, even according to Louis? Is it because it has a
black mayor? No! Is it because Newark has 54 percent of its
population black? No! The basic cause of Newark's low standing is due to lack of police protection and, in a larger
sense, the indifferent delivery system of the government.
With all respect to Louis, he tried to manipulate the data
to see whether Newark could rise from the bottom. He was
unable to do so. Through his in-depth research, Louis only
reinforced the evidence that murder and negligent homicide,
rapes and robberies were due to poor police protection and
lack of a governmental delivery system. Local governments
are notorious for spending more money per capita in the
suburbs than in the central city where most blacks live.
Kenneth Gibson has his work cut out for him. But, if Gibson
is to improve the blighted environment of Newark, it must

be done with the help of business as well as the help of
state and federal government. Newark is locked in by the
suburbs.

Whites who work in the city by day, flee the city
by night. The inner city becomes like an abandoned ghost
town that has been looted and left to struggle for survival in an atmosphere of hostility and scorn. In his first
administration, Gibson had a very poor tax base and the
inflexibility of property taxes. Is it any wonder that
Gibson and his council could not raise sufficent revenue
to rehabilitate the city? Also, with the City Council
constantly at odds with the Mayor, the groundwork for inac-
tion and the maintenence of the status quo had been laid.
Co-operation for the betterment of the entire city and
region was almost beyond the capabilities of the local governing structure.

However, the basic problem of Newark, as with most
large urban areas, is the high unemployment rate. The recent
recession of 1974-75 is still a recession for blacks and the
cities.

In May, 1974, Gibson won reelection. These first
four years under Gibson brought to the city administration
honesty and credibility. The corruption of Addonizio was
gone. Property taxes had been cut. Former delinquent taxes
were moving back on the tax rolls. Infant mortality due to

lead poisoning was wiped out. Construction was taking place
in the city. The state of New Jersey was planning a large
educational center in Newark, thus the hope of Newark under
Gibson was the meshing of forces for constructive change,
reducing racism white or black and improving the city's
delivery system.

The severity of the recession for 1974-75 was revealed in North Jersey with construction workers unemployed
at the rate of 18 percent. Mayor Kenneth Gibson of Newark
revealed plans to lay off 291 city employees. He was hoping
to salvage the city's pending deficit of $35 million and
explained that the layoffs were necessary to offset the
recession, cutbacks in state aid to education, and the eroding tax base and increased costs on government. In the
spring of 1975, these reductions in city personnel first
affected policemen, firemen, and miscellaneous city personnel. With a police force of 1361 persons in Newark, a 10
percent reduction as well as an 8 percent reduction in the
number of firemen would save the city about $2 million. A
city councilman was alarmed with these reductions. In times
of such dire straits in Newark, crime was apt to increase.
With the incidence of crime increasing because of high unemployment, a reduction of police personnel would only exacerbate criminal activity in the North Jersey city.

A few blocks from Newark another North Jersey city

was in fiscal difficulty. Jersey City officials negotiated an agreement with their police to forego overtime and paid holidays, in order to avoid a large layoff of policemen. This agreement was expected to save the city $800,000. It was to be returned when good times returned.

Detroit, Michigan

A second large city near the bottom of the Louis data is Detroit, Michigan. Coleman Young was elected mayor of Detroit in 1973. Coming from the background of state senator, Coleman Alexander Young won over John F. Nichols, Police Commissioner, in November, 1973. The campaign was free of the race issue. Using as a base the United Auto Workers Local with its 167,000 members in Detroit, Young won over Nichols.

How did Coleman Young win in Detroit? Immediately after the election, a precinct analysis was made by a local civic action group called the Urban Alliance. It was found that the wily, sagacious Young and his staff of cohorts had put together a cohesive group of blacks, white liberals and unionists. Since Young was already a Democrat, many political observers in Detroit felt that Young could conceivably develop the clout of Mayor Daley in Chicago.

John F. Nichols, the former police commissioner had run on a law and order theme. Young ran on a conciliator campaign - "Let us bring the people together".

Young, at his prayer breakfast in Detroit prior to
his inaugural, vowed to attack such problems as crime,
drugs, economic development, gun control, downtown revi-
talization, tax reform and transportation. At the breakfast were two of Detroit's powers, Henry Ford, II, and
Leonard Woodcock of the United Automobile Workers.

Young was elected mayor of Detroit when the economy
in Detroit was headed for one of its worst downturns in
history. In November, 1973, the energy crisis hit the United
States like a clap of thunder. United States citizens, in
their usual care-free manner, did not dream that it could
happen to them--limitations on gasoline for their Sunday
chariots. The Arabs and the Near East countries, as well
as Venezuela, placed higher prices on oil as well as limit-
ing the supply. United States citizens began to shift to
the compact car. Now, since General Motors, who is the king
of Detroit, had been realizing large profits on the medium-
sized cars, it felt the impact of reduced sales on these
medium-sized cars, far more than did Ford or American Motors.
Layoffs in the thousands were made by General Motors. Re-
flections on the local economy of Detroit and politics placed
Young in a position of Hobson's Choice. Black mayors are
usually elected in the riptide of change, population out-flow,
erosion of the tax base, and economic downturns.

As Young moved into city hall, the motor city was
undergoing drastic changes. The famous Pick Fort Shelby
Hotel closed its doors. Atlas Brewery could no longer
afford losses, so it was closing down. As the year 1974
wore on, the auto industry announced more layoffs until
there were 187,000 people in the Detroit region out of
work. It has often been said that when the United States
has a cold, Detroit catches pneumonia. Things were so bad
in Detroit in December, 1974, that Henry Ford, II, went to
Washington to plead with President Ford for relief for the
auto industry. The president promised tax relief.

The Department of Housing and Urban Development had
foreclosed on 80,000 homes in the United States. More than
16,000, or 25 percent , were in Detroit alone in 1974.

As black mayors are caught in the forces of change,
they must always assure their white constituents that this
is not a black take-over. This black take-over seems to
haunt whites in this country. This indicates a glaring guilt
complex.

The black mayor must assure his black constituents
that he is not a lackey for whites and that he stands for
respect and equality for all of his constituents. The black
mayor treads a hazardous path as he seeks to maintain a
balanced administration. He appears always to be on guard.

Young says he starts out confronting the thing that has infected him with fear and frustration since he was a baby in Alabama: "I think the biggest problem facing any black or white mayor in America today is to recognize that racism and polarization are major problems that confront each and every citizen in America and that they must be dealt with.

I think we must recognize that there is a commonality of interest for the white population and the black population in the cities and in the suburbs and deal with it from that point of view. The problems of the cities cannot be isolated from the survival of nation. If the cities go down, the suburbs go down; if the suburbs go down, the nation goes down.

Young's old counselor, Judge Crockett, believes that "sooner or later Chrysler, Ford and General Motors are going to realize these people in the inner city make it possible for them to live in Grosse Pointe. They'll have to turn some of their interest back".

But Young stops short of putting it to the big three: give us our due or we will no longer make it possible for you to live in Grosse Pointe. Even an old radical like Young, mellowed and made wise by experience, approaches that point with caution, for it would put to test the country's most powerful forces.

Grim as Detroit seems to outsiders, Young's easy-going manner seems to have relieved tensions in the city. On the morning after his election a white patrol-man saluted a black patrolman at the main police station: "Good morning, Inspector." A black gang sent word to toughs along downtown streets: "Don't embarrass Coleman." Judge Crockett rated Young's administration a "dynamic success" even before it started, "be cause the goddam town didn't blow up." In Detroit they measure progress that way.

The Career of Coleman Young

What a man! What a politician! What a mayor! Coleman Young is that man, politician and mayor. The fifty-seven year

old Young comes from a background that would make Horatio
Alger appear as a little boy in rompers. He has had a
varied, interesting career that spans forty years of tra-
vail, hard work, labor union activity, political activism,
state senatorship, then the mayoralty.

In the fall elections of 1977, Coleman Young was
overwhelmingly re-elected to the Mayor's office for a
second term over a Black candidate, City Councilman Ernest
Browne.

Born in Tuscaloosa, Alabama, in 1919, Young
experienced terrorism at a young and tender age. The Ku
Klux Klan paraded through the black section of town. The
hooded Klansmen terrorized the black section. When Young
was five his parents migrated to Detroit. This was the post-
World War I great migration of blacks from below the Mason-
Dixon line to the North. Young's parents were attracted by
high wages in Detroit. Detroit in those days of the early
twenties was an ethnic flotsam. Ford Motor Company was king.
Walter Chrysler was a flamboyant motor tycoon. General Motors
had not as yet come on stream. The ethnic types of Germans,
Italians, Greeks, Syrians, Poles and southern blacks made up
a racial melange which was spirited but not hostile. The
Young family settled on the east side of a section called
Black Bottom. The old man was a tailor and he plied his trade
among the hard working blacks who wanted to look nice on

Sunday when they went to church. The "sweetbacks" also had
their clothes made, and business was good, measuring, cutting, stitching the bell bottoms, padded shoulders and
high waists. In the immediate vicinity was a neon lighted street
called Paradise Valley. Paradise Valley in Detroit was
like so many of the tinseled streets of broken dreams. A
country boy meandering along this street could get lost
and wasted by the activity on the street. Hotels, greasy
spoon restaurants, painted dames and bootleg liquor flourished . Paradise Valley was where many a black Detroit boy
was caught up in the soft life. The life was so soft that
he perished. He got hooked on gambling, bootlegging, numbers, or had a harem of dames. This life enticed many of
the young black boys, and once they became enmeshed in it,
their doom was sealed. Such a life was not for Coleman
Young. He worked in his father's shop, taking spots off of
clothes, pressing suits and dresses and smoothing wrinkles.
Young had a purpose in mind; he had objectives in life.
Matriculating under the Jesuits at St. Mary's School, he
served as an usher in the church. At St. Mary's, Young
earned top grades with honors in mathematics. But even after
winning a scholarship to a Catholic high school, he could
not attend. At DeLaSalle High School, a priest shredded his
application. The incident startled Young. He talks about it
to this day. Equality had not arrived yet in Catholicism in

Detroit. After such a confrontation, Young went to Eastern High School, one of a number of public schools in Detroit. After graduating with honors from Eastern, Young qualified for a scholarship to the University of Michigan. But he could not go there either. His scholarship did not qualify him for full costs, only partial. But always reaching for the golden cup, Young would not be derailed from his main quest - outstanding achievement.

The depression of the thirties was a mean, lean time for this country, and more so for blacks. Drifting from job to job, and trying his hand at typing and shorthand, Young enrolled in a Ford apprentice electricians' school. His mathematical skills placed him in a preferred position. He scored 100 on the test, but the job was given to a white man who scored far below Young. Denied the job as an apprentice, Young went on the assembly line. In the motortown pecking order this was one of the lowliest, humdrum jobs in the rank order order of car production.

Always restless, yearning and striving, Young reached out again and found himself involved in union recruiting activity. In the banter, jousting, and needling over the assembly line with fellow workers, one of the company men found that Young was doing union recruiting. In those days union recruiting on company time was a dangerous activity. This was during the time of the Battle of the Overpass in

Ford Motor Company. This was during the time of Harry Bennet, Henry Ford's FBI and CIA all rolled into one. The company man came at Young across the belt. Young hit him beside the head with a three-foot steel bar. The man was knocked cold. He fell across the assembly belt unconscious and was conveyed on the belt into a box of waste. Young was fired.

The Post Office was the next stopping off place for Young. This government agency has long been a dead end street for black talent. Prior to the end of World War II, such a job was the sine qua non for black males. The private world of business was closed to them, and in the daily routine of casting mail and toting mail pouches, it became a way station in the quest for achievement.

Young's will would not drown. He challenged the superintendent in the Detroit Post Office. In his colloquy with this official, Young found that the superintendent was bigoted, and that he didn't even know the United States Constitution. For the fifth time in his budding career, Young was fired again. In retrospect, Young looks back on these firings as victories. They were victories of the spirit over racism, intolerance and oppression. They were also victories of the individual over the mass.

In his intense struggle for achievement and accomplishment, Young was always shooting for the bull's eye. Along the way he met Charles C. Diggs, the mortician. The

House of Diggs was well known in Detroit. The son of this mortician, Charles C. Diggs, Jr. has carried on the will of his father and he is now the senior member of the Black Caucus in the House of Representatives.

Coming out of the depression of the thirties, blacks began engaging in boycotts and demonstrations for jobs. Adam Clayton Powell in Harlem led movements against merchants who did not hire blacks but sold their goods and wares to them. In Detroit, Young joined in with a local group which was seeking to break jim crow housing. In this effort Young saw a coalescing of civil rights. Joining him on the picket line were union men, preachers and other professionals. A catalyst had been discovered by blacks in civil rights. This discovery would propel blacks through the forties and fifties until the enactment of the Civil Rights Act of 1964.

After the Japanese bombed Pearl Harbor in 1941, Young joined the Army Air Corps. He was assigned to Freeman Field in Indiana. He did not make it as a flight officer, but as a bombardier. During those parlous times, the officers' club at Freeman Field was off limits to black officers, although blacks paid dues to the officers' club. This is similar to taxation without representation. Together with other black officers, a march was made on the post commander. The group was immediately surrounded by the MP's and herded into the post stockade. Later, all the black officers were released when information seeped out of the post to the NAACP and the black press, that the Army Air Force had jailed blacks for protesting against discrimination. A directive came from Washington stating that discrimination was illegal in all military establishments.

After the war, Young returned to the post office. From this second stint of casting the mail, Young became an organizer for the Wayne County CIO. He also soon lost this job when he supported the Progressive Party and Henry Wallace in the elections of 1948, when Truman squeaked into the presidency over Tom Dewey. Again being branded a pinko or Communist, Young was fired from his job as a union organizer. Returning briefly to the dry cleaning business, at which he was an old hand, Young founded the National Labor Council. In this period of McCarthyism, the Council was branded as a Communist front organization. The House Un-American Activities Committee, which was recently disbanded, labeled Young as subversive. Young was vehement in his denial of being a Communist. He had never been disloyal to this country, nor did he have any designs to overthrow the United States Government, but the name of the game was protesting and fighting for your rights. In the fifties, after two marriages which both ended in divorce and ,having no children to support, Young moved from job to job as an

insurance man, cab driver, truck driver. This was during
the recession of 1954-61.

In 1960, John F. Kennedy defeated Richard M. Nixon.
Young's chance came to make a political strike when Michigan called a Constitutional Convention to write a new
state Constitution. Young ran as a delegate and won. In
1962, he lost a race to become a State House representative
but won in 1964, when he was elected to the Senate. In 1966,
Young became a Democratic National Committeeman. While in
the Senate, Young became a power to reckon with. His colleagues rated him high as a person who was able to bring
factions together. Michigan politics were racked with dis-
sension. Young's staying ability in long sessions, and his
hearing out both sides, enabled him to offer compromises.

Always on top of developments, Young observed that
whites were leaving the city of Detroit and migrating to
the suburbs. He could not run for mayor in 1969, because
a court ruling held that a state legislator could not run
for mayor. In 1973, it was found that blacks outnumbered
whites at the polls by 8,000 votes. There were 228,000
registered blacks and 220,000 whites. Young won over John
Nichols, a white who was the darling of the police department, by 14,000 votes. Young received only 6 percent of
the white votes and Nichols received 8 percent of the black
votes.

After one year in office, Young found Detroit
deep into a recession. He is hunkering down to the task
of welding a community of interest. Crime was still Young's
nemesis. Seeking to overcome this monstrous apocalypse,
Young began building up his police force. Being a realist,
Young allowed at least a two-year lead time to bring crime
under control. Housing was his second big need. Through
his political clout, he was able to get the Department of
Housing and Urban Development to convey to the city 2,000
abondoned Detroit homes for $1.00 each. What was the report
card on Young after eighteen months in office? Detroiters
respectfully pass average on their black mayor. He needs
more time. If Young can pull off the Detroit miracle, he
can possibly move on to the U.S. State Senate or take a
crack at the governorship.

Atlanta Underground

Prior to the runoff election for mayor of Atlanta
on October 2, 1973, Maynard Jackson appealed to the Atlanta
electorate to consider candidates on their character, not
their color. In the regular election on October 2, 1973,
Jackson led an eleven man race. He got about 47 percent of
the vote. Sam Massell, his number one opponent, polled about
20 percent of the vote. Jackson, in his portly manner, chortled that his was a victory for all Atlanta classes and races.
Winning along with Jackson were blacks who won five of nine

seats on the city school board. The black population was assured of at least half of the seats on the city council. Hosea Williams, the civil rights activist, outpolled two white aldermen and won a runoff spot for the post of City Council President. Blacks in Atlanta had reached 50 percent of the population. Of the 206,270 registered voters, blacks represented about 49 percent.

After a two-week break from the general election, Jackson won over Massell in the runoff on October 16,1973. Jackson polled about 59 percent of the vote. Massell got 41 percent. On Tuesday, October 4, 1977, Maynard Jackson, incumbent mayor of Atlanta, Georgia, won reelection for another four-year term, over six opponents. Jackson won with 63.3 percent of the votes cast, or 52,838, over his nearest opponent who had 17.8 percent, or 14,842 votes. By winning over Massell, Jackson became the first black mayor of a major southern city. It should be noted here that in winning, it was probable that Jackson received only about half of the black registered vote. The rest was white. The race for president of City Council was won by a white, Wyche Fowler. Hosea Williams was defeated 75,799 to 43,693.

While Jackson was serving Atlanta as a Vice-Mayor and preparing to run for mayor, Arthur Louis was doing his research on the fifty cities. Where did Atlanta rate among the fifty? There were thirty-six with a rating of 30.0.

Atlanta was above Detroit which was worst in four categories: 1, 3, 16, 18. Detroit was best in only one: 10. Atlanta was worst in three: 1, 4, 5. Atlanta was best in one: 23. In the first category, murder and non-negligent manslaughter per 100,000 residents, Atlanta had the worst record of the fifty cities. Based on FBI data for 1972, 255 cases of murder and non-negligent manslaughter were committed in the city. Among the worst cities in this category, Atlanta led Cleveland, Detroit, Newark and Baltimore. When Jackson assumed office he promised to do something about cleaning up Atlanta crime, dope, poor housing and promoting a constructive Affirmative Action program in race relations. As a complement to the federal affirmative program, Maynard Jackson introduced a city Affirmative Action program for the city of Atlanta. He has required that any business gaining a city contract must use 15 to 25 percent of blacks on the job. Jule Sugarman, the city's chief administrative officer, has been ordered to implement the plan wherever possible. White businesses, of course, are crying foul. This is virtually always done when the majority are _required_ to conform to policy or law. The majority never seem to realize that power alone enforces compliance upon the minority. The law that is well administered is the saving grace for the minority. In his zeal to become an excellent mayor, Jackson no doubt did not realize the latent hostility which lurked in

the hearts and minds of white Atlantans. He was elected over
Sam Massell who had alienated the white downtown business
establishment and because of the overwhelming support of
the black Atlantans.

Because of the intransigence of the white police chief
Jackson called for the firing of the chief and the hiring
of a black commissioner. The control of crime in Atlanta is
only one of the problems. Irrespective of who the mayor is
in American cities, crime has been increasing at an alarm-
ing rate. Crime is a problem in Atlanta not only for the
police but also for the politician and businessman as well.
Other problems that have beset Atlanta are the lack of downtown parking and poor transportation. These are problems of
most big city areas. Hanging over Jackson's head is the
threat that the downtown businessmen will move to the suburbs.
Since Atlanta has a fence built around it through the inability to expand and annex land contiguous to it, it is locked
in just as the northeastern cities are.

The group of businessmen which has become disenchanted
with Jackson call themselves Central Atlanta Progress, a
euphemistic term for the Chamber of Commerce. These businessmen want a good liaison with city hall as well as a solution
to the problems of the inner city.

Maynard Jackson must think of all the people in
Atlanta, not just the power structure in downtown Atlanta.
The white power structure in Atlanta for fifteen years had

had an uneasy alliance with the black elite. These two forces were able to keep the Georgia Rednecks in line. Atlanta and Georgia had moved deeply into racial harmony since the days of suspender-snapping Gene Talmadge, but a politician must wear many hats. Because of the need of expressways to bring the outlying whites into downtown Atlanta, white businessmen made a pitch for building these expressways. To build these expressways the route was not only through the poor black areas, but also through the white areas. The white power structure had never had any trouble with the poor blacks. After a few rumblings from the ghetto, quiet would descend, and the next order of business was at hand. It was the white area which protested vehemently the building of the expressways. Maynard Jackson sided with the whites who opposed tearing up their neighborhoods to build such expressways. Thus, construction of the expressways was defeated. This defeat dismayed the downtown bankers and corporate lords, but the downtown power structure still held the trump hand.

In cities where the economic power is in the hands of whites and the voting strength is in the hands of the blacks, there is bound to be a clash of wills. Maynard Jackson was caught between these forces. Whites controlled the economic power to the extent that 97 percent was in their hands and only 3 percent was in the hands of the blacks.

Hosea Williams rallied at this mal-distribution in his run for the office of mayor. How to redistribute this imbalance was the basic problem of Maynard Jackson. Such restructuring through taxation was bound to run head-on into the power structure. The Atlanta downtown power structure furnished the money for Jackson in his run for mayor. Strains in the alliance of the black elite, black poor and the downtown power structure were showing. It was apparent to Jackson and to most other black mayors that there was no kind of solid white vote. When the white middle income class was threatened by the downtown power structure, such divisions strengthen the politician's hand. Jackson could gain strength from these differences. Trying to govern under these conditions was difficult, but possible. Being able to maintain a balance was the main problem of Jackson in Atlanta and any other black mayor under similar circumstances.

Writing in the New York Times, Drummond Ayers, Jr. gave a brief assessment of Atlanta's problems as 1975 waned. When the city's newest building, the Peachtree Center Plaza Hotel topped out in October, signs of a new vitality seemed to be brewing in the city that Sherman had laid waste to more than a century ago. This newest of hotels was built like a cylinder. Concrete and glass, the seemingly new motif of architects were lavishly displayed. This new symbol of the new Dixie offered to Atlanta a rallying cry of new energy and optimism for the future. Not so long ago, Atlanta boasted of a city too busy to hate. But as the recession bit deeper into the economy of this capital city, business interest quickly became disillusioned with the slogans of past years. Squabbling became a breakfast and dinner conversation piece. The basic issue was new sources of revenue. Like most cities fenced in by state laws, Atlanta was not able to expand its geographic boundaries to increase it tax base. This was the nub of the problem.

The inner city school system is now 85 percent black. Whites have fled to the suburbs and are still fleeing. The white business interests have invested millions of dollars in downtown Atlanta. The white business district is surrounded by a black belt. The constant imbalance of economic power which is controlled by the white interests and the political power that is controlled by the blacks, causes deep rumbling in both ethnic groups. Whites who work in the city and live in the suburbs, do not pay city taxes. The excuse the whites give is that the city is going black. Not so, says black Atlantans. Blacks take the attitude that whites have shirked their responsibility of paying taxes and paying for services which are done by the city. Whites again, as is seen in so many of the eastern cities, are fleeing (so-called from blacks) in order to forego paying taxes. This is an age-old dodge.

Wanting to become a greater than great city only

exacerbates Atlanta's problems. Trying to expand has created
strains in the political and economic climate of the city.
The answer, of course, is for the legislature to permit
Atlanta to annex the suburbs which have hemmed in the city,
but, to do this, the legislature will come under a searing
flame from the suburbs as well as the black electorate.[1]

The City of Angels

For a number of years the citizens of Los Angeles
had lost their confidence in Sam Yorty, the former mayor of
Los Angeles. It was hard for Sam Yorty to stay home; he was
always on the road. Bradley promised that if he were elected,
for at least the first year in office, he would attend to
the business of Los Angeles and not hit the road. Yorty had
beaten Bradley the first time he ran, but on the second time
around Thomas Bradley, former policeman, lawyer and City
Councilman defeated Sam Yorty. Bradley's victory was somewhat similar to Edward Brooke's victory in Massachusetts in
winning a seat in the United States Senate in 1966. Brooke
came from a state where the black population was only 3 percent. He ran against a white candidate. In Los Angeles, the
mild-mannered Bradley got 56 percent of the vote. Yorty
received about 44 percent. Bradley won over Yorty by 431,222
votes to Yorty's 334,297. There are 3170 precincts in Los
Angeles. Bradley's election could be termed an upset because
blacks only represent 15 percent of the 3,000,000 people in

Los Angeles.

The late Chief Justice Earl Warren administered the oath of office to Bradley. In his inaugural address Bradley promised a "turn to tomorrow." But even while he was speaking, forty American Nazi Party members dressed in the garb of the German Storm Troopers of a generation ago, paraded across the street in full view of the ceremonies at City Hall. The Jewish Defense League exchanged catcalls with the Nazis. No incidents occurred. The police kept members of the Jewish Defense League and the Nazis from mixing.

Less than six months after his vitory over the irascible and peripatetic Sam Yorty, Thomas Bradley had so endeared himself to Los Angeleans that he had become "one of them". To the blacks of Los Angeles as well as the whites, Bradley was a symbol of success. With visible evidence it had been proved that a black man could ascend to the mayor's office in Los Angeles. People were happy to see a black man as mayor of Los Angeles.

A poll in California, as late as May 12, 1974, showed that Tom Bradley was the most popular figure in California politics. It is apparent that Bradley has been able to rise above race and communicate with the body politic of the Golden State. This is a remarkable feat inasmuch as California has been known as a convoluted state, and Los Angeles

as rampant with racial probelms. The former Mayor, Sam
Yorty, had untold racial problems with blacks and Mexican-
Americans which kept him constantly under criticism. Bradley has an open door policy. Not only does he work long
days, but he also sets aside time to listen to all citizens
at a kind of town meeting. As Bradley settled down for his
four-year term what were his problems? One was the need of
a rapid transit system. Over the past twenty years, Los
Angeles had built an extensive freeway system. The auto has
been indispensable in Los Angeles. The freeway has become
the major means of transportation. However, recent environmental restrictions and an eroding tax base have curtailed
freeway construction.

The second major problem in Los Angeles is crime.
On the Louis analysis of fifty cities, Low Angeles ranks
worst on forcible rapes per 100,00 residents; hospital beds
per 10,000 residents; micrograms of particulate matter per
cubic meter of air. She ranks best in median value of owner
occupied single-family dwellings (estimated by owner); percentage of housing units lacking some or all plumbing facilities; and places of amusement and recreation per 100,000
residents. Los Angeles ranks among the five worst cities in
the crime of forcible rape. The three cities which outrank
her in rape are St. Louis, Newark, and Washington. Los
Angeles shows up best in median value of owner-occupied

single-family dwellings, percentage of housing units lacking some or all plumbing facilities and places of amusement
and recreation per 100,000 residents. Los Angeles ranked 22
among the fifty cities with an average of 24.6.

Our analysis of the four largest cities with black
mayors,using some of the Louis data can only view Newark,
Detroit, Atlanta and Los Angeles in a period of transition.
The fifty cities that Louis researched are only eyeopeners.
Even if a researcher fed into a computer more than 100
variables it is hardly likely that the researcher could come
up with which was really the best and which was worst. Moti-
vational researchers maintain that cities have personalities
like radio stations, TV stations, universities and corporations. The frame of reference is local. The politics
are local. Nowhere in Louis's data do we find the deadly hand
of racism. Whites seek to manipulate blacks for their own
ends.

The manipulation of East St. Louis, Ill. is a study
in retrospect of what should not happen to a medium-size
city in this country. In the medium and smaller cities,
mayors in general are limited in power. These smaller cities
usually have councilman - manager control. More will be said
about managerial control subsequently. But the problems of
the medium-sized cities are similar to those of the larger
cities. The difference is in degree. The inner cities of

this country are plagued with high unemployment, low educational attainments, low income, high welfare and poor housing. Some of these cities are political wastelands.

Tom Bradley, mayor of Los Angeles, California, is president of the National League of Cities. All of the mayors named in the foregoing pages attended the 50th Convention of the National League of Cities in Houston, Texas, December 5-8, 1974. At this convention, in one of the workshops, James E. Williams, mayor of East St. Louis, Illinois, complained that his city had an unemployment rate of 28 percent. Williams had been mayor of East St. Louis since 1971. Its population at this time was 70,000. It had grown by 22,000 since the 1970 census. The black population was extimated at 80 percent. Williams submitted four resolutions to the Convention; most of them concerned the poor and the rehabilitation of the depressed inner city core. The quality of living was considered the most important factor in the environment by the mayor of East St. Louis, who stated, "We can live with some pollution if people have jobs. I don't want a totally clean city with high unemployment."

The decline of East St. Louis began a long, long time before the change in mayors from white to black. In April, 1975, another change took place in mayors when William E. Mason, the school system superintendent, defeated the incumbent mayor, James E. Williams.

The economy of the once prosperous city of East
St. Louis was based on meat packing, iron forging, chemicals
and refineries. The decline started about twelve years ago,
when the white flight began and accelerated. The black population in 1975 was at 80 percent. Seventy percent of these
were either on relief or working at the poverty level. With
only 70,000 people in the city, 56,000 of these were black.
Of these 56,000, 39,200 were on relief or working at the
poverty level. With a declining population and a high poverty class, the tax base of the city shrank from $277,000,000
to $197,000,000, or 29 percent. A shrinkage of this magnitude
in the tax base can only have dire effects upon the education of the children living and going to school in the city.
In most Illinois cities real estate taxes provide 52 percent of most educational costs for the public schools. In
East St. Louis real estate taxes provided only 21 percent.
Not being able to float bonds for city improvements because
of the erosion of the tax base, East St. Louis was hard
put to raise finds for its city schools. If a city cannot
do this, then it is inevitable that the State of Illinois
should be expected to assume this responsibility, or, if the
state cannot or will not assume this function, then it is
up to the federal government to bear such responsibility.

We are concerned with the people of East St. Louis.

And so long as the solution will help people, then the solution can come from private, philanthropic and government sources. To abandon East St. Louis is no solution. The conditions which afflicted East St. Louis will only be transmitted to other places by the forces which caused these conditions in East St. Louis. These things have been white flight, black indifference, white intransigence, lack of commitment by the federal government, as well as by state government and by private avoidance of responsibility, a high crime rate, and corruption of city government as well as school officials. Replacement of the 10,000 jobs which have been lost will make East St. Louis more viable again. State and federal governments can bring jobs into the city by locating government agencies in the city.

Small Black Towns in the South

At the second annual Convention, the Southern Conference of Black Mayors in Atlanta, Georgia, April 10,1976, revealed to the delegates that conditions were slowly improving for the small black towns with black mayors in the South. These once poverty-stricken towns were getting sewers, water conduits, better housing and new businesses. Bennie Thompson, the youthful mayor of Bolton, Mississippi,was enthusiastic over these new developments. Attending the conference were sixty mayors from fourteen States and the District of Columbia. The organization has ninety members.

Mayor Thompson was running a health center in Bolton. He was receiving no salary as mayor. His town had received a Rockefeller Foundation grant of $274,000. Matching funds must be made by the State of Mississippi. Mayor Thompson stated that the white mayor he replaced was wealthy. The white mayor did not think that Bolton needed any help from the outside world. Everything was fine. Neglect of these black towns was based on racial prejudice. Now that these small towns were getting black mayors, even the poor whites were beginning to realize that the black mayors were trying to bring economic development to their towns. Thus there was a nascent beginning of a poor white-black coalition for better government, better housing and more jobs in these small towns in the South.

It appears that, in this society where institutionalized racism has been so ingrained that it has just about become a way of life for some of the population, the body would expect more out of an exceptional black man than a white man. The black athlete is expected to excel. If he does not, he is sent packing. A mediocre black athlete in baseball, football or basketball is soon traded or cast into limbo. Similar expectations are prevalent in politics. The black politician is expected to do more. Nuances of the voting public flow through all facets of the political faucets. When the black mayor is elected he is expected to do three basic things:

1. Clean up crime

2. Revive business conditions

3. Represent all facets of the population in the city

The first condition on cleaning up crime has frustrated not only most politicians in the cities, but also the voting public as well. For crime to be cleaned up, first the police must be cleaned up. Corruption among the police and politicians can preclude any kind of crime purification in the near future.

One way of helping the business community is easing up on some kinds of taxation on businesses, but the real help for the inner city businessman must come from the inner city residents and the suburbs. Better inner city housing, recreation, and education will help the businessman. Help for the businessman goes beyond the politician. Federal grants as well as state grants can do far more for the businessman than the local politician.

In a city with large enclaves of ethnics, it is a most difficult task to be sensitive to all segments of the city. If the mayor can appoint ethnic aides, this may help. But responding to all demands of ethnics as well as vested interests are beyond the realm of the kith of the mayor. The mayor's real purpose must be to know what he can do,

and what he cannot do. He cannot be all things to all
people. He must get some kind of clear-cut understanding
of what people want and the probability of achieving these
wants. The black mayor's job becomes one of a healer and
compromiser. Just about every large city in this country
has become polarized. Racism has caused this blight.

Beginning in 1977 there were 152 black mayors.
Many are in small southern cities. In cities of 50,000 or
more, there are sixteen black mayors, fifteen men and one
woman. In cities with white majorities there are forty
black mayors. The major cities with black mayors are
Washington, D.C., Los Angeles, Detroit, Newark, Gary,
Atlanta and New Orleans.

On Saturday, November 12, 1977, Ernest "Dutch"
Morial became the first black mayor of New Orleans, La.
Morial won over City Councilman Joe DiRosa in a runoff
election. After the 428 precincts had filed final tallies,
Morial had 89,823 votes and DiRosa 84,352 votes.

Morial's previous political experience was as the
first black state representative and the first black judge
on the state Court of Appeals.

One of the dilemmas of the minority politician is
seen between the backing of the political machine or party
in a particular locality and the necessity of minority constituents who are opposed to the party politician. A recent

example of this was the victory of Ralph Metcaff in Chicago. Metcaff, who placed second to Jesse Owens in the 1936 Olympics, and who was a Marquette graduate, ran on a platform for Congress in Chicago but did not have the backing of the powerful Daley Democratic Party. In the March, 1976, primary, however, Metcaff polled 71 percent of the Democratic vote in this district against Erwin France, who had the backing of the Daley machine. Black politicians have bucked the machine before and won. This recent example of Metcaff is notable.

Statutory Power

In the rush for political office, following the Civil Rights Act of 1964, and the trend to elect black mayors in small and medium-sized cities, what is the real or statutory power of these mayors? Do they really possess any political clout? Are they effective in a local government which has been derelict in its delivery system to the poor and middle income citizen? The time has not fully passed when blacks were given hand-me-downs to satisfy a measure of their demands. The time has not passed when blacks and other minorities usually moved into old houses which had previously been occupied by whites. The time has not passed when blacks and other minorities occupied the slums of this nation more often than did the whites. Are the whites deliberately turning these small and medium-sized cities over to the blacks, even though blacks are not in the voting majority? There is no evidence that whites are doing this.[1] However, these same whites come back to the city to work, shop, play, visit the recreation areas, parks, zoos, museums, sports and educational facilities. With the great uncertainty over energy, it is possible that we will see an influx back to the cities.

In constitutional law, it is known that cities are the creatures of the state. There is a dual system of government in this country-federal and state. Cities obtain charters from the state. But the anomalous nature of the dual system, really a tri-system, is metropolitan government. Some of the metropolitan areas are larger than states. In recent years the megalopolis is really interstate. Under these forms of government, governing is made more difficult for those who have the least power to govern as they are in smaller and medium-sized cities.

City charters usually stipulate the conditions to govern. Since the basis of all governing is the power to tax, all cities lack inherent power to tax except within limitations prescribed by the state. The main tax base of most cities in the small and medium class is the property tax. The sale tax or payroll tax has been developed as sources of revenue since the end of World War II. To get such power to tax, the city fathers must go to the state

legislatures. It is highly possible that New York City
could go bankrupt. When Mayor Beame needs additional funds
to run New York City, he must go to Albany with hat in hand
and ask for permission to do such and such. Grants from
the federal government will help, but they are not sufficient to bail a city like New York out of its financial
difficulties.

A second fallacy in this tax structure is the in-
flexible nature of the property tax. Inflation or recession
can hit a city, and yet there is little change in the property tax. It remains like an iceberg, although at times
the tax assessor's office may arbitrarily revalue property
to raise more revenue. But opposition from political foes
and taxpayers deter such taxing authorities from frequently
revaluing property.

Within such context fall the black mayors of the
small and medium cities to which they have been elected
over the past ten years. At the end of 1973, there were
ninety-five black mayors in the United States. Of these
ninety-five, one was a black woman-the first black woman
elected mayor in this country, Doris A. Davis, a former
city clerk of the city of Compton, California. She became
Compton's 25th mayor in 1973. Since the mayor's position is
parttime, she is paid $400 per month. At the end of 1974
there were 108 black mayors.

In a study by Herrington J. Bryce of the Joint Center for Political Studies, it was found that half of the black mayors lead from weakness instead of from strength. Students of government know that weak mayors are found usually in cities of medium sized population of 25,000 to 250,000. Bryce also found that these mayors are usually elected in constituencies where whites of voting age outnumber blacks, and a disproportionate number of the poor in these medium sized cities are black. The paradox here is that blacks are the poor and needy, whites are in greater numbers and are more affluent. The black mayor in such a situation is caught between two diametrically forces. How can he serve the poor and needy and at the same time satisfy the needs of the affluent without severe conflicts eroding his credibility among the blacks as well as the whites? An instance of where this happened involves Carl Stokes who won a second two-year term as mayor in Cleveland in 1969. During this second term a riot broke out in the Hough section. Some black militants had holed up, allegedly with machine guns, and threatened any whites coming into the area. The Cleveland police wanted to move into the area and clean out these "niggers". Stokes prevailed upon the police not to go in but to "cool it". Stokes and a number of influential blacks went into the hostile area which was at flash point. Because of Stoke's presence and the presence of other

influential blacks, the shooting did not take place. The
white police force in Cleveland never forgave Stokes for
this ploy. He had upstaged them. The masters of law and
order wanted to exert their authority over some hapless
blacks. In this instance Stokes lost his credibility in
the white community.

In another situation Stokes wanted to relocate
some low income blacks in public housing in a white area.
The howls what went up from these whites could be heard
all over the lake front city. Stokes desisted. Again, seeking to relocate these Cleveland low income blacks in public
housing, Stokes swung to the affluent black neighborhoods.
Again, such howls   went up from these affluent blacks
that Stokes again desisted. The issue in these instances
was not race, but economics - housing values. The people,
both whites and blacks,did not want their private housing
values lowered vis a' vis public housing. Stokes was frustrated to no end. He could understand the racist whites,
but he did not understand the affluent blacks. Carl Stokes
did not run for mayor in Cleveland again.

How Mayors are Chosen

Mayors are selected in various ways to head city
governments. These ways are the council-manager form, mayor-
council and commission. Under the council-manager form of
government, the city manager is appointed by the council

while the mayor is elected by the people. Under the mayor-council form, it is found that the mayor wields most of the powers of the chief executive such as appointing the cabinet members, making the budget, and controlling legislation. In the commission type of government he is an elected

member of the city council and representing some section of the city and is over a specific department over which the mayor has no control.

In Bryce Herrington's study of twenty-three cities with black mayors he found four with mayor-council. They were Pritchard, Alabama; Highland Park, Michigan; East Orange, New Jersey and Detroit, Michigan. Six had a mayor-council form with Chief Administrative Officer. There were New Brunswisk, New Jersey; Gary, Indiana; Newark, New Jersey; Atlanta, Georgia; Washington, D.C.; and Los Angeles, California. Council-manager was the most popular form, These were: College Park, Maryland; Ypsilanti and Inkster, Michigan; Chapel Hill, North Carolina; Compton, California; Boulder, Colorado; Pontiac, Michigan; Berkley California; Grand Rapids, Michigan; Raleigh, North Carolina; Dayton, Ohio; Cincinnati, Ohio. Only East St. Louis, Illinois had the commission form. Table XXXI below shows the size and class of the city with population.

Table XXXI

Twenty-three Cities With Black Mayors
Showing Size and Form of Government

Name and Size of City	Form of Government			
	Mayor-Council	Mayor-Council w/ Chief Adm. Officer	Council-Manager	Commission
25,000-49,999				
1. Pritchard, Alabama	X			
2. College Park, Maryland			X	
3. Highland Park, Michican	X			
4. Inkster, Michigan			X	
5. Ypsilanti, Michigan			X	
6. New Brunswick, New Jersey		X		
7. Chapel Hill, North Carolina			X	
8. Compton, California			X	
9. Boulder, Colorado			X	
10. E. St. Louis, Illinois			X	
11. Pontiac, Michigan				X
12. East Orange, New Jersey			X	
100,000-249,999				
13. Berkeley, California			X	
14. Gary, Indiana		X		
15. Grand Rapids, Michigan			X	
16. Raleigh, North Carolina			X	
17. Dayton, Ohio			X	
250,000-449,999				
18. Atlanta, Georgia		X		
19. Newark, New Jersey		X		
20. Cincinnati, Ohio			X	
500,000-999,999				
21. Washington, D.C.		X		
22. Los Angeles, California		X		
23. Detroit, Michigan	X			

Source: Focus Vol. 2, No. 12, October, 1974. Joint C enter For Political Studies, Washington, D.C. pg. A4.

Conclusion

Because of the nature of the city's status in this country-obtaining the right to govern by sufferance of the state-the mayors of all cities in this country are mere conduits in the process. Since mayors and cities lack inherent taxing power, of necessity they must go to the state and federal government for funds to operate their cities. Second, because of the type of government imposed upon cities by the electorate, it is apparent that city governments are not trusted or do not have as much credibility as state and federal government. The fear of ethnic groups because of the upsurge in black mayors is a throwback to their own fears among each other. The rip-off of Boston by the Irish, or Newark by the Italians are a few examples. Ethnics are fearful of other ethnics. It is because of these governing deficiencies that cities are difficult to govern.

Among the cities that black mayors govern, it is found that half of them are governing from a position of weakness. The weak forms of city government are the council-manager and commission. These are the forms in about half of cities that have black mayors. Bryce Herrington revealed these findings in his study.

One of two specific black political organizations for better municipal government is the Southern Conference of Black Mayors, Inc. incorporated in June, 1974. Boasting seventy member mayors located mainly in the southeastern quadrant of this country, the Conference named its first executive director, Bernard M. Porche, November 30, 1974. The major thrust of the Conference is to provide expertise to these mayors in the areas of management, engineering, economics, taxation, revenue sharing and other matters of local government. Since most of these small towns with black mayors do not have the resources to fund these experts, the Conference was organized to close this gap. The director, Bernard M. Porche, came to the organization from his position as director of Grants and Administration for the Environmental Protection Agency.

The second black political organization, the National Black Caucus of Local Elected Officials, met in Houston, Texas, December 1-5, 1975. The Black Caucus has more than 250 members. Pre-convention workshops were held. The Caucus sponsors the Joint Center for Political Studies in Washington, D.C. Board members include chairman Henry L. Marsh,Vice Mayor of Richmond, Va.; Mayor Maynard Jackson, Mayor of Atlanta, Georgia; Mayor Warren Widener, Mayor of Berkley, California; and Edward Bivens, Mayor of Inkster, Michigan. Besides the big city mayors who are members of the Caucus such as Tom Bradley, Kenneth Gibson, Coleman Young, Ted Berry and Richard Hatcher, there are a large number of municipal office holders who are also gaining professional expertise in running a city government by means of attendance at the

convention. These men and women are councilmen, comptrollers
and department heads. Small city mayors were represented
by Penfield W. Tate of Boulder, Colorado, A.J. Cooper of
Pritchard, Alabama, Wallace Holland of Pontiac, Michigan,
Howard M. Lee of Chapel Hill, North Carolina, William Haw-
kins of Phoenix, Arizona, Nathaniel Vereen, Eatonville,
Florida, Rev. Walter S. Taylor of Englewood, New Jersey
and Lyman S. Parks of Grand Rapids, Michigan.

Workshops and panels were held on modernization,
decentralization, crime, taxation, and drugs, the multifaceted problems of city government.

Resolutions at the convention called on Congress
and the administration to:

1. Continue the Office of Economic Opportunity,
   retaining funding local OEO offices at an
   80 percent level with 20 percent local funds.

2. Extend the Voting Rights Act, due to expire
   in August, 1975.

3. Establish an "inner city development" trust
   fund to be administered like the Highway Trust
   Fund.

4. Not cut back funds for drug abuse programs until
   legislation to halve the flow of heroin into the
   U.S. is effective.

5. Increase funding for the Comprehensive Employment
   and Training Act and devise a formula to eliminate
   excessive unemployment among minorities, youth,
   veterans and the elderly.

6. Renew revenue sharing if it is restructured to
   respond to community needs and is anti-discrimina-
   tory.

7. Call upon all levels of government to revamp
   civil service systems and end discrimitation,
   particularly through use of "result-oriented
   criteria" in hiring.

These resolutions submitted in Houston sum up the
plight of the cities in America in general and the plight
of the cities with black mayors in particular. Crime is
the number one problem for alleviation. Others are standard
housing, transportation, education and recreation. The
South is ripe for dynamic changes. In the eleven states of
the old Confederacy there were seventy-five elected officials
in these southern states, the small number of black elected
officials represents only 2 percent. There is still a long,
long way to go before the potential number of blacks holding elective office could reach 14,000.

Chapter XVIII

Crime and the Minorities

The fault, dear Brutus, is not in our stars,
But in ourselves, that we are underlings.
    Julius Caesar, Act I, Scene II

This statement is apocryphal. There is doubt and
hesitation in the quotation. Is there doubt and hesitation
among minorities and because of this doubt and hesitation
on achievement and accomplishment, does it lead to crime?
There is not a scintilla of evidence that such doubt and
hesitation lead to crime. However, there is evidence that
there exists among minorities and people in general a dwarf
complex. This kind of complex can envelop the individual
making him feel that he cannot achieve, cannot accomplish.
The dwarf complex can make the individual shrink from bigness and holistic endeavors. Such a complex can lead to
paranoia.

In the American milieu there is a definite hang-up
on bigness. To be big, one must think big. The bigger a
thing is the better it is loved, or worshipped. If bigness
is exponential, then smallness is inverse. Hence, we hold
here that the great society in which we live imposes a
terrible weight on smallness. This weight can be shifted by
the small person, through achievement and accomplishment.
It is not insurmountable.

But our analysis here is how can a feeling of being a

non-person which besets some minorities lead to crime-crime committed by the person as well as a "crime" committed by minions of the laws? Can a person cope with the system? Yes, once he learns the operations of the system. But will a person who is controlled by a dwarf complex ever learn the system? These are crucial questions and they are open questions. If a person feels that he cannot do, that he cannot cope with the system, the tendency is to strike back out of frustration. Our free enterprise-democratic system gives some license to this. The system has yet to control unemployment, racism, poverty, abuse by public authority and the constraint of bigness. These issues are so pervasive and abstract that they boggle the minds of even the most learned people. To the unlearned and unlettered they are an abyss, a vast chasm, or an endless hill to climb.

Since the minorities are the victims of unemployment, racism and poverty as well as abuse by public authority and the monopoly power, they are the first ones to fall before the pervasive requirements of the system. One of the basic requirements of the system is to go to school. Learn something well. Well, the black and Chicano boy in his teens is apt to drop out or be pushed out. He does not relate to either academic or vocational subjects. He knows that the system protects him, based on various state laws, up to age sixteen. So, he plays hooky from school, or the school officials slough off

the black or Chicano boy as another boy gone over the brink.
Now, that he is on his own with little guidance from his
family, he finds that jobs are hard to come by - those that
are paying wages of $4-$5 per hour. He does not want the low
paying jobs of $1.75 or $2   per hour. But he does   want
a girl. He learns early that he is not a eunuch. And also he
learns that girls like what he likes, and that is money. He
learns early that this is a highly skilled system. There is
not much need for the unskilled person. Self doubt creeps
deeper into him. Now he turns to those who have empathy with
him and consideration for his plight. These individuals are
similar to him, or they may be operating on the thin edges of
the law. His associates can become the numbers runner, dope
pusher, petty gambler, pimp, fence, burglar, car thief, rob-
ber or shoplifter. Or they can become the non-achievers, those
who are given to rhetoric, but can never defend their points
of view. Those are the individuals who will argue vehemently
that man has never gone to the moon, that the establishment
has pulled a snow job on the electorate.

This school dropout is not necessarily stupid, and he
can be highly intelligent. He begins to challenge the system,
but through the avenue of petty crime. In the black communities the ripoff is usually done by black teenagers looking for
color television sets, radios, stereos and any loose cash lying
around the house. Robberies, heists, and hijacking are usually

done by the habitual criminal. If the black teenager turns to the drug culture he becomes hooked. The pusher creates a market and the addict supplies the revenue. The ramifications of hits are endless. He is possibly caught before he withdraws himself or he may be killed by the pusher or killed by accomplices in the network of crime within which he has become enmeshed. In these instances, the criminal sows the seeds of this own destruction. Those who turn to crime and can avoid prosecution know that they are under constant surveillance by the police.

Police Power

In the broadest sense the police power of a state includes the health of its citizens--things that are harmful to health of its citizens, consumer complaints, violation of pollution laws. But in our analysis we are concerned with criminal law. Writing in the Center Magazine for September/October, 1975, Norval Morris states there are five areas of criminal law he would like to isolate. These are entrapment, conspiracy, the defense of insanity, compensation and sentencing. [1] Our discussion and analysis will not take us through all five, but will develop the three areas of entrapment, conspiracy and sentencing as they affect minorities.

Entrapment

Entrapment is one of the easiest ways of committing a crime. First, let us take the case of a hapless John Doe

in the ghetto. He is a teenage dropout. He has never committed a crime of any kind before. But he has <u>heard</u> about
the blue shirts, the men in blue, and how hard they are on
blacks and the ignorant. Actually such fear of cops can be
planted in a black teenager's mind so firmly that all cops
become devils in his mind. From this context, a policeman
can induce entrapment by his presence alone. If a person
is paranoid, just seeing a cop may cause the person to flee.
In so doing, the cop takes after the person thinking a crime
has been committed. As the cop pursues the person, contingent
on the time of day, and crowds, a great hubbub can occur
in the course of the chase, and may possibly bring in its
chain a number of compound misdemeanors.

Police forces in this country are known to set traps
for victims. Radar traps are set along the highways for
those exceeding the speed limit. Traps for jaywalking in
some cities are well known. Traps set by female members of
the police force to lure male victims who are seeking a
prostitute have been used. Norval Morris in his paper says
this is highly objectionable.

> A system of law that sets up this pattern of
> luring people into crime and then convicting them
> for it because of their "predispositions" or past
> convictions is wholly objectionable.[2]

The victims in these cases of entrapment are invariably
the poor, the minorities, the unlearned, the unlettered.

Conspiracy

Conspiracy and entrapment are almost similar. Only conspiracy implies an accomplice. Plea bargaing is a kind of conspiracy between the prosecution and the defense attorneys. Planting evidence, setting a victim up for the commission of an act is a much abused device in police-District Attorney procedure in this country. Again, such victims are those who have the least protection. True, public defenders are now being used and costs of such trials are borne by the state. But can a public defender match the awesome power of the district attorney? No.

Sentencing

It is commonly thought that sentencing for criminal acts in this country is done by the judge on the bench. It is not. It is done by the prosecution and defense counsel. The reference point is the judge. People who are demanding mandatory minimum sentencing are generally unaware of their ineffectiveness. Under such conditions of sentencing, prison terms are increased. Norval Morris inveighs against this form of minimum mandatory sentencing. However, it must be emphasized here that again it is the minorities who are victimized by such a form of sentencing.

Crime in the Ghetto

Crime in the ghetto in this country is at times the rawest kind of criminal behavior. Most of the writers on the problems in the inner city, however, have failed to show a cause and effect relationship between crime and the people who live in the inner city in the sprawling metropolitan cities of this country. The homicide rate in some of these cities, such as Atlanta, Georgia, and Detroit, Michigan,is the highest in the country. More than 60 percent of these are gun homicides. (See Chapter XVI This is one of the worst crimes of violence which takes place in the inner city. A caveat is in order so that the reader must understand that the crimes committed in the ghetto are not always committed by residents of the ghetto, but by individuals who drift in and out of the ghetto.

Sociologists and criminologists who have researched this problem have found that a black woman is subject to greater criminal hazards in the ghetto than a white woman would be subject to in a white environment. This means that there is a constant ripoff taking place in the black community by the black mugger, rapist, thug, hoodlum and thief. It is a well-known fact that blacks in the inner city are not protected by the police as well as are whites living on the periphery or whites living in the suburbs.

The age at which the young criminal is apt to become involved in a life of crime is between 18 and 34 years.[3]

This group has the highest unemployment rate of any group
in the country. They are denizens of pool rooms, school
dropouts, dope addicts, with all the terrible disadvantages
which appear to be visited on this age group. The social
values of this group are highly distorted. They are raised
in the ethos of the hustler, pimp, dress-off and the individual who always appears to be skirting the edge of crime.
Because of recessions, crime has jumped enormously in the
ghetto. But the social scientists have not as yet been
able to show whether the relationship is due to a lack of
income or to a malaise of despair or hopelessness.

There is much ambivalence in the ghetto. If there is
a black mayor with a white police chief in a given city, the
black mayor is hesitant to ask for gun control, because he
may feel that he is trampling on the rights of his constituents.
This hesitancy on the part of the black mayor can cause untold
problems for the white police chief. In a situation of this
kind the black hoodlum may feel that he has a license to
commit whatever act he so desires outside of the law, because
he thinks he **will not be** prosecuted to the full extent of the
law. The white police chief, therefore, must carry out his
duties in the face of adverse circumstances.

The greatest threat within the power of a state is
its criminal law. Criminal law is the haunting specter in
a a democratic society. Within this society it is found that

the usual victims of criminal law and its vast machinations
are the poor and the minorities. In almost any prison in
this country on the state level you will find that the majority
of the felons and miscreants are black, brown, Indians and poor
whites. Of course, the incarceration of these ethnic groups
will be derived from their population in the state or the
country.

Table XXXII below shows a comparison of whites, blacks
and Mexican-Americans in the Texas Department of Corrections
for a   sixteen-year period, 1958-1974. Texas is the third
largest state in the Union and at present has a population of
12,500,000. Anglos, or whites, represent 68 percent, Mexican-
Americans, 18 percent, black 12 percent and others or Orientals
tals 2 percent. The data from the Texas Department of Corrections show that the number of whites who are incarcerated,
runs from a high of 58 percent over the sixteen-year period
to a low of 43 percent in 1974.

Blacks incarcerated in the state prison system show
a low of 28 percent to a high of 42 percent. In 1973, almost
as many blacks were sent to the state prison as whites. This
was at a rate of more than three times their proportion in
the population.

The rate of incarceration of Mexican-Americans parallels their rate of population. The low was 13 percent in
1962 and 19 percent in 1959. Records were not available
for the years 1970-71-72.

Table XXXII

New Receives at the Texas Department of Corrections
Huntsville, Texas, 1958-1974

Year	White	Percent	Black	Percent	Mexican-American	Percent	Total
1958	2,675	56	1,329	28	738	16	4,742
1959	2,627	52	1,461	29	956	19	5,044
1960	2,761	55	1,452	29	822	16	5,035
1961	3,008	54	1,666	30	924	17	5,598
1962	3,244	58	1,651	29	713	13	5,608
1963	2,993	53	1,690	30	976	17	5,659
1964	2,959	52	1,727	30	1,037	18	5,724
1965	2,836	51	1,797	32	981	17	5,614
1966	2,520	51	1,587	32	814	17	4,921
1967	2,400	48	1,761	35	859	17	5,020
1968	2,236	46	1,712	35	896	19	4,844
1969	NA		NA		NA		NA
1970	NA		NA		NA		NA
1971	NA		NA		NA		NA
1972	2,937	44	2,730	40	1,082	16	6,749
1973	3,129	43	3,085	42	1,059	15	7,273
1974	3,194	43	2,884	39	1,289	18	7,352

Source: Texas Department of Corrections, Huntsville, Texas, March 5, 1976
Percents will not equal 100 in all cases because of rounding.

The Regional Planning Council of Allegheny County in Pittsburgh, Pennsylvania reports that blacks are victimized most. There was a higher percentage in prison in the county in 1973 than any other ethnic group. Of 9,300 cases going to court in 1975, only about 1,000 resulted in prison terms. The most likely victims of robbery, assault, burglary, larceny and auto theft are black. For cases which received a court verdict in 1975, a higher percentage of blacks than whites were sentenced to institutions for all major crimes. More blacks than whites went to trial for murder, robbery and larceny. Blacks held in the county prison increased by 18 percent in 1975 (a recession year) to a rate of 50 percent with whites increasing 10 percent. Head of the Council, the Rt. Rev. Msg. Charles Owen Rice, held that police can apprehend persons, but they can do nothing about the conditions which cause crime. There are distinctions between rich and poor and the high unemployment rate that affects the poor far more than the rich. Poor cooperation between municipal political factions exacerbate the problem. By focusing on McKeesport, a third-class city near Pittsburgh, crime was reduced. Tensions were relieved.[4]

Overall crime increased by 23 percent in Pittsburgh in 1975, a recession year. Rape was up 56 percent, robbery with the use of firearms up 23 percent and aggravated assault and battery with the use of firearms up 20 percent.

It has been shown that because of their blackness, brownness or poverty, these people are victimized by the criminal justice code, the district attorneys and the judges. Very seldom does a rich man, black or white, go to jail or serve any extended term of years. Thus, if the trials in our courts system are mainly for miniorities, then it flows from this thesis that minorities are in prison far out of proportion to their numbers in the population.

Federal Prisons

Data from the Statistical Report of the Federal Bureau of Prisons for fiscal year, 1973, show that there were 30,170 individuals committed to Federal Prisons in the United States. Distribution by race and sex are:

	White	Black	Red	Yellow	Other
Male 96%	65%	31%	2%	.2%	.2%
Female 4%					

The average age of the felon is thirty-one years. The average sentence is eighty-eight months. The data show that 31 percent are black, far out of proportion to the black population in this country. Some investigators will try to prove that blacks are more prone to crime than whites. Of course, spurious data can be used to prove anything, but there is no evidence that blacks are more prone to crime than any other thnic group. These data only show that disproportions exist in a society which is still racist-prone and hard on

poverty people. The designation of "Red" means that these
are Indians. Since Indians only represent about 700,000
people in this country, their federal prison population is
far, far out of proportion to their numbers.[5] Indians only
represent three-tenths of one percent of the U. S. population,
or three out of every one thousand Americans. It must also
be said that since most Indians reside on reservations,
Federal jurisdiction would be predominant and not state jurisdiction.

State Prisons

It is estimated that the prison population on the state
level is approximately 250,000. The largest prison populations
are found in the most populous states--California, New York,
Pennsylvania, Texas, Illinois and Ohio. Again, it is found
that blacks outnumber, in proportion to population, all other
ethnic groups.

Severe overcrowding of prisons in the South is causing
constant complaints and lawsuits aimed at preventing overcrowding. The Alabama prison system is made up of four main
prisons: Holman, Fountain Correctional Center, Draper Correctional Center and the Medical and Diagnostic Center at Mt.
Meigs. These four prisons were built to house 2,212 felons.
The Poverty Law Report in November, 1975, stated that these
prisons had an overload of 1,550 felons. An additional 600

convicts which had recently been sentenced were being held in county jails prior to being transferred to these prisons.[6]

Based on criminal statistics furnished by the FBI, our prison population is increasing. In Houston, Texas, Federal judges have ruled that Harris County must build better facilities for its increasing prison population. It is presumed that better facilities or new prisons are needed in most of the states. But Jessica Mitford in her book, Kind and Usual Punishment, says that the people who live in these disgraceful dungeons are not clamoring for new prisons.[7] Prisoners are in opposition to new facilities. New prisons only increase the prison bureaucracy. More prisons mean more money for the guards and the administrators of these prisons. So, again, we see much evidence for maintaining a built-in labor force of convicts. It is possible that a better case for tax-payers could be made by using money for new prisons for real rehabilitation of prisoners for our prisons are not run for rehabilitation, but for punishment. Early release from prison to the half-way houses accomplishes far more rehabilitation and costs far less than any spate of new prisons or correctional facilties.

The patent fear spread by police forces against early release or paroles for the criminal is that "do we want to not loose murderers and robbers on the unsuspecting public?" Of course, this is an over-simplification of this issue. The

public does not want the habitual criminal released to prey
upon the public, but they do want the cost of administering
the prison population reduced. The victims of this system--
those who are in the prisons--believe implicitly that this
country wants a large prison population, an underclass to
work at low wages to support the establishment.

The secret of this immense profitability is not
hard to discover; in fact it is laid out for us in
the board of directors' report. Pay rates for inmate
workers in the federal industries range from 19¢ to
47¢ an hour (in California the great majority are
in the lower pay brackets; the average wage is 26¢
an hour). In 1970, 5,478 inmates earned $3 million
for an average of $547 a year. In the same year, the
report informs us, annual production for each inmate
worker was $12,168, and the average profit per worker
stood at $2,350.

This report does not mention that in early 1971, a
full-fledged strike, supported by over 90 percent of
the convicts, broke out in McNeil Federal Penitentiary,
largely over the inadequacy of job training provided by
prison industries and the demand for a 35 percent wage
increase. I asked Mr. Norman Cousin, director of the
Federal Bureau of Prisons, why the bureau refused a demonstrably modest demand for an increase that would have
raised the average wage from 26¢ to 35¢ an hour. He
answered, as employers are wont to do, "We'd go broke
if they got a 35 percent increase." This, in a year
when net profits were close to $10 million.

Texas boasts a comparable success with prison industries. "The enemy is inmate idleness, so you put him to
work," writes Jack Waugh in the Christian Science Monitor.
"Working that philosophy, George Beto (director of the
Texas Department of Corrections) has built the Texas
prison system into a clean, highly disciplined industrial dynasty." Of the 60¢ a day per inmate allotted
for food, only 13¢ worth has to be bought. Prison
industries in Texas, says Waugh, generated $7,083,077
in sales from September,1970,through August,1971, and
he described the new prisoner's introduction to the
clean industrial dynasty: "The first job every inmate

coming into the Texas system gets, if he is able-bodied is six months on the line--hard, back-bending labor in the fields, and recalcitrant, rebellious prisoners are often sent back to the line as punishment. Armed bosses on horseback supervise as the inmates stoop in the fields. A boss called the 'long arm,' with high-powered rifle over his saddlehorn, watches from a distance for any sign of an attempted break.

From the convict's point of view the changeover from contract labor to prison industries is merely a switch in labels, as comments from two widely disparate sources show. In an interview with Mark Lane, published in the Black Panther, Huey P. Newton explains why he refused to work while imprisoned in California, choosing instead to suffer the punishment of solitary confinement for more than a year: "The prison is a capitalistic enterprise. It differs very little from the system where inmates are 'farmed out' to growers. In those instances the growers compensate the state. Most civilized people agree that the system is abhorrent. Yet the California method is to employ the reverse system. The convicts are not farmed out, the work is farmed in. What factors remain the same? The convicts are still exploited by the state; the work is still accomplished; the state is still compensated.8

The underground in this country also believes that there is a studied purpose to keep a large prison population of blacks, browns, Indians and poor whites working at slave wages to supply license plates, and other commodities for themselves and various entities. The concentration complex is uppermost in prisoners' minds that prisons are used to confine the aggressive, rebellious type of individual who does not fit into the system. Prisoners are a form of captive labor which is shared in by all citizens whether they know it or not. Mitford reports that Federal Prison Industries is a most profitable line of business. Over a thirty-five year period, 1935-1970, the Federal Prison Industries had a gross income of $986 million, "increasing their net worth by $50 million and contributing $82 million in dividends to the U. S. Treasury." [9]

Summary

What are the chances for improvement in the criminal justice system in this country? Not much. The Criminal Justice Reform Act of 1975, which was supposed to revise the criminal code in this country, was introduced in the Senate in January, 1975, by Senator John L. McClellan. The document runs to a 753-page bill. The bulk and complexity of the bill in, of, and by itself is forbidding. The press has begun criticising the bill on the grounds that it is weak on the first amendment. The need based on how it affects minorities is the fact that it does not de-criminalize offenses such as vagrancy, minor drug, prostitution and gambling. There is a need of deferring first offenses when they are not of a capital nature or felony.

The Criminal Law Bulletin has reported that 80 percent of the cases tried each day in this country originate in the lowest income group. Again and again, it is obvious that these individuals come from the poor, black and brown groups. The evidence is now overwhelming that the prison system is used as a club against the poor and black people in this country.

Is there a high correlation between increased crime
and a recession? Yes, say the police enforcement officers.
The recession of 1973-75 saw a decided increase in crime in
American cities over the previous years. Colin Frank, administrator of mental health services in the Federal Bureau
of Prisons, says there is a direct correlation. The time
lapse between the commission of a crime and incarceration,
in a federal prison, is about fifteen months. High unemployment, job layoffs, are felt by prison officials to be a cause
of fights, homicides, felonies, increase in pilfering, shop-
lifting, burglaries and petty thefts.

The difficulty of establishing a close connection betwe-
en increasing crime and recession is that we have no data to
base the linkage on. The great depression of the thirties saw
an increase in crime, but no cause and effect relationship was
established. But irrespective of the gap in theory, police
chiefs in general feel that there is a general connection between
high crime and the level of the economy. The lower the level
of the economy, the more the crime. The higher level of the
economy, the lower will be the crime level.[10]

Crime in the cities varies widely from city to city.
In the Southwest in Houston, Texas, a hectic, raucous city
sprawls over 503 square miles. It is the oil marketing capital of the world and is growing at such a rapid rate that
the recession of 1973-75 did not pause long enough to cause
ripples in its burgeoning economy. Minorities within the city-

blacks and Mexican Americans with a sprinkling of Chinese and other Orientals live throughout the city. Blacks represent about 30 percent of the population and Mexican-Americans 12 percent of the population. In the school population blacks are more than 50 percent of the student body. There are ghettoes in Houston, but they are not heavily concentrated ghettoes such as in Chicago's Southside or New York's Harlem. Because unemployment is low, Houston ranks about thirty-fourth in crime among the large metropolitan centers in this country. Fear of walking in the city does not stalk the citizen as in other large metropolitan areas.

On the local level, crime can be reduced. We cite Atlanta as a case in point. Sending white policemen into the inner city is almost like an occupying force. There is a need of more and more black policemen/women. The Atlanta case is an example.

When Maynard Jackson appointed A. Reginal Eaves as the police commissioner in 1974, Atlantans were aghast. at least the white ones. This thirty-nine year old law school graduate seemed naive and unqualified for the job. Atlanta had a 1500 man police force which appeared inadequate to cope with a rising crime rate. When Eaves took over, Atlanta was the murder capital of the United States. After about eighteen months on the job, violent crimes in Atlanta had dropped by about 10 percent. Homicides had been reduced from

248 to 195. Break-ins and burglaries had dropped from
16,802 to 14,501. Stickup artists and hijackers had reduced
their activity from 4,357 to 3,887. In comparison with the
rest of the country where crime in 1975 increased by 11 percent, in Atlanta it increased by only 3 percent. Observers
have attributed this decrease in violent crimes to Eaves'
hard approach to black on black. This city which Margaret
Mitchell made famous with her Gone With The Wind now has
three out of every five Atlantans black. But it was in the
black areas where most of the crime occurred . Either the
largely white police force did not care or provided inadequate police protection which caused the crime rate in the
black areas. Eaves demoted about 10 percent of the police
force and promoted black officers who had been held back
for years by the white police chief. The white officers
immediately labeled this as reverse discrimination yet they are
still 70 percent of the police force.

REFERENCES

1. Norval Morris, Dean of the School of Law, University of Chicago, Center Magazine, Vol. VIII, Number 5, September/ October, 1975, pg. 44.

2. Ibid.

3. Crime in the United States, 1972, issued by Clarence M. Kelley, Director, FBI, August 8, 1973, pp. 123, 136, 137, Supt. of Documents, Washington, D. C.

4. Regional Planning Council, 1425 Park Building, 355 Fifth Avenue, Pittsburgh, Pa. 1976.

5. Federal Bureau of Prisons, Fiscal Year, 1973, U. S. Department of Justice, Federal Bureau of Prisons, Management Programs Branch, Washington, D. C.

6. Poverty Law Report, Review of Advance in the Legal Rights of the Poor, Vol. 3, Number 5, 1001 South Hull Street, Montgomery, Alabama, 36101.

7. Jessica Mitford, Cruel and Usual Punishment, Alfred A. Knopf, Inc., New York, 1973, pg. 183.

8. Ibid., pg. 197.

9. Op. cit. 196

10. Wall Street Journal, Vol. LV, No. 38, February 25, 1975, pg. 1 - 23.

Chapter XIX

Minorities in Sports and Professional Baseball

The Sport of Kings

The Kentucky Derby is the sport of kings in this
country. Until the advent of Plessy v. Ferguson, blacks
participated widely as jockeys in the Kentucky Derby. The
first running of the Derby was in 1875. Oliver Lewis, a
black, hunched low over Aristides, won the event in a field
of fifteen. Small black teenagers dominated the running of
the first Derby. Fourteen of the fifteen in the first Derby
were black.

Thus the early years of the Derby saw blacks domina-
ting the event. In 1877 William Walker riding Baden-Baden
won the event. Isaac Murphy, winner of three subsequent
Derbies, made his entry in 1877, but finished fourth riding
Vera Cruz. Winning the 1880 was George Lewis with Appollo.
It was not until 1884, when Isaac Murphy, the spindly
young black jockey, won the first of his three Derbies.
As reported in the Louisville Defender[1] Murphy came from
behind and won, riding Buchanan. Murphy had a knack of knowing horseflesh and how to handle horses. In this same
Churchill Downs meeting Murphy led the field in the Kentucky
Oaks and the Clark Stakes, an accomplishment which has never
been repeated. The other two Derby wins for Murphy were in

1890 and 1891 when he rode <u>Riley</u> and <u>Kingman</u>. These three wins for the diminutive jockey rode in the record books for thirty-nine years, and was not beaten for fifty-seven years.

During Murphy's remarkable career he rode 628 winners out of 1,412 mounts, riding his first winner at the age of fourteen. Murphy was a multiple winner at the Latonia Derby and the American Derby at Washington Park. When the National Museum of Racing at Saratoga Springs in New York was dedicated, Murphy was the first jockey voted into the Jockey Hall of Fame.

The Halcyon days of the black jockey were in the years before the turn of this century. Black jockeys won fifteen Kentucky Derbies, ten in Latonia, six in America, six in St. Louis and five in Tennessee. Jimmie Winkfield, almost an equal to Murphy, rode Derby winners in 1901 and 1902. He placed second in 1903.

After Winkfield's triumph in 1902, the dominance of the black jockey started to decline. Racing enthusiasts started to organize at this time. Purses on these races began to increase. White jockeys, realizing the financial gains to be derived from booting home a winner, began to exclude blacks. The fallout from Plessy v. Ferguson began to take its effect. Highly unorganized, the black jockeys were by-

passed. The few black jockeys, who continued to ride, rode
a race of terror. They were subject to taunts and dangers
in riding for those two minutes in races dominated by whites.
The black jockey was an outcast among strangers. The 1911
Derby was the last in which a black rode. Jess Conley riding
Colston, finished third. The era of the black jockey was at
an end. For two generations a black jockey has not ridden
in the Derby. However, just as suddenly as he disappeared
from the Sport of Kings in this country, he can return just
as suddenly. Today is it unsportsmanlike and unconscionable
that any sport should be all white or all black. There are
forces which are urging the return of the black jockey. Will
the black jockey ride again?

In harness racing, the first outstanding black driver at the Yonkers Raceway had a winning season in 1975. Lew
Williams won with more than 20 percent of his horses during
the season at the New York track.

Boxing

It was not until the art of Boxing, which originated
in England and thence came to America, that minorities, especially blacks, came into their own. The commercialization
of boxing which made a sport, a business to the business
man, and an art to the practitioner as well as a business,
developed the black practitioner to the very height of his
attainments.

Boxing is a sport where we have a one on one situation. The art of boxing, like so many contact sports is highly brutal. Nearly always there is a winner or loser. Very seldom is there a draw. The blood lust of the spectator cries out for combat. It is a kind of throwback to the Roman gladiators. The boxers receive the accolades of the crowd. A hand (s) is waved in acknowledgment. The contestants are saying "Morituri turi tu salutami:" we who are about to die salute you. One must lose and one must win. Thunderous applause rises from the crowd. Once hands are shaken, the deadly business of brutality begins. The spectators want a winner. The feint, jab, half crouch, left hooks and right crosses highly appeal to the boxing fan. Boxing seems to bring out the primeval instinct in man, and also, in women. The female of the species goes in heavily for boxing as well as having an affinity for wrestling.

In the art of boxing the ethnic affiliation of the participants takes on the major aspect of a battle. It is not that ethnics have an inferiority complex, but that they feel they are carrying their race on their shoulders. So, usually, when a black boy fights a white boy, he feels he is representing all black people. All of his feelings of conquest are in his clenched fist encased in skin tight leather gloves. The black boy must win at all costs. He

must not lose. He would be a discredit to his race. Of
course, this psyched up feeling permeates his entire being
when winning. When he loses, as he eventually must, he
becomes like any other mortal.

It is possible that the greatest athlete who has
ever lived is this country was the legendary Jim Thorpe,
an Indian who completed his education at the Carlisle
Indian School. At the 1912 Olympics in Stockholm, Thorpe
won the pentathlon and decathlon.

For the first half of the 20th century, Thorpe was
recognized as America's greatest athlete. He was a star
in college and in professional football. Walter Camp
named him twice in 1911, and 1912, on his All-American
teams. Thorpe scored 25 touchdowns and 198 points for
Carlisle Institute in Pennsylvania. At Carlisle he was
under the tutelage of famed Glenn "Pop" Warner. He also
attended Haskell Institute at Lawrence, Kansas. Thorpe
ended his athletic career in 1919. He played six seasons
with the Boston Braves. He hit .327 while playing in
sixty games in 1919. Thorpe was a superior performer in
baseball, football and track. However, it is alleged that
he appeared in a semi-professional baseball game in 1911.
His amateur status was revoked and all of his medals were
forfeited. President Ford has asked the Olympic Committee
to restore the gold medals to Jim Thorpe. Grace Thorpe,

daughter of Jim and staff worker for Senator James Abourezk, Democrat of South Dakota, is also trying to get her father's medals restored.

From the time of Jack Johnson and Harry Wills down to George Foreman, Joe Frazier and Muhammed Ali, blacks have dominated the heavyweight ranks. Jack Dempsey was an exception. The Manassa Mauler had fast hands as well as a lethal punch. Another exception was Gene Tunney. This ex-Marine, who had built up a reputation in the Marine Corps, bested Dempsey in the Battle of the Long Count. Dempsey, in 1927, had virtually knocked out Tunney, but the master boxer bested the puncher and Tunney walked off with the championship. Instead of going immediately to a neutral corner, Dempsey, momentarily lingered over his fallen foe, possibly savoring his conquest. The referee motioned him to a neutral corner, so he could begin counting. But in those few seconds of indecision, Tunney was able to recover. Before the count went to ten, the bell sounded. Tunney's seconds hustled him to his corner and feverishly went to work on him. Having recovered sufficiently from the blows of Dempsey, Tunney was able to outbox Jack the rest of the fifteen rounds and win the fight. With the title back securely in white hands--during the time of Johnson, Langford, Willard--the sports writers talked of a white hope-- there was a period of taking stock of the game. But

immediately a cry went up for Tunney to fight Harry Wills.
The black sports writers called Wills the Black Panther.
Wills made a fetish of fasting for a week or two during
the year. He fasted to cleanse his body of impurities
and to keep in trim. Practically all during Wills'life he
kept trimmed down and ready for a go at Tunney, but he
never got the chance. Racial feelings during this period
in the United States history were at a fever pitch. You
see, Jack Johnson had married a white woman, and the white
press had never forgiven Jack for doing this. This former
longshoreman, who was born in Willis, Texas, a bucolic village north of Houston, devastated his foes with such dis-
patch that he was feared and hated throughout sportdom.
It was the irony of our times that when all the miscegnation
laws of various states were declared null and void; the case
was based on a white man, married to a black woman in Virginia, who challenged these miscegnation laws. The Supreme
Court in Loving vs Baker declared in the white man's favor.
The couple had three children and lived in the western part
of the state of Virginia.

The dominance of blacks in boxing is not because of
superior ability over whites, but because of a greater concentration of their mission. However, during the long,
tortuous ascendancy of blacks in boxing, other people have
had their reasons for such dominance.

During the great depression, when Joe Louis cut such a huge swath through the heavyweight rank, he was thought of as a superman or super heavyweight. The Brown Bomber, as he was known to the sports writers, practically annihilated such opponents as Jim Braddock, Primo Carnera, and Max Schmeling among others. Hugh Johnson, the administrator over the Blue Eagle during the great crash, who was known as the price administrator in the thirties, stated that blacks were superior to whites physically because they had just come out of the jungle. This late, hoary handed administrator, was as usual resorting to so-called cultural differences. Also to explain why Jesse Owens was so fast, according to a coach at Penn State, he had a spur on his heel.

In the light of what has gone on in the past, and what we know from the present, statements such as the above evoke laughter from the reader. These were pure myths and shibboleths. But all of these were not from the white side of the street. Blacks had hangups also. When Joe Louis came out of Alabama and went to Detroit, he worked for Ford Motor Company. His handlers were John Roxborough and Julian Black. These Detroit businessmen hired the wily Jack Blackburn to train Joe. The fortunes of most Americans were down, way down, and, to a greater extent were the blacks. When Joe began winning, he was looked upon as a savior of his race. When he was beaten by Max Schmeling in his first fight with the German, despair was rampant among blacks. It was not until Joe regained the crown in a return match that blacks again boasted of their champion.

While blacks have long dominated the fight game, promotion of the fights and entree into the executive suites have been a white preserve. With the Ali-Foreman fight in Zaire, came the first black promotor. Don King, the ex-numbers baron of Cleveland, Ohio, was able to snatch the plum of plums--as a promoter. How did King pull this off? He appealed to the race instincts of Muhammad Ali. He knew that Ali was the greatest drawing card in the fight game. The former Cassius Clay of Louisville, Kentucky was not only a great fighter, but highly articulate and a poet of sorts. Sports writers trailed after him because he was usually good copy. Clay had changed his name to Muhammad Ali and was a follower of Elijah Muhammad, the Black Muslim leader. At the height of the Vietnam War, Ali mentioned that he had no quarrel with those Vietcongs. Immediately he was vilified in the press. But when American youth turned against the war, and the demonstrations and recriminations against the war in Vietnam caused the late President Johnson to withdraw from the 1968 Presidential race, Ali had moved from hero to anti-hero and back to hero again in the short span of five years.

Track

When Jesse Owens won three gold medals in the Olympics in 1936, he no doubt had Hitler in mind. This evil genius, as Churchill called him, saw Owens win his medals, but he left the Berlin Stadium because he did not want to shake Owens' hand. In these individual sports, ethnics breached the wall of prejudice early. In college competition the great black track stars form a long, long line from the days of Duke Slater down to Bob Hayes. When the track coach at Penn State could not find any spurs on Owens' heels to explain his speed, scientists gave up seeking a cause and effect relationship to explain why black boys could outrun white boys in the 100 yard dash, the 220 and the 440. More of them went out for track. They were well motivated. They wanted to excel.

Whereas the individual sports such as boxing and track encouraged ethnic participation in their early development, the three great team sports, baseball, football and basketball, resisted such participation.

Baseball

History does not record the ethnic group that played the first sandlot baseball game was played in 1839, in Cooperstown, New York, home of the baseball Hall of Fame. The game was sponsored by General Abner Doubleday. Cooperstown is a little, sleepy hamlet in upstate New York, about seventy miles from Binghamton, New York. Every August, this area takes on worldwide proportions when baseball's greats are inducted into the baseball Hall of Fame.

The first organized game was played in Hoboken, New Jersey, in 1857, between the teams of Brooklyn and New York. It was a nine inning game. The first team scoring 21 "aces" or runs was declared the winner. In 1869 the first professional game was played in Cincinnati, Ohio. In 1867, the National League was organized.[2]

Because blacks were excluded in the early years of baseball, they formed their own teams. In the twenties and thirties the Negro leagues had teams such as the Homestead Grays, Indianapolis Clowns, Birmingham Black Barons, Newark Eagles, Philadelphia Stars, Pittsburgh Crawfords, New York Black Yankees, Chicago American Giants, Kansas City Monarchs and Baltimore Elite Giants.

It was recently revealed by Ulish Carter, sports editor of the Pittsburgh Courier, that the committee formed by the Hall of Fame to select black players for the Hall of Fame that played in the old Negro league could be discontinued in a year or at the most five years. The committee set up to select black stars will then go out of business. This was done to expiate the guilt of the whites who made the selections from the majors, long before the majors included blacks.

The first seven black players selected thus far have
been Satchell Paige, Josh Gibson, Monte Irvin, Buck Leonard,
Cool Papa Bell, William "Judy" Johnson, and Oscar Charleston. If the committee is discontinued, contends Carter,
there is a platoon of blacks eligible for induction. Some
of these future selections could be Andrew (Rube) Foster,
pitcher and manager; Ted Page, star outfielder; Smokey Joe
Williams, pitcher; John Henry Lloyd, shortstop; Vic Harris,
outfielder; Cum Posey, manager.

A player must receive 75 percent of the votes from
the committee to be chosen. Players are chosen from a list
of twenty candidates. Present members of the committee
are Monte Irvin, RBI leader in the National League in 1951
with 121, assistant to Bowie Kuhn; Eppy Barnes, white
player who played against blacks; Roy Campanella, Frank Forbes, Eddie Gottlieb and Judy Johnson. Sam Lacy recently
resigned from the committee. These teams produced great
stars in the persons of Josh Gibson, Satchel Paige, Roy
Campanella, Cool Papa Bell, Buck Leonard, Monte Irvin, Larry
Doby, Judy Johnson, Oscar Charleston, Smoky Joe Williams,
Rube Foster, Ted Page and Willie Wells. It has been said
by those baseball buffs who lived in the halcyon days of
the past, that the late Josh Gibson hit more home runs in
one year than Babe Ruth or Rodger Maris. It was also
claimed that he hit them farther. Norman Tweed, the black

sports historian has followed these black players for more
than a generation.

Tribute to Vic Harris

Vic Harris, now living in Los Angeles, managed the
legendary Homestead Grays for nine years. In his baseball
career, Vic won six pennants as manager of the Homestead-
Washington Grays from 1937 to 1942. On his team he had such
stalwarts as Buck Leonard, Cool Papa Bell and the longest
long-hitting catcher at the time--Josh Gibson. After Vic
left the team, in 1942, to take a job in the war industry,
the Grays won three more pennants.

In Cleveland, in 1934, Vic hit one of Dizzy Dean's
first pitches for a triple. In Diz's own way, he called
Vic a clean name. As Vic rounded second, he told Vic he
would not hit a pitch again. When Vic came up again he
threw a first pitch over Vic's head. The Grays beat Diz's
team in Cleveland and beat them in Pittsburgh.

The late Dizzy Dean admitted that Satchel Paige was
the best pitcher he ever saw. It was the usual custon in
the thirties when the World Series was over to barnstorm
with a white team and black team. Games were played in the
South during October and early November. The players could
test themselves in a black-white, white-black contest. The
games usually drew large crowds because the black population

gloried in their stars and the white population came to
see the black stars lose to the white stars. It was while
playing these games, matching Paige and Dizzy, that Satchel
would beat Dizzy. Of course, these results were seldom if
ever published in the white press because it would challenge the owners of the major leagues teams on quality. But
Dizzy admitted Paige's superior pitching ability. Even prior
to the great base stealing of Maury Wills and Lou Brock,
Cool Papa Bell, who was inducted into the Hall of Fame in
1974 was the fastest. Satchel Paige remarked that Bell was
so fast that he could turn the light off in the room and
jump in bed before the room got dark.

On August 29, 1977, Lou Brock of the St. Louis
Cardinals broke Ty Cobb's record for stealing bases. Before
the 1977 season had ended Brock had stolen 893 bases. He
broke Cobb's 49 year record of 892 stolen bases. In 1974,
Brock broke Maury Wills' record of 104 stolen bases in
one season when he pilfered 118. Cobb's old record for
stolen bases in one season was 96.

While breaking Cobb's record, Brock needed only 2,376
games. The Georgia "Peach" stole his bases in 3,033 games
over a span of 20 years, 1908 - 1928 during which time he
played with Detroit and the Philadelphia Athletics. Brock
made his record in 16 seasons with the Chicago Cubs and
St. Louis Cardinals.

The most recent stars in the majors, Willie Mays,
and Hank Aaron, got their start playing in the black league.
Getting into the majors was a long, traumatic experience
for blacks. The black press and black sports writers had
for years virtually pleaded with the major league owners
to let the bars down. Pressure began to build at the beginning of World War II.

The first spokesman for blacks in sports was Paul
Roberson, the great baritone, screen and stage star. Roberson had an established reputation as a great leader. He had
won fame as an athlete competing in football at Rutgers. He
had gone to Lincoln in Pennsylvania where his father matric-
lated, but later transferred to Rutgers. The white
players at Rutgers were so prejudiced and hated blacks so
much, that they did everything possible to make Roberson's
participation unpleasant, but his ability prevailed in the
end. He became an All-American at Rutgers. From the
athletic field he went into stage, movies and concerts. The
establishment hated Roberson because he defied them.

At a meeting of the major leagues in Cincinnati in
1941, Roberson made a plea before the baseball magnates to
employ blacks in the majors. These baseball men listened
politely but continued business as usual. It was six years
later that Jackie Robinson, one of the greatest athletes
produced in this country, donned a Montreal uniform. The

next year he moved up to the then Brooklyn Dodgers, now
known as the Los Angeles Dodgers.

Roberson made frequent trips to Russia, and on racial
matters he believed at this time that Russia did not discriminate against races such as blacks in the way ingrained
segregation existed in the United States. Roberson praised
Russia in her race relations and told how the October Revolution in Russia, in 1917, had overcome race prejudice and
had passed laws forbidding racial discrimination. The
American Legion was so incensed at Roberson, at one time in
his career, that they wanted to know why, if he loved Russia
so well, he did not live there.

The United States still had the blight of legal
prejudice, mainly in the South. In later years Roberson
softened his criticism of the United States, but only after
the case of Brown vs School Board 1954 and the Civil Rights
Acts of 1964-65.

For a while Roberson imposed a self-exile upon himself. He returned to the United States in 1963 and retired
to Enfield, Connecticut. In 1973, ten years after his
self-imposed exile, 3000 persons squeezed into Carnegie Hall
in tribute to Paul Roberson on his 75th birthday. He died
on Friday, January 23, 1976 in Philadelphia, Pennsylvania.

The late Branch Rickey had brought Jackie Robinson
into the majors in 1947. Rickey was accorded acclaim by

sports fans for his courage in taking this great risk, but
for breaking the color line he would be condemned by the
hard line segregationist as well as by the lily white competitor. The southern players in the majors hated blacks
and did not want to compete with them. The southern boys
knew it was an economic problem, but, as usual, it was
cloaked in sex and shibboleths. White sports writers for
the Associated Press, United Press International and United
Press would often say, "Would you want one of them to marry
your daughter?" As if marrying one's daughter had anything
to do with playing baseball.

After reams of writing and speculation, the first
black manager was announced to the baseball world on Thurs-
day, October 3, 1974. The Cleveland Indians had selected
Frank Robinson to manage their club for the 1975 season. Thus
Frank Robinson, the ex-Marine, who came into baseball in
1956, the year in which Jackie Robinson retired, became
baseball's first black manager. This was indeed a mile -
stone. It was twenty-seven years after Jackie Robinson broke
the color line in baseball with the old Brooklyn Dodgers. In
his interview with the press, Frank Robinson asked to be
judged on his ability as manager not by his color.

Frank Robinson was fired as manager of the Cleveland
Indians on June 18, 1977. He was later hired as a coach by
the California Angels.

Probably more than most individuals selected to manage
a group of high strung athletes, Robinson weighed in with
impressive credentials. He had been named as the most
valuable player in each league. He had 533 career home
runs. Only three players are ahead of him in home runs: Hank
Aaron, Babe Ruth and Willie Mays. He has played on four
pennant winners and two world champion teams. In his twenty-
year career he played on the Cincinnati Reds, Baltimore
Orioles, Los Angeles Dodgers, California Angels and the
Cleveland Indians. In the winter season he managed the Santurce
Club in Puerto Rico for five years. With this club he had
two firsts, two thirds and one fifth.

Hank Aaron felt that Robinson's main problem would be
with the press. He would be under a microscope. Every move
he made would be watched. His handling of players would be
observed closely, especially the white ones.

After twenty-nine years, minorities are well represented in the majors. The latest data are for 1973. At the end
of the 1977 baseball season twenty percent of the 650 players
were black. Eighteen percent were foreign born of which eighty
percent were black.

During the major league baseball season in 1973, 823
players competed against each other on twenty-four teams. Of
these 823 players, 141 were black Americans or about 17 percent, and 86 Latin-Americans, or about 10 percent. These

minorities constituted about 27 percent of the players in
major league baseball in 1973. Among the black North Americans, six were from Canada. It was in 1973 that the high-
water mark in the use of minorities was reached by the major
leagues. From the date in 1941, when Paul Roberson had made
his plea to the major league owners meeting in Cincinnati
to use blacks, down through 1947, when the late Branch
Rickey signed the late brilliant athlete, Jackie Robinson,
to a Brooklyn Dodger contract, by 1973 the use of the minority
athlete had reached unprecedented proportions.

In Table XXXIII below are presented the eight
countries which have Latin-American and Carribbean players.

Table XXXIII

Latin-American Players In Major Leagues - 1973

Country	Number	Percent
1. Puerto Rico.	27	31.40
2. Dominican Republic	16	18.60
3. Cuba	15	17.44
4. Mexico.	9	10.47
5. Venezuela.	8	9.30
6. Panama.	6	6.98
7. Virgin Islands.	3	3.49
8. Bahama.	2	2.33
	86	100.01

Source: Office of the Commissioner of Major League Baseball, January, 1974.

Puerto Rico leads the list with twenty-seven players, or almost a third of the total. This territory of the United States produced the late, great Roberto Clemente of the Pittsburgh Pirates. The Dominican Republic and Cuba run a close second and third among the Latin-American players in producing stars in the majors.

The reasons that minorities are represented in major league baseball in greater percentages than their relative percentage of the United States population are the open competition on the playing field for talent, the love of sports by the people of the United States, and the ego-mania of the owners. With a few exceptions, the twenty-four cities in which the major leagues are located, compose the twenty-four major metropolitan markets in this country.

But while extolling the open policy of the major leagues on the playing field, it is also held suspect that the treatment of minorities suffers in comparison with the white ball players. Whether it can be proved or not, blacks appear to think that a white mediocre player will be carried. However, blacks and minorities must all be outstanding and almost superstars to command a salary which a white mediocre player can command.

Another caveat that blacks and minorities must endure is the race baiting that takes place by some of the clubs.

Some general managers, who are the only conduit for the owner's money, seem to feel that in negotiations with black players, the players should take what he has to offer--that the general manager is doing him a favor and that the black player should not be ungrateful by refusing to sign in the first round of negotiations. If a black player ever becomes a hold-out, it is generally only a matter of time before he is traded to some other club, or may be sent back to the minors.

Since the open door policy of the major leagues, a whole new dimension has opened to the owners. Two expansions had taken place in 1962 and 1967. Another expansion took place in 1977. The caliber of baseball was improved. Larger crowds are now attending the games. New stadiums have been constructed in Houston, Los Angeles, Anaheim, San Francisco, Oakland, Philadelphia, Pittsburgh, New York, Atlanta, Washington, D. C., Kansas City, Cincinnati, Minneapolis, St. Paul, New Orleans and San Diego.

Blacks, Latin-Americans and Foreign Born in the Major Leagues

Broadcasters, newscasters and the media are a little wary of announcing or reporting on the ethnic origin of the baseball players. The reason for this is that broadcasters, newscasters and the media are paid by their employers and the impression they want to give is one of pure objectivity. However, blacks and ethnics from the Islands and Mexico want to

Table XXXIV

Black and Latin-American Baseball Players in
American League for 1973

| Teams | Number of Players | |
	Latin-Americans	Blacks
1. Baltimore	3	6
2. Boston Red Sox	5	3
3. California Angels	3	3
4. Chicago White Sox	7	7
5. Cleveland Indians	5	4
6. Detroit Tigers	4	3
7. Kansas City Royals	5	2
8. Milwaukee Brewers	5	2
9. Minnesota Twins	1	3
10. New York Yankees	5	2
11. Oakland Athletics	9	2
12. Texas Rangers	2	4
	54	41

Table XXX V

Black and Latin-American Baseball Players in
National League for 1973

| Teams | Number of Players | |
	Latin-Americans	Blacks
1. New York Mets	3	3
2. Philadelphia Phillies	2	1
3. Pittsburgh Pirates	7	2
4. Chicago Cubs	4	3
5. Atlanta Braves	3	6
6. Houston Astros	9	3
7. San Diego Padres	6	3
8. San Francisco Giants	4	3
9. Los Angeles Dodgers	4	5
10. Cincinnati Reds	4	3
11. St. Louis Cardinals	6	4
12. Montreal Expos	6	2
	57	38

Source: Baseball Commissioners Office, 1974.

Table XXXVI

Black and Latin-American Baseball Players in
the American League for 1975

		Number of Players		
Teams		Latin-American	Black	Other
1.	Baltimore	2	6	
2.	Boston Red Sox	4	3[a]	
3.	California Angels	4	4	1 German
4.	Chicago White Sox	1	5	
5.	Cleveland Indians	1	5	
6.	Detroit Tigers	2	3[a]	
7.	Kansas City Royals	2	7	1 Samoan
8.	Milwaukee Brewers	4	4	
9.	Minnesota Twins	3	4	1 Holland
10.	New York Yankees	1	9[a]	
11.	Oakland Athletics	3	7	
12.	Texas Rangers	2	3[a]	
		29	60	

Table XXXVII

Black and Latin-American Baseball Players in
the National League for 1975

		Number of Players		
Teams		Latin-American	Black	Other
1.	Atlanta Braves	2	8	1 Hawaiian
2.	Chicago Cubs	4	5	
3.	Cincinnati Reds	6	3	
4.	Houston Astros	2	5	
5.	Los Angeles Dodgers	3	6	1 Hawaiian
6.	Montreal Expos	3	2	
7.	New York Mets	2	4	
8.	Philadelphia Phillies	1	4	
9.	Pittsburgh Pirates	5	6	
10.	San Diego Padres	3	4	
11.	San Francisco Giants	1	4	
12.	St. Louis Cardinals	1	6	
		33	57	

[a]One is a Canadian
Source: Baseball Commissioner Office, 1976.

read of their heroes. Wanting to read about their heroes
does not mean to discount or play down the accomplishments
of the white players.

Latin-American players are those players from the
Caribbean Islands and Mexico. Also, some of the black players
are from Canada, such as Reggie Cleveland and Ferguson Jen-
kins. Other foreign players are from Hawaii, Germany and
Holland. The data for 1973 show fifty-four Latin-American
players and forty-one blacks in the American League. In the
National League for the same year there were fifty-seven
Latin-American players and thirty-eight blacks.

In 1975, there was an almost 50 percent gain in
blacks in the American League and in the National League
there was a 72 percent gain. There were sixty blacks in the
American League and fifty-seven in the National League.
Between 1973 and 1975, the New York Yankees made the biggest
gain in the number of blacks in the American League and
the Montreal Expos in the National League.

As of July 16, 1975, there were 19½ percent of blacks,
9 6/10 percent of Latins and one percent from the Bahamas,
Virgin Islands, Hawaii and Samoa. These data show non-whites
in major league baseball as high as 30 percent.

With the exception of Johnny Bench of the Cincinnati
Reds, a white player has not led the National League in
home runs in the past fourteen years. Over the past five

years, only three players, Willie Mays, Hank Aaron, and the late Roberto Clemente have gained the plateau of 3000 hits. Willie Mays has hit 646 home runs. Aaron had hit 733 career home runs when the Atlanta Braves ended the season on October 2, 1974. There are only two players beside Babe himself who have hit more than 600 home runs in their playing careers. In just about every category, black players have outplayed white players. Between 1969 and 1973, the batting averages were blacks, .270, Latins, .265 and whites, .251.[3] In the pitching category black and Latin-American pitchers since 1961 have consistently attained better records than white pitchers.

During the 1974 baseball season, Lou Brock, of the St. Louis Cardinals, stole 118 bases. This was a new record. It was only through the efforts of Brock that the Cardinals were in competition in the National League East, right up to the last two games of the season Pittsburgh won only by one game. In each game in September the baseball world followed Brock. He overtook Maury Wills' old record of 104 bases, and this thirty-five year-old seasoned outfielder became the premier base stealer in baseball history.

Since he has broken this record, Brock nurtured hopes of becoming the most valuable player in the National League, one of baseball's most coveted awards. But to the chagrin of Brock, the baseball writers of America selected Steve

Garvey, first baseman of the Los Angeles Dodgers. Garvey received 270 votes and Brock 233. During the season Garvey hit .312, polled 21 home runs and was responsible for driving in 112 runs. Besides stealing 118 bases, Brock hit .309 and scored 105 runs. However, it is necessary to be a baseball buff to understand this selection. The award usually goes to a member of a division winning team or a pennant winner in each league.

Notwithstanding their outstanding achievements, black players do not have as great longevity in the major leagues as do white players. Here we have a latent, veiled form of racism. Owners, general managers, and field managers want and seek any player who can perform on the field. But when the black or Latin-American falters at the bat in the field, he goes. The white player generally can have two or three mediocre seasons, batting .235, and he can be traded time and time again. The problem for owners and general managers is, of course, not to keep mediocre ball players white or black and Latin-American coaches and managers. There have been two Latin-American managers, Al Lopez, who managed the Cleveland Indians and the Chicago White Sox, and Preston Gomez, who managed the San Diego Padres and the Houston Astros.

Prior to Frank Robinson's appointment as a manager, blacks picketed the All-Star Game in Pittsburgh on Wednesday,

July 24, 1974 in order to bring to the attention of the owners, management, players and fans that there was not one black manager in major league baseball. The hue and cry for a black manager in baseball gained momentum during the balance of 1974 and continued through the winter meetings and up to the spring training in 1975.

Marvin Miller, executive director of the Major League Baseball Players Association, contended that a strong case of racial discrimination could be made against the owners over-looking blacks in their quest for managers. Every year, because of poor attendance on the part of fans, mediocre team play, or lack of ability to get along with players or the front office, a manager may have to seek employment elsewhere. Practically all of the managers and coaches are hired from year to year. Only in exceptional cases, such as Walt Alston, former manager of the Dodgers, Red Schendienst former manager of the St. Louis Cardinals and the late Danny Murtaugh of the Pirates, are managers hired on a long term basis. Certainly Alston and Murtaugh were outstanding managers. They appear to have their teams as contenders year after year. Earl Weaver has good longevity with Baltimore in the American League, but, just about every year, there is a high turnover of managers in the majors. Thus, not having black managers is crass discrimination. Gabe Paul of the Yankee front office said a manager should have

some minor league experience. Miller challenged Paul. Many
whites have managed major league teams without serving as
managers of the minors. In July, 1974, when Eddie Mathews
was fired as manager of the California Angels, Frank Robinson,
who had won the Most Valuable Player title in both leagues,
was an Angel. Robinson showed interest in the manager's
job, but the Angels picked Dick Williams, former manager
of the Oakland's A's.

In August, 1974, Whitey Lockman stepped down as manager
of the Chicago Cubs. The job was turned over to Jim Marshall,
third base coach. Bowie Kuhn, Commissioner of major league
baseball commented that a black manager was one of the situ-
ations with which baseball was confronted. Ron Santo of
the Chicago White Sox thought that the personable Ernie Banks
should have been given the Cub job. Besides the managerial
prospects named above, other blacks mentioned as possible
managerial timber were Maury Wills, Jim Gilliam and Tommy
Aaron.

What do the players earn in baseball? What are the
sources of income for the owners? The data below are for
1973. Broadcast Magazine shows income for the major league
clubs from TV-radio broadcast payments.

Table XXXVIII shows that income from TV-radio to
the twenty-four major league teams amounted to more than
$24 million. For 1973, NBC paid $18 million for rights to

Table XXXVIII

TV-Radio Broadcast Payments
To Major League Baseball
Clubs for 1973

National League Team	Amounts	American League Team	Amounts
Los Angeles	$ 1,800,000	New York Yankees	$ 1,300,000
Philadelphia	1,600,000	Chicago White Sox	1,050,000
Cincinnati	1,300,000	Boston	1,000,000
New York Mets	1,250,000	Detroit	1,000,000
Chicago Cubs	1,200,000	California	1,000,000
San Francisco	1,100,000	Oakland	1,000,000
Pittsburgh	1,000,000	Minnesota	950,000
Atlanta	1,000,000	Cleveland	800,000
Houston	1,000,000	Baltimore	775,000
Montreal	800,000	Texas (Dallas/Ft. Worth)	700,000
St. Louis	800,000	Kansas City	650,000
San Diego	710,000	Milwaukee	600,000
Total	$12,311,250	Total	$11,825,000

Source: Broadcast Magazine, 1973

the World Series, the division playoffs, the All Star
Game and the network's Game of the Week presentation.   The
total for broadcasting is more than $42 million.[4]

For the 1977 season the national networks,
local stations and regional affiliates
will pay an estimated $52,000,000 to the major baseball
leagues for television and radio rights.[5]

The revenue from radio and broadcasting is at times
the difference between making a profit and suffering a loss
through the baseball season. The Baltimore Orioles in
their 1976 annual financial statement show that 25 percent
of their operating income was derived from broadcasting and
radio rights. In 1976 this amounted to $1,275,000. From
this figure it is derived that the operating income for the
Orioles in 1976 was $5,100,000.

Operating a major league baseball team is therefore
not a big business, but, as a group and its influence in
sports, it is big business.

Broadcast Magazine for 1977 shows this breakdown for
air rights:

Event	Network	Amount Paid
Monday Night Base-ball and World Series	ABC-TV	$12,500,000
Saturday Game of the Week, All Star Game and the Leagues' Championship Series	NBC-TV	$10,700,000

Event	Network	Amount Paid
Radio Broadcasts	CBS-Radio	$75,000
Season Games	Local TV and Radio and Regional Chains	$29,285,000

One soft spot in the majors is down in Arlington, Texas, where the Texas Rangers are split between Dallas and Fort Worth. Bob Short, who moved the Senators from Washington, later sold the club, renamed the Rangers, to a group of local people. He was known in Washington for giving out cans of Right Guard to patrons who came to the Senator's games. Dr. Bobby Brown, former Yankee Third Baseman, became president of the new setup. The other soft spot is the San Francisco franchise.

Other income is derived from fans' attendance at home games. Assume an average game attendance is 15,000 at $3.25 per patron, for 72 home games, 1,080,000 would come into the park paying gross revenues of $3,510,000. For each game played on the road (72) the visiting team is paid 15 percent of the gate. The variable is half of the attendance at home, or 540,000 paying ($3.25 x 540,000 = $1,755,000). Fifteen percent of this amount is $263,250. Other sources of income for the major teams are parking, concessions, advertising, gifts, restaurants, souvenirs and travel. The profit centers in major league baseball are numerous. The trick is to have a contender, a team that is in the thick of the pennant race. All the world loves a winner. People will come out to see a winner.

The main expense for major league baseball is the player salaries. Minimum salaries for 1974 were $16,000. In 1973, the minimum was $15,000. In 1967 the minimum was $7,000 per season. Over the eight-year period, salaries for major league baseball players have gone up 128 percent, or an average of 16 percent per year. The median salary was $31,000 and the average salary was $37,000. The highest salary was $225,000. In 1973, of the 600 players on active rosters, or 25 per 24 teams, 30 of these players had earnings of $100,000 per season. These were the super stars. Leonard Koppett, in the New York Times, reported that in major league baseball about 17 percent of the gross income goes for player salaries.[6] Shrewd entrepreneurship in major league baseball knows that once a fan is in the ball park he is a captive audience. A stadium such as the Astrodome in Houston, Texas, is a huckster's paradise. The Astrodome is all-weather. Seats are opera-like. Men and women can come to a game well-dressed. There is a constant 72 degree temperature. All games are played at night with the exception of Sundays when they are played at 2:00 p. m. By inching up on prices on choice seats, selling season tickets, parking fees, food and drinks, management can grow almost as much off concessions as prices paid for a seat.

The drama of major league baseball appeals to all
those who find the sport attractive. Owners are for the
profits and the association of exceptional talent, the
players are for the high salaries and the glory of competing for the ultimate prize of the World Series, and
the fans identify with the players and reflect in the
achievements of the players. In 1973, 823 players played
in the majors. With a legal capacity of 600 or 25 per
team, 223 came and went during the season. This was a
27 percent turnover. Thus, theoretically, five years is
the usual longevity of a major league baseball player. The
competition is so keen and the price is so high, that
although many are called, few are chosen. It is no wonder
that   minority baseball players play so hard and always
strive for excellence because there is no other endeavor
where these 141 North American blacks and 86 Latin-Americans
during 1973-75 could have earned such salaries and be
assured of a good pension if they could last a minimum of
five years.

Research in major league baseball by Scully[6] reveals
that the average player salary in 1969 was $25,000, or a
roster cost of $625,000. The roster cost is determined by
multiplying the average player salary by twenty-five players,
the limit to be carried by a major league team. In the same
research by Scully, minimum game costs were estimated to be
$800,000.

Capital investment in a major league franchise is difficult to pinpoint. In conventional capital investment, we
think of plant and equipment which is used in the production
process. In the world of sports, capital investment implies
purchasing a monopoly (the franchise for a market area) and
player contracts. The player contracts carry the greatest
impact. Estimated costs by Scully of a major league franchise
is $8,400,000. It is alleged that Bill Veeck, the innovative
and peg leg owner of the Chicago White Sox, purchased this
club for $9,750,000 in December, 1975. This article by
Gerald W. Scully, professor of Economics at Southern Methodist
University is unique. Very little research has been conducted
by writers on player salary determinants or costs of fielding
a major league team from a scientific point of view. However,
in his article, Scully mentions that "one percent increase in
the percentage of black players on the team reduces revenue
by $59,000."[7] It is felt that Scully in this instance is on
tenuous ground. How he reaches such a conclusion is not clear.
It is recognized by baseball savants that the inclusion of
blacks in the game of baseball has somewhat revived it, and
that whites want to see the black stars as well as white
stars.

The Most Valuable Player Award of professional baseball is one of the highest acclaims that can be awarded to
a major league player. Over a thirty-year period, 1947-1976,

of the thirty outstanding players chosen, blacks have captured this toga of outstanding acclaim eighteen times. These
outstanding black players, along with numerous white ones,
have been Roy Campanella, three times, Mays, Morgan and
Ernie Banks twice each, Frank Robinson, the late Roberto
Clemente, Hank Aaron, Don Newcombe and the late Jackie
Robinson; Bob Gibson, Willie McCovey, Orlando Cepeda and
Maury Wills. Table XXXIX shows the list of the Most Valuable Players from 1947 to 1976.

Table XXXIX

Major Leagues' Most Valuable Players From 1947 to 1976

	Name	Position	Team	Year
1.	Bob Elliott	First Base	Milwaukee	1947
2.	Stan Musial	Outfield	St. Louis	1948
3.	Jackie Robinson	First Base	Brooklyn	1949
4.	Jim Konstanty	Pitcher	Philadelphia	1950
5.	Roy Campanella	Catcher	Brooklyn	1951
6.	Hank Sauer	Outfield	Chicago	1952
7.	Roy Campanella	Catcher	Brooklyn	1953
8.	Willie Mays	Outfield	New York Giants	1954
9.	Roy Campanella	Catcher	Brooklyn	1955
10.	Don Newcombe	Pitcher	Brooklyn	1956
11.	Hank Aaron	Outfield	Milwaukee	1957
12.	Ernie Banks	Shortstop	Chicago	1958
13.	Ernie Banks	Shortstop	Chicago	1959
14.	Dick Groat	Shortstop	Pittsburgh	1960
15.	Frank Robinson	Outfield	Cincinnati	1961
16.	Maury Wills	Shortstop	Los Angeles	1962
17.	Sandy Koufax	Pitcher	Los Angeles	1963
18.	Ken Boyer	Third Base	St. Louis	1964
19.	Willie May	Outfield	San Francisco	1965
20.	Roberto Clemente	Outfield	Pittsburgh	1966
21.	Orlando Cepeda	First Base	San Francisco	1967
22.	Bob Gibson	Pitcher	St. Louis	1968

Table XXXIX   (continued)

Name	Position	Team	Year
23. Willie McCovey	First Base	San Francisco	1969
24. Johnny Bench	Catcher	Cincinnati	1970
25. Joe Torre	First Base	St. Louis	1971
26. Johnny Bench	Catcher	Cincinnati	1972
27. Pete Rose	Outfield	Cincinnati	1973
28. Steve Garvey	First Base	Los Angeles	1974
29. Joe Morgan	Second Base	Cincinnati	1975
30. Joe Morgan	Second Base	Cincinnati	1976

Pensions for Baseball Players

Baseball players get the most lucrative pensions of all the players in major sports. The figures below show pensions at various ages and years of service. The age column shows the ages from 45 to 65. The horizontal column shows the years of service and the amount of pension based on years of service in the majors. If a player with ten years of service wanted his pension to start at age 50, he would receive $600 per month. Or, if a player had a bare minimum service of four years, at age 45 he could collect a pension of $174 per month. It must be considered that the major league pension plan is noncontributory. Pensions for players come from the All Star Games.

The 227 minority players in 1973 represent 27 percent of the players in major league baseball. Blacks and other minorities are represented much higher in baseball than

Table XL

Monthly Pensions for Baseball Players

Age	4	6	8	10	15	20
45	$174	$262	$350	$436	$509	$582
47	198	296	396	494	577	659
49	224	338	450	562	656	749
50	240	360	480	600	700	800
51	256	384	513	641	748	854
53	291	437	582	728	848	968
55	329	494	659	824	959	1091
57	372	559	745	931	1088	1224
59	421	831	842	1052	1212	1372
60	447	671	895	1119	1286	1452
61	476	715	953	1191	1364	1538
63	541	812	1082	1353	1540	1726
65	618	927	1236	1545	1745	1945

their proportion in the general population. Blacks are only 12 percent in the general population. Baseball is seeking this good talent and is willing to pay for it. The opportunities in this medium for minorities are much more promising than in business, government and the managerial elite.

The second mass team sport that has great crowd appeal is football. We now turn to that sport and examine the part which minorities have played in its development.

REFERENCES

1. The Louisville Defender, May 1, 1976.

2. Baseball, The First 100 Years, Poretz Brothers. 2nd Edition, 1976. Research provided by Monte Irvin, Assistant to Baseball Commissioner Bowie Kuhn.

3. The Sports Enclyclopedia, Baseball, 1974.

4. From an article in Sports Magazine by Oscar Kahan, April 9, 1977.

5. New York Times, March 11, 1973, Section 5, pg. 4.

6. "Pay and Performance in Major League Baseball," Gerald W. Scully, The American Economic Review, Vol. LXIV, Number 6, December, 1974.

7. Ibid, pg. 921.

Chapter XX

Blacks in Professional Football

Under the astute guidance of Pete Roselle, Commissioner, the National Football League is now a well-entrenched,
vastly rich spectator sport in this country. For decades baseball enjoyed the spotlight as America's national pastime.
But in recent years football, the game of violence, as it
is played on Sunday afternoons in the fall of the year, is
coming to compete on an even basis or even to surpass baseball as America's favorite sport. Because of its action -
fast breakaway backs, the threading of a needle by the quarterback, and the quickness of its line backers, it brings
thrills to the spectators that the slow game of baseball cannot muster.

Similar to baseball, football is divided into two
divisions - the American Conference and the National Conference. There are teams· in each conference. Again we have
twenty-eight major market areas. With only a few exceptions,
the cities where football is played, parallels the cities
where baseball is played. In fact, the football owners rent
the stadiums from the baseball owners, or the cities or
counties which have title to the stadiums.

There are 1198 football players in the NFL. Each
team has an average of forty-six players. The number of

American blacks is 435, or 36 percent. This figure is more
than double the number of blacks in baseball. Is the National
Football League more democratic than baseball? Yes. The use
of blacks testifies to this. Also, out of 172 assistant
coaches, five are black: Emlen Tunnel* of the New York Giants,
Willie Wood of San Diego, Lionel Taylor of the Pittsburgh
Steelers, Al Tabor of the Cleveland Browns and Earnell Durden
of the Houston Oilers. Also, there are more black officials
in the National Football League per team than there are black
umpires in the baseball leagues. Art Williams is one of the
black umpires in the National Baseball League.

From the time thirty years ago when there was only a
handful of black football players in the old National Football League such as Ray Kemp of the Steelers, Kenny Washington and Woodie Strode of Los Angeles, the NFL has come a long
was in including blacks and minorities in the game of football.

One of the earliest black football players was Fritz
Pollard, famous All-American from Brown University in 1916.
After his college days he became a player-coach at Akron and
Milwaukee. From Akron and Milwaukee, Pollard moved to the
Hammond Pros in the old National Football League. Pollard
had a two-year tenure at this post from 1923-25.

Another early black football player was Fred E. "Duke"
Slater who was said to have put Iowa football on the map.

In the Notre Dame game in 1921, this towering tackle helped
defeat Notre Dame 10-7. The great Knute Rockne was stunned.
Iowa went on to win the Big Ten Title. In those days players
purchased their own shoes and helmet. Because Slater came
from a modest family, they could not afford a helmet, so
Slater played bareheaded. After graduating from Iowa (later
Slater went back and earned his law degree), Slater played
professional football for ten years. He played with Rock
Island Independents, Milwaukee Badgers and along with team-
mate Paul Roberson on the Chicago Cardinals. Slater later
became a municipal judge in Chicago. He died in the Windy
City at age sixty-eight in 1966.

Professional football never had a rigid color line
as deadly as the WASP's in professional baseball. As early
as 1919, blacks were playing in the National Football league.
In the mid-thirties, blacks in professional football had
practically dwindled down to a handful. Ray Kemp was playing with the Pittsburgh Steelers. The hiatus of the lack of
blacks in football during the thirties was due to the great
depression and the extreme racism practiced on the part of
the WASP's. In the early forties, because of the war against
Hitler, football as a sport was at a low ebb. After the war,
change was rapid. In 1946, Woody Strode and Kenny Washington
signed with the Los Angeles Rams. Paul Brown, the highly
successful Ohioan who coached at Massillon High School, Ohio

States Great Lakes Naval Station, Cleveland Browns and then
the Cincinnati Bengals gave blacks the first great break in
professional football. At Great Lakes, Brown noticed the
formidable, durable quality of the black athlete. With his
Great Lakes team, Brown practically blew away all the college
and service teams in the region of the Mid-west. When the old
Cleveland Rams moved to Los Angeles and called themselves the
Los Angeles Rams, Brown moved into Cleveland and organized
his own team and named it after him. He immediately signed
Bill Willis, lineman from Ohio State and Marion Notley, a
back from Nevada. Paul Brown was instrumental in helping to
organize the old All-American Conference. Later, the conference was disbanded and the Browns were absorbed into the
National Football League.

As football took on a new meaning after World War II,
we have yet to hear from the predominantly black colleges in
this country and their athletic prowess. Most of the great
black athletes in the early twenties and thirties came out
of the Big Ten and a few other eastern colleges. Sure, Roberson had come out of Lincoln in Pennsylvania and went to Rutgers, but none had contributed to professional sports. After
World War II, Grambling became the first black college to
contribute to the National Football League. Tank Younger became a fullback for the Los Angeles Rams in 1948. Since that
time of 29 years ago, Grambling College in northern Louisiana,

has contributed as much or more than Notre Dame or any other
college to the National Football League. Eddie Robinson, the
stellar coach at Grambling, is a fundamentalist. Robinson
was elected president of the American Football Coaches Association for 1976. His teams are always noted for their sturdy
lines, good blocking and tackling. There is hardly a predominantly black college playing in a conference that has not
contributed to major league sports. Morgan State, Jackson
State, Texas Southern University, Prairie View A.& M., Tennessee State, Maryland Eastern Shore, all have made major
contributions to the National Football League. James Gaither,
legendary coach of Florida A.& M. sent forty of his players
to the pro football leagues.[1] During the 1977 National Football League season Grambling had nineteen players, and Texas
Southern University ten. The final step again is one of
ownership. Expansion can do this. The National Football League
expanded into Seattle and Tampa Bay in 1976. Other cities
beckoning for expansion are Memphis, Birmingham, Louisville
and Columbus, Ohio.

In Tables XLI and XLII there are lists of the teams
and players in the National Football League and the number
of blacks on each team for 1973.

In the American Conference in 1973, just about half
of San Diego's players were blacks. The Miami Dolphins had
the lowest representation of 27 percent. In the National
Conference more than half of the Chicago Bears players were

TABLE XLI

BLACK PLAYERS IN
THE NATIONAL FOOTBALL LEAGUE
AMERICAN CONFERENCE
1973

Team	Number of Black Players	Percent
Miami Dolphins	12	27
New York Jets	15	34
Buffalo Bills	15	34
Baltimore Colts	11	25
New England Patriots	21	48
Pittsburgh Steelers	19	43
Cincinnati Bengals	13	30
Cleveland Browns	20	45
Houston Oilers	19	43
Oakland Raiders	17	39
Denver Broncos	20	45
Kansas City Chiefs	18	41
San Diego Chargers	22	50
Total	222	

Source: National Football League

TABLE XLII

BLACK PLAYERS IN
NATIONAL FOOTBALL LEAGUE
NATIONAL CONFERENCE
1973

Team	Number of Black Players	Percent
New York Giants	11	25
Philadelphia Eagles	17	39
Minnesota Vikings	12	27
Green Bay Packers	20	45
Detriot Lions	16	36
Chicago Bears	25	57

TABLE XLII (Continued)

Team	Number of Black Players	Percent
Los Angeles Rams	15	34
San Francisco 49ers	15	34
Atlanta Falcons	17	39
New Orleans Saints	9	20
St. Louis Cardinals	13	30
Washington Redskins	20	45
Dallas Cowboys	21	48
Total	211	

Source: National Football League

blacks, 57 percent. Only one fourth of the Giants players
were black in 1973.

With more than a third of the players in the National
Football League black, another 10 percent are of other ethnic
groups. Recently the football teams have been hiring soccer
players as placekickers and extra point and field goal specialists. These soccer players who are ethnics are usually
from Europe where soccer enjoys the same popularity as football in this country.

As in baseball, football has player unions. These
unions have been responsible for placing a floor or minimum
on salaries paid to rookies. The minimum salary in the
National Football League is $12,000. The median salary is
$26,000 and the average salary is $27,500. The highest salary
in the NFL is $250,000. There are ten players in the NFL earn-
ing $100,000 or more for a season's work. These players are

usually outstanding quarterbacks or halfbacks such as Joe
Namath and O.J. Simpson. In 1974, the player union in the
NFL struck for about one month, but they went into camp in
August, because the owners stood fast on their negotiations
with the unions. Ed Garvey, Executive Director of the union,
called a cooling off period for two weeks, so that the veterans could report to camp to get ready for the season.

The lack of black managers and front office personnel
in baseball is similar in football. Dick "Night Train" Lane,
former star cornerback of the Detroit Lions, scathingly
attacked the "establishment" for its lack of hiring more
black coaches, officials and front office personnel. Lane
spoke at his enshrinement into the Hall of Fame at Canton,
Ohio on July 28, 1974. His audience included President
Gerald R. Ford, who at that time was Vice President, and
was also a former football player at the University of Michigan.

Trying to make a start using blacks as coaches,
Ralph Goldston, a black, was appointed to coach the Portland
franchise but it was shortlived and before they could field
a team, Goldston was reassigned back to the Chicago Bears
on May 5, 1974. Goldston had begun his career in pro football with the Philadelphia Eagles in the early 50's.

Winning professional football teams begin with recruiting and the draft. Of course, the head coach and his

staff   design plays, establish basic strategy and make ad-
justments to bring home a champion. Most of the teams in the
National League have black assistant coaches and black re-
cruiters or directors of player personnel. Two of these
black recruiters and directors of player personnel are Bill
Nunn, Jr. of the Steelers and Lloyd Wells, formerly of the
Kansas City Chiefs. Hank Stram, formerly coach of the Kansas
City Chiefs and now of the New Orleans Saints, has employed
Wells in the capacity of personnel selection.Bill Nunn, Jr.,
formerly Sports Editor of the Pittsburgh Courier and a star
basketballer at West Virginia State, has worked for Chuck
Noll, the two-time Super Bowl Champion Pittsburgh Steelers.
These two men have roamed the black colleges, observing,
taking notes, inquiring about potential players, hoping and
praying that a naive, green kid in college will eventually
become an O.J. Simpson, Joe Greene, Fran Tarkenton or Johnny
Unitas. In college football, Case Jackson was appointed head
football coach at Oberlin College and Tommie Smith, athletic
director.

What happens to the black pro football players when
his playing days are over? Many, if not most, of the black
pro football players never finished their college curriculum.
Those who attended the predominantly white colleges played
out their eligibility and after that were forgotten. If one
of them got a pro contract this was a god-send. According to

Eddie Robinson, coach of the highly successful Grambling
Tigers, when a black boy can earn $30,000 or $50,000 a year
in pro-football and do this for five or more years he becomes
a male Cinderella. Grambling has more players in pro-football
than any other college.

However, when his playing days are over, when the
great ovations from the stadiums fade from his memories, the
black athlete stands almost as a sheep shorn for slaughter.
The plight of some of the ex-black pros is lamentable.Cookie
Gilchrist, former Denver, Buffalo and Miami player in the
Aermican Football League has organized the United Athletes
Coalition of America to counsel, advise and help the pro-
football player. Gilchrist can document cases of a great
back, a Hall of Famer who is sleeping on a park bench in a
city where he was a star. The late Big Daddy Lipscomb, fearsome lineman of the Baltimore Colts and Pittsburgh Steelers,
died on an overdose of herion. Lenny Ford died drunk and
broke in a rundown hotel. Warren Wells, former Texas Southern
University star and Oakland wide receiver ran afoul of the law.
He served a prison term, attempted a comeback in 1972, but
was still dogged by the law.

Basically the ex-pro black athlete should complete
his college education. When he is in his glory days of full
adulation, and he hears the roar of the crowd, he must
realize that when his reflexes dim and his timing is off, it
is only a matter of time when he will no longer hear the roar

of the crowd. He must quit pretending that the world loves

him. He must realize that there is no more pitiful figure

than the broken down hulk of an ex-athlete. The pretty girls

are no longer at his beck and call, and the banquet circuit

has long ago passed from his thoughts. People faintly recall

him, and his newspaper clippings are a poor substitute for

substance.

---

*Tunnell, died at the Giants training camp on July 23, 1975.
He was a great defensive back for the Giants for eleven
seasons and three for the Green Bay Packers. He was
named to the pro football Hall of Fame in 1967.

Chapter XXI

Basketball

The third team sport of mass appeal is basketball. It
is in this sport that the greatest representation of blacks in
proportion to their population is found, greater than in baseball or basketball. Again history does not record that when
the first basketball game was played, who played on it. History does record that Professor James Naismith of   Spring-
field, Massachusetts, invented basketball in 1870.

The two major leagues in basketball are the National
Basketball Association and the American Basketball Association. The National Basketball Association is the stronger of
the two. It is stronger by virtue of getting started early,
just after World War II, and thus being able to attract the
best stars produced by the colleges. Where baseball must develop its own talent through farm systems, football and basketball have their talent developed free by the colleges. Also,
basketball has the fewest players per team, as well as the
widest participation in high schools, junior colleges and
colleges each year. There are twenty-two teams in the National
Basketball Association and twelve in the American Basketball
Association. Each team carries a roster of twelve players.
At any time on each of the teams in the league all five
starters can be black. In the twenty-two teams participating

there is a total of 264 players. Blacks represent 83 percent, or more, of the players in the two leagues.

The Black-White Thing in Sport Attendance

It appears that when there is a drop in attendance in any sport, promoters, sports writers, and the benefactors from these games that men play, look for a scapegoat to blame for such a drop in attendance. In the winter of 1974-75, there was a decided drop in attendance in professional basketball. Some of the sports writers, promoters and owners were blaming the number of blacks in pro-basketball for the drop in attendance. It is strange that this news article, which came out of the Los Angeles Times and Washington Post News Service, did not mention that the recession could have been the main reason for such a drop in attendance, as well as the high prices charged for the game. The writers of the article mentioned that professional hockey outdrew professional basketball. The implication was that, because blacks dominate professional basketball with about 83 percent of the players being black, since whites do not identify with blacks, therefore, they were not attending the games as much as they did in the past. The reasons these writers and promoters were giving are so superficial that they hardly bear comment. Comment, however, does not just refute such baseless contentions, but shows that racism is used again and again to hide shortcomings of promotion, high prices and even onerous comparisons.

To compare hockey and basketball is like comparing
apples and oranges. Each sport draws different spectators. A
few seasons ago, soccer appeared on the American scene as a
spectator sport. It was competing with baseball. The professional sport of soccer did not last a season. Hardly any
blacks competed in soccer. Pele' is the exception. This Bra-
zilian is reputed to be the highest paid soccer player in the
world. He is contracted to the New York Cosmos. There were
only a few from Brazil or one or two other South American
countries. The sport was dominated by whites. But Americans
did not care for soccer and they stayed away in droves. Racism
was not mentioned. Color is not the only point of identification of a sport. Identification is in performance, location,
nationality, religion, ethnic group, college or university,
age, sex and class.

Other odious comparisons were made by these writers
from the Los Angeles Times and the Washington Post News Service. The article stated that boxing promoters rued the day
that blacks dominated the sport. They only wished for a white
hope to come riding in on his white horse and take the world's
heavyweight championship away from the black. The chicanery
of such comparisons is that these promoters seem to think
that boxing attendance started to sag when blacks began to
dominate the sport. Instead, boxing was revived by black
fighters. Starting with Joe Louis, the Brown Bomber down

through Muhammad Ali, the sport took on a new dimension.
The white promoters are now sad, not because of poor boxing
as they once did. Black fighters earn far more by fighting
out of the United States than within the United States. Tax
laws, corruption in boxing, managerial tangles, all have cast
aspersions on boxing. Black boxers and minorities are the
world's greatest fighters.

Other cities which made comparisons between basketball and hockey were Atlanta, Philadelphia, and St. Louis.
Each of the cities had a second-rate basketball team. They
were not contenders in 1974-75-76 in their respective leagues

In mid-March of 1975, the St. Louis entry in the
American Basketball Association was twenty-five games out of
first place in the Eastern Division. Philadelphia was in last
place in the Atlantic Division of the Eastern Conference of
the National Basketball Association. Atlanta was in fourth
place, or twenty-four games out of first place in the Central
Division of the NBA. Certainly Americans are still racist.
They would not admit as much, because they are unaware of
their racism. It is ingrained. It is institutionalized. It
will take time to get it out of them. There are other reasons
for a drop in attendance. Black is not the cause. It is superficial to use such reasons. The promoters and businessmen of
these sports should not use such ploys. They only deface the
sport. They are only covering up their own shortcomings. To
use racism shows their own meanness and hypocrisy.

Blacks dominate play in the two leagues so thoroughly
that there is a possible cause for alarm among whites on reverse discrimination. Again, the reasons that persist can be
compared to those in the other sports, desire for achievement,
eager to earn big money, out-performing the opposition.[1]
When one observes the black youngsters in the ghettoes, play-
grounds, back alleys, side streets and in the open countryside, he will find them playing basketball. The black youngster starts at an early age, and when he is ready for junior
high school, he is already a nearly complete basketeer. On
the sandlots and the recreation centers he has come up against
big and little boys. These boys are rough and are not above
playing gut basketball. Elbows and knees are used to beat
their opponents. They learn early how to block a man out of
a play. On rebounds an adept skill is mastered in riding a
man out of the play. Keeping arms extended and flailing the
air to keep his opponent off balance, feet wide apart in
guarding have all been virtually mastered by the time the
youngster reaches high school. The coach's job now is to
bring in the fine points of the game, polishing up on his
shooting ability, knowing when to shoot from the open and
above all keeping in good condition. In an Indiana high
school tournament, the black high schools consistently beat
the white high schools. The white boys became so exasperated
from losing that they conceded that they could not beat the
black boys because the black boys had long arms, large hands,

big feet, sharp eyes, and just ran too fast.

In basketball, Walt Frazier feels that blacks can outperform whites because blacks are not team play oriented. He says that whites do not have the talent basically, that is why they are team players.

Pete Maravich is an exception. In this interview in Penthouse, Frazier feels that it is in the coaching that blacks get. Black coaches believe in a run and shoot game in basketball. This is because the guys are quick and they can jump.[2]

Achieving the ultimate in basketball competition, when he is selected by either league, is the cap and crown of the black competitor. Of the two leagues, the National Basketball Association has the highest salaries. The minimum is the same in either league, which is about $20,000. But the median salary in the NBA is $65,000 and in the ABA, $31,000. Average salaries in the NBA are $90,000 and in the ABA, 37,000. The highest salaries in the NBA are $400,000 and in the ABA $200,000.

The super stars were such as Wilt Chamberlain, Willis Reed, John Havlichek, Kareem Jabbar, Jerry West, Julius Irving, Walt Frazier and Oscar Robertson.

At the beginning of the 1975-76 basketball season in the NBA, five head coaching jobs were held by blacks, and there were two general managers. The coaches and teams were:

Ray Scott, Detroit Pistons; Bill Russell, Seattle Super-
sonics; K.C. Jones, Washington Bullets; Al Atles, Golden
State Warriors; and Lenny Wilkens, Portland Trailblazers.
The two general managers were Wayne Embry of the Milwaukee
Bucks and Bill Russell of the Supersonics. Russell is the
only black coach who is serving in a dual capacity. Before
the season ended in March, Ray Scott was let out by the
Detroit Pistons, and after Washington lost to the Cleveland
Cavaliers in the playoffs, K.C. Jones was fired. The two
black coaches in the American Basketball Association were
also without jobs because of the folding of four franchises
in the ABA in 1975-76.

Wayne Embry,formerly general manager of the Milwaukee
Bucks,was let out at the end of the 1976 basketball season.
Simon Gourdine is Deputy Commissioner of the National Bas-
ketball League serving with Larry O'Brien who replaced
Walter Kennedy.

Playoffs

The playoffs in the National Basketball Association-
when division leaders meet to decide the winners of the East
and the West for the championship - is a bonanza for the
owners. It is possible that over an eighty-two game schedule,
a team can lose money, but if they can make the playoffs, they
can recoup these losses and turn a profit for the year. In
the 1974-75 season, the Washington Bullets won their divi-

sion handily and went on to defeat Buffalo and Boston for
the eastern title. In the playoffs the Bullets make between
$40,000 and $50,000 at the gate. In the playoffs, the home
team gets 55 percent of the gross after expenses. The
National Basketball Association gets the remaining 45 percent and pays for each team's playoff expenses as well as
the player prize money pool. When the Bullets whipped Buffalo and Boston, the Bullets shared in $128,000, or $10,666
per man.

The owners of the team share in parking revenue,
concessions and telecasting-broadcasting. During 1974-75 CBS
had the telecasting - broadcasting contract. It called for
$9 million. Each of the eighteen NBA teams shared equally
for the thirty-eight televised games. All games over the
fourth game of the championship series, must be paid for by
CBS on a per game basis. All of the eighteen teams in NBA
split this money, too. The three mass team sports - baseball,
football and basketball have been great for minorities because of the high salaries and competitive nature of the
sports. In Table XLIII below it is shown that the highest
salaries are paid in the NBA. Hockey ranks among the highest
paid, but at present there is only one black in pro hockey,
Mike Marion, a black Canadian.

Table XLIII

Selected Salaries In Professional Sports In 1973

	National Football League	Major League Baseball	Former American Basketball Association	National Hockey League	National Basketball Association
Minimimum Salary	$ 12,000	$ 15,000	$ 17,500	$ 15,000	$ 17,500
Minimum Salary, 1974	NA	16,000	NA	NA	20,000
Median Salary	26,000	31,000	31,000	25,000	65,000
Average Salary	27,000	37,000	37,000	40,000	90,000
Highest Salaries	250,000	225,000	200,000	200,000	400,000
Number of players on active rosters	1,040	600	120	304	204
Number of players at $100,00 or higher	10	30	15	45	50
Proportion of players at $100,00 or higher	1%	5%	12½%	15%	25%
Gross Income	$140M	$130M	$14M	$50M	$40M
Player Payroll	$28.5M	$22M	$4.5M	$12M	$18M
Proportion of Income paid to players	20%	17%	32%	24%	45%

Source: New York Times, March 11, 1973, Section 5, pg. 4.

NA: Not available.

The highest salaries in the National Basketball Association have been subsidized by cooperation among the teams in the NBA. Bill Bradley, Princeton graduate and one of the top forwards in the NBA from 1967 through 1976, received the following salary:

Table XLIV
Salaries

Year	Salary	Loan	Summer Camps	Endorse- ments	Personal Appearance
1967-68		$82,000			
68-69	$750,000	over			
69-70	over	4		2,125	$1,000
70-71	4 years	years	1,125	925 total	....
				1,963 total	....
1971-72	$214,000	50,000		1,400 total	
72-73	250,000	50,000	1,417	16,447	12,000
73-74	300,000	50,000	2,858	4,856	2,000
74-75	350,000	12,000	....	Not Stated	....

Source: New York Times, Vol CXXV #43,156, Section 5, Pg. 1-6, March 21, 1976.

Some of the other high priced stars in the NBA were Spencer Haywood, $302,000; John Havlicek, $250,000; Rick Barry, $237,500; Elvin Hayes, $202,000 and Jim McMillian, $200,000, Rudy Tomjanovich, $100,000; Bob Dandridge, $80,000; Bob Love, $75,000 and Stev Mix, $60,000.

Included in most of the star's contracts are bonuses for signing and deferred compensations for as long as into the eighties for some of them.

Meeting in Bloomington, Minnesota on May 8, 1975,
the five commissioners of the big pro sports were skep-
tical as to whether they could continue to operate paying
the high salaries demanded by the super stars. Joining hands
in this discussion were: the late Walter Kennedy of the
NBA, Clarence Campbell of the NHL, Pete Rozelle of the NFL,
Bowie Kuhn, Commissioner of Baseball, and Deane Beman, professional head of golf. There was a mutual agreement that
professional sports were here to stay, but at reduced costs.
Twelve years ago, in the NHL, average player's salary was
$16,333 annually. Ticket prices averaged $2.50, arenas were
occupied to a 96 percent capacity. It cost $850,000 to field
a team. By 1971, conditions of the NHL economics of operating
a team had changed drastically. The six-team league of ten
years ago had expanded to fourteen. Average ticket prices
had shot up to $4.50 and average player's salary had increased
to $28,000. In 1975, the NHL had expanded to eighteen teams.
Average ticket prices had shot up to $6.61. It now cost $3.5
million to operate a team. The average player salary had
increased to $75,314. Capacity at games had dropped to 90
percent.

Whether these conditions obtain in the other four pro
sports can only be revealed by the owners and the Commissioner's
office. The sports fans, through observing sales of franchises, shifting of franchises, attendance at games and

salary negotiations can reach his own conclusions.

Golf

The ranking black golfer on the pro circuit is Lee Elder. Lee gained this distinction when he won the Monsanto Open Golf Tournament April 21, 1974. In a sudden death play-off he sank a twenty-one foot putt and won over Peter Oster-huis. By winning the Monsanto, for the first time in history, a black qualified for the Masters tournament, which is one of the four major golfing events in the world. To qualify for the Masters, a golfer must win a tournament recognized by the professional Golfers Association.

Before the change from point leaders to tournament victors, other blacks would have qualified for the Masters. The black golfers who would have made the Masters under the old system were Pete Brown and Charley Sifford. It is possible that there are not many blacks in golf because most of the black colleges do not have golf teams.

Since 1967, when Elder pushed Jack Nicklaus to five holes in the highly regarded American Golf Classic, no black golfer has come close. Over the three-year period, 1968-71, Elder earned $49,933, $70,401 and $84,730. In 1971, Elder attracted world-wide attention when Gary Player, a native of South Africa, invited this black man to play in the South African PGA. Since the Republic of South Africa still holds

to an unwavering policy of racism, blacks in this country
challenged Elder on accepting this invitation. While on
this African trip, Elder won the Nigerian Open. During the
1973 season Elder moved among top golfers in this country
when he had a total of eight wins and finished in the top
ten.[3]

Auto Racing

Another individual sport that has been cracked by
blacks is auto racing. No black has ever started in the
Indianapolis 500. Randy Bethea, a young black has set his
sights on the brick yard. Why not many black racing
drivers? For one thing the cost of entering is high. The
cost of a baseball and glove is cheap. It is similar in
basketball, but the cost of a racing stock car is tremendous
as well as the cost of the standard racers.

Notwithstanding the great contributions of blacks in
other fields of achievement, it is possible that their greatest
contribution has been in sports. Why is it, one may ask, that
whites like to see blacks compete in all sports, but by the
same token resist competition in business, education, government, politics and science? It is possible that, due to their
combative nature, the spectators want to see the best possible
boxer, baseball player, basketeer, golfer, football player,
jockey, racing car driver, swimmer, or tennis player. The

spectator is looking for the excellent player or superior player. He is looking for the gladiator who stands above all his competitors and receives the accolades of the crowd. What blacks have done in sports, they have not done in education, business, government, politics and science. We submit to the reader here that in these cases there are hard monopolies in existence which prevent blacks and other minorities from achieving their potential development.

Sports, a Growth Industry

One of the least known and recognized growth industries in this country is sports--baseball, football, basketball, hockey, soccer, swimming, surfing, golf, tennis, boxing, camping, hunting and fishing. Sports to the participant is an athletic contest. If he is doing it for pay he is classed as a professional. If he is a college boy and doing it for fun or scholarship he is classed as an amateur. The owners of the professional teams have made the promotion of these contests into a business.

Table XLV   below shows the growth in attendance of these major sports between 1964 and 1974. Increase in attendance has been phenomenal. Horse racing leads the entire pack. The increasing urbanization of people has been one of the reasons for the expansion of all of the major sports since 1960. Other reasons are the rapid growth of

Table XLV

Total Professional Attendance
1964-74 in the United States

Sports	1964	1974
Baseball	21,280,341	30,025,608
Basketball (NBA & ABA)	4,772,841	10,975,256
Football (154 Games)	6,010,924	10,236,323 (182 Games)
Hockey (NHL & WHA)	2,882,086	13,616,529
Auto Racing (USAC)	N. A.	2,500,000 Plus
Auto Racing (All Types)	N. A.	50,000,000 Plus
Golf (PGA)	1,324,744	2,851,195
Horse Racing	N. A.	78,000,000 Plus
Tennis (U. S. Open)	101,496*	153,287

*Total professional tennis attendance not available (N. A.)

Source: Harper's, Vol. 251, No. 1506. November, 1975, pg. 90.
From an Article, The Angry Fan by Randall Poe.

retirees. People over 65 now number 22,000,000. Early retirement at 55 has added to leisure time and has increased the
number of spectators at all sports events. Since 1949,
median income in the United States has almost quadrupled for
families. Half of the families now have a median income of

more than $12,450 annually. These are the families which
provide the great mass of spectators at sporting events.

The uniqueness of each sport produces its own following. Baseball is a middle-aged male's sport with a
history of more than one hundred years. The action in baseball is slow but the skills are appealing. Football has more
action than baseball, and appeals not only to the middle-aged
male, but also to the youth of the country. Baseball has a
one-hundred year history as a professional sport, but football came from the colleges to the procircuit. Basketball
also came out of the YMCA and the colleges. Hockey is not
only the fastest professional sport but also the most brutal.

One of the startling developments in the four major
sports are the high salaries paid these stars and superstars
on the diamond, gridiron, court and the rink. Since most
of the owners of these clubs are businessmen, they can get
tax writeoffs for losses, and they can use these teams to
advertise their products, such as beer, and, because cities
have absorbed and made concessions to these club owners in
the form of taxes, owning a professional team can be a
lucrative venture. Owners in some cases are frustrated
athletes, who often bask in the glory of their charges. This
exposure satisfies the owner's ego and is a kind of reflected
glory for him, especially when his team is a division, pennant,
World Series or Super Bowl winner.

Salaries of the participants in the four major sports in 1975 are shown below in Table XLVI   These high salaries are also justified on the basis of the average playing span of the professional athlete.

Table XLVI

Salaries of Four Major Sports

Sports	Average	Minimum
Football (NFL)	$ 42,338	$16,000
Baseball	41,000	16,000
Basketball (NBA)	65,000	20,000
Basketball (ABA)	80,000	17,500
Hockey (NFL)	70,000	15,000
Hockey (WHA)	$40-50,000	20,000

Source: Harper's Vol. 251, No. 1506, November, 1975, pg. 88. From an article, The Angry Fan by Randall Poe.

The average playing life of a basketball player in the National Basketball League is three years, in the major baseball leagues, it is five years, and seven in the National Football League. In professional sports, an athlete can easily delude himself into thinking he has arrived as a rookie and can expect a long tenure in his chosen sport. Facing the stiffest kind of competition, if he survives beyond the average three to five or seven years, he is the exception rather than the rule.

Those players who have exceptional talent and certain
longevity, have become millionaires. When a contract is
negotiated now, the player hires a lawyer. If he has personal charisma he can obtain advertising contracts which
further enhance his income. Milking his talents further are
the movie producers who may cast the star in a class "B" or
"C" movie or a blaxploitation cinema. It appears that a
star's fans will see their hero under all and every circumstances.

In recent years fans are becoming jaded. The strikes
in baseball and football have given them second thoughts on
their heroes. Furthermore, costs of admission have risen
faster than salaries and wages. Fans do not like to see
their stars as money grubbers. This is what they see when
the players are constantly bickering over pensions for a
life time for only five years work. Some of the stars have
an inflated conception of themselves. In the recession of
1973-75, the World Football League went out of business.
This league was the brainchild of Gary Davidson, the organizer of the World Hockey League. Prices for seats for the
WFL were just about as high as those for the NFL. The fans
did not buy the WFL and it threw in the towel midway through
their 1975 season. In December, 1975, the Utah Stars called
it quits. It is alleged that Bill Daniels, owner of the
Stars, lost $3,100,000 on this team. Other ABA teams that

folded in 1975 were the San Diego Sails and the Baltimore
Claws. Earlier in ABA history, the Pittsburgh Pipers did
not survive, nor did the Houston Mavericks. In the NBA,
franchises have shifted from San Diego to Houston, and
from St. Louis to Atlanta.

The old Brooklyn Dodgers became the Los Angeles
Dodgers. The New York Giants became the San Francisco
Giants. The Boston Braves became the Milwaukee Braves, and
then the Atlanta Braves. These shifts around the country
in professional sports have further left fans disenchanted
with their stars as well as with the owners. In the four
major sports there are 3,500 players. With all of these
shifts taking place and expansion to almost every nook and
cranny of the nation, big time sports may just be saturating
the market. There is a limit to the sports dollar. As
this country settles into a slow growth pattern and city
governments as well as the Federal government reduce tax
incentives to the professional teams, salaries of the stars
will be reduced because owners will not be able to use
expenses as tax writeoffs.

The ambition of most professional athletes is to
play in the "world series" of their sports, whether it is
hockey, tennis, soccer, basketball, football or baseball.
Since most minority professional athletes are in basketball,
baseball and football, then it is in these three major

sports where the final diadem in the championship of their

league is in the culmination of a career. Not alone is

pride a major factor, but the money that goes along with it.

As Eddie Robinson, the legendary coach of Grambling, once

stated, for a black athlete to make the National Football

League where he can earn from $20,000 to $250,000 a season

is the impossible dream. Nowehere, nowhere else in this

land can a black man go to school for three years or four

years, play gruelling football, and possibly earn $200,000

a year. By turning out excellent football players, similar

to those from Notre Dame, Grambling College in northeastern

Louisiana has produced more college football players who

have made it in the big time than any other college with the

possible exception of Notre Dame. Fame is not the only

spur, but also the lucrative contracts which await the player

who can make them team.

Always, at the end of a successful football season,

there is the Super Bowl. Those on the winning side can expect

something like this, according to Mickey Herskowitz writing

in the Houston Post: [4]

Super Bowl Victory	$15,000
Conference Championship	8,500
Playoff Victory	3,000
College All Star Game	3,000
	$29,500

A whole season's pay is wrapped up in the Super Bowl

victory. The pot of gold at the end of the rainbow is a

powerful lure for the minority or the majority football

player. Even if he loses or does not play after the Super,

he has the alternatives of coaching, teaching, advertising,

recreation, summer camps or going into the professions. Thus

football is not only a sport but a business. The benefits for

the winners are beyond the wildest dreams of the participants.

Tennis

In one-on-one sports, such as boxing, track, golf,

swimming, and tennis, minorities have always been competi-

tive. For reasons other than race, minorities have not

always competed as whites have in swimming, golf and tennis.

However, in golf and tennis, Mexican Americans have won

their share of championships with Lee Trevino in golf and

Pancho Gonzales in tennis. The real black victory in tennis

came for blacks when Arthur Ashe defeated the brash and

arrogant Jimmy Conners in July, 1975 at Wimbledon, England

and became the Wimbledon Singles Champion. With this triumph,

Ashe , the tennis pro from Richmond, Virginia,became the top

singles pro in the country. After twelve years of playing at

Wimbledon, he finally won the male singles championship.

Prior to the Wimbledon match, Conners had beaten Ashe three

times. The victories for Conners were on cement or clay

courts. The last time a black won at Wimbledon was Althea

Gibson in 1957 and 1958. Ashe was a losing semi-finalist in

1968 and 1969. In 1975 Ashe had two main objectives:

to win the World Championship Tennis and Wimbledon.   He won both.[3]

Arthur Ashe attributes the few blacks in tennis to the lack of emphasis on tennis in the public schools. Tennis is a highly individualistic sport and expensive in relationship to basketball and football. In basketball all you need is a ball and a basket and you can drum up a dozen or more kids on the lot or in the park for a game. In football you need a football and an open lot and drum up twenty-two players and you have a game. But not so in tennis. You need a court with nets and racquets. There are few public schools with tennis courts. However, tennis is played in the black colleges, but the gap in developing a tennis player, which is about five years before the kid reaches college, is not a hindrance in developing basketball and football players. These players do not have the high school gap to overcome. Until this gap is closed, Ashe believes that there will be a dearth of black tennis players. Along with developing tennis in college, however, there are black middle class families who are sending their children to tennis clubs in the hope that they will develop into top notch tennis players.

It is reported that about 34,000,000 Americans are playing tennis. There are about 400-500 college and professional tennis players. One black pro that ranks high in tennis is Arthur Ashe·

Black Women Tennis Players

In recent years probably the most promising black
woman tennis player was Althea Gibson, but as early as
1924, there was the first outstanding black woman tennis
player in Ora Washington. She wanted to play the renowned
Helen Wills Moody, but blatant segregation prevented such
a match. When Ora Washington was inducted into the Black
Athletes Hall of Fame in 1976, her whereabouts were unknown.
Charlie Mays, founder of the Black Sports Hall of Fame is
seeking to locate her. In 1924, Miss Washington became
the first black woman to win the singles title in the
American Tennis Association competition. She held the
title for twelve years, longer than any other woman player.[3]

Conclusion

The economics of professional sports hinge on the
state of the economy and the records of the teams in the
highly competitive world of baseball, football, basketball
and hockey. During the recession of 1974-75, professional
sports suffered from a drop in gate attendance, the demise
of about eight teams in the World Football League, dropouts
in the world tennis league, and severe losses in professional baseball, football and basketball.

During the 1974 season, the National Football League
suffered a drop of 4 percent in attendance. This league had

been riding a high tide of profitableness for years. However, because of the players' strike in the summer of 1974, many of the football fans became disenchanted with their Sunday heroes, and there was a decided drop in season ticket sales as well as fans who reflect in the glory of the fast break-a-way backs and wide receivers and the burly line backers. Of the twenty-six teams, half lost money or just barely broke even.

It is well known in economic theory that a recession respects no enterprise. During 1974-75, the sports business was caught between a fall-off in income in most of the cities where they played and the rising costs of player salaries. The Detroit professional teams in 1974-75 came under severe financial strains. As an entry in the new WFL, the Detroit Wheels stumbled through about two-thirds of their schedule of twenty games before the owners threw in the towel and took their losses. When the Wheels filed bankruptcy proceedings, they owed about $2.5 million to about one hundred twenty businesses and individuals. Following the Wheels into oblivion were the Detroit Loves who participated in World Team Tennis. The Loves were sold to an Indianapolis group of investors. Coming fast on the heels of the Wheels and Loves were the Detroit Stags in the World Hockey Association. Not being able to pay their rent, and missing a few payrolls, the Stags were taken over by the League and moved to Baltimore.

The above examples, as seen in Detroit, show the hazards of operating a sports franchise in a declining market. The recession of 1974-75 hit Detroit harder than any other major city in this country. Unemployment in Detroit,because of the lack of demand in car sales,rose as high as 16 percent. This was twice the rate of the nation as a whole. It is also apparent that the ego trip of some business owners for a pro sports franchise to compensate for their own shortcomings as athletic heroes in college has boomeranged. Also, the subsidizing of sports tax writeoffs is ending. In former years,owners,who are usually brewers, shipping magnates, real estate developers, horse racers and sportsmen,have been able to write off and depreciate losses. A federal court in 1975 ruled that the NFL Atlanta Falcons could not depreciate the full amount of player contracts. The Falcons tried to depreciate $8 million over more than five years on forty-two players contracts. The court only allowed half this amount.

REFERENCES

1. In an articel in <u>Sporting Review</u> for February 7, 1976, pg. 9, Art Spander quotes Dick Vertlieb,a white man, as saying that (Vertlieb is general manager of the Golden State Warriors) his job is to put together the best coach and team available to win. The only thing that matters is ability. Golden State won the NBA Championship in 1975, and has two black coaches in Al Attles. Of the twelve players, ten were black.

2. <u>Penthouse Interview</u> by Terry Buerin, Vol. 6, Number 3, November, 1974, pp. 123-124.

3. <u>San Francisco Examiner</u>, April 22, 1974, p. 51.

4. <u>Houston Post</u>, Sunday, January 18, 1976, pg. 3-C.

Chapter XXII

The Minority College in the United States

The minority colleges and universities discussed in this chapter are primarily the predominantly black colleges in this country. The predominantly black colleges in this country have multi-racial faculties, as well as multi-racial student bodies, but the majority of the students are black. Other minority colleges are those colleges and universities which are predominantly Jewish, Chicano, Catholic, or ethnic oriented. All of their problems are not similar, but their ideals of higher education are similar. The main differences between the ethnic colleges and the non-ethnic colleges are basically those of administration, teaching and research.

It is a foregone statement that the organization of any ethnic group is based on non-acceptance of its religion, social customs and mores by the inner groups or majority. Hence, the black colleges were organized basically because blacks could not enter white colleges. Lincoln University in Pennsylvania lays claim to being the first black college of higher learning. This university was organized in 1854 in Chester County, Pennsylvania. John Miller Dickey, a Presbyterian minister from Oxford, Pennsylvania, learned that an ex-slave from Maryland could not enter Princeton.

Incensed at such discrimination, Dickey established Ashmum
Institute, whose name was later changed to Lincoln Univer-
sity. Other colleges or universities laying claim to this
title as the oldest black college in the United States are
Wilberforce in Wilberforce, Ohio and Livingston College in
Livingston, North Carolina.

These claims are based on "firsts" in given areas
such as first black college with a black president, or the
first black sectarian college, or the first black co-educa-
tional college, or the first black girls college.

As of 1967, these predominantly black colleges numbered 104. Table XLVII shows the names of these colleges
and their location.

Table XLVII

Geographical Locations of Negro Colleges & Universities

Colleges	City
ALABAMA	
Alabama Agricultural and Mechanical College	Normal
Alabama Lutheran Academy and College	Selma
Alabama State College	Montgomery
Miles College	Birmingham
Oakwood College	Huntsville
Selma University	Selma
Stillman College	Tuscaloosa
Talladega College	Talladega
Tuskegee Institute	Tuskegee
ARKANSAS	
Arkansas A. M. & N. College	Pine Bluff
Arkansas Baptist College	Little Rock
Philander Smith College	Little Rock
Shorter	North Little Rock

Table XLVII (continued)

Colleges	City
DELAWARE	
Delaware State College	Dover
DISTRICT OF COLUMBIA	
Howard University	Washington, D. C.
FLORIDA	
Bethune-Cookman College	Daytona Beach
Edward Waters	Jacksonville
Florida A & M College	Tallahassee
Florida Memorial College	St. Augustine
Suwanne River Junior College	Madison
GEORGIA	
Albany State College	Albany
Atlanta University	Atlanta
Clark College	Atlanta
Fort Valley State College (The)	Fort Valley
Morehouse College	Atlanta
Morris Brown College	Atlanta
Paine College	Augusta
Savannah State College	Savannah
Spellman College	Atlanta
KENTUCKY	
Kentucky State College	Frankfort
Simmons University	Louisville
LOUISIANA	
Dillard University	New Orleans
Grambling	Grambling
Southern University	Baton Rouge
Xavier University of Louisiana	New Orleans
MARYLAND	
Bowie State College	Bowie
Coppin State College	Baltimore
Naryland State College	Princess Anne
Morgan State College	Baltimore
MISSISSIPPI	
Alcorn A & M College	Alcorn
Coahoma Junior College	Clarksdale
Jackson State University	Jackson
Mary Holmes Junior College	West Point

Table XLVII   (continued)

Colleges	City
Mississippi Industrial College	Holly Springs
Mississippi Valley State College	Itta Bena
Natchez Junior College	Natchez
Piney Woods County Life School	Piney Woods
Prentiss Normal & Industrial Institute	Prentiss
Rust College	Holly Springs
Tougaloo College	Tougaloo
Utica Junior College	Utica

MISSOURI
Lincoln   Jefferson City

NORTH CAROLINA
Agricultural & Technical College	Greensboro
Barber-Scotia College	Concord
Bennett College	Greensboro
Elizabeth City State College	Elizabeth City
Fayetteville State College	Fayetteville
Johnson C. Smith University	Charlotte
Kittrell College	Kittrell
Livingstone College	Salisbury
North Carolina Central University	Durham
Saint Augustine's College	Raleigh
Shaw University	Raleigh
Winston-Salem State University	Winston-Salem

OHIO
| Central State University | Wilberforce |
| Wilberforce University | Wilberforce |

OKLAHOMA
Langston University   Langston

PENNSYLVANIA
| Cheyney State College | Cheyney |
| Lincoln University | Lincoln |

SOUTH CAROLINA
Allen University	Columbia
Benedict College	Columbia
Claflin College	Orangeburg
Clinton Junior College	Rock Hill
Friendship Junior College	Rock Hill
Mather School (The)	Beaufort
Morris College	Sumter

Table XLVII (continued)

Colleges	City
South Carolina State College	Orangeburg
Voorhees College	Dermark
TENNESSEE	
Fisk University	Nashville
Knoxville College	Knoxville
Lane College	Jackson
Lemoyne College	Memphis
Meharry Medical College	Nahsville
Morristown College	Morristown
Owen College	Memphis
Tennessee A & I State University	Nashville
TEXAS	
Bishop College	Dallas
Butler College	Tyler
Huston-Tillotson College	Austin
Jarvis Christian College	Hawkins
Paul Quinn College	Waco
Prairie View A & M University	Prairie View
Southwestern Christian College	Terrell
St. Philip's College	San Antonio
Texas College	Tyler
Texas Southern University	Houston
Wiley College	Marshall
VIRGINIA	
Hampton Institute	Hampton
Norfolk State College	Norfolk
Saint Paul's College	Lawrenceville
Virginia Seminary & College	Lynchburg
Virginia State College	Petersburg
Virginia Union University	Richmond

Table XLVIII shows the number of these colleges and their states. The states with the largest number of these colleges are North Carolina, Mississippi, Texas, Alabama and Georgia.

Table XLVIII

Number of Colleges and Their States

States	Number
Alabama.	9
Arkansas	3
Delaware	1
District of Columbia	3
Florida	5
Georgia	9
Kentucky	2
Louisiana.	4
Maryland	4
Mississippi.	12
Missouri	1
North Carolina	12
Ohio	2
Oklahoma	1
Pennsylvania	2
South Carolina	9
Tennessee.	8
Texas.	11
Virginia	6
Total.	104

The great majority of these colleges began as private and church related schools. Some of them were purely vocational but most were teacher-education oriented. Wilberforce,in Ohio, was used to educate the black off-spring of white parents in the South. Of the one hundred-four colleges in 1967, 40 percent were land grant or state assisted institutions. By state assisted it is meant that the state only supports these colleges to the extent of about forty-nine cents of each dollar of expenses. The remainder of the funds come from tuition, fees, alumni contributions, private foundations and federal grants.

Young blacks enrolled in these colleges in 1967, male and female, numbered 156,000. Females attending these colleges were 57 percent. Males were 43 percent. Enrollment of blacks in all institutions of higher learning in 1968 was 434,000. Black colleges represented about 36 percent of the total. In 1970, enrollment in the predominantly black colleges jumped to 160,000, or 2.56 percent. Enrollment of blacks in all institutions of higher learning in 1970 went up to 470,000, or 8.29 percent. By 1975, enrollment of blacks in the black colleges had increased to 311,584. Enrollment of blacks in all institutions of higher education in 1976 had increased to 948,000, or about 9 percent of the total population in higher education.

Now, although blacks are approaching a par with whites in attendance at the college level in this country, they have yet to reach such parity on the graduate and professional level. On the graduate and professional level, among minority students, blacks predominate, only 6 percent are in master's and doctoral programs. Based on a study by the National Board of Graduate Education in 1974 blacks received only 3½ percent of the doctorates granted that year. Among these doctorates earned by blacks, more than 60 percent were in education, whereas only 25 percent granted to the candidates as a whole were in education.

The table below shows a five-year growth of the number of blacks in higher education in this country. From 1970-74 it is estimated that there was a net increase of 292,000 blacks in higher education in this country. This increase ranges from individuals working on bachelor degrees through those working on professional and terminal degrees. The data only show figures of the total number of blacks in relation to the total students in higher education in this country. The percentage of blacks in higher education increased each year from 7 percent in 1970 to 9.2 percent in 1974. The decline between 1972-73 was because of the recession that year and it is estimated that there will be a decline in 75-76 because of the recession in 1974-75. The great upsurge in blacks attending colleges and universities

in the 70's ,is of course, an outgrowth of the Civil Rights
of the 60's as well as a continuously high unemployment
rate among blacks which is now running at 12 percent for
black families and 40 percent for black teenagers.

Table XLIX

Blacks in Higher Education
in the United States   1970-1975

Year	Number of Blacks	Total	Percent of Blacks
1970	522,000	7,400,000	7.0
1971	680,000	8,000,000	8.5
1972	727,000	8,300,000	8.8
1973	684,000	8,100,000	8.4
1974	814,000	8,800,000	9.2
1975	778,960	11,128,000	7.0

Source: Statistics of Higher Education, Washington, Government Printing Office, 1975.

1975 data from Department of Health, Education and
Welfare, reported December 15, 1975. The percent
of blacks is estimated as seven percent of the
total.

Community College or Two Year Colleges

Community colleges have had a very rapid expansion
since the end of World War II, and especially in the sixties.
Bronx Community College in New York City has 12,700 students,
of which the majority are blacks and Puerto Ricans. Seventy

percent of these students cannot read, write and compute figures on a college level. Fifty-two percent come from families with annual income of less than $7,000 per year, and only about 7 percent have fathers with a college education.

Gene I. Maeroof, writer for the New York Times, reports that in this country in 1973, there were 2,866,062 students in 1,141 two-year institutions of education beyond the high school. In 1900 there were fewer than a dozen two-year colleges in the United States.

Community colleges have a greater attraction for minorities than four-year colleges and universities. One reason for this is that tuition costs may be non-existent, or they are much lower than in four-year colleges and universities. A second reason is that community colleges provide practical vocations and trades for the student who works full or part-time. A third reason is that an open admissions policy is available for the applying student. Because of low tuition policy or non-existent tuition in high education, black student enrollment in this country has increased 211 percent over the past ten years.

As early as 1948, there were 465,815 students in these two-year community colleges. By 1968, based on data from the Association of Junior and Community Colleges, there were 1,924,970 students in 1,038 two-year colleges. Miami-Dade

Community College in Florida has 36,000 students, the largest
in the country. Enrollment in Bronx Community College for
two selected years is shown below:

Percent of Ethnic Enrollment

Year	White	Black	Puerto Rican	Other
1969	54.8	31.6	11.3	2.3
1973	34.7	45.8	17.9	1.6

In the aforementioned article by Gene I. Maeroff,
Jerome Karabel, a Harvard graduate student writing in the
November, 1973 issue of the Harvard Educational Review,
stated that the community college is the lowest rung of
educational opportunity in this country. Mr. Karabel holds
that the community college inflates higher education and is
thusly far more costly than higher education. Having this
article published in the Harvard Educational Review is not
such a distinction. This Review also published the spurious
findings of Jenson on the inferiority of black ghetto children vis a vis whites.

The community college is paying off. What Karabel
does not realize or refuses to recognize is that (1) this
country does not have any kind of educational elite which
calls the shots on the business, governmental and social
life of this nation. (2) Educational opportunity should
be open to all and not to just the wealthy people whose
sons and daughters can go to college because their parents

are rich. (3) Community colleges provide an opportunity for
the poor and modest income families to have their children
seek to improve themselves. And (4) would these young men
and women be better or worse citizens if they had not attended
a community college.

Because of the financial crisis through which New York
City went in 1975-76, there were demands that students pay
tuition for enrollment in the Bronx Community College. It was
alleged that non-payment of tuition was one of the causes of
New York City's financial crisis. However, the direct cause
of lack of revenue is the eroding of the tax base by those
people who work in New York, but live in New Jersey and Connecticut.

Dr. James A. Colston, a black who gave up a life-time
appointment as president of Knoxville College,was appointed
president of Bronx Community College.

The Drop-Out Rate in Black Education on the College Level

What are the survival rates of the black college
entrant? For the general population, recent studies show
the following survival rates. On August 31, 1974, the City
University reported that 50 percent of their college students
fail to complete their college courses. This drop-out rate
is 50 percent, which is equal to the national average. City
officials think that this high drop-out rate is a reflection

of the open admission policy. Under the former selective-
admission policy, 70 percent of the students completed college. Open admissions policy started in 1970.

The dire predictions of opponents of open admission
that college education would become diluted and that the
A. B. degree would be cheapened have not materialized. The
American Council on Education found that 38 percent of students who had finished high school with an average of "C"
completed four years of college. A study at Pennsylvania
State University showed that 30.8 percent of the high school
students in the bottom fifth of their classes completed college after five years.

Questions that are raised about the high drop-out rate
are not answered by the open admissions policy, but improvement of the quality of teaching, offering better counseling
and compensatory education could no doubt reduce the high
drop-out rate. These factors have really severely affected
minorities such as blacks, Puerto Ricans, Latin-Americans
and Indians. Poor counseling is the chief fault. Oftentimes
college freshmen have not one iota of information about the
job market. They do not know that there are more than 50,000
occupational specialities open for penetration. Even most
counselors do not know this statistic.

It is suggested that the "Now Generation" with greater
sophistication derived from instant experience and instant
reaction is a valuable adjunct to general education. However,

unless such instant experience is blended in with proficient
reading and analytical skills, this generation can grow up
with softness of heart as well as softness of mind. The
skills of the preelectronic age must be a complement to the
present-day skills of the computer and solid state electronics.

In the spring of 1974, James A. Harris, president
of the National Education Association, made a speech before
the South Carolina Education Association. His speech was a
grim reminder of the problems facing this country in the
education of its youth. These are some of the stark realities
which were revealed in speech. Two million children of
school age who should be in school have dropped out. These
children live in the central city. Because of the permissive,
ness of society, it is highly likely that a greater number
of these drop-outs will spend some portion of their lives
in correctional institutions than will the students attending all the schools and colleges of higher education. On
any given school day, 13,000 school children are in correctional institutions and another 100,000 are in jail or in
police lineups. Out of every 100 students attending school
across the nation, 23 drop out, 77 graduate from high school,
43 enter college, 21 receive a B.A.,six earn an M.A., and one
earns a Ph. D. In all the statistics above, there is no
mention of what groups suffer most from the lack of funds

spent on education. You guessed it. It is the minorities. Minorities are the heavy drop-outs, and the ones who are usually incarcerated in correctional institutions. The percentage of these minorities runs as high as 80 percent. In the central city schools it is well known that crime and violence abound. There are students who have no interest in education who roam the halls disrupting classes and intimidating teachers and officials.

One of the more disturbing aspects of this report is that many states now spend more money to place a student in a correctional institution than to provide this child with an adequate education. In Iowa, the state pays $9,000 a year to keep a student in a juvenile home but only $1,050 a year for the average student in school. Maryland spends $18,000, Illinois and Michigan $10,000, Virginia $3,877 and Washington, D.C. $7,469. All of these amounts are far in excess of the amounts which each of these states spends on a child in the school system.

Harris feels that by reduction in the class size, we could add 400,000 new teachers to improve educational programs. Just to improve educational programs we need an additional 670,000 teachers. For special education and kindergarten classes an additional 266,000 teachers are needed. It is lamentable that education is not at the top of the nation's priority list. Bond issues should not be

voted down for education. The long-term advantage accruing
from the effects of education are far more beneficial than
the short-term losses from prisons, jails, and drop-outs.

During the period 1973-76 and continuing into
1977 and beyond there is the perennial question, can the
black college survive? This question has become increasingly unsettling to blacks since the decision on Brown v School
Board and the Civil Rights decision of 1964-65. Blacks
generally have a nagging fear that whites would like to get
rid of the black colleges because the black colleges constantly remind whites of racism and neglect in this dynamic
economy. But by the same token, there is a school of whites
who would like to keep the black colleges as going concerns
because the black colleges, in their present condition,
could never compete with the Ivy League colleges, the Big
Ten and colleges in the Southwest and on the Pacific Coast.
The colleges in these regions, especially the state colleges and universities rank as super universities. With
huge enrollments, swollen budgets, political clout in the
state capitals, these colleges and universities are power-
houses in just about getting all they want, and with the
legislatures of the various states, boards of regents and
administration, these colleges and universities are run
like fiefdoms. Higher education in this country is a growth
industry. Where does all of this activity in higher educa-

tion leave the black colleges and universities?

It can be stated succinctly that black colleges have always struggled for survival. This new twist in recent years is nothing new to the black colleges. Since the founding of Lincoln University in Pennsylvania in 1854, black colleges have fought to keep the wolf from the door. There are now about 114 predominantly black colleges in this country. Of the 948,000 blacks in higher education in this country during the 1976-77 academic year, about half were attending black colleges. Over the years, these black colleges have graduated 75 percent of the black Ph. D's, 85 percent of the black surgeons and physicians, 60 percent of the black dentists and the great majority of the black officers in the armed forces. These 474,000 blacks attending black colleges are in attendance at the thirty-six state-assisted institutions and eighty-four private institutions. But in the state assisted-institutions, are those which are fighting for survival.

Presently under threat of absorption by their big white brother institutions are these predominantly black universities: Florida A&M University in Tallahassee, Tennessee State in Nashville, Morgan State, Bowie, Coppin and Maryland State in Maryland. The threat of absorption by the large white state universities comes from two sources: the intense efforts of the HEW bureaucracy to integrate faculty and staffs of the predominantly black state-assisted colleges and from the state legislatures. Some of these black administrators who are protected by political hacks who are masked as regents, and by governors and state legislatures, run their black state-assisted institutions like a plantation. They do not recognize even their faculty senate of faculty organizations. These boards of regents who are really political appointees by the governor virtually ignore their faculties. However, it is amazing that the best teaching in the black colleges takes place in the midst of these adversities. Yet, the private black colleges which are really educating their students and doing an excellent teaching job and research have no fear of survival, although it is true that a few of them are experiencing financial constraints. These institutions are non-profit with no profit centers or stockholders. They are purely service-oriented colleges supplying graduates for an ever-changing economy. First, black colleges are bereft of wealthy corporate alumni who can endow a college. Second, corporate giving to the black colleges is on a small scale. The vast consumer market of blacks, about $60 billion, which is funneled into gasoline, food ,beverages, clothing, autos, housing and myriad other goods and services see only one to two percent of corporate giving to black colleges and universities in this country. Third, government grants, including the Department of Health,

Education and Welfare and the National Science Foundation, are very low in comparison to their grants to the predominantly white colleges and universities. Fourth, grants from private foundations such as the Ford Foundation have also been small in comparison to what have been given to the predominantly white colleges and universities. In a free market economy which is heavily dependent on the college graduate for staffing corporate boards and line functions, it is the duty and responsibility of these foundations, corporations and governments to supply financial assistance to the black colleges. It is suggested that, for every graduate who is hired by the government or a corporation, a stipend, matching the salary that the graduate is receiving should be given to that college. The great contribution of the black college to the milieu of this country is that it has taken the black boy and girl and has educated him/her to a level in this highly competitive society where they can compete and make a living. These colleges more than any other agency have been instrumental in moving these blacks from a low income status to a middle income status. The deprivation of blacks in a racist culture has been documented. It is the refusal to recognize this deprivation that inhibits the black colleges. However, in spite of this deprivation, the black college has taken the young black and has made him into a productive citizen.

Black Studies

It has often been asked, how did black studies come to be a major thrust in education in the sixties, when not much had been said about it prior to this time? First, much had been said of it prior to the sixties. The majority of the black scholars who had received their degrees at predominantly black colleges and universities had been exposed to black studies in the thirties, forties, fifties and sixties. However, it was not called black studies, but Negro History, or the Negro in Labor, the Negro in Western Culture or some other esoteric name. Black historians who founded the Association for the Study of Negro Life and History, long ago pleaded for recognition of blacks in western civilization. Early blacks who came upon the scene in these strident times pushed for education of blacks. Among these men and women were, Alain Locke, the philosopher; Carter G. Woodson, historian; A. Philip Randolph, labor leader; Abram Harris, economist; Scott Joplin, composer; Duke Ellington, musician; Bert Williams, entertainer; Bishop Wright, theologian; Kelly Miller, educator; Madame C.J. Walker, businesswoman; C.C. Spaulding, businessman; and General Benjamin O. Davis, military. A.J. Rodgers' research on black contributions to western culture, which were long carried in the Pittsburgh Courier, opened areas to the study of Negroes in history.

In the twenties, black writers such as Langston Hughes

and Claude McKay; black poets such as Countee Cullen, Paul
Lawrence Dunbar and Melvin Tolson were in the vanguard of
the Negro Renaissance. During this period there was an outpouring of black culture in the arts, music, theatre, literature and athletics.

Because of the great depression in the thirties, there
was a slackening in the development of this country on a
broad scale. Not alone was the economy in a holding action,
but there was actual retrogression. Education did not flourish
during this period, nor did it gain much momentum during the
forties. World War II claimed the youth of the country to
fight Hitler and the Japanese, but with the end of the War
and the enactment of the GI Bill in 1945, there was a great
upsurge in education for whites as well as blacks, which
carried over into the sixties after the passage of the Civil
Rights Act of 1964. In the meantime, Kwame Nkrumah had gained
independence for Ghana and Richard Wright had long since
published his Black Boy and Native Son. This writer, who was
born in Mississippi and raised in Chicago, came out with
Black Power in the mid-fifties. Adam Clayton Powell, who was
in Congress, seized on this phrase and in his own flamboyant
manner conveyed it over to Stokeley Carmichael. This smooth,
black spellbinder began to walk the land with the Student
Non-Violent Coordinating Committee, an adjunct to Martin
Luther King's Southern Christian Leadership Conference. Seeking to arouse the black youth who were marching in Mississippi,

Selma and Birmingham, the phrase Black Power began to be
painted on walls to further encourage blacks to stand up and
fight for their rights. From Black Power came the phrase
Black is Beautiful. To some of the black intellectuals these
phrases meant nothing. They were mere fillups to bulwark the
ego of blacks. However, when blacks began to matriculate in
greater and greater numbers into the white schools a cry went
up for the black studies program. Black studies were to justi-
fy Black Power and Black is Beautiful. The black studies movement gained a prairie-fire acceptance after Martin Luther King
was assassinated in Memphis on April 4, 1968. From universities
in the Ivy League, Harvard and Columbia, through the Big Ten
and the Pacific Coast, white universities created black
studies departments. They were done in such haste that most
of the experienced black scholars held them suspect. The great
question was what were they teaching. It was found that history and literature were the main fare. Furthermore, even
after a person received a degree in black studies he could
use it in only a limited way in the world of work. Areas of
business and government would be closed to him, but there
would be a place in an educational institution for him. It
was found that the instructors in these black studies programs were mainly Africans who had come over here for an
education and who represented blacks more strongly than
American blacks.

Black studies gained acceptance through the black
student unions in white colleges. These black activists as
well as their white brethren virtually screamed at the white
administrators to put black studies programs in the curriculum. J.K. Obatala, writing in the Smithsonian stated that
207 black studies directors attended a meeting in Philadelphia
in 1970.[2] In 1974, Cecil Glenn, a black who took over the
Black Education Department at the University of Colorado in
1970, reported that after "a bubu-clad nationalist was shot
and killed in Denver one day before school was to open" there
were only eight black studies directors in attendance at the
New York meeting in that year.

In just a four-year span can black studies be written
off? No. Black studies were cast in the light of frenzy and
a need to identify. Yet, in most of the black studies courses
more whites were enrolled than blacks. Oftentimes black studies
were looked upon in academia as "sop courses" and "snaps".
When politics tries to become greater than hard, serious
study, which is the hallmark of scholarship, then all the
king's men cannot sustain a program which is not substantive.
Within the white colleges and universities, the budgets for
black studies were siphoned from other departments. When
money became tight in 1973-75, black studies budgets were cut.
Nothwithstanding the shrill cries of the black activists of
wanting something to hang their hat on, black studies needed

to broaden its concepts to fulfill the needs of its students.
History is the framework within which black studies fall. However the art, literature, sociology, economics and science in
the general university can be made relevant to the black as
well as to the white student,   so that both the black and
white student can play his part in advancing this democracy.
Black studies must fulfill a need beyond just the knowledge
of black accomplishments and achievements.

Conclusion

In the coming of age of black studies, it has gene
ated ethnic studies of other racial groups in this country.
These have been Scandinavian, Polish, Italian and Greek
Studies.[1] Jews have always had their own study groups, so
that it should not be strange that other ethnics would want
to learn more about themselves. As black studies move more
and more into the warp and woof of the academic structure in
this country, there is a need of better teaching. The African
and West Indian black who moved into this vacuum when black
studies came upon the scene as instructors in the sixties
have just about run their course. Teachers, whether they are
black or white, must be well educated in ways in which blacks
and whites can rehabilitate the ghetto. Why is it that the
governmental delivery system for minorities is so inept and
fractional? How can the establishment overcome its racism
and utilize personnel on the basis of competency in lieu of

having a white skin in preference to a black skin? Why is it so difficult for a black businessman to borrow funds even though he is highly successful? These are the great issues that black studies can throw some light on. The need is for excellent teaching. The teacher can be black or white, but he must be sincere and well ingrained in the milieu around him.

Chapter XXIII

Minorities and the Military

At the end of the Vietnam War, minorities, especially blacks, had achieved a level of development in the
military undreamed of three decades ago. Minorities have always served in the armed forces. Participation of the American Indians in World War I and II have been covered in Chapter VI. . The Japanese Nisei did yeoman work in World War
II in Italy and Southern France. It was called the Gung-Ho
battalion. Mexican-Americans have distinguished themselves
in both of the great wars as well as in Korea and Vietnam. In
this chapter we emphasize the progress of blacks in the military and their significant achievements in the Officers Corps.
As we move beyond the bicentennial, the percentage of blacks
in all branches of the military - Army, Navy, Air Force and
Marine Corps have reached unprecendented heights.

A quarter of a century ago, President Harry S. Truman, of the Missouri twang and the tart tongue, created the
Committee on Equality of Treatment and Opportunity in the
Armed Services. The Committee submitted its final report to
the President in 1950. Prior to this time, the most segregat-
ed of the armed forces were the Marine Corps, Navy, Air
Force and Army, in this order. The Army was the most liberal,
to use an overworked phrase. The late eminent George C. Marshall, who armed the Republic for the onslaught on Hitler and

Tojo, prevailed over the late Hap Arnold, who was the chief
of the Air Corps in World War II. Arnold wanted to exclude
blacks completely from the Air Corps. He wanted a lily white
Corps but Marshall said no. As Chief of Staff and one of the
few men President Roosevelt listened to, he created the black
Air Corps Squadron at Tuskegee Institute. This outfit flew
combat in Italy and downed more Nazi planes at Anzio and other
parts of Italy than any other Air Force Squadron.

Benjamin O. Davis, a West Pointer, whipped the
squadron into combat efficiency and led it into action. Our
brief mention of the exploits of blacks can only be in capsule form. Volumes have been written and are to be written on
black infantry and artillery in World War I, and the 92nd and
93rd Divisions in World War II, as well as the black tankers
under the legendary George Patton in France and the Battle of
the Bulge. Beginning with the Revolutionary War, blacks engaged in all of its battles. We cite here only a few of the
many blacks in the American Revolution.

Black Heroes of the American Revolution

The battle of Bunker Hill was fought on June 17,
1775. The names of the great leaders and soldiers who fought
this battle have gone into history as heroes chiseled into
the memory of millions of Americans. However, there were numbers of black men who fought in this battle whose names have
been long forgotten. This little vignette is being written to

recall the names of some of those blacks who fought in the
Battle of Bunker Hill. These men were Peter Salem, Caesar
Basom, Cuffee Whittemore, Titus Colburn, Alexander Ames, Basi-
lai Lew, and Caleb Howe.

As the British stormed Bunker Hill Peter Salem fought
valiantly. Salem has been credited with killing the British
Major John Pitcairn at the Battle of Lexington in April.
Caesar Bason, and Cuffee Whittemore fought under Colonel
William Prescott. Prescott's company was formed at Groton and
Pepperell, Massachusetts. From the village of Andover came
Colburn, Ames, and Lew. Howe fought with the men from Plymouth. These seven black immortals along with their white
counterparts fought the British to a standstill. It is only redundant for us at this date in history to once more go over
the exploits of these men, but as the years pass we cannot
help but recall these seven men who were fighting the British
not only physically for their freedom, but also fighting for
their philosophy of all free men who are and were held in
bondage through the institution of slavery and those inden-
tured whites who were virtually slaves.

The charge of the British at first swept the Americans back, but the musket of Peter Salem fatally wounded
Major Pitcairn. Caesar Basom was fighting a rear-guard action
when he was hit in the thigh by a musket ball. It was reported
that Captain Aaron Smith of Shrewsbury, Massachusetts, was firing

at the British, Basom was loading his musket for him. In the
heat of the battle Smith's musket was destroyed. He then
lifted Basom on his back and with his sword charged the British. As the British bore down upon Smith, Bason entreated
Smith to leave him to go and save himself. It was later learned that the British overwhelmed the position Smith left and
in the aftermath of the battle, Basom was known to have been
captured and taken prisoner to Boston.

This Texan's Name Nobody Knows

After the Revolutionary War a black veteran, named
Thomas Savoy, journeyed to Texas and took up the cause of
Texas's independence with General Sam Houston. It was in the
year 1839, when a Texas expedition under Jordon marched to
Saltillo to bulwark the infamous Mexican Commander Canales
who,with his armed Federalist troops, were fighting against
the Mexican Anti-Federalists. The traitor Canales betrayed
the small group of Texans, but this small band of Federalists
and the states rights Mexican army whipped the Mexican Anti-
Federalists thoroughly and then later returned to Texas.

Thomas Savoy, the black Texan, in this group, ac-
quitted himself well in the skirmishes against the Mexicans.
He had established such a reputation among the Texans that
they called him "Black Tom," and he was known as Black Tom in
Texas thereafter. In 1842, General Woll invaded Texas with a
Mexican army, and was soundly trounced at the Battle of Salado.

Black Tom again participated in this battle and was wounded.
As the Texas and Mexican War gained momentum, Black Tom,
fighting under Taylor's banner fought in the Battle of Mon-
terey. Before the war with Mexico was over he also fought in
the Battle of Buena Vista.

After the Mexican War ended, Black Tom was in a number of Indian engagements in Texas. He now made San Antonio
his home and became well-known in and around Bexar County. He
was a likable man and a great favorite. However, being an ad-
venturer and a soldier of fortune, Black Tom ranged far afield.
It was known among the bar habitues in San Antonio that Black
Tom would every now and then go off on jaunts into the countryside. Such a wandering spirit kept him in close touch with
nature. He would be missing for days and weeks. At various
times he would be in the area now known as Fort Clark and in
the Comanche Indian country in central Texas. About five years
after the Mexican War was over, on the 15th day of July, 1853,
a cowhand found the body of a man two miles west of San Antonio. At the coroner's inquest it was found that this was the
body of Black Tom. The cause of death was unknown as well as
the identity of the perpetrator.

Black Tom was a legend in Bexar County. However,
when Texas won its independence and the Civil War was over,
younger generations completely forgot Black Tom. He was omitted
from the history books of Texas. Yet in light of the pioneer
service he gave to the state, he must go down in the annals of

Texas history along with Davy Crockett, Jim Bowie, and others.

The End of Segregation

With the breakdown of segregation and after thirty-four years with a draft Army and other branches of the military, we have now draft-free armed forces. The percent of blacks in the armed forces has increased remarkably over the seven years ending in 1974. The table below shows the percent of blacks in the various branches of the armed forces at this time.

Table L

Percent of Blacks Enrolled in the
Armed Forces in December 1974

Branch of Service	Percent of Enrollment
Army	22
Marine Corps	18
Air Force	15
Navy	9

Source: Department of Defense

Basic reasons for such a large increase in the strength of blacks in the armed forces can be attributed to four conditions:

1. Freedom of choice stemming from the Civil Rights movement.

2. Equality of opportunity in the armed forces.

3. The stability of military life vis-a-vis the

uncertainty of civilian life.

4. The recession of 1973-75.

Promotion and advancement in the armed forces are much more available for blacks than advancement and promotion in the industrial complex in this country. The table below shows the number of blacks by rank in the Officer Corps in the various branches of the armed forces.

Table LI

Blacks in the Officer Corps of the Armed Forces in 1974

Rank	Number of Black Officers in		
	Army	Air Force	Navy
1. Four Star General		1	
2. Major Generals	3		
3. Brigadier Generals	11		
4. Full Colonels	132		
5. Admirals (Rear)			2
6. Lt. Colonels	600	205	
7. Majors		1,393	
8. Captains		2,534	

Source: Department of Defense

It appears that there is a gap in the number of black officers in the Navy as compared to the Army and Air Force, but the Navy equivalents in Lieutenant Colonels, Majors,

Captains, and Junior Officers are about the same as the Army and Air Force. Figures for the Marine Corps are included in those of the Navy.

Not by any stretch of the imagination can we say that blacks have reached their ultimate development in the armed forces. Only about 3 percent of the combined Officer Corps are black. The Army is highest with about 5 percent. The Navy has one percent, the Air Force, 2 percent and the Marine Corps, 2 percent. To all the blacks who served in World War I and II it was a remote thought that a black would ever become a Four Star General in any branch of the service in the Defense Establishment.

General Daniel "Chappie" James is the highest ranking black in the armed forces. He is a graduate of Tuskegee Institute and was in Pensacola, Florida. James came fron the rank of fighter pilot. He flew 101 combat missions during the Korean War. He was also a protester against unfair treatment. As a First Lieutenant in the Air Corps, he and a number of other black officers tried to integrate Freeman Field in Seymour, Indiana in 1945. He and the other officers were promptly arrested. Little or nothing came of the incident because white-hot publicity was thrown on the incident and the Air Corps decided to proceed no further with the case at this time, entering the record of nolle prosequi. The young officers were released with no charges brought against them.

As a big, burly fighter pilot, James came to the
attention of Melvin Laird after he had flown 78 combat missions over North Vietnam. As Secretary of Defense, Laird
brought James to the Pentagon, where he was installed in the
office of Public Affairs. A determined and dedicated man,
James has been the main thrust in carrying the equal opportunity theme to members of the armed forces. It is up to the
blacks to pursue all opportunities possible in the armed forces. Institutionalized racism no longer remains in the armed
forces. With the draft-free enrollment, the armed forces present one facet of life in America where a black man or woman
or any other minority can achieve the ultimate potential.
General Daniel "Chappie" James moved from his position as
vice commander of the Military Air Lift Command on Saturday,
August 30, 1975, when he assumed command of the North American
Air Defense Command in Colorado Springs, Colorado. He succeeded General Lucius Clay, Jr.

The two highest ranking naval officers are Rear
Admirals Gerald E. Thomas and Samuel L. Gravely, Jr.

Predominantly black colleges and universities that
have contributed ROTC graduates to the armed forces are
Howard, Wilberforce, Central State, and Prairie View. Howard
University, located in Washington, D.C., is a federal govern-
ment-sponsored university, named after General O.O. Howard of
Civil War fame. Wilberforce and Central State in Wilberforce,

Ohio, have a long heritage of educated young blacks, and the
city of Wilberforce was a spot on the Underground Railroad.
Charles Young, the first Colonel in the U.S. Army lived in
Wilberforce, Ohio.

At the end of 1973, the Department of Defense compiled the following data showing the percentage of blacks in
the Officer Corps relative to all officers.

Branch of Service	Total	Blacks	Percent
Army	93,779	3,927	4.19
Air Force	113,486	2,375	2.09
Navy	64,215	705	1.10
Marine Corps	17,432	351	2.01
	288,912	7,238	2.51

Source: Department of Defense

Out of more than a quarter of a million officers in
the armed forces, blacks have 7,238 slots of a small 2½ percent. These data show that there is much more work to be done.

Other high ranking officers in the armed forces are:

Coast Guard: Commander Bobby C. Wilks

Army: Brig. Gen. R.C. Cartwright, Washington, D.C.
Major Gen. Frederic E. Davison, Washington, D.C.
Brig. Gen. Julius W. Becton, Jr., Bryn Mawr, Pa.
Brig. Gen. Roscoe Robinson, Jr., St. Louis, Mo.
Brig. Gen. George B. Price, Laurel, Miss.
Brig. Gen. Edward Greer, Gary, West Va.
Brig. Gen. Geo. M. Shuffer, Palestine, Texas
Brig. Gen. Thomas E. Clifford, Washington, D.C.
Brig. Gen. Charles C. Rogers, Claremont, W. Va.
Brig. Gen. Fred Sheffey, McKeesport, Pa.
Brig. Gen. Oliver W. Dillard, Margaret, Ala.

> Brig. Gen. Arthur J. Gregg, U.S. Army
> Lt. Gen. B.O. Davis, Jr. (retired) U.S.
> Army Reserve
> Brig. Gen. Cunningham C. Bryant, U.S. National
> Guard
> Brig. Gen. William Brooks, Jr., Indianapolis,
> Ind.

Marine Corps: Colonel Kenneth H. Berthoud, Jr. U.S.M.C.

Without the equal opportunity and the affirmative action programs issued under executive orders, it is highly doubtful that such promotions would have been made. It is notable, however, that the armed forces have done far more in the quest for equal opportunity than the civilian sector. Supervising the equal opportunity program has been the top echelon of the Department of Defense: Dr. John L. McLucas, Secretary of the Air Force; William P. Clements, Secretary of Defense; Howard H. Callaway, Secretary of the Navy; Robert E. Cushman, Jr., Commandant of the Marines; and H. Minton Francis, Deputy Assistant Secretary of Equal Opportunity, Department of Defense.

Chapter XXIV

Communication Industry

What is the employment picture and the outlook for
minorities in the communication industry in this country?
Still bleak. Our analysis of communications and their treatment of minorities and blacks must first begin with newspapers. This is one of the oldest mass media. Mewspapers have
a built-in leverage. The Constitution guarantees freedom of
sppech, freedom of assembly and freedom to write as one
chooses so long as he does not commit libel. Freedom of the
press is nurtured and worshipped by the press. This freedom
is guarded jealously by the press in this country, and the
press takes great delight in having been the main instrument
in bringing Nixon down. A zealous reporter of the style of
Richard Harding Davis, who probes and probes when he scents
wrong doing can cause upheavals in government and business
with his "nose for the news".

Minorities have complained and rightly so, that for
all the vaunted freedom enjoyed by the press, it does not
pursue with similar zeal the guarding of freedom of minorities
in various facets of living. Minorities complain that the
press very seldom, if ever, presents the minority view point,
whether it is Chicano, black, Indian, Oriental, or foreign
born. Basically, the press is out to sell papers. Through

the sale of newspapers and advertising - and advertising is the main source of revenue - the press is controlled by big business. The journalist in today's scheme of things has bowed to the cost accountant. We will take one case in point which has been in the front pages of the newspapers for about four years - busing. Every school year, beginning in September, for the past four years, there has been some kind of violence in this country over busing, but busing is not new to minorities. Blacks and Chicano children - those living in areas where access to elementary and high school education is in short supply - have been bussed most of their lives. Brown v School Board introduced desegregation into school systems in this country, but the fulfillment of Brown v School Board has not yet been achieved after more than twenty-four years. Treatment of busing and desegregation has almost always been anti-minority by the press. It has been pro-establishment.

Another area where the cause of minorities has been underwritten by the press is in crime. Certainly it is not our purpose here to qualify crime, but it should be one of the purposes of the press to analyze the causes of crime. This is necessary because the workhouses, jails, correctional institutions, prisons and security institutions are filled with minorities far out of proportional numbers in the population, and you will find that just about 50 percent of the incarcerated individuals are minorities - blacks and Chicanos.

Jessica Mitford in her Kind and Usual Punishment, severely excoriates our prison system and rightly so. However, the press does not challenge the basic causes of crime in this country, only the effects. Certainly, the system is amiss when most of the prison population are minorities, and it is the system which is going unchallenged by the press.

One of the basic reasons why minorities are shunted onto the back pages of the press is that so few are employed by the press in this country. Black Enterprise made a survey of blacks employed by major newspapers in this country in 1974. Results are in Table LII below. Of these twenty-nine papers employing blacks as reporters or rewrite men and editors, The Washington Post led the field with seventeen. The second paper was The New York Times with sixteen, and The Washington Star News employed twelve, The Boston Globe employed ten. These four newspapers, all noted for their liberalism and their policy of coming to grips with vital issues, had double digit employment. On the other twenty-four papers, employment ranged from nine down to one. The 160 blacks on these twenty-nine newspapers were indeed a minority. Because of this lack of employment of blacks and other minorities, it is possible that little empathy is given to unpopular causes or causes which will not sell newspapers or garner advertising.

Yet the owners of the white press should not be written off. Minorities need them and they need minorities.

TABLE LII

Blacks Employed In Major Newspaper Publication

In The United States In 1974[1]

NEWSPAPER	BLACKS EMPLOYED
The Boston Globe	10
Detroit Free Press	6
The Seattle Times	2
Minneapolis Star	3
The Christian Science Monitor	1
The Dallas Morning News	1
San Francisco Chronicle	5
Philadelphia Inquirer	6
Minneapolis Tribune	2
Pittsburgh Post-Gazette	2
The Atlanta Constitution	4
The Courier Journal	3
The Louisville Times	3
St. Louis Post Dispatch	9
The New York Post	3
Newsday	8
The Los Angeles Times	4
The Atlanta Journal	6
Oakland Tribune	3
Chicago Sun Times	6
Denver Post	3
The Plain Dealer	5
Washington Star News	12
Chicago Daily News	6
Washington Post	17
The Sun	1
San Francisco Examiner	5
Daily News	8
New York Times	16
Total	160

The minority population can improve their image in the nation's press through hammering on the presentation of the news. Long before the Civil Rights Act, the white press, when finding that the guilty party in a rape was in the minority group, would mention that a black or Chicano had raped the woman.

This was rank racism, for when a white man had committed the act, no mention of race was made. This is a kind of slimy journalism, and, in the days of William Randolph Hearst, was called yellow journalism.

Probably the only champions of minorities are the minority newspapers - Chicano and black. The black press has an organization called the National Newspaper Association. It has about sixty members - mostly weekly or bi-weekly papers published from New York to Los Angeles. Operating, as they do, under certain handicaps, these newspapers do a commendable job in filling the gaps of minority coverage committed by the white press. The black press is seeking to close these gaps. Since the publication of the Freedman's Journal and Frederick Douglas' North Star, the black press has been in the forefront fighting for justice for all minorities in this country. Long ago the gauntlet was thrown down and there is no surcease in the struggle for equality of justice under the Constitution of this country.

Radio and Television

A second communication media which is found lacking in its recognition of minorities is in radio and television. Of the more than 900 commercial TV stations in this country, only one is black-owned. This station is WGPR-TV, Channel 62, in Detroit, Michigan, the first black television station in the United States. It was organized in September, 1975, by

Dr. William V. Banks, president and general manager, who had purchased Radio Station WGPR 107.5 FM in 1964. The combined television and radio station occupies about two acres at 3140 Jefferson Avenue. Its range covers a 70 mile radius in the Detroit area.

Dr. Banks has had a long history in economic development in the black community. His rich experience as president of the International Masons and Eastern Stars, with a combined membership of 350,000, has caused him to become well aware of the need of blacks becoming a major force in the American milieu. The motivating purpose behind these two ventures was the belief of Dr. Banks that blacks needed their own radio and television station to give talented young blacks an opportunity to develop their ability to express themselves and at the same time interpret themselves to the black community.

Channel 62 is not a black station per se. Its listening audience is composed of 20 percent whites, 60 percent blacks, and 20 percent of other ethnic groups including Spanish, Puerto Rican, and French.

However, the real meaning of this Detroit TV station is that it portrays blacks in their own interpretation instead of being portrayed through the eyes of whites. Distortion of blacks by whites is seen in the overplay of crime and in the burlesquing of black life in presenting the daily

scenes of American life. Local programming by WGPR focuses
on a talk show, sports, blacks' involvement in improving of
jail features, business in the inner city and drugs. It emphasizes presentations of black-oriented program material
through news, sports, cultural and public events.

The main programming of Station WGPR-TV is local.
However, it is able to generate a number of programs that
appeal to a national audience. Repeats of former high visibility programs such as "I Spy," "Have Gun Will Travel,"
"Rawhide" and others have produced an unusual reception.
George White, station manager, and Tom Winters, sales manager, are optimistic on the ratings and the promise of better
things to come. Advertising revenue is excellent and expected
to increase. Local businesses in the Detroit area have assured
the operation of the station for another year through $3 mil-
lion in advertising commitments. Dr. Banks expects profits to
be a reality.

WGPR-TV is a UHF station which is in competition
with three other stations under the same label. A survey in
December, 1975, showed that this black-owned station was
attracting one to 2 percent of the potential market in the
Detroit area. For an established VHF station, this would
amount to a "skin and bones" showing, but, in the UHF class,
this shows a market penetration which is promising.

Seeking to start a television station in the city

of Detroit was an endeavor which could hold all kinds of pitfalls. However, Dr. Banks, in his own sagacious way, was able
to overcome all of these obstacles. The cost of starting this
station was $6 million. He raised this money through the sale
of property which his organization owned in Florida and through
contributions from his fraternal organization. For the first
18 months the going was rough. In the beginning, Dr. Banks
had to settle for second-grade white personnel. There were
just not any blacks available. The white personnel, and, in
so doing, were able to bring black personnel up to a competent
level of performance.

This station was innovative in that it was the first
station in Detroit to operate for 24 hours, and also to show
all night movies. Of its 70 employees at the present time,
about 20 percent are white and 80 percent are black. Black
females compose about 20 percent of the staff.

In August, 1977, Channel 62 was able to break even.
In other words, advertisement revenue and other income now
covered the payroll of the 70 employees as well as the costs
of station operation and other expenses. The station is a
corporation.

Of the 350 radio stations in the country, only
seventeen are black owned, or about 5 percent. Of the 2750
cable TV circuits in this country, only one is black-owned,
and that one is in Gary, Indiana. There is a certain irony

in the lack of ownership of radio and TV, because the A.C.
Nielsen company study shows that the number of blacks looking
at TV is proportionally greater than others in the general
population.

Preferences of blacks for TV programs in the winter
of 1975 were for "Sanford and Son", "Good Times" and "That's
My Mama." These ratings were surveyed by the National Black
Omnious Poll produced by National Black Opinions, Ltd. of
New York. "The Jeffersons" was number 5 on the poll, and
"Chico and the Man" was number 4. Sanford and Son got 58 7/10
percent of the black audience.

In the news category, Walter Cronkite of CBS held
6 percent more of the audience than John Chancellor of NBC.
Harry Reasoner of ABC was third with a difference of 10 percent.[2]

WNET/13, it was stated, beamed its tube directly
to the Germans, French cooking, Russian ballet and the British
drama.[3] Since WNET/TV is a public station, it should serve the
public and not a bunch of snobs. Hooks thought such arrogance
on the part of the station should not endure. Since he is only
one of seven members, Hooks lost, but the Puerto Ricans in
New York are not finished with the station yet.

Dr. William Venoid Banks

Dr. William V. Banks was born in Geneva, Kentucky
on May 6, 1903, the son of Richard D. Banks, a tenant farmer,
and his wife Clara Bernett Banks.

Music

It has been said that music soothes the soul. Those who do not like music are "fit for steals, stratagems and spoils, beware of them." These lines have been woven into the fabric of literature. And it is in the world of music that the blacks have made their greatest contribution in this country. Our lines here cannot do justice to the contributions of the vast number of black musicians who have contributed to American folklore, but we can cite one who laid the groundswell for jazz which has permeated music in this land for nigh onto 100 years. Our first real music which emanated from black musicians in this country was known as ragtime.

The King of Ragtime was Scott Joplin. Martin Williams, writing in the <u>Smithsonian</u>, says that early on a summer evening in 1899, a local man named John Stark, owner of a Sedalia, Missouri, music store, stopped in at the local Maple Leaf Club for a beer. Blacks and whites were nursing their mugs, and at the piano was a black man gently stroking the keys, and playing Maple Leaf Rag. Stark asked that the player stop by his store the next day. Joplin, the piano player, with a little boy in tow, saw Stark, played his Maple Leaf Rag with the boy stepping off. The music captivated Stark, and he agreed to publish the music, arranging royalties for Joplin. An advance was also arranged. Joplin chortled to friends that Stark agreed to publish his work, and this would make him king of "ragtime composers". Joplin was right, Maple Leaf sold more than 1,000,000 copies. According to critics, Joplin was the first real American composer.

Scott was born into a family of five children in the border town of Texarkana, Texas, which sits astride Texas and Arkansas and founded by the Missouri-Pacific Railroad. The year was 1868, a short time after emancipation. Scott's mother was a free black, that is, born free, and his father was an ex-slave. His father was a laborer, who had emigrated from North Carolina. Early in life Scott showed an affinity for music. By the time Scott was seven he had discovered the keyboard of a piano. His father became interested and scraped enough money for a second hand piano. A German music teacher heard about the talented nature of Scott's music inclinations and decided to teach him free. Later in life, writes Williams, Scott sent gifts of money to his former teacher.

Wandering through the heartland of America, Joplin played the piano in honky-tonks in St. Louis and Chicago. He returned to Missouri where he composed his celebrated Maple Leaf Rag. After an unsuccessful marriage, Joplin went to New York in 1909, and married Lottie Stokes. Joplin continued his writing and composing. He plunged into composing "Treemonisha", an ambitious opera depicting the life of blacks in the United States. After two years, the opera was finished, but Joplin could not find anyone to publish it. He financed the opus out of his own pocket, but the opera was poorly attended. Joplin declined rapidly after this failure. In 1916, he was admitted to Manhattan State Hospital. His deterioration, according to Williams, was complete. Joplin died on April 1, 1917. Musicologists credit Joplin with being the main popularizer of ragtime. A revival of his work is going on today.

Coming after ragtime were the blues which W.C. Handy popularized, and later there was jazz from New Orleans. In the hurly-burly of the early mid-western frontier of this country, it is significant that a black man became the first American composer, with his achievements being recognized after almost a century.

Art

Classification of peoples began in Western Europe as white and the rest of the world as non-white. It is interesting to note that if blacks did not live in a predominant western culture, they would not think of themselves as black. However, black art is based on a world culture. Black civilization stems from Ethiopian culture. In the black Ethiopian ethos the black man was looked upon as being of the most humane and just being. His endowments came from God.

Black art is a derivative from African Art. Since the beginning of America, the term Negro art or art by Negroes has been used. During the fifties and sixties the word "Negro" was gradually abandoned (not having an historical, ethnic or geographic meaning) and substituted the term "black" or Afro-

American. Just as black art delineates black culture, so does "yellow" art explain oriental culture and Indian art explain the red man's culture.

Visitors to the campus of Texas Southern University, while viewing the murals of students of Dr. John Biggers, head of the art department, marvel at the stark nature of the paintings. One white viewer was amazed at the details of a mural showing the police brutality in the Birmingham riot. He said, "What thoughts are going through these students heads?" These murals grip the viewer. The mural just will not let the viewer go.They almost pull the viewer toward them. These are the great protest murals. This is protest art by the black artists challenging the System. Running as a thread through the art of the black artist is this challenge. He cannot escape it. It is a part of his soul. He must challenge the system of which he has been a victim.

Poetry

Just as the black artist challenges the system in his art work so does the black poet challenge the system in this poetry. Again we may refer to the violent sixties in reference to the former Leroy Jones, now Amari Baraku. This little, short, stubby man, in the Newark riots rode around the city on a motorcycle with two guns on his hips. He didn't fire at anybody, but he was arrested by the brutal Newark cops because he had the guns on his hips. In his poetry he

moves along rhythmically,   until all of a sudden a number of
vile epithets fly at the reader from the pages. This is shock
action. Baraku is telling the system to wake up, "the night
is far spent, the day is at hand".

A counterpart to Baraku is Nikki Giovanni. This pert
Ms. constantly pulls and tugs at her reader in challenging
the system. She has a way of shocking her audience or reader
by using ghettorick that is almost too sheer coming from a
smooth, olive-skinned beautiful girl.

The Movies, Dancing, Theatre, and Opera

The silent movies showed blacks only in virtually
subservient roles. They were just about always maids, cooks,
chauffeurs and sambos. The small black boy in Our Gang Comedy
was virtually the only representative part. D.W. Griffith in
his "Birth of a Nation", showing the cruel nature of the Ku
Klux Klan, set the advent of blacks entering movies on a
higher plane, back a generation. Louise Beavers enacted subdued roles as a house servant. Hattie McDaniel in Gone With
The Wind was commendable. She won an Oscar for her performance. She not only played the role of a black mammy, but
stood out in her own right as an actress. But we still do not
yet see the black male emerging as a leading man or supporting character actor in the movies. Of course there were all
black casts in Emperor Jones and Carmen and Porgy and Bess.
It was not until after World War II, that we see actors such

as James Earl Jones, Sidney Poitier, Woody Strode, Brock
Peters, and Paul Winfield coming into their own.

In the television series of ROOTS, for the first
time was the black man/woman as shown as heroes and heroines.
Prior to this and in a narrow context they were depicted as
buffoons, prostitutes, pimps, dope pushers and racketeers.

As a large black middle class began to emerge
following the Civil Rights Act of 1964, more pure black movies
were produced. Identity was not the word. Get with it. Look
upon yourself as moving on up. A rash of these blaxpoitation
movies came out with big bosomy, brown wenches who could perform karate and make love with black and white men so intense
that your skin would burn. The black stud was also an outgrowth of blaxpoitation movies. Like all cycles in Hollywood,
these movies will run their course.

As the late H.G. Wells said, the blacks have super-
lative rhythm. This rhythm is the envy of whites. As a communication medium, the dance is an expression of joy, hate,
love, envy, jealousy and happiness. And this tap dancing came
from patting one's feet to music or keeping time. From tapping
one's feet we turn to a synchronization of other parts of the
body. When these are coordinated into a rhythmic pattern, the
individual is carried away with the performance. The dance
here, like most art forms, acts as an escape mechanism. While
he is isolated now from all conflict, his body is in harmony

with self. Alvin **Ailey** expresses this harmony to a fine degree.

"Bubbling Brown Sugar", the rage of Broadway for the 1976 season, covers the period in Harlem from 1910 to 1940. In the fast moving sixties and early seventies, it appeared that that period had vanished. But it hasn't. This musical has woven into it the songs of Eubie Blake, Cab Calloway, Duke Ellington, W.C. Handy, Earl Hines, Billie Holiday, Andy Razaf, Noble Sissle and Bert Williams. This was the real Harlem as Bojangles, Bill Robinson,knew it and where the Lindy Hop was created. Rosetta Le Noire,who conceived the project,wanted people to see Harlem as it was. The cast is headed by Avon Long, Josephine Premice, Vivian Reed and Joseph Attles. Direction is by Robert M. Cooper.

The world of opera appears to be the Waterloo of the black male, whereas the black female has cracked opera.

The theatre and opera are somewhat similar. But where James Earl Jones has been able to crack the theatre wide open with his performance in The Great White Hope, the black male in opera has still to come across. MeHenry Boatwright has had success in Europe where he scored in "The Visitation" by Gunther Schullar,but he has not had success in this country. Boatwright, like many of his black brothers feel that whites are so sex conscious that they cringe when they see a black man embracing a white woman. Strange that this happens in opera and not in the movies or on the stage. Just the opposite has taken place with black women. Marian Anderson broke through at the Met about thirty years ago. Since then black females have had leading roles on through Leontyne Price, Grace Bumbry, Martina Arroyo and others. No question arises when they are cast opposite white males. So, in many ways, it could be the women who do not encourage the black males. Is it possible that a black woman relishes love being made to her by a white male in preference to a black male? This could be so in opera. The black female can gloat in her superiority over the white male. Could she do likewise over the black male?

Advertising

Five years ago there were seven (7) black advertising agencies in New York. Today there is only one. Just six years back Black Enterprise named the following with their billing:

NAME	BILLINGS IN 1973
1. John F. Small, Inc.	$7,000,000
2. Zebra Associates, Inc.	4,600,000
3. Junius Edwards, Inc.	3,500,000
4. Uniworld Group, Inc.	3,500,000
5. Phat Advertising Consultants, Inc.	1,200,000
6. Howard-Sanders Advertising, Ltd.	1,200,000
7. Eden Advertising and Communications, Inc.	1,000,000

Source: Black Enterprise, 1973

The Uniworld Group is the only survivor of the list
on the previous page. It is alleged that there are only four
other black-owned advertising agencies throughout the country
out of an industry total of more than 7,000.

Pluria Marshall, former director of the National
Black Media Coalition, along with the Black Caucus, is inves-
tigating the reasons for the failure of the black advertising
agencies to survive in such a highly competitive industry.
The NBMC is also monitoring 200 broadcasting licenses on
their handling of minority newscasts.

The withdrawal or failure of blacks in the $13 bil-
lion advertising industry in this country has promoted charges
of discrimination and conspiracy on the part of the white-
owned agencies. The black agencies made their pitch with the
Civil Rights movement in 1965. Lyndon Johnson's Great Society
was the progenitor of these agencies. White-owned companies
gave business to the black agencies out of a guilt feeling
rather than productivity. Could blacks do more for them than
the established agencies? Evidently they felt blacks could
not do this. With the denouement of the black agencies, black
employment in the advertising industry rose from 5 percent
in the New New York City area around 1960 to 15 percent today.[4] It is possible that the black agencies failed because
they did not work hard enough. They were seeking courtesy
business and this is a weak prop for any on-going business.

After the initial period was over and the blacks were accepted
into the industry, the established white-owned agencies
began going after the same business black agencies had. No
holds were barred. Creativity is the name of the game in
advertising. New ideas to get the consumer to buy are dinned
into the ears and eyes by the advertising industry. Demand
is created by advertising. In the commercial world it is
hard for the blacks to compete as fledglings. But they can
compete for government advertising - Federal, state and
local. Affirmative Action could be implemented in these
agencies.

REFERENCES

1. Black Enterprise, Vol. 5, No. 2, September, 1974, pp.
   39-45.

2. Atlanta Constitution, October 26, 1974, by Irving
   Kupcinet of the Chicago Sun Times.

3. The New York Times, Vol. CXXIV, #42,799, March 30, 1975,
   Section 2, p. 25.

4. The New York Times, Vol. CXXV, #43,275, July 18, 1976,
   pg. 35.

INDEX

Title	Page

Title	Page

Title	Page

Title	Page

Title	Page